Sociology

Seventh edition

Themes and Perspectives

AS and A2 level
Student Handbook

Martin Holborn, Pam Burrage, Peter Langley

William Collins's dream of knowledge for all began with the publication of his first book in 1819. A self-educated mill worker, he not only enriched millions of lives, but also founded a flourishing publishing house. Today, staying true to this spirit, Collins books are packed with inspiration, innovation and practical expertise. They place you at the centre of a world of possibility and give you exactly what you need to explore it.

Collins. Freedom to teach.

Published by Collins
An imprint of HarperCollinsPublishers
77-85 Fulham Palace Road
Hammersmith
London
W6 8JB

Browse the complete Collins catalogue at
www.collinseducation.com

© HarperCollinsPublishers Limited 2009

10 9 8 7 6 5 4 3 2 1

ISBN-13   978 000 731 0722

Martin Holborn, Pam Burrage and Peter Langley assert their moral rights to be identified as the authors of this work.

British Library Cataloguing in Publication Data. A Catalogue record for this publication is available from the British Library.

Commissioned by Charlie Evans
Project management and editing by Tim Satterthwaite
Index by Sally Parker
Original concept design by Nigel Jordan
Page layout and cover design by Angela English
Production by Simon Moore
Printed and bound by Printing Express, Hong Kong

CONTENTS

Introduction   1

Chapter 1 Social stratification   4

Chapter 2 Families and households   26

Chapter 3 Education   46

Chapter 4 Religion and beliefs   68

Chapter 5 Culture and identity   92

Chapter 6 Wealth, welfare & poverty   108

Chapter 7 Power and politics   132

Chapter 8 Health, medicine & the body   150

Chapter 9 Communication & the media   164

Chapter 10 Crime and deviance   178

Chapter 11 Methodology   206

Chapter 12 Sociological theory   224

Useful websites   242

Index   244

USING THIS HANDBOOK

The handbook is a companion to the best-selling textbook *Sociology Themes and Perspectives* 7th edition (Collins, 2008). It is designed mainly for AS and A2 students following the AQA, OCR or WJEC specifications, and provides all the essential information you need to succeed in the exams. It is also useful for Access students and for other sociology courses.

The *Student Handbook* can be used both as a revision guide, and as a companion to help you through your course and make the most of the main textbook. It can also be used on its own as a short textbook, including summaries of all the themes and perspectives you will come across in your studies.

Specifications

At the start of each chapter are details of the modules for each examination board that are covered in the chapter. You will also find pointers throughout the chapters to show which sections are relevant to AQA, OCR and WJEC. References at the start of all the main sections point you to pages in the *Sociology Themes and Perspectives* textbook, where you will find each topic covered in much more detail. Books and articles by sociologists are listed by author name and date; full details are included in the Textbook's bibliography.

Essay plans

Each chapter includes a section designed to help you plan and write first-class AS and A2-level essays. *Develop your analytical and evaluation skills* includes essay titles on key themes in the chapter, that are often the focus of exam questions. There are notes guiding you to the key sociologists and their arguments, and suggestions on how you might plan and structure an essay. The last plan in each chapter is developed into a model answer, to give you an idea of what examiners are looking for in a good student essay.

Resources

At the back of each chapter is a range of resources, including tables, summaries and mind maps. These provide a quick guide to all the key sociologists and their work, and you will find them very useful in your revision.

Useful websites

The handbook is supported by a website which includes many additional resources: mind maps, quizzes and notes on exam-style questions. To make the most of the *Student Handbook* visit:

www.collinseducation.com/sociologyweb

A list of other useful sociology websites is included at the end of the handbook.

INTRODUCTION

Sociology is one of a number of **social sciences** which explains human behaviour.

Unlike psychology it is much less concerned with individuals and much more concerned with **social groups** including whole **societies** and even **international** and **global** groups.

Although there are **biological** influences on human behaviour, sociologists generally see these as much less important than **social** influences, particularly the way humans learn the behaviour expected of them in a particular society.

These expectations about behaviour are part of what sociologists refer to as **culture**.

CULTURE, INEQUALITY AND SOCIETY

AQA, OCR, WJEC   Textbook pp. 2-5

Culture and socialization

Ralph Linton (1945) sees **culture** as the way of life shared by members of a society. It is learned and is a vital part of human society. Cultures vary from society to society, and the values of one culture may be rejected by others – for example, amongst the Sioux Indians of South Dakota it was considered impolite to answer a question in the presence of others who did not know the answer. This is very different to what is expected in a classroom in the USA today.

Socialization is the process through which individuals learn a culture, and it continues throughout life. Socialization is essential for participation in human society.

Primary socialization is the first phase, usually taking place in the family.

Peer groups (groups of a similar age and status), the education system and occupations are important agents of **secondary socialization**.

Values are general guidelines about what is considered good and desirable or bad and undesirable in a society. In contemporary Britain, widely held values include the acquisition of material possessions, honesty and so on. In Sioux society, generosity was a key value.

Norms are specific guides to action that derive from general values. Norms define when, for example, it is acceptable to remove clothes. Norms are regulated by **negative sanctions** (punishments) and **positive sanctions** (rewards).

Culture and **norms** change over time – for example, text messaging has led to a whole new culture and language.

Most societies do not have a single culture, but also include a variety of **subcultures** – social groups within society with a distinctive lifestyle which is significantly different from that of other members of society (including, for example, minority ethnic groups and youth subcultures).

Culture and subculture are important sources of **social identity** – an understanding of who we are.

Inequality and social divisions

Inequality is concerned with differences in access to scarce resources.

There are two main types of inequality:

- Inequalities of power – the ability of individuals or groups to get what they want regardless of the wishes of others.
- Material inequality – access to wealth and income which may also give greater access to power.

Inequality is a major basis of social divisions between groups; it is linked to **identity** (how people see themselves and are seen by others) and can cause **conflict**.

Social classes are the key social division for many sociologists, who believe that there is a division between a wealthy upper class, a middle class which has well-paid non-manual jobs, and a working class which has less well-paid manual jobs.

Social divisions include:

- gender divisions between males and females;
- ethnic divisions;
- age groups.

Other divisions might be related, for example, to religion, sexuality, disability.

DEVELOPMENT OF HUMAN SOCIETIES

AQA, OCR, WJEC   Textbook pp. 5-7

Some sociologists see societies as having gone through broad developmental phases, described as **premodern**, **modern** and **postmodern**.

Premodern societies

Anthony Giddens (1997) distinguishes three types:

- hunting and gathering societies based on hunting animals and gathering fruit and vegetables;
- pastoral and agrarian societies in which animal herding and settled agriculture have developed;
- non-industrial civilizations such as the Aztecs, Ancient Egyptians, Greeks and Romans.

Modern industrial societies

These started developing in the late eighteenth and nineteenth centuries. **Lee & Newby** (1983) identify four key features:

- **Industrialism** – the Industrial Revolution started in the late eighteenth century; it greatly increased human productive power and reduced the degree to which nature shaped social life.
- **Capitalism** involved the employment of labour for wages and businesses based upon making profits.

- **Urbanism** resulted in populations being increasingly concentrated in towns and cities.
- **Liberal democracy** eventually replaced monarchical rule, giving people a say in how society was run.

The above changes have been seen as creating modernity, which involves a belief in the ability to plan, achieve progress and solve problems using science and technology. Some see sociology as closely involved with modernity.

Postmodernity

Some sociologists claim modernity is now being replaced by **postmodernity**.

Postmodernity tends to involve a loss of faith in science and rationality, a loss of belief in progress, and increased **scepticism** about any theories that claim to be able to produce a better future.

Some **non-rational** beliefs (such as **New Age** beliefs) have become more popular. According to some postmodernists, the changes are linked to a **postindustrial** (service- or information technology-based) economy.

For some postmodernists older theories of society have become outdated. Other sociologists question the value of postmodernist theories.

THEORIES OF SOCIETY

AQA, OCR, WJEC   Textbook pp. 7-13

Functionalism

Functionalists see society as having a **structure**, with key institutions performing vital **functions**, and **roles** directing people in how to behave.

They identify the functions of each part of the structure – for example, the family socializes the young and produces a shared culture.

Institutions are there to meet the basic needs, or **functional prerequisites**, of society – for example, producing food and shelter for people.

A **value consensus** (shared beliefs about right and wrong) helps society to run smoothly and to integrate the different parts.

Early functionalists borrowed their ideas from biology. They saw each part of society as having a function like each part of the body – for example, the government of a society is like a human's brain.

Leading functionalists include **Emile Durkheim** 1858-1917) and **Talcott Parsons** (1902-79).

Conflict perspectives

Conflict perspectives argue that there are differences of interest between groups in society – what is good for one group is bad for another. This creates the potential for conflict between groups. There are a range of conflict theories.

Marxism

Marxism is based upon the work of **Karl Marx** (1818-83), though it has been adapted by later writers.

Marx argues that societies result from humans getting together to produce food. The forces of production (the technology used to produce things) shape social relationships.

The economic system, consisting of the forces and social relationships of production, forms the **infrastructure** of society. The infrastructure shapes other parts of society, such as the government, family life, the education system and religion – collectively known as the **superstructure**.

Most societies are based upon exploitation of some groups by others. Those who own the **means of production** (such as the land, factories, raw materials or capital) exploit those who work for them, who lack the means to produce things themselves.

Contemporary societies are described as **capitalist** – meaning that the owners of capital are dominant. Capitalists (the **bourgeoisie**) exploit their workers (the **proletariat**) by paying them less in wages than the wealth created by their work. Capitalists accumulate **profits** (or **surplus value**) and get richer and richer.

In capitalist societies, the ruling class owns the means of production. It tries to use the superstructure (including the government, legal system, religion and the mass media) to persuade workers that society is fair and just, and prevent workers from rebelling against their exploitation. Where it succeeds, **ruling-class ideology** is dominant and creates **false class consciousness** (a mistaken belief that society is fair) amongst workers.

Eventually workers will come to realize that they are being exploited and will overthrow capitalism and create a **communist society**. In communism the means of production (land, factories etc.) will be communally owned, so there will be no ruling class, no exploitation and much less inequality than in capitalism.

Feminism

There are different versions of **feminism** but all see society as divided between men and women.

Feminists tend to see women as exploited by men, and society as **patriarchal** (male-dominated). Examples of patriarchy include men monopolizing high-status and well-paid jobs, doing less housework than women and holding the most senior positions in politics.

Most feminists tend to see women as having shared interests, and believe that progress towards ending patriarchy is possible. **Difference feminists** argue that different groups of women may have different interests, and that not all women are equally exploited.

Many feminists criticize sociology (particularly older sociology) as being ‘**malestream**’ – that is, written by men, largely about men and from a masculine viewpoint.

Interactionism

Unlike **macro theories** (which look at society as a whole – for example, Marxism and functionalism), **interactionism** (a **micro theory**) looks at social behaviour in smaller groups.

Interactionists stress the importance of meanings – the way people interpret the behaviour of others.

Meanings develop during **interaction**, as people try to get a feel for the intentions behind other people's actions.

Humans possess a **self-concept**, or idea, of what sort of person they are. Self-concepts develop in response to the reactions of others – i.e. you end up thinking of yourself in the same way as others think of you.

Like functionalists, interactionists believe that **roles** exist, but they see them as much more flexible and negotiable. For example, married couples develop their own interpretations of the roles of husband and wife.

Society is seen as more fluid, less rigidly fixed, than in macro theories.

Postmodernism

Postmodernist perspectives have developed since the 1980s.

Some versions see important changes taking place in society. Other versions question the ability of conventional sociology to produce worthwhile theories of society.

Some postmodernists argue that social behaviour is no longer shaped by factors such as class, gender, ethnicity and different types of **socialization**. It is now simply a question of **lifestyle choice**.

Some postmodernists argue that sociological theory can never objectively describe the social world.

Lyotard (1984) criticizes all grand or general theories, and many postmodernists stress that everybody's viewpoint on society is equally valid.

Postmodernists emphasize differences between individuals rather than similarities between members of the same social group.

HUMAN BEHAVIOUR

AQA, OCR, WJEC   Textbook pp. 14-16

There are three main sociological approaches, which reflect different ways of understanding human behaviour.

Positivism

Positivists believe that human behaviour can be objectively measured.

Direct observation can produce **objective data**, and only that which can be observed should be studied.

Human behaviour is shaped by **external stimuli**.

Sociologists should use **natural science methods**.

Statistical data can be used to uncover cause-and-effect relationships between two or more things.

Social action perspectives

Social action perspectives argue that sociology is not like the natural sciences because it involves the study of conscious human beings.

Humans interpret the meaning of things before reacting and do not react passively to external stimuli.

In order to explain behaviour, sociologists need to examine what is going on inside people's heads – these **internal meanings** cannot be directly observed.

Proponents of social action approaches include **Max Weber** (1864-1920) and **interactionists**.

Phenomenology

Phenomenologists deny that any objective classification of the social world is possible.

All **categorization** is **subjective**; statistics are simply based upon personal opinions.

Without factual data, causal explanations of human behaviour cannot be produced.

Sociologists can only really study the factors that influence the way people categorize the world (for example, what makes them decide that a death is a suicide or that a particular action is a crime).

SOCIOLOGY AND VALUES

AQA, OCR, WJEC   Textbook pp. 16-17

Positivists believe that an objective, unbiased, value-free sociology is possible, but many sociologists argue that it is not. Critics of positivism argue that a researcher's **values** (or personal beliefs about right and wrong) are bound to influence what they study, how they study it and how they interpret the data.

Functionalism has often been seen as supporting the status quo and opposing change because it views all institutions as having useful functions. It is therefore seen as having a **conservative ideology**.

Marxism advocates change in order to remove exploitation and oppression. It is described as having a **radical ideology**.

The sociological imagination

Some sociologists, such as **Giddens** (1977, 1979, 1984), argue that different perspectives should be combined and that both social structure and social action are important for understanding society.

C Wright Mills (1959) advocates a similar approach. He argues that links should be made between public issues (such as unemployment) and personal troubles (such as the experience of the unemployed individual).

Sociology can be seen as successful when it achieves this imaginative connection; the theories and studies examined in the rest of the book can be judged in these terms.

SPECIFICATION COVERAGE

Specification	Details
AQA A2 Unit 4: Stratification and Differentiation	
OCR A2 Unit G674: Exploring Inequality and Difference	All sections are relevant. This is the synoptic unit; you are required to understand the connections between sociological thought, methods of sociological enquiry and social inequality
WJEC A2 Unit SCY4: Understanding Social Divisions Option 2, Social Inequality	

INTRODUCTION

AQA, OCR, WJEC   Textbook pp. 19-20

Social inequality refers to any differences that result in some people having more socially valued characteristics than others. Degrees of power, prestige and wealth may be significant.

Social stratification refers to a situation in which people are divided into distinct groups ranked at different levels. The Hindu caste system is an example – different castes have different levels of status depending on their supposed degree of religious purity.

Those at different levels in a stratification system may develop a common **subculture** or way of life.

Social mobility refers to movement between strata.

Status in stratification systems can be **ascribed** (given at birth – for example, the caste system), or **achieved** (resulting from what you do – for example, class systems).

Life chances are an individual's chances of having or acquiring socially desirable things (for example: money, education, longevity), and are affected by that person's place in the stratification system.

Stratification systems have sometimes been based on what were thought to be natural inequalities or biological differences – for example, apartheid in South Africa assumed that whites were superior to blacks. However, sociologists see such views as **rationalizations** to legitimate the position of powerful groups. In modern Britain four types of stratification have been identified: social class, gender, ethnicity and age.

FUNCTIONALIST PERSPECTIVE

AQA, OCR, WJEC   Textbook pp. 20-23

Parsons – stratification and values

Parsons (1964) sees all societies as having a **value consensus** – a general agreement about what is desirable and valuable (or undesirable and valueless). Whatever these values, individuals will be ranked in accordance with them.

Stratification is inevitable as all societies have some values and will make judgments.

In complex industrial societies, planning and organization require some individuals to have more **authority** than others.

Stratification unites people because it derives from **shared values**.

Criticisms

Critics argue that many values are not shared and that stratification can be highly divisive.

Davis & Moore – role allocation

Davis & Moore (1967, first published 1945) argue that all societies share certain functional prerequisites. One of these is **role allocation** – ensuring that roles are filled and performed effectively and conscientiously by properly trained people. Some jobs are more functionally important and some people have more ability than others.

To match the most able to the most important jobs, and to ensure that tedious, unpleasant or dangerous jobs are filled, a rewards system is needed. The better-rewarded will form a higher stratum. This process is inevitable, universal (found in all societies) and beneficial because it helps society to function better.

Criticisms

Melvin Tumin (1967) argues that:

- many low-paid and even unskilled jobs are just as vital as higher-paid or more skilled jobs.
- there is a greater pool of talent than Davis & Moore assume.
- training is a pleasant experience and does not require extra rewards to persuade people to undertake it.
- stratification systems can demotivate those at the bottom.
- stratification systems do not provide equality of opportunity and tend to prevent those from lower strata achieving their potential.
- stratification systems encourage 'hostility, suspicion and distrust'.

MARKET LIBERAL PERSPECTIVE

AQA, OCR, WJEC   Textbook pp. 23-26

The **market liberal** or **New Right** perspective believes in **free market** capitalism. Market forces encourage competition which ensures that goods and services are high quality and low in price, making them available to a wider section of the population. Markets are based on **choice** and encourage **individual liberty**. Inequality is motivating and promotes economic growth. Capitalism has widened opportunity for everyone. Socialist societies are more repressive.

Saunders – stratification and freedom

Saunders (1990) believes there are three types of equality:

1 **Legal equality** – everybody is subject to the same laws. This is a characteristic of Western capitalist societies.

2 **Equality of opportunity** – everybody has an equal chance to become unequal.

3 **Equality of outcome** – everybody is treated exactly equally whatever they do. This requires positive discrimination in favour of those who would otherwise get less. Those who would have achieved more will feel aggrieved, and nobody needs to make much effort.

Society, in Saunders's view, should be based on legal equality and equality of opportunity. People strive for rewards and their success will add to the productive power and wealth of society. People must be allowed to keep the rewards they have gained.

Saunders argues Britain is almost a **meritocracy**; inequality of outcome is based on merit. Middle-class children succeed because they inherit higher ability and work harder.

Criticisms

The harmful effects of stratification on **cohesion** and **integration** are ignored.

Freedom and the free market do not necessarily occur together.

Marshall & Swift (1993) argue that Saunders has misinterpreted the figures. Even when factors such as effort and intelligence are taken into account, working-class children still do considerably worse than middle-class children. The free market does not ensure merit is equally rewarded.

MARXIST PERSPECTIVE

AQA, OCR, WJEC   Textbook pp. 26-29

In **Marx**'s theories, stratification is a key aspect of the capitalist system. All stratified societies have two major classes: a **ruling class** and a **subject class**.

The ruling class owns the **means of production** (land, capital, machinery etc.) and the subject class does not. The ruling class exploits the subject class.

The ruling class uses the **superstructure** (for example, legal and political systems) to **legitimate** (justify) its position and prevent protests by the subject class.

In capitalist societies the main classes are the **bourgeoisie** (the capitalist class that owns the main means of production: capital) and the **proletariat** (the working class that has to sell its labour to survive).

The bourgeoisie exploits the working class through the system of wage labour. Capitalists pay wages to workers, but make a **profit** (surplus value) because they pay workers less than the value of what they produce.

Capitalism is the newest type of class society but it will also be the last. Eventually it will be replaced by a **communist** society in which the means of production (land, capital, factories, machinery etc.) will be communally owned.

The **transition to communism** will not be straightforward because it requires **revolutionary action** by the proletariat. However, the bourgeoisie uses the superstructure (for example: the media, education system, and political and legal systems) to suppress the proletariat by creating **false consciousness** (which means that workers do not realize that they are being exploited). Eventually, though, **class consciousness** will develop – workers will realize that they are being exploited and will rise up to change society.

Class consciousness develops for the following reasons:

- There is a basic **contradiction** in capitalist societies between the interests of workers and capitalists.

- Workers will become concentrated in large factories, making it easier to communicate with one another and organize **resistance**.

- Workers' wages will decline in relation to the growing wealth of capitalists, in order to maintain profits. There will be a **polarization** of classes, with the rich getting richer and the poor poorer, making inequalities more obvious.

- **Skill divisions** between workers will be reduced as new technology is introduced, resulting in a more homogeneous and united working class.

- The **petty bourgeoisie** (small capitalists such as shopkeepers) will be unable to compete and will sink into the proletariat.

- Capitalist economies are unstable, and **economic crises** and periods of high unemployment will cause growing resentment.

- Workers will join together to form unions, political parties and revolutionary movements as class consciousness grows, enabling them to overthrow capitalism and replace it with **communism**.

Criticisms

Many other theories, and much of the research we will look at in this chapter, provide evaluations of the Marxist perspective.

WEBER'S PERSPECTIVE

AQA, OCR, WJEC　　　　　　　Textbook pp. 29-32

Max Weber accepted some of Marx's ideas but rejected others. Weber argued that classes develop from people's **market situation** (their situation in relation to buying and selling things, including their labour power) in market economies.

Weber differs from Marx in a number of ways:

- Like Marx he saw a basic division between those who have considerable property (and can live off the proceeds) and those who do not – the **propertyless** – who have to sell their labour. However, there are also significant differences within the two groups as well as between them.

- Within the propertyless group there are some who can sell their labour for a higher price (those with scarce but sought-after skills such as professionals and managers). They have an advantaged market situation compared to other groups of workers. Unlike Marx, Weber therefore believed that different **occupational groupings** could form classes.

- Weber saw no evidence of a polarization of classes. Instead he thought that the middle class of **white-collar workers** in bureaucracies would expand.

- Weber did not believe that a revolution by the proletariat was likely.

- He thought that some, but not all, power came from wealth.

- He argued that class was not the only basis for group formation. **Status groups** (groups of people who enjoyed similar levels of status or respect in society) could also be formed. Status groups might,

for example, be based on ethnicity, age, nationality or gender; individuals within groups tended to share similar lifestyles. Class and status could be closely linked (for example, ethnic minorities might be excluded from highly-paid jobs in a society) but this was not always the case. Status groups often cut across class divisions (for example, members of the gay community in today's society).

Organized groups which seek to exercise political power or influence those with power are called **parties** by Weber. Parties may be political parties (for example, the Labour and Conservative parties) or they may be pressure groups. They may be based on class (for example, the 'old' Labour Party), status groups (for example, gay rights organizations) or neither (for example, Greenpeace).

CHANGES IN STRATIFICATION

AQA, OCR, WJEC　　　　　　　Textbook pp. 32-41

Changes in the occupational structure

During the twentieth century the proportion of manual workers and personal service workers in Britain fell steadily, from over three quarters of all employees to well under a half, while the proportion of **non-manual workers** rose from under a quarter to over a half. Manufacturing industry declined, particularly in the last quarter of the twentieth century, while service industries grew.

There was a continuing shift towards **managerial** and **professional** employment at the start of the twenty-first century and the drop in routine and intermediate occupations continued. **Private sector** service jobs have increased rapidly over recent years.

Women, especially married women, now form a bigger proportion of the workforce, but women are more likely to work part-time and are concentrated in intermediate and junior non-manual jobs.

The changing distribution of income

Income has an important effect on **life chances**. Official statistics measure income in a variety of ways:

- **Original income** refers to all income apart from state benefits.

- **Gross income** includes state benefits.

- **Disposable income** deducts tax and national insurance.

- **Final income** includes the value of benefits such as healthcare, which are not given in cash.

Government figures show that the poorest 20% of the population receives less than half the average final income, while the richest 20% receives nearly twice the average. However, taxes and benefits do equalize and redistribute income to some extent.

The **Royal Commission** on the Distribution of Income found that there was some **redistribution** of income away from the richest groups between 1949 and 1979, but middle-income groups benefited most. From 1979 to 1997 changes in taxation and benefits under Conservative governments generally benefited the well-off at the expense of the poor. From 2001 to 2005 income inequality fell slightly. However, the rapidly increasing incomes of the highest earners (chief executives, city workers, sports and entertainment stars) has prevented a move to greater equality, despite the introduction of tax credits and a fall in unemployment.

The changing distribution of wealth

There are no direct measures of the distribution of wealth, but surveys and data on the value of the estates of those who have died give some indication of wealth distribution.

Wealth can be defined in different ways: **marketable wealth** includes only things that can be sold; **non-marketable wealth** includes the value of pensions etc. Home owners, who make up an increasing share of the population, saw the value of their properties increase rapidly over a number of years – until 2007, when the housing market went into decline.

Available figures suggest that wealth inequalities narrowed from 1900 to the early 1990s, then widened through to the end of the 1990s.

Wealth remains quite highly **concentrated**: in 1999 the richest 1% of the population owned 23% of all marketable wealth, and the richest 50% owned 94%.

The proportion of people in Britain owning **shares** has increased in recent years, but shares make up a declining proportion of personal wealth (16% in 1995), and most people have only small shareholdings.

The **super-wealthy** have increased their share of wealth due to lower taxes, enormous bonuses and profits from the global economy.

The taxation system in Britain favours the wealthy. Inheritance tax can be avoided by handing over assets early or setting up trust funds. Corporation tax can be avoided by registering companies abroad. Income tax can be avoided by living abroad. Wealthy foreigners living in Britain pay very little tax.

Lansley (2006) argues that the great majority of the population pay their dues whilst the richest individuals and largest corporations increasingly opt out of their tax obligations.

THE UPPER CLASS

AQA, OCR, WJEC   Textbook pp. 41-45

Westergaard & Resler – a Marxist view

Westergaard & Resler (1976) put forward a **Marxist** view that there is a **ruling class** in Britain consisting of the richest 5-10% of the population, whose position comes from the ownership of capital. Private share ownership is highly concentrated in this minority group. The ruling class is made up of company directors, top managers, higher professionals and senior civil servants, many of whom are big shareholders.

Saunders – a New Right view

Peter Saunders (1990) puts forward a **New Right** view of the upper class. He agrees with much of what Westergaard & Resler say about the concentration of wealth, but he sees this group as an influential **economic elite** rather than a ruling class.

Most big companies are run by managers with only small shareholdings in the company. Much wealth is not privately held but is in pension schemes, insurance policies etc., meaning that most people have a stake in capitalism.

Saunders claims that the economic elite do not have most of the power; power is **decentralized**. Class divisions have weakened and a ruling class no longer exists.

Scott – Who Rules Britain?

John Scott (1982, 1991,1997) is influenced by **Marxism**, **elite theory** and **Weber**. He sees Britain as retaining an **upper/ruling class**, though this is much changed since the nineteenth century.

The upper class evolved from nineteenth-century **interlocking networks** of landowners, financiers and manufacturers. During the twentieth century, family-controlled companies became less common (though important ones remained) and **joint-stock companies** developed. Furthermore, professional managers took a greater role in running companies.

A **capitalist class** persists. The ownership of property for use (for example, housing) has become more widespread, but the ownership of property for power (for example: stocks and shares, privately owned businesses etc.) remains highly concentrated.

The decisions of big companies and big financial institutions are controlled by a network of managers and directors who often have directorships in many companies (**interlocking directorships**).This capitalist class comprises around 0.1% of the adult population.

The policies of all governments (even Labour ones) are strongly influenced by the interests of the capitalist class, and governments cannot go against the interests of capitalists without risking grave economic problems.

Lansley (2006) argues that a **super-class**, a small number of very wealthy, powerful people, dominates Britain. It is largely drawn from privileged backgrounds but includes successful entrepreneurs, entertainers and sportspeople.

Sklair – globalization and transnational capitalism

Leslie Sklair (1995) argues that **globalization** and the global system have produced a **transnational capitalist class** associated with major transnational corporations. Members of this class are not loyal to particular countries; they see their interests in terms of the capitalist system as a whole (see Textbook pp. 551-554).

Criticisms

Sklair underestimates the importance of finance capitalists and the continuing power of nation states. He may be right to add a transnational dimension to ruling-class theory.

Elite theory and **pluralism** provide alternative views (see Textbook pp. 525-534).

THE MIDDLE CLASS

AQA, OCR, WJEC   Textbook pp. 45-46

Marx's ideas on the middle class have influenced later research. Marx argued that classes would be increasingly polarized between the bourgeoisie and the proletariat. Small-business people and the self-employed (the petty bourgeoisie) would sink into the proletariat.

Marx recognized the growing number of white-collar workers but said little about their significance. Many critics of Marx argue that there is a growing middle class, which undermines his theory of two polarizing classes.

Weber believed the middle class was distinguished from the working class by its superior **life chances** and more advantaged **market situation**; middle-class workers had skills and qualifications which were in demand, which allowed them to command higher wages than the working class.

The conventional way to distinguish between the middle class and the working class is to equate them with **non-manual** and **manual workers**. However, the idea that non-manual workers make up the middle class can be criticized:

- Unlike Marxist and Weberian theories, it has little theoretical basis.
- Non-manual workers are a diverse group which may overlap with other classes.

THE UPPER MIDDLE CLASS

AQA, OCR, WJEC   Textbook pp. 46-50

Until the 1980s the **petty bourgeoisie** of self-employed individuals and small employers declined in line with Marx's theory. However, from the 1980s it increased.

The professions

The professions grew from around 4% of those employed in 1900 to 14% of men and 12% of women by 2005.

Professionals are employed both in growing **private businesses** and in the welfare state. They can be divided into **lower professions** (for example: teachers, social workers, nurses) and **higher professions** (doctors, lawyers, accountants etc.).

Savage et al (1992) distinguish between professions and **welfare professions**. Professionals generally have above-average incomes, but higher professionals/non-welfare professionals are particularly well paid. Both tend to have greater security and more fringe benefits than most other workers.

Functionalist perspective

Functionalists such as **Bernard Barber** (1963) see professional jobs as having distinctive attributes:

- possession of a body of specialist knowledge;
- concern for the interests of the community;
- control of behaviour through a code of ethics;
- high rewards and prestige, reflecting their contribution to society.

Criticisms of functionalism

Many commentators have criticized the professions – for example, lawyers have been accused of mystifying the law; teachers have been attacked for allowing underachievement. **Illich** (1975) accuses doctors of hiding the damaging effects of the environment.

Weberian perspective

Parry & Parry (1976) believe that professions serve their own interests rather than community's interests:

- They restrict entry to the profession in order to limit the supply of qualified workers, thus maintaining their high wages.
- Professional associations tend to protect and defend the image of the profession rather than protecting the public.
- **Professional associations** ensure that their members have a **monopoly**, thus protecting their interests.
- Professionalism is seen as a **market strategy** designed to maximize the security and rewards of a particular job, not as a characteristic of particular types of work.
- Higher professions get paid more than lower professions simply because they have achieved **monopoly status** – for example, doctors are paid more than teachers because the BMA ensures that only their members can practise medicine, and doctors are therefore in short supply. However there are many routes into teaching and few shortages, so teachers get paid less.

Macdonald – the professional project

Macdonald (1997) argues that groups of workers undertake what he calls the **professional project** – they organize to get their work accepted as professional using techniques such as **social closure** (excluding others), establishing their own jurisdiction and attaining respectability.

The deskilling of professions

Braverman (1974) argued that professional work was being **deskilled** (the skill was being removed from it) and the work was increasingly controlled by managers rather than the professionals themselves.

Declining independence of the professions

Several sociologists have pointed to the declining independence of professionals. For example, **Johnson** (1972) argues that accountants have to be loyal to their company above their profession.

The professional-managerial class

Ehrenreich & Ehrenreich (1979) do not see the professions as a separate group. They put forward a neo-Marxist view that there is a distinct **professional-managerial** class making up 20–25% of the population. They see this class as carrying out vital functions for capitalism:

- organizing production;
- controlling the working class;
- promoting ruling-class ideology;
- developing a consumer goods market.

There is **conflict** between this group and the working class, because the professional-managerial class serves the interests of the ruling class, and the working class sometimes resists their control.

Criticisms

Marxists such as **Wright** (1978) do not see this group as a distinctive class but merely as an intermediate stratum.

Weberian theorists see the middle class in terms of **market situation** rather than the functions it performs for capitalism.

THE LOWER MIDDLE CLASS

AQA, OCR, WJEC   **Textbook pp. 50-52**

Marxist perspective

This includes clerical workers, secretaries and shop assistants. According to the **proletarianization thesis** (supported by Marxists) this group has been proletarianized: they have become working-class.

Braverman (1974) argues that they have been **deskilled** – for example, clerical workers have gone from a semi-managerial role to doing very routine work.

Weberian perspective

Weberians tend to argue that the lower middle class remains distinct from the working class.

Lockwood (1958) argues that the lower middle class has:

- a better **market situation** than the working class, with higher wages, job security and promotion prospects;
- a better **work situation**, working closely with managers and not being closely supervised;
- a superior **status situation**: their work has more prestige than manual work.

Stewart et al (1980), in a study of large firms, argue that most male clerical workers remain middle-class because their jobs are often stepping stones to junior management positions.

Criticisms

Crompton & Jones (1984) argue that:

- most clerical workers are female and their promotion prospects are much lower than those of men.
- many supposed managerial positions to which clerical workers are promoted are themselves routine.
- clerical jobs have been deskilled and are now proletarian, whatever the prospects for individuals holding those positions.

Marshall et al (1988), in their survey of 1,770 British people, found no evidence of deskilling or loss of autonomy at work among clerical workers. However, they found that **personal service workers** such as wedding consultants and personal shoppers, who are largely female, had very little control or autonomy at work, and they could be regarded as working-class.

MIDDLE CLASS OR MIDDLE CLASSES?

Giddens – the middle class

Giddens (1973) uses a Weberian perspective to claim that the middle class form a single group, with educational qualifications and the ability to sell their mental labour power.

Goldthorpe – class divisions

Goldthorpe (1980) is also a Weberian but he distinguishes between a **service class** (larger employers, professionals, managers) and an **intermediate class** (clerical workers, small proprietors, technicians etc.). The service class forms a higher class of employees, who get increments on their salary and have pension rights and promotion prospects.

In later work, Goldthorpe divides up the middle class according to whether they are employed, employers or self-employed.

Criticisms

Goldthorpe has been criticized for:

- failing to identify a difference between managers and employers and professionals;
- disagreeing with the Marxist view that big employers constitute a ruling class.

Savage et al – middle-class assets

Savage et al (1992) claim that the middle class can possess three different types of asset:

- **property assets** – owned in particular by the petty bourgeoisie;
- **organizational assets** – held, for example, by managers with jobs in large organizations;
- **cultural assets** – deriving from educational attainment and credentials, which are particularly concentrated amongst professionals.

Members of the middle class use their different types of asset to help their children gain middle-class positions.

These different types of asset can lead to differences of interest and **division** in the middle class.

In recent years another line of division has opened up between **public sector** professionals and better-rewarded **private sector** professionals, managers and the petty bourgeoisie.

Different middle-class groups tend to adopt different lifestyles:

- Public sector professionals tend to have a relatively healthy, ascetic lifestyle.
- Well-paid private sector professionals have a more extravagant postmodern lifestyle.
- Managers and civil servants do not have a distinctive lifestyle.

Evaluation

This study may underestimate the power and influence of managers and oversimplify lifestyle differences. However, it does highlight important sources of division and the changing nature of the middle classes.

Wynne – middle-class divisions

Derek Wynne (1998) uses the ideas of **Pierre Bourdieu** (see p. 12) to identify divisions within the middle class on a private housing estate. Managers and professionals on the estate had developed different lifestyles:

- **Managers** largely gained middle-class status through the possession of **economic capital** and many based their lifestyle around drinking.
- **Professionals** owed their middle-class status more to **cultural capital** and based their lifestyle more around taking part in sport.

Differences in leisure activity reflect differences in class background, education and occupation, but differences in **consumption patterns** are increasingly important and these are starting to have the biggest role in shaping class.

Criticisms

Wynne's own research seems to suggest that class background remains more important than lifestyle choice in creating class differences.

THE WORKING CLASS

AQA, OCR, WJEC Textbook pp. 56-58

The working class tends to receive lower wages, enjoy less job security and receive fewer fringe benefits than the middle class.

Working-class individuals have significantly poorer life chances, including lower life expectancy.

The issue of whether the working class share a distinctive lifestyle has been controversial. **David Lockwood** (1966) identified a group that he called **proletarian traditionalists**, who lived in close-knit working-class communities (for example, coal miners) and exemplified traditional working-class culture. The main features of the culture were:

- loyalty to workmates;
- the spending of leisure time with workmates;
- a belief in pursuing goals **collectively** rather than individually;
- a **fatalistic** attitude to life (a belief that life chances depend on luck);
- a **present-time orientation** with an emphasis on **immediate gratification** ('enjoy yourself now');
- a tendency to see class in terms of a division between 'us' (working people) and 'them' (the rich and powerful);
- **segregated conjugal roles**, with men as the main breadwinners and women as home-makers.

These characteristics are diametrically opposed to supposed **middle-class values** such as individualism, a belief in deferred gratification (planning for the future), an image of society as a status hierarchy with opportunities for individuals, and joint conjugal roles.

Marx predicted an expanding and increasingly homogeneous and **class-conscious** working class, but some sociologists have argued that the working class is becoming smaller, more **fragmented** and less class-conscious:

- Since 1945 manual work has fallen by 54% and jobs in services have increased by 45%.
- **Deindustrialization** has particularly affected the jobs which produced proletarian traditionalists such as mining, ship building and steel work.
- The expansion of non-manual jobs has created opportunities for **social mobility**.
- The standard of living has risen for the population as a whole.
- The working class is increasingly divided by occupations and differing levels of success.

EMBOURGEOISEMENT

AQA, OCR, WJEC Textbook pp. 58-63

This theory, first advocated in the 1950s by **Kerr et al** and **Bernard**, suggested that well-paid affluent workers were becoming middle-class in terms of attitudes and lifestyle. If true this would undermine Marx's theory of an increasingly united and class-conscious working class.

Goldthorpe, Lockwood et al (1968a, 1968b, 1969) investigated the theory in a study of affluent manual workers and white-collar workers in Luton in the 1960s.

Although affluent workers earned as much as routine white-collar workers they had inferior conditions of work and a poorer **market situation** (for example, fewer promotion prospects). They retained a collectivist outlook but support for unions was no longer based on unconditional loyalty. **Instrumental collectivism** (collective action if it would improve wages) had replaced solidaristic collectivism (based on strong loyalty).

Both affluent workers and white-collar workers had adopted a **privatized**, **home-centred** lifestyle, but the manual workers did not mix socially with the white-collar workers. Most saw society in terms of a **pecuniary model**, in which position was largely determined by income. They continued to be Labour voters, but for instrumental reasons rather than loyalty.

Goldthorpe et al concluded that **affluent workers** made up a new working class of **privatized instrumentalists**, located between the traditional working class and the middle class.

Savage (2005) re-examined Goldthorpe & Lockwood's data and concluded that workers had a basic **working-class orientation**, seeing themselves as ordinary/normal because they worked for a living whilst the upper class did not.

Devine (1992) returned to Luton in the late 1980s to see how things had changed. She found that workers:

- continued to support unions but remained **instrumental collectivists**.
- continued to choose largely working-class friends and retained fairly traditional conjugal roles.
- still had a **pecuniary model** of society.
- retained fairly left-wing political views, but some were disillusioned with the Labour Party, and some intended to vote Conservative.

Devine concluded that they were less individualistic than the affluent workers in Goldthorpe et al's study, and she felt that they had retained significant features of traditional working-class attitudes and lifestyle.

Marshall et al (1988) conducted a large survey on class in Britain in the 1980s, and found evidence of some **sectionalism**, **instrumentalism** and **privatism**. But they argued that these characteristics were nothing new – they dated back to the nineteenth century – and they therefore denied that there had been any major change in the working class.

Divisions in the working class

Dahrendorf (1959) argued that the working class was increasingly divided by skill level, with a growing proportion of skilled workers anxious to maintain higher wages and status. He claimed that there had been a 'decomposition' of the working class.

Penn (1983) studied cotton and engineering industries in Rochdale between 1856 and 1964 and found that skill divisions had long existed, and there was no evidence that they were becoming much more significant.

Crewe (1983), on the other hand, claims that there is an increasing division between a growing 'new working class' and a shrinking 'old working class'. The new working class:

- live in the south;
- are not union members;
- work in private industry;
- own their own home;
- tend to vote Conservative.

The old working class, in contrast, live in other areas of the country, are union members and council tenants, work in the public sector, and tend to vote Labour.

However, **Marshall** *et al* (1988) found that class continued to have more influence on voting than the **sectoral divisions** identified by Crewe.

Warwick & Littlejohn (1992) studied mining communities in the 1980s and found some divisions between the more successful workers, who were able to buy their council houses, and the less successful, who suffered from unemployment. However, these divisions were based on economic differences not level of skill.

Class consciousness

While Marx predicted growing class consciousness, the evidence suggests that it is not happening.

Goldthorpe *et al*'s 1960s study of affluent workers in Luton showed the proletarian traditionalists already in decline. **Roberts** (2001) argues that most workers still see themselves as working-class, but that the working class is disorganized, disempowered and devalued.

Some sociologists believe that the seeds of **class consciousness** are still there. **Devine** (1992) found that 1980s Luton workers, conscious of inequality and injustice, still looked to unions and the Labour Party to tackle such issues, but they had little faith that they could achieve much.

Blackburn & Mann (1975) argue that the working class show inconsistencies and contradictions in their views. They experience exploitation and subordination at work, which encourage class consciousness, but the mass media and the ideology of the dominant class undermine class consciousness.

Marshall *et al* also found contradictory beliefs: many of the working class in their sample were aware of injustice and inequality but were ambivalent about taking steps to reduce inequality. Overall, Marshall *et al* found considerable potential for class consciousness, in terms of individuals seeing society as unfair, but they criticized the Labour Party for failing to mobilize and harness this sense of dissatisfaction.

THE LOWER STRATA

AQA, OCR, WJEC   Textbook pp. 63–66

Some sociologists have argued that there is a class underneath the working class. This class is often referred to as the **underclass**.

Murray – the underclass

Charles Murray (1989) puts forward a **cultural view** of the underclass. He argues that, in America and more recently in Britain, there is a growing underclass defined in terms of behaviour and attitudes. It includes:

- single parents;
- the unemployed who don't want to work;
- those making a living from crime.

In America, a large proportion of the underclass is black.

Members of the underclass reject values such as honesty and hard work. **Welfare payments** allow people to become single parents, and children lack the role model of a hard-working father, thus perpetuating underclass attitudes.

Criticisms

This cultural theory neglects economic divisions.

It ignores structural factors which might cause lack of economic success – for example: lack of employment opportunities; the decline of manual work.

It blames the disadvantaged for their problems (see p. 17 for other criticisms).

Giddens – the dual labour market

Giddens (1973) has a more economic theory of the underclass. It is made up of workers who tend to find jobs in the **secondary labour market** (low-paid, insecure jobs with few prospects). Employers tend to recruit women and ethnic minorities into such jobs, partly because of discrimination and prejudice.

The underclass have more radical views than the working class who are in secure employment.

Criticisms

Mann (1986) argues that there is no clear dividing line between the primary (secure, well-paid work) and secondary labour markets. He claims that Giddens fails to give a convincing explanation of why women and ethnic minorities are in secondary employment (see p. 17 for a discussion of ethnicity and the underclass).

Gallie – heterogeneity of the underclass

Gallie (1988, 1994a) argues that the underclass is too **heterogeneous** to be seen as a single class. He finds big differences in the employment situations of women and members of ethnic minorities, and points out that there is a big flow into and out of unemployment.

The underclass also includes diverse **age groups**, and they often have different interests. They are therefore unlikely to develop shared consciousness.

Gallie found no evidence that the long-term unemployed were resigned to being without work and little evidence of a political split between the working class and the underclass.

Roberts (1997) argues that the underclass:

- are more deprived than the working class.
- experience **long-term** deprivation.
- have different **social networks** and lifestyles from those in employment. He points out, however, that they are a very **diverse** group.

Runciman – underclass claimants

Runciman (1990) sees the underclass as consisting of those reliant upon benefits, with little chance of being able to participate in paid employment. This places them in a different economic situation from even low-paid workers.

Criticisms

Dean & Taylor-Gooby (1992) criticize Runciman for failing to take into account the large numbers who escape from reliance upon benefits. This makes any supposed underclass highly unstable.

Dean (1991) argues that the term underclass is used imprecisely in a variety of ways, often with the implication that the disadvantaged are to blame for their own problems. He therefore argues that it should no longer be used.

CLASS IDENTITY AND CULTURE

AQA, OCR, WJEC   **Textbook pp. 67–75**

Savage (2005) suggests that class identities cannot merely be predicted from structural processes. They are actively created through cultural processes interacting with economic inequality.

Lawler (2005) shows, for example, how people resist the label 'chav' because of its negative connotations.

Pierre Bourdieu

Bourdieu (1984) sees cultural aspects of class as being as important as economic aspects. **Economic**, **cultural** and **lifestyle** factors interact to shape an individual's life chances. There are four types of capital related to class:

1. **Economic capital** consists of wealth and income.
2. **Cultural capital** includes educational qualifications and knowledge of the arts.
3. **Social capital** consists of social connections and friendships.
4. **Symbolic capital**, similar to status, concerns reputation.

The value of cultural capital is socially constructed:

- **Legitimate culture** belongs to the dominant classes and is equated with good taste – for example, classical music.
- **Middlebrow culture** belongs to the middle classes.
- **Popular taste** belongs to the lower classes and is seen as having little value – for example, pop music. Cultural capital also relates to lifestyle and consumption – for example, food and diet.

Different types of capital can be used to achieve upward mobility. Sometimes one type of capital can be used to gain another; for example, economic capital can be used to pay for private education which gains cultural capital.

Groups whose position is based on different types of capital tend to develop a different **habitus**. The habitus consists of the different ways a group perceives the world and the different tastes and perceptions they have. The habitus of a group changes over time.

Criticisms

Some see the theory as underestimating individual choice by assuming that people tend to conform to their habitus.

Bourdieu may neglect the importance of institutions such as the welfare state in shaping class.

Charlesworth – culture of necessity

Simon Charlesworth (2000) studied working-class life in Rotherham. The **habitus** of the working class was reflected in the way they dressed, their comportment and their nights out.

Lacking symbolic and cultural capital, life is a daily struggle which creates a **culture of necessity**.

Education, argues Charlesworth, plays a crucial role in encouraging people to devalue themselves.

Skeggs – class and gender

Skeggs (1997) studied working-class women on caring courses in an FE college. The women lacked economic, cultural, social and symbolic capital.

The women sought to **disidentify** themselves from the working class by trying to show that they were respectable and responsible, and by avoiding being seen as 'tarts' or 'sluts'.

However, they also wanted to be seen as desirable, to maximize their value in the 'marriage market'.

Savage *et al* – class identities

Savage *et al* (2001) studied class identities near Manchester.

Few thought Britain was becoming **classless**. The majority were **defensive** and **ambivalent**, seeing themselves as individuals, in control of their lives, but recognizing the existence of class.

A small group of the upper middle class and working class had strong class identities. The working class were most threatened by their class identity and most likely to disidentify with class.

Criticisms

Payne *et al* (2005) criticize the methodology of Savage's research. Their research shows that people recognize social class. Respondents identified a total of 14 criteria including financial inequalities, educational qualifications, aspirations, lifestyle and housing. Payne argues the confusion in expressing views on class was a result of the complexity of the concept not a rejection of **self-identification**.

Conclusion

These studies suggest that class continues to exert a strong influence on people's lifestyle and life chances through the interaction of cultural and economic aspects of class.

SOCIAL MOBILITY

AQA, OCR, WJEC   Textbook pp. 75-82

Social mobility is movement from one stratum of society to another.

In preindustrial societies status is largely **ascribed** – based upon who you are (for example: kinship, gender, ethnicity, and class background).

In industrial societies status is increasingly **achieved** – based on what you do. People's social position is based on merit, talent, ability, ambition and hard work.

Rates of social mobility are higher in industrial societies.

Sociologists study social mobility because:

- it shows whether society has **equality of opportunity**;
- where social mobility is low distinctive class cultures may form.

There are two types of social mobility:

- **Intragenerational mobility** refers to mobility within one generation – for example, a person being promoted at work.
- **Intergenerational mobility** refers to mobility between generations; it is measured by comparing the occupational statuses of parents and children.

The Oxford Mobility Study

Glass (1954) did the first major study of social mobility, but the study has significant methodological flaws.

In 1972 the **Oxford Mobility Study** provided more up-to-date and reliable data. It divided the class structure into three main groups: the service class (highest), the working class (lowest) and an intermediate class.

The study found higher rates of **long-range** mobility than Glass's study and high rates of **absolute** mobility (the total amount of social mobility). This was largely due to a considerable expansion of the service class, creating more room at the top of the stratification system. There were high rates of **upward mobility**.

However, **relative mobility** chances (the chances of those from different backgrounds achieving particular positions) remained unchanged. Thus children from the service class were much more likely to achieve positions in the service class than children from the working class. **Kellner & Wilby** (1980) summarize this as the **1:2:4 rule of relative hope** – for every child from the working class who ends up in the top class, two achieve this from the intermediate classes and four from the service class.

Trends since the Oxford Mobility Study

Goldthorpe & Payne (1986) used data from British election studies to show that from 1972 to 1983 relative mobility chances stayed about the same, despite further growth of the service class.

At the very top of the stratification system there is evidence that mobility is low. **Elite self-recruitment** tends to take place, whereby elite positions are filled by the children of those already in the elite.

The **National Child Development Study (NCDS)** (1997) found that 55% of sons stayed in the working class (compared to 57% in the Oxford study). However,

there was more chance of working-class sons getting service-class jobs than in the Oxford study (26% as opposed to 16%).

Gender and mobility

Most studies of mobility have used the class of the main breadwinner (usually a man) to determine the class of family members.

Goldthorpe & Payne (1986) argue that other ways of determining the class of women (for example, using their own jobs rather than their husbands' jobs) make little difference to the overall findings of mobility studies.

Heath (1981), however, found that women from service-class backgrounds were more likely to be downwardly mobile than men from this class, while women from working-class backgrounds were more likely to be upwardly mobile than men. Heath believes that, overall, this disadvantages women rather than men.

- The **NCDS** (1997) also found that women from service-class background were less likely than men from this background to maintain their class position. Women were more likely than men to be upwardly or downwardly mobile to the intermediate class.

International studies of mobility

Breen (2004) studied mobility in eight European countries. He showed that men achieved more **upward mobility** than **downward**. Upward mobility had increased for women, but they still had higher rates of downward mobility than men. The study examined class of origin and educational success. It found no evidence of a decrease in the influence of social class on educational achievement in Britain.

Blanden *et al* (2005) showed that Britain had lower upward mobility rates than most of Europe and the rate had fallen between 1958 and 1970. He found a strengthening link between **parental income** and educational success. More pupils stayed on at school post-16 between the mid 1980s and mid 1990s, but the rates rose faster among the affluent groups. After the mid 1990s the relationship between staying on post-16 and income weakened, but there was a marked strengthening of the relationship between parental income and achieving a university degree. Blanden argues that **equality of opportunity** is decreasing.

GENDER AND SOCIAL CLASS

AQA, OCR, WJEC   Textbook pp. 82-83

The position of women in the class structure was neglected in many early studies – women were often assumed to simply have the same class as their husbands. However, increasingly this has been disputed.

Parkin (1972) argues that the life chances of women are largely determined by the position of the male breadwinner in a family.

Britten & Heath (1983) disagree, pointing out that there are an increasing number of **cross-class families** in which women have a better-paid, higher-status job than men.

Goldthorpe (1983) largely agrees with Parkin, arguing that the family is the **unit of class analysis**. However, he does concede that the class of the family should be taken from the head of household. This is usually the man, but it can be the woman – for example, in single-parent households or where the woman has more commitment to paid employment than the man.

Stanworth (1984) argues that men and women should be placed in classes as individuals according to their jobs, not as members of families.

Rose & Marshall (1988) found that **class fates** (for example, mobility chances) were more affected by the class of individuals, while **class actions** (for example, who you voted for) could be better predicted by the family's class.

CONTEMPORARY THEORIES

AQA, OCR, WJEC   Textbook pp. 83-89

The death of class?

The postmodernists **Pakulski & Waters** (1996) claim that class is losing its significance. People no longer feel that they belong to classes, and supposed classes include a big variety of people. New **cleavages** are more important in shaping people's social and political beliefs than class.

Towards the end of the twentieth century, stratification became based on **cultural differences** rather than economic ones. **Lifestyle** and **identity** have become more important than economic differences – for example, status is more to do with the décor of a person's house than the job they have.

Some low-paid jobs (for example, in the media) have higher status than better-paid jobs. As a result, stratification systems are more fragmented and fluid than previous class systems – it is easier to change status than it once was.

Pakulski & Waters explain the death of class in terms of:

- the increasing importance of educational qualifications in shaping status;
- the declining importance of privately owned property compared to property owned by organizations;
- a wider distribution of wealth, giving more people greater **lifestyle choices** and more opportunity to choose what they consume according to their taste;
- **globalization**, which has reduced the importance of class inequalities within countries;
- the growth of **new politics** based around non-class issues such as ethnicity and religion.

Criticisms

Bradley (1997) argues that Pakulski & Waters have no consistent definition of class. They ignore the extent to which economic class differences still affect what people can afford and therefore what lifestyle choices they can make.

Marshall (1997) argues that they are highly selective in the arguments and evidence they use and tend to neglect evidence that economic class inequalities are still a major factor in shaping people's lives.

Ulrich Beck – Risk Society

Beck (1992) believes societies have moved from **simple modernity** to **reflexive** or **late modernity**.

In **simple modernity** most conflict is about the distribution of wealth.

In **reflexive modernity** technology increases production and reduces material need, making class divisions less important.

There is increasing concern with **risk** created by science and technology rather than material need. Risks are associated with obesity from processed foods, the possibility of nuclear accidents and toxins in the environment.

All social classes are subject to these risks, not just lower classes.

Late modernity involves **reflexivity**, or reflection on these risks.

People experience risk as individuals, and society becomes **individualized** as class identities become weaker.

Criticisms

Scott (2000) argues that wealth does enable individuals to avoid some risks.

Beck may underestimate the extent to which wealth still shapes life chances.

Beck ignores empirical research which shows that class still shapes identity.

Westergaard – hardening of class inequality

Westergaard (1995) argues that, far from disappearing, class inequalities are hardening.

He sees class in Marxist/Weberian terms as determined by a person's position in the economic order.

There is strong evidence of increasing inequality:

- In Britain the highest-paid 10% of white-collar workers had a 40% increase in real wages from 1980 to 1990, while the poorest 10% of manual workers had no rise in pay.
- From the 1970s to the 1980s the share of all income earned by the richest 20% of households increased from 37% to 44%, whilst the share of the poorest 20% of households fell from 10% to 7%.
- Privately owned wealth was becoming more concentrated in the hands of a few in the 1980s.
- The power of big business has been growing as a result of **privatization** and the adoption of **free-market policies**.

Westergaard sees the reasons for these changes as lying in government policies and the growth of **transnational corporations**.

He accepts that **lifestyle** and **consumption** have become increasingly related to **identity**. However, he sees these as strongly influenced by economic differences such as wage inequality.

Gender divisions tend to reinforce class inequality. In middle-class families, the man and the woman may have well-paid jobs, whereas few working-class families benefit from one partner's higher white-collar salary.

Ethnic divisions are closely related to class, with some ethnic minorities tending to be concentrated towards the bottom of the stratification system.

Westergaard accepts that **class consciousness** may have declined but he partly attributes this to the Labour Party's failure to express and mobilize dissatisfaction in society.

Class consciousness has the potential to revive, as surveys show continued dissatisfaction with inequality in British society.

GENDER INEQUALITY

AQA, OCR, WJEC   **Textbook pp. 100-104**

Firestone (1970) argues that the **sexual class system** is the most fundamental form of stratification in society. **Feminist** theories try to explain inequalities and differences between men and women and suggest what should be done about them. There are several broad approaches:

- **Radical feminism** – radical feminists believe that women are **exploited** by, and subservient to, men. Society is **patriarchal**, or male-dominated. Men are the ruling class and women the subject class. Radical feminists explain the inequality in various ways, some seeing **biology** as the cause, others seeing **culture** or **male violence** as more important. **Female supremacists** see women as superior to men, while **female separatists** believe that women should stay completely independent of men.

- **Marxist and socialist feminism** – Marxist and socialist feminists see the **capitalist system** as the main source of women's oppression and stress the importance of the exploitation of women as paid and unpaid workers. Some would like to see a communist society established.

- **Liberal feminism** – This perspective is associated with **equal rights** campaigners, who want **reforms** to improve women's position, rather than revolution. They often attribute inequality to **sexism**, **discrimination** and **sex role stereotyping** and socialization.

- **Black feminism** – Black feminists believe that racial/ethnic differences between women have been neglected by white feminists, and they stress the particularly deprived position of black women. **Brewer** (1993) argues that **class**, **race** and **gender** combine to give black women multiple sources of deprivation.

GENDER AND EMPLOYMENT

AQA, OCR, WJEC   **Textbook pp. 121-131**

In 1970 the **Equal Pay Act** legislated that women should be paid the same as men for doing the same or broadly similar work. In 1984 an amendment stipulated that women should get equal pay for work of equal value.

The 1975 **Sex Discrimination Act** made discrimination on the grounds of sex illegal in employment, education and the provision of goods and services.

The 2006 **Equality Act** required all public bodies to take an active role in removing illegal discrimination against women.

Despite these changes in the law, and some improvements in the position of women in Britain, women remain disadvantaged at work:

- The proportion of the labour force who are female has risen considerably. In 1971 92% of men of working age were employed and 56% of women. By 2005 80% of men were employed and 70% of women.

- In 2005 42% of women were part-time workers and 10% of men.

- In 2004 67% of women with **dependent children** worked.

- Women continue to be less well paid than men. In 1970 women working full-time earned 63% of the average full-time male wage; by 2005 they were still only getting 82% of the average male wage.

Horizontal segregation – where men and women tend to have different types of job – also continues. Women tend to be employed in areas such as personal services, administration, hotels and restaurants. Most routine clerical and secretarial workers are women, as are most primary teachers. Men tend to dominate in areas such as manufacturing, construction and transport. The proportion of women managers and professionals has increased recently. In 2005 the **Women and Work Commission** found 75% of pharmacists, 40% of accountants, almost 50% of lawyers and over 30% of doctors were women.

The Equal Opportunities Report (2006) reveals the absence of women in **elite positions** across a number of occupations, and comments that at the present rate of progress it would 50 years before half of top directors were women and 200 years before women were equally represented in the House of Commons.

Vertical segregation continues – i.e. men predominate in higher paid jobs whilst women predominate in lower paid ones. For example, in 2005 83% of directors and chief executives were men, 74% of waiting staff were women.

Explanations for gender inequalities

Textbook pp. 124-131

Human capital theory suggests that women are less valuable to employers than men because they are less committed to work and more likely to take career breaks to raise children. This gives employers less incentive to promote women and invest in their training.

However, a study by **Peter Sloane** (1994) found that gender continued to influence pay even when qualifications and experience were taken into account.

Hakim (2004) argues that women now have more choice, and inequality stems from **personal preference**. Women have better labour market opportunities than ever before due to:

- the contraceptive revolution;
- the equal opportunities revolution;
- the expansion of white collar occupations;
- the expansion of jobs for secondary earners.

Increased affluence means personal preference is more important than necessity.

This has led, according to Hakim, to the emergence of three types of women:

- **adaptive women**, who combine paid work and family without prioritizing either. This group is about two thirds of women. They seek flexible or part-time work.

- **work-centred women** – a minority, who focus on career and fit family life around it. This group is less than 20% of women, so men will continue to dominate the workplace.

- **home-centred women**, who prefer not to work. This group is about 20% of women, including some who are well qualified.

Crompton (1996), however, found no evidence of clear-cut categories among women working in banking and pharmacy in Britain and France. **Houston & Marks** (2003) found many factors other than **personal preference** influenced women's attitude towards paid employment. **Abbott et al** (2005) criticize Hakim for ignoring **structural constraints** which limit and shape women's choices.

The **dual labour market theory** developed by **Barron & Norris** (1976) distinguishes between:

- the **primary labour market** of well-paid, fairly secure jobs with prospects;
- the **secondary labour market** of poorly paid, insecure jobs with few prospects.

Employers try hard to attract and retain **primary workers**, who are seen as key to the success of their enterprises, but **secondary workers** are seen as easily replaced. It is difficult to transfer from the secondary to the primary labour market, and women tend to be concentrated in the secondary sector. This is due in part to employer sexism but also to factors such as lack of unionization.

Beechey (1986) sees women as a cheap **reserve army of labour**, brought in during economic booms but thrown out during slumps. This creates flexibility for capitalists and depresses overall wage levels. Women tend to be in the reserve army because: they are often not in unions; they may be prepared to work for less if their wage is a second income; they are seen as combining work with domestic responsibilities.

However, this theory cannot explain horizontal segregation. Also, the continued growth of female employment suggests that women are not being used purely as a temporary, reserve army of workers.

McDowell (1992) applies **post-Fordist** theory to female employment. Post-Fordism suggests that there has been a move away from mass production to more **flexible production** of specialist products. Businesses keep a core of highly skilled workers, but most other workers are temporary or part-time, or work is contracted out to other firms. Women tend to be concentrated in the more flexible jobs, particularly part-time work, although some have benefited from gaining **core jobs**.

Research by **Lovering** (1994) found evidence to support this theory in some companies but not in others, suggesting that post-Fordist trends affect only some workers.

Some feminists stress the role of **male trade unionists** in restricting women's opportunities. **Walby** (1986) argues that in some areas (for example, engineering) trade unions have used exclusion to disadvantage women, while in industries such as textiles, women have been disadvantaged by confinement to certain lower-paid areas of work. Low-paid work ensures that women are more likely to take on domestic responsibilities than men.

Radical feminists see **patriarchy** rather than capitalism as the main cause of female disadvantage. **Stanko** (1988) argues that **sexual harassment** in the workplace is used to keep women in their place. Men use their power in the workplace to protect their position. Women in jobs such as bar work and secretarial work are **sexualized**, and are not taken as seriously as workers or considered for promotion.

Adkins (1995) goes further, arguing that **sexual work** has become integral to many women's jobs. In service sector jobs where women have contact with men they are expected to engage in **sexual servicing**: looking attractive, engaging in sexual banter, tolerating sexual innuendo and so on.

The Women and Work Commission (2006) argues that reform, legislation and tackling sexist socialization can solve the problem of unequal pay. They argue that:

- **gender stereotyping** in schools, in careers advice, and in work experience programmes, is based on traditional roles. This results in the concentration of women in lower-paid occupations. The Commission pointed out that the media could challenge these cultural expectations – two thirds of forensic science students are now women.

- combining work and family life leads to women taking career breaks and working part-time. **Gosling** (2005) found a single year working part-time before returning to full-time work led to a 10–15% reduction in pay, largely due to the quality of the part-time work available.

- women need more opportunities for **lifelong training**.

- **workplace practices** often disadvantage women. Job evaluations which rank male-dominated jobs more highly than female ones, even though these jobs have a similar skill level, need to be challenged.

ETHNIC INEQUALITIES

AQA, OCR, WJEC Textbook pp. 174-176

It can be argued that **ethnicity** is an important form of stratification in society. There is clear evidence of **inequality** between different ethnic groups in Britain. Various government statistical sources provide useful data. The **Labour Force Survey** of 1998-2000 showed that:

- 41% of white men were in the highest two social classes compared to 47% of Indian men, 44% of Chinese men, 33% of Black men, 31% of Pakistani men and 23% of Bangladeshi men.

- patterns were different among women: 41% of Chinese women, 34% of white women, 34% of black women, 33% of Indian women and 29% of Bangladeshi/Pakistani women had jobs in the top two classes.

A Cabinet Office Report in 2000 showed big differences in earnings between ethnic groups, with white men earning twice as much as Bangladeshi men. Some of the differences in pay were related to qualifications but racism played some part in explaining them as well.

In 2004 5% of white British men were unemployed compared to 14% of black Caribbean men, 13% of Bangladeshi men, 11% of Pakistani men and 7% of Indian men.

Social Trends (2006) shows that in 2004 25% of white British women were economically inactive compared to over 70% of Pakistani and Bangladeshi women. It suggests that religious and cultural explanations may explain part of this difference.

Pilkington (2005) argues that ethnic minorities are disadvantaged in their housing. They are more likely to live in deprived areas of cities and other urban areas and also more likely to live in overcrowded homes.

The Home Office (2005) calculated that even when educational qualifications were taken into account ethnic minorities were still less able to find employment than other groups. They calculated an **ethnic penalty** for each group. Pilkington (2005) argues that **racial discrimination** continues to play a role in the disadvantaged position of ethnic minorities in the labour market.

Ethnic minorities and the labour market

AQA, OCR, WJEC Textbook pp. 204-207

A number of attempts have been made to explain the tendency for people from some ethnic minorities to get lower pay and to have lower-status jobs.

Discrimination

Brown & Gay (1985) used bogus job applications to measure the extent of racial discrimination by employers in the 1980s. They found evidence that more than a quarter of employers discriminated against ethnic minority applicants by denying them job interviews.

In a 1990s survey by the **Policy Studies Institute** substantial minorities amongst ethnic groups (for example, 28% of Caribbean people) claimed to have been denied a job because of their race or religion.

Ethnic minorities as an underclass

Some sociologists have seen ethnic minorities as making up an underclass.

Charles Murray (1984) argued that in the USA there was a growing **black underclass** made up of single mothers, young men unwilling to work, and criminals. Their problems stemmed from their **culture**, which was characterized by **dependency**. Welfare payments made single parenthood possible and encouraged dependency on benefits rather than earned income. However, Morris (1994) points out that there is no automatic entitlement to benefits for the unemployed in the USA.

An alternative view of the US underclass in the USA is put forward by Wilson (1987). He sees blacks and Hispanics living in inner cities as making up an underclass, but because of disadvantage rather than because of cultural differences.

A combination of **racism** and lack of skills has held these groups back, and their lack of economic success has reinforced racial stereotypes.

Successful blacks and Hispanics have moved out of the inner cities, leaving the least successful behind. Wilson suggests that the term underclass should be abandoned because it has been used by some to unfairly blame the disadvantaged for their problems. He prefers the term **ghetto poor** which has no such connotations.

Giddens (1973) argued that there was an **ethnic minority** and **female underclass** in Britain, as a result of structural problems such as low skills and discrimination.

Rex & Tomlinson (1979) studied the area of Handsworth, Birmingham, in the late 1970s and found evidence of an **ethnic minority underclass**. They found that blacks and Asians were concentrated in **secondary labour market** jobs – those with few prospects and little security. For example, a high proportion worked in metal or metal goods manufacturing but only a low proportion in the better-paid vehicle manufacturing sector.

Marxist approaches

An alternative view is put forward by Marxists such as **Castles & Kosack** (1973).

From a study of immigrant groups in various European countries, they acknowledge that such groups are concentrated in low-paid and low-status work.

In Britain this is mostly due to **discrimination**. However, in France, Germany and Switzerland many members of ethnic minorities are **migrant workers** who lack **citizenship rights**. Here restrictive laws and regulations prevent them from getting better work.

Castles & Kosack see immigrants as a **reserve army of labour** – easily hired and fired – who are needed to cope with the booms and slumps of capitalist economies. They see them as the most disadvantaged group in the working class rather than as a separate underclass.

Pilkington (1999) questions all of the above theories which see ethnic minorities as forming a distinct **stratum** below or at the bottom of the working class. He points out that a substantial proportion of all ethnic minorities have **non-manual jobs**. African Asian men are more likely to be in high status employment than white men.

Although ethnic minorities overall have lower pay and lower-status jobs, there is a great deal of overlap and no evidence of ethnic minorities as a whole forming an underprivileged stratum. Over time all ethnic minority groups have made greater gains in the labour market than whites.

Bangladeshis and Pakistanis remain the most disadvantaged. There is **polarization** within these groups between the successful and unsuccessful.

Mirza (1992) highlights the success of some black women in Britain. She argues that a range of factors (such as class, background, gender, age and cultural difference, as well as ethnicity) need to be examined in order to understand the labour market.

AGE

AQA, OCR, WJEC Textbook pp. 747-756

Vincent (1995, 2006) argues that age is an important form of stratification in society. It creates barriers to and opportunities for status, power, wealth and income. The significance of age varies between societies and over time, and the experience of ageing depends on social class, gender and ethnicity. In rural economies age was irrelevant but in capitalist societies age became associated with legal rights and restrictions – for example, compulsory education and work became the basis of status and income. Vincent describes three types of age classification:

- **Age strata** or **age classes** are groups of people of the same age. They share the same life chances and social rights. Jackson & Scott (2006) argue that childhood in Britain is a form of subordination.
- **Generation** refers to position in the family and can also be a source of conflict.

- **Cohort** refers to groups of people born at the same time. They experience the same historical changes which can influence their outlook.

Vincent shows how old people, especially working-class women, are more likely to be poor than other age groups. The value of the old age pension has declined since 1979, and women who work part-time or in low-paid jobs may have restricted entitlements to pensions. At the same time women live longer than men so have more years of **dependency**. Vincent argues there is a growing divide between the elderly and the working population, and growing divisions amongst older people. Vincent believes that the problem of old age is **socially constructed** and the moral panic over Britain's ageing population is an ideological distraction.

Feminist perspectives

Feminist perspectives link inequalities of age with those of **gender**. One approach links the **oppression of children** with the **oppression of women**; a second links the way ageing affects men and women differently:

- **Oakley** (1994) argues that women and children are minority groups locked together in **patriarchal oppression**. They are regarded by society as physically or culturally different and have fewer citizenship rights.
- **Gannon** (1999) argues that women are materially disadvantaged in old age because they tend to be paid less and to have caring responsibilities.

Interactionist perspectives

Interactionists see old age as socially constructed rather than biological or natural.

Hockey & James (1993) argue that childhood and old age are linked: the elderly are often treated like children as **dependent, passive and powerless**. This is demonstrated in old people's homes where the elderly are not allowed access to their own money or choices about their food. **Disabled people** may be similarly **marginalized**.

Hockey & James suggest that both the elderly and children could be more independent. They quote examples of these groups resisting their status – teenagers pretending to be 18 and elderly men exerting patriarchal power over female carers.

Postmodernist perspectives

Postmodernists suggest that differences in the stages of the life course are breaking down.

Pilcher (1995) argues that in the modern world the life course is strongly influenced by the **labour market**. Exclusion from the workforce has extended **powerlessness** and **dependency** in old age whilst the extension of education has prolonged childhood and youth. As modernity breaks down, the borders between the different stages become blurred – children dress as adults whilst the middle-aged dress as young people. However, Pilcher believes that age-based divisions continue to be important.

Featherstone & Hepworth (1991) argue that childhood has become less separate from adulthood and the elderly regard old age as a **chronological mask** which hides their **personal age** – the age they feel themselves to be. Even after retirement middle-class people

continue to contribute to their community, for example through voluntary work, and may often retain considerable economic, cultural and social capital.

Blaikie (1999) argues that stereotypes of ageing have broken down and those over retirement age are an important market for **consumer goods**. He notes **positive ageing role models**, such as Cliff Richard and Joan Collins, and argues people are no longer restricted by age. However class, gender and ethnicity continue to shape the experience of old age.

For more information on childhood see Textbook pp. 756-765.

LATER LIFE AND OLD AGE

AQA, OCR, WJEC　　　　　　　Textbook pp. 782-5

Laslett (1989) suggests it is helpful to distinguish between the **third age**, when people retire and have fewer responsibilities, and the **fourth age**, when physical and mental decline limits activities.

Arber (2006) notes that **ageism** and **sexism** combine to make the lives of older women very difficult. Women live longer than men so are more likely to have caring responsibilities but are less likely to be cared for by a partner. Women are also more likely to experience poverty. However, some older women find new intimate partners but live separately – 'living apart together'.

Nazroo (2006) argues that ethnic minorities have poorer health in old age and this is linked to income inequality. However, they have more family contacts, stronger social networks and more opportunities to take part in the community than white people.

Giddens (2006) argues that members of ethnic minority groups have lower incomes in old age.

Walker & Foster (2006) argue that social class impacts on pensions, health and life expectancy.

Functionalist perspectives

Functionalists see old age as a time of **disengagement** from society.

Cumming & Henry (1961) argue that the marginalization of the elderly is good for society because they become less able to do the work and they block opportunities for the young. Gradual disengagement allows both society and the individual to adapt to their ultimate disengagement.

Criticisms

Hunt (2005) argues that disengagement theory ignores the fact that some people may not be able or do not wish to disengage. Disengagement may be a waste of human resources.

Hockey & James (1993) argue that the role of the elderly results from **social construction** rather than disengagement.

Vincent (1995) argues that the elderly are dependent and disadvantaged because of **social structure** not because of biological decline or disengagement.

DEVELOP YOUR ANALYTICAL AND EVALUATION SKILLS

Essay plans

For each of the following questions write your own essay plan before comparing it with the suggestions given here. For the final question you can write a full answer and compare it with the provided model answer.

Does social class still shape people's life chances and lifestyle?

Background

This is about the economic and cultural aspects of social class. Studies show considerable ongoing economic inequality, but the growth in class consciousness predicted by Marx has not happened. Weber spoke of lifestyle and status. Studies of class culture suggest that class continues to influence lifestyle (see Bourdieu, Charlesworth and Payne). Postmodern sociologists suggest class is no longer important (see Pakulski, Beck).

For	**Against**
● Westergaard (p. 14)	● Pakulski & Waters (p. 14)
● Weber (p. 6)	● Ulrich Beck (p. 14)
● Studies of social mobility, and income and wealth (p. 6 and 13)	● Bourdieu, Charlesworth, Payne (p. 12)
● Bourdieu, Charlesworth, Payne (p. 12)	

Top Tip

You can argue that class is changing rather than ceasing to be important. There are lots of discussions in the chapter about changes in different classes – such as the embourgeoisement of the working class (p. 10), proletarianization of part of the middle class (p. 9) and Sklair's ideas on the globalization of the upper classes (p. 7).

Evaluate the Marxist theory of stratification.

Background

Marxist theory describes conflict within a two-class system and predicts growing class consciousness and a revolution. However, studies have shown fragmentation of social classes and divisions based on ethnicity and gender. Wealth is concentrated in the hands of the few and economic inequality is increasing. Marxism offers one explanation, Weberians another and postmodernists another still.

For	**Against**
● Marxist theory (p. 5)	● Postmodernism (p. 18)
● Westergaard (p. 14)	● Weberian views of the middle classes (p. 8)
● Braverman (p. 8)	● Arguments that the working class lacks class consciousness (p. 10)
● Figures on the concentration of wealth (p. 7)	● Risk society (p. 14)

For and against
● Scott (p. 7)
● Weber (p. 6)

Top Tip

You can also evaluate Marxism by considering whether it can really explain gender and ethnic inequality as well as class.

Stratification is an inevitable and desirable feature of human societies.

Background

Parsons supported this view, and saw stratification based on common values. Davis & Moore see stratification as inevitable because of the need for role allocation, and desirable because it ensures the most able do the most important jobs. Market liberals see unequal rewards as motivating. Tumin is a particular critic of Davis & Moore. Marxist theory suggests stratification is not inevitable (because of communism) or desirable (because it is based on exploitation). The section on social mobility is useful for suggesting that some talent might be wasted by stratification.

For	Against
● Davis & Moore (p. 5) ● Parsons (p. 4) ● Saunders (p. 5)	● Tumin (p. 5) ● Marx (p. 5) ● Some studies of social mobility (p. 13)

Top Tip

Treat the questions of whether stratification is inevitable and desirable as two separate issues; you might agree with one claim but not the other.

Evaluate explanations of the changes in the structure of inequality since the 1970s.

Background

Inequality has a number of strands including wealth, income and occupation. Changes in the occupational structure such as the deindustrialization and the growth of white-collar jobs affect people's life chances. The increasing employment of women is important too. Whilst the wealthy have largely maintained their advantage and some workers have become more affluent, those in the lower strata have seen their incomes fall.

Theory	*Explanation*
● Marxist theories (p. 5)	● Proletarianization ● Class inequalities hardening
● New Right theories (p. 5)	● Meritocracy ● Emergence of the underclass
● Postmodern theories (p. 14)	● Fragmentation of social class ● New cleavages more important

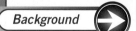

Top Tip

First establish the changes you are going to evaluate. Then evaluate sociological explanations. How far does the data match each explanation?

Britain is a meritocracy; inequality is based on ability and hard work.

Background

Meritocracy means the most able and hard-working achieve the highest rewards. If ability is randomly distributed amongst the population then Britain should have high levels of social mobility, both upwards and downwards, and people in higher social groups would not be able to use their position to advantage their children. Gender would be irrelevant. Studies of mobility show this is not the case, but Saunders believes this is because ability is concentrated in higher social classes.

<table>
<tr><td>

For

- Davis & Moore (p. 5)
- Saunders (p. 5)

</td><td>

Against

- Oxford mobility study (p. 13)
- Kellner & Wilby (p. 13)
- NCDS (p. 13)
- Scott (p. 7)
- Lansley (p. 7)

</td></tr>
</table>

Top Tip

Think about how to use the information on downward social mobility and changes in the occupational structure.

Model answer

Britain is a meritocracy; inequality is based on ability and hard work.

In a meritocracy rewards are given on the basis of achievement, and achievement is seen to be the result of ability, intelligence and effort. This essay will consider theoretical approaches to this issue, and then discuss the evidence on social mobility.

According to functionalists, meritocracy ensures that key roles in society are filled by people who have the appropriate aptitudes and training and are prepared to work hard to fulfill their role. Davis & Moore identified the importance of education in selecting students by aptitude and ability and allocating them roles in society. Thus those of higher ability would get higher grades, go on to university and fill more functionally important roles in society. In these higher roles they would achieve higher rewards, which Davis & Moore believed was entirely fair – rewards earned through merit.

Saunders, a New Right thinker, believes that Britain is almost totally meritocratic. The economic inequalities that exist are a reflection of the ability and effort of different sections of the population. Thus the success of middle-class students in the education system and beyond is due to their greater genetically inherited ability and the fact that they work harder than their working-class peers. Their greater success is earned in an open system where everybody has a chance to achieve, and the increase in middle-class jobs ensures everyone has the chance to be upwardly mobile.

Marxists would strongly disagree and believe that the ruling class use their power to ensure they can pass their advantage onto their children. They can point to richer people buying superior educational opportunities for their children, and a strong 'old boy' network advantageing the children of the ruling class, whilst the middle classes benefit from their cultural capital.

If Britain is a meritocracy, and if ability is distributed equally amongst the population, studies of social mobility should show both upward and downward mobility, and levels of mobility would probably be similar to those of other European countries. The Oxford mobility study showed relatively high rates of long-range mobility and high rates of absolute mobility. Every social class consisted of at least half of those born into a different social class. There was more upward mobility than downward – a reflection of the growth of middle-class jobs in the second half of the twentieth century. This evidence supports the idea of Britain as a meritocracy.

However, studies of relative mobility have shown that the high levels of upward mobility are largely due to changes in the occupational structure; Kellner & Wilby have shown that those higher up the social structure have better chances of upward mobility – the 1:2:4 rule of relative hope. This evidence does not show Britain to be fully meritocratic.

The Oxford mobility study was based on data for male occupations, and there is some evidence that women have different mobility patterns to men. Heath found women had greater downward mobility than men, and Abbott argued that women's jobs still relate to housewife/mother roles, so men have a career whilst women have a job that fits round that career. Abbott found very few women were upwardly mobile into the top social classes. Heath found working-class women were more likely to be upwardly mobile into routine non-manual occupations than working-class men, but argued that these jobs have little advantage over working-class jobs. Studies of the social mobility of women show less opportunity for social mobility than studies of men.

Work on the National Child Development Study has shown that although the class structure has continued to change, the majority of working-class children enter working-class jobs. The increase in service-class jobs gives opportunities for upward social mobility, so 40% of the service class had working-class origins; however, the majority of service-class children enter service class. Roberts argues that wide inequalities that tend to favour the middle class will continue, and as the middle class grows it will increasingly become self-recruiting.

Marxists have long believed that there is an upper class in Britain that is self-recruiting. Scott showed a capitalist class consisting of about 0.1% of the population who monopolize politics, business and the state. More recently Lansley argued that a super-class, drawn from privileged backgrounds, dominates British society. However, Lansley believes the traditional establishment has lost some of its influence and successful entrepreneurs, sports people and entertainers have joined the ranks of the wealthy.

So is Britain a meritocracy? There is substantial evidence of upward social mobility which represents opportunities for the working class, and the new business elite has wider social origins than other elite groups. However, Britain has less upward social mobility than its European neighbours. Blandon attributes this to the rising educational advantage of the middle classes. The data shows that the majority of children of the service class get service-class jobs, whilst the majority of working-class jobs are filled by children of the working class. Other theorists identify a ruling class which dominates British society. Overall, although Britain has some meritocratic features, it is not a meritocracy.

RESOURCES

Social stratification theories

Perspective	Basis of stratification	View of inequality	Key theorists	Key critics
Functionalism	Value consensus. Specialist roles needed by advanced industrial societies	Society pays the most important people at the highest level. High rewards encourage competition	Parsons Davis & Moore	Tumin Marxists
Market liberal	Meritocracy. Those in higher positions earn them through merit and deserve higher rewards	Motivating. Without unequal rewards force would be needed to ensure all jobs done	Saunders	Tumin Marshall
Marxism	Ruling class dominates resources and power. Exploits subordinate class	Ruling-class ideology and false consciousness prevent revolution	Marx Westergaard & Resler	Functionalists Weber Saunders
Weberian	Market situation; combination of occupation, wealth, social status and political influence	Market strategy by powerful groups of the population ensures their social and economic position	Weber Parry & Parry Macdonald	Ehrenreich & Ehrenreich Johnson
Postmodernist	Stratification based on cultural factors. Class no longer important	Status no longer depends on occupation or salary. Lifestyle is important	Pakulski	Westergaard

Writers and their work

Writer	Perspective	Concept	Study
Parsons	Functionalist	Value consensus	Stratification is inevitable, based on shared values
Davis & Moore	Functionalist	Role allocation	Shows that society needs differentiation
Marx	Marxist	Two-class system	Shows how the ruling class dominates and exploits the subordinate class
Westergaard	Marxist/ Weberian	Hardening of class inequality	Shows how inequality has increased under free market
Saunders	Market liberal	Economic elite	Study of meritocratic basis of inequality
Scott	Marx, Weber, elite theory	Upper class	Shows capitalist class remains a ruling class
Sklair	Marxist	Transnational capitalist class	Shows the emergence of a global ruling class
Weber	Weberian	Market situation	Shows differentiation based on class, status and party
Parry & Parry	Weberian	Professionalism	Shows how professions ensure they get well paid
Barber	Functionalist	Distinctive attributes of professions	Shows professions as serving society
Ehrenreich & Ehrenreich	Neo-Marxists	Professional-managerial class	20-25% of population carry out vital functions for capitalism
Braverman	Marxist	Deskilling	Work is increasingly becoming routine
Charlesworth	Interactionist	Culture of necessity	The daily struggle leads to a culture based on immediate needs
Runciman	Weberian	Market situation of underclass	Benefit claimants have no prospects of moving to paid employment
Kellner *et al*	Influenced by neo-Marxism	1:2:4 rule	Study of social mobility
Goldthorpe & Lockwood	Weberian	Affluent worker, proletarian traditionalist	Study of workers in Luton
Crewe	Political scientist	New working class	Differences between working class in north and south
Giddens	Weberian	Secondary labour market	Jobs with low pay, insecurity, no prospects
Murray	New Right/ market liberal	Underclass culture	Study of the 'undeserving' poor
Gallie	Sociology of economic life	Heterogeneity of underclass	Study of differences in the underclass

(Continued)

Writer	Perspective	Concept	Study
Bourdieu	Marxist	Cultural capital	Different types of capital can be used to ensure upward mobility
Beck	Postmodernist	Risk society	Study of risks affecting all social classes
Savage	Studies of complexity of stratification	Class ambivalence	Study of northwest England. Working class disidentify with class
Wynne	Based on Marxist ideas	Differences in middle-class lifestyles	Study of middle-class status on a private housing estate
Pakulski & Waters	Postmodernist	Death of class	Shows fragmented and fluid stratification system

Chapter 2 | FAMILIES AND HOUSEHOLDS

SPECIFICATION COVERAGE

Specification	Details
AQA AS Unit 1 SCLY1: Families and Households	All sections are relevant to AQA except the final section, *The Ageing Population and Society* (p. 38)
OCR AS Unit 672: Sociology of the Family	All sections are relevant to the OCR specification
WJEC AS Unit SY1: Families and Culture	All sections are relevant except *The Family, Politics and Social Policy* (p. 36) and *Demography* (p. 37). Note that this topic also covers family aspects of Unit SY 1: Acquiring Culture

FAMILY TYPES

AQA, OCR, WJEC   Textbook pp. 459-460

A simple definition of the family is a group of people related by marriage or blood or adoption. However, families types vary:

- The **nuclear family** is the smallest family unit and consists of a mother, father and their dependent children.

- The **extended family** is a larger family grouping, consisting of other members related by birth, marriage or adoption.

Another distinction is between **co-resident** families (who live together) and **kinship networks**.

FAMILIES AND THE SOCIAL STRUCTURE

AQA, OCR, WJEC   Textbook pp. 460-473

Is the family universal?

In 1949 **George Peter Murdock** looked at 250 societies and claimed that some form of family existed in each. He defined the family as a social group characterized by:

- common residence;
- economic cooperation;
- reproduction;
- having adults of both sexes, two of whom maintain a socially approved sexual relationship;
- including one or more (own or adopted) children of these adults.

He concluded that the nuclear family is **universal**, either on its own or as the base unit within an extended family.

Evaluation of Murdock

Murdock's definition of the family includes at least one adult of each sex. However, many children, both today and in the past, have been raised in households that do not contain adults of both sexes.

Kathleen Gough's analysis (1959) of the Nayar society in pre-colonial India, describes women with several 'husbands' who took no responsibility for the care of their offspring.

A significant proportion of black families in the West Indies, Central America and the USA are **matrifocal** (female-headed) families and do not include adult males.

Sheeran (1993) argues that the 'female carer core' is the most basic family unit. In Britain, for example, children usually have one woman who is primarily responsible for their care. This primary carer is not always the biological mother: it could be a grandmother, elder sister, aunt, adoptive mother or other female.

Gay and lesbian households may well contain children, either from a previous heterosexual relationship or as the result of new reproductive technologies.

Callahan (1997) argues that gay and lesbian households should be seen as families because their relationships are not significantly different from those in heterosexual households.

Whether the family is regarded as universal ultimately depends on how the family is defined. It may not be useful to insist on a single definition that embraces all the types of household and relationship that can reasonably be called families.

FUNCTIONALIST PERSPECTIVE

An analysis of the family from a functionalist perspective involves three main questions:

1   What are the functions of the family for society?

2   What are the functional relationships between the family and the wider social system?

3   What are the functions of the family for individuals?

Murdock's universal functions

Murdock (1949) argues that the family performs four basic functions for individuals and society, and that these are applicable to all societies:

- **Sexual** – essential for continuation of the society
- **Reproductive** – essential for continuation of the society
- **Economic** – essential for survival (for example, the production and preparation of food)
- **Educational** – essential for passing on the society's culture to the next generation

Criticisms

Murdock does not consider whether the above functions could be performed by other social institutions. **Morgan** (1975) points out that Murdock presents the nuclear family as a totally harmonious institution. Many writers, below, question this view.

Parsons's theories of the family

Talcott Parsons (1955, 1965b) argues that the family retains two 'basic and irreducible' functions that are common to all societies. These are: the primary socialization of children; the stabilization of adult personalities.

- **Primary socialization** refers to socialization during the early years of childhood. The child's personality is moulded to absorb the central values of the society's culture. Parsons could think of no other social institution providing the warmth, security and mutual support necessary for the successful socialization of individuals.

- **Stabilization of adult personalities** emphasises the marital relationship and the emotional security the couple provide for each other. This acts to balance out the stresses and strains of everyday life. The family also allows adults to 'act out' the childish parts of their personalities.

Parsons (1959, 1965b) argues that the **extended family** was typical of preindustrial societies. Most people worked in agriculture and each generation tended to stay on the land farmed by the family, leading to the formation of extended families.

Parsons describes the **isolated nuclear family** as the typical family form in modern industrial society. It is 'isolated' in that relationships between the nuclear family and wider kin are a matter of choice rather than obligation. There are three key reasons for its suitability in industrial societies:

1   **The evolution** of society involves a process of **structural differentiation**. This means that institutions evolve that specialize in fewer functions. Specialist institutions such as businesses, schools and hospitals take over many of the functions of the family.

2   There is a functional relationship between the isolated nuclear family and the **economic system**. In modern societies individuals are required to move to places where their particular skills are in demand. The isolated nuclear family is more suited to **geographical mobility** as it is not tied down with binding obligations to wider kin.

3   The isolated nuclear family is the best family form for societies where **status** is **ascribed** rather than **achieved** (fixed at birth). If adult children remained as part of an extended family unit, conflicts could arise if a son achieved a higher social position than his father, because within the family the father has a higher status.

Parsons also believes that society functions more effectively if fathers specialize in earning a living while mothers specialize in emotional roles, particularly being housewives and mothers.

Criticisms

Parsons presents an idealized view of the family, based largely on the American middle class. Like **Murdock**, Parsons fails to explore alternative family structures – for example, among different classes and ethnic groups.

Parsons sees socialization as a one-way process and he ignores the active role that children play in creating their own personalities.

Feminists reject as sexist the idea that women should stay at home as mother-housewives.

Research in Britain does not support the idea that the Industrial Revolution led to a change from extended to nuclear families. **Laslett** (1972, 1977) found that only about 10% of households contained extended kin before the Industrial Revolution. **Anderson** (1971) found high rates of extended household in Preston in 1851. **Young & Willmott** (1973) found that as late as the 1950s extended kinship networks were still strong in Bethnal Green, a working-class area of London.

MARXIST PERSPECTIVES

AQA, OCR, WJEC   Textbook pp. 464-465

Engels – the origins of the family

Friedrich Engels (1972, originally published 1884) attempted to trace the evolution of the family through time. In Engels's theory, the monogamous nuclear family developed to solve the problem of the inheritance of private property. Property was owned by males, who needed heirs to whom they could pass it on. They needed greater control over women so the paternity of their offspring was certain. The **monogamous family** provided the most efficient device for this purpose.

Zaretsky – capitalism and the family

Eli Zaretsky (1976) sees the family as a major prop to the capitalist system. The capitalist system is based on the **domestic labour** of housewives, who reproduce to create future generations of workers. The family **consumes** the products of capitalism and this enables the bourgeoisie to maintain its profits. The family provides comfort to **alienated** workers so they can carry on working.

Evaluation of Marxism

There is a lack of direct evidence for Engels's view, though **Gough** (1972) argues the general outline is broadly correct.

Somerville (2000) believes Engels exaggerates how well the family provides comfort, as there is much conflict within families.

FEMINIST PERSPECTIVES

AQA, OCR, WJEC   Textbook pp. 465-466

In recent years, feminism has had more influence on the study of the family than any other approach. Feminists have strongly criticized the effects of family life upon women. Feminist approaches have:

- introduced the study of areas of family life such as **housework** and **domestic violence**;
- challenged established views about **male dominance** in families;
- highlighted the economic contribution to society of women's domestic labour;
- focused on **power relationships** within the family, in particular the ways in which men benefit from families at the expense of women.

Some recent feminist writers have questioned the tendency of many feminists to make generalized condemnations of family life, and have emphasized the different experiences of women in families.

Marxist feminist perspectives

Marxist feminists argue that the family and its exploitation of women serves the needs of capitalism.

Benston (1972) points out that the husband's obligation to pay for the production and upkeep of the next generation weakens his bargaining power at work: he cannot go on strike because he has a family to support.

Ansley (1972) argues that the emotional support of wives acts as a safety valve for husbands' frustration caused by working within the capitalist system.

Cooper (1972) argues that the family is an **ideological conditioning device** in which children learn to submit to authority, thus keeping capitalism stable.

Criticisms

Variations in family life, such as those of class and ethnic group, are ignored.

Morgan (1975) points out that Marxist approaches often assume the existence of highly traditional families, a type of family that is becoming less common.

Marxist feminists may exaggerate the harm done to women in the family. They are reluctant to concede that there may be positive sides to family life. They also tend to portray women as the passive victims of exploitation, ignoring women who fight back against exploitation. Marxist feminism assumes that men are dominant in all families, with little evidence to back up this assertion.

Radical feminist perspectives

Radical feminism is a distinct body of theories, rather than adapted from existing theories. It sees the oppression of women as the most significant aspect of a **patriarchal** and male-dominated society.

Delphy & Leonard (1992) argue that the family is a patriarchal and **hierarchical** institution through which men dominate and exploit women. It is an **economic** system in which the male head of household gets unpaid domestic, sexual and reproductive work from women in return for subsistence and the occasional gift.

Greer (2000) argues that wives get less out of marriage than husbands; for example, single women tend to be happier than married women though the opposite is true for men. This is partly because wives remain **subservient** to their husbands, although the increased divorce rate shows women are less willing to accept this situation than they were. **Motherhood** can be rewarding, but is not valued by society, and mothers take the blame for many of society's problems. **Daughters** often suffer **sexual abuse** from male relatives. Greer concludes that women would be better off living away from **patriarchal families**.

Criticisms

Many of the criticisms of Marxist feminism also apply to radical feminism. In addition, radical feminists largely ignore the progress made by women and simply assume that all families are male-dominated or patriarchal.

Liberal feminist perspectives

Somerville (2000) offers a more moderate assessment of women's position in contemporary societies. She argues that:

- many feminists fail to acknowledge the progress made by women in Britain;

- women have more opportunities and choices open to them than in the past, and some men advocate greater **gender equality**;
- although many men do not live up to their responsibilities, most women do not wish to live without a male partner.

Feminists, Somerville concludes, need to adopt **principled pragmatism**, by which practical policies produce greater equality – such as improved childcare provision for working mothers.

Criticisms

- Somerville's claims are not backed up by detailed empirical evidence.
- Radical feminists believe that pragmatic, gradual, liberal feminist policies have not produced genuine gender equality, so they are unlikely to succeed in the future.

Difference feminism

Neither **Marxist** nor **radical feminism** is very sensitive to differences between families. Both can be criticized for failing to acknowledge the variety of domestic arrangements and the range of effects family life can have. Increasingly, feminists have begun to highlight these differences. These feminists have been referred to as **difference feminists**. Their work often has links with **postmodern** theories of the family.

Nicholson (1997) believes that there is a powerful **ideology** that supports traditional families but devalues other types. She believes that alternative families are often better than traditional ones for the women who live in them. Nicholson concludes that all types of family and household should be accepted because they could suit different women in different circumstances.

Calhoun (1997) focuses on **lesbian families**. She argues that modern family life is characterized by choice, and lesbian and gay families are 'chosen families'. Calhoun believes that gay and lesbian relationships are just as much family relationships as those of heterosexual couples.

Criticisms

Some difference feminists lose sight of the **inequalities** between men and women in stressing the range of choices open to people. They also tend to neglect the common experiences shared by most women in families – for example, of still having most responsibility for caring work.

POSTMODERN PERSPECTIVES

AQA, OCR, WJEC   **Textbook pp. 512-519**

Postmodern sociologists have many perspectives in common with difference feminists. They do not believe that a single type of family is dominant or is the norm in contemporary society. They disagree with functionalists, Marxists, and radical, Marxist and liberal feminists, that a single theory of family life is possible. They argue that there can be no **metanarrative** (see p. 230) of how family life is or should be.

Stacey – the postmodern family

Judith Stacey (1993) believes that contemporary societies such as the USA have developed the **postmodern family**. She associates changes in the family with a movement *away* from a single dominant family type and *towards* a greater variety in family relationships. Arrangements in the postmodern family are 'diverse, fluid and unresolved'.

The development of the postmodern family has destroyed the idea that the family progresses through a series of logical stages. There can be no assumption that any particular form will become accepted as the best, or normal, type of family. Diversity is here to stay.

Stacey illustrates her idea by citing the lives of two women in California, Dotty and Pam, whose family lives changed frequently and who both moved away from living in traditional, male-dominated nuclear families. Dotty split from her violent husband but took him back after he had a heart attack and could no longer dominate her.

Stacey acknowledges that the postmodern family can create unsettling instability but she generally welcomes it as an opportunity to develop more **egalitarian** family relationships.

Criticisms of postmodernism

It is questionable to what extent diversity and the postmodern family have become commonplace. It is possible that Stacey exaggerates the extent of change.

The examples of families in California may be unrepresentative.

MODERNITY AND THE FAMILY

AQA, OCR, WJEC   **Textbook pp. 512-514**

Some sociologists accept that important changes have taken place in the family, but they think we still live in the **modern** era and have not entered **postmodernity**.

Anthony Giddens

Giddens (1992) argues that **intimate relationships** have undergone important changes.

In the 18th century the idea of **romantic love** developed, where a marriage partner was idealized as the person who would make an individual's life fulfilled. Marriage was seen as a lifelong arrangement. Women would retain their virginity waiting for the right partner.

In the most recent era of modernity, **plastic sexuality** has developed, where better contraception has meant sex can be for pleasure rather than conceiving children. Relationships are no longer based upon the idea that a relationship is permanent.

Relationships are now based on **confluent love** – love depends on both partners getting what they want from the relationship. In the resulting **pure relationships** divorce and other break-ups become much more common.

People are unwilling to stay with unsatisfactory partners because of the **reflexive project of self** – a constant reflection on and attempt to improve one's life.

Individualization

Beck & Beck-Gernsheim (1995) see **individualization** as the main characteristic of modern life: individuals expect to make their own decisions about more and more aspects of their lives. More opportunities are open to everyone, especially women.

There is little **security** or **intimacy** in everyday life so people seek emotional security in families.

There is much more choice over the way that love and families work, so people have to work out a formula for their relationships. Without fixed, clear-cut roles, there is more conflict. The '**normal chaos of love**' results and leads to high divorce rates.

Another important perspective on the family is put forward by the **New Right** (see p. 36).

HISTORICAL DEVELOPMENT OF THE FAMILY

AQA, OCR, WJEC   Textbook pp 473–482

Young & Willmott – four stages of the family

In their book *The Symmetrical Family* (1973) **Young & Willmott** suggest that the family has gone through several main stages.

Stage 1 – the preindustrial family

The **preindustrial family** is a **unit of production**. It was gradually supplanted as a result of the Industrial Revolution. It did, however, continue into the nineteenth century and there are still some examples in farming families today.

Stage 2 – the early industrial family

This type of family developed in the nineteenth century and reached its peak in the early twentieth century. The family ceased to be a unit of production and responded to the new industrial society by extending its **network** to include relatives beyond the nuclear family. The early industrial family was still found in working-class Bethnal Green (London) in the 1950s, where mothers and their married daughters often lived near to one another and kept in close touch.

Stage 3 – the symmetrical family

By the early 1970s the *stage 2* family had largely disappeared. The *stage 3* family is **nuclear** and **home-centred**. Free time is spent doing chores and odd jobs, and leisure is mainly home-based. The bond between husband and wife is strong and they share work in the home. Young & Willmott use the term **symmetrical family** to describe the *stage 3* nuclear family.

The rise of the symmetrical family is promoted by:

- a reduction in the need for kinship-based support because of rising wages and the welfare state;
- increased geographical mobility;
- a reduction in the number of children per family (see p. 37);
- more amenities and entertainment in the home, making it a more attractive place.

Stratified diffusion

Young & Willmott argue that their theory of **stratified diffusion** explains many of the changes in family life. The theory states that what those at the top of the stratification system do today, those at the bottom will do tomorrow. The home-centred nuclear family began in the middle classes and eventually filtered down to the rest of society.

Families – 1980s and 1990s

In a comparison of attitudes to the family in 1986 and 1995, **McGlone *et al*** (1996) argue that families remain very important to people in contemporary Britain.

Families remain an important source of help and support. Family contacts are still maintained even though family members tend to live further apart than in the past.

Differences between social classes remain significant, with the working class more likely to have frequent contact than the middle class.

In terms of attitudes, most people are **family centred**; for example, most people think parents should continue to help children after they have left home.

The *British Social Attitudes Survey* (**Park *et al***, 2001) found that only 10% of those who had a mother surviving saw her less than several times a year, and 61% of grandparents saw their grandchildren at least once a week. Therefore both face-to-face and other contacts between family members remained quite frequent.

Dispersed extended family

Attempts have been made to characterize the contemporary family, taking account of the continuing contacts between relatives.

Willmott (1988) claims that the **dispersed extended family** is becoming dominant in Britain. It consists of two or more related families who cooperate with each other even though they live some distance apart. Cars, public transport and telephones allow dispersed extended families to keep in touch.

Brannen (2003) argues that contemporary family structure resembles a **beanpole**, as there are strong **intergenerational** links between parents and children across two, three or four generations, but **intragenerational** links (for example, between siblings and cousins) tend to be weaker.

FAMILY DIVERSITY

AQA, OCR, WJEC

Leach (1967) calls the image of the happily married couple – a male breadwinner and a female carer/housewife with two children – the '**cereal packet image**' of the family. This image remains prominent in advertising. Recent research suggests, however, that contemporary societies are characterized by a **plurality** of household and family types, so the idea of a 'typical' family is misleading.

Households in Britain

There has been a steady decline in the proportion of British households consisting of **married couples with dependent children**, from 35% in 1971 to 22% in 2005.

There has been a corresponding increase in **single-person households**, which rose from 18 to 29% in the same period.

The proportion of **single-parent households with dependent children** rose from 3% in 1971 to 7% in 2005.

Types of diversity

Rhona & Robert Rapoport (1982) identify five types of family diversity in Britain:

1 **Organizational diversity** – there are variations in family structure, household type and patterns of kinship, and differences in the division of labour in the household. There are also increasing numbers of reconstituted families, such as families formed after divorce and remarriage.

2 **Cultural diversity** – there are differences in the lifestyles of families of different ethnic origins and religious beliefs. (For discussion of ethnic diversity, see p. 32.)

3 **Class diversity** – there are differences between middle- and working-class families in relation to child-rearing and adult relationships.

4 **Life-cycle diversity** – differences result from the stage in the life cycle of the family. Newly married couples without children may, for example, have a different family life from those with dependent children.

5 **Cohort diversity** – this refers to the periods at which the family has passed through different stages of the family life cycle. High rates of unemployment during the 1980s, for example, may have increased the length of time children lived with their parents.

Allan & Crow (2001) see the trend towards diversity as being caused by:

- a rising **divorce rate**;
- a rise in lone parenthood, which partly reflects an acceptance that pregnancies do not have to be **legitimized** by marriage;
- acceptance of **cohabitation** before marriage;
- declining **marriage rates**;
- a growth in **stepfamilies**.

Gay and lesbian families

Gay and lesbian households have become more common since the 1980s. **Weeks et al** (1999) argue that gays and lesbians look on their households, and even their friendship networks, as '**chosen families**'. They choose who to include in their families and negotiate their relationships.

New reproductive technologies

New reproductive technologies such as **surrogate motherhood** add an entirely new dimension to family diversity. The implication is that biology will no longer restrict the possibilities for forming and enlarging families by having children, for example by gay and lesbian people, single women and older women.

Single-parent families

Single-parent families have become increasingly common in Britain. The figures must be interpreted with caution because they are only a snapshot and do not represent the dynamic nature of many families. For example, children may start their life in a single-parent family, but the single parent may find a new partner, so that the children then live with two parents.

The causes of single parenthood

People who are married can become single parents by **divorce**, **separation**, or the **death** of a spouse. Single parents who have never married:

- may have been living with the parent of the child but have subsequently separated.
- may not have been living with the parent of the child when the child was born.

The rise in lone motherhood and fatherhood (about one in eight single-parent families is headed by a male) is closely linked to two factors: increases in the **divorce rate** (see p. 35) and increases in **births outside marriage**.

Allan & Crow (2001) argue that both these trends reflect an increased acceptance of diversity.

Brown (1995) suggests that in previous eras 'shotgun weddings' (couples getting married to legitimize a pregnancy) were common. Now partners may choose to **cohabit** rather than marry. **Park et al** (2001) use data from the *British Social Attitudes Survey* to show that younger age groups are much more accepting of births outside marriage than older age groups.

Rapoport & Rapoport (1982) argue that the single-parent family is an important 'emerging form' of the family, which is becoming accepted as a legitimate alternative to other family structures.

Murray (1989) (see below) believes that over-generous welfare payments allow and even encourage unmarried women to become single parents. However, there is little evidence that a large number of single parents actively choose it as an alternative to dual parenthood. In a small-scale study by **Burghes & Brown** (1995), all of the lone mothers in the sample aspired to forming a two-parent household.

The consequences of single parenthood

Charles Murray (1989), a **New Right** sociologist (see p. 36), has gone so far as to claim that single parenthood has contributed to the creation of an antisocial **underclass** (see Textbook pp. 64-66). In some social classes, Murray suggests, young women choose to get pregnant, fathers remain unemployed and refuse to support their children, and the children grow up to be involved in crime.

Many sociologists disagree. **McIntosh** (1996) claims that lone mothers have been stigmatized and blamed for problems such as youth crime and unemployment.

However single parenthood is viewed, there is little doubt that it is associated with low living standards. The *General Household Survey* (2005) found that 41% of single-parent households had an income of £200 per week or less, compared to 11% of cohabiting couples with children.

Some research finds that lone parenthood has negative effects on children. **McLanahan & Booth** (1991) review the findings of American studies, which seem to indicate that children are harmed by single parenthood – that they are more likely to experience **poverty**, become **delinquent** or engage in **drug abuse**. However, as the authors themselves point out, these differences tend to stem from low income rather than the absence of a second parent.

Cashmore (1985) argues that it is often preferable for a child to live with one caring parent than with one caring and one uncaring parent. Single parenthood can also give women greater independence than they have in other family situations.

Ethnicity and family diversity

Statistical evidence from *Labour Market Trends* (2002) suggests that there are differences in household types among different ethnic groups:

- Black African and black Caribbean families have much higher rates of **single parenthood** than other groups.
- Rates among Indian families are very low, with white and Pakistani/Bangladeshi families having rates near the average.
- Asian families are more likely to have **extended kin** in the household than the families of other ethnic groups.
- **One-person households** are most common among black ethnic groups and least common among Pakistani/Bangladeshi ethnic groups.

South Asian families

Ballard (1982, 1990) has examined South Asian families in Britain:

- Many children had the experience of **two cultures**. They behaved in ways that conformed to the culture of wider society for part of the time, but at home conformed to their ethnic **subculture**.
- Although children expected to have some say in their marriage partner, they did not reject the principle of **arranged marriage**.
- Despite the distance involved, most families retained links with their village of origin in Asia.
- In Britain, close family ties remained. By living close together, people were able to retain strong family links.

Bhatti (1999) found that ideas of *izzat*, or family honour, remained very strong, as did the roles of the traditional male breadwinner and female child-rearer. However, in a minority of families there were **generational clashes**, especially where the sons sought to marry outside their own ethnic group. Overall, distinctive patterns of family life remained.

African Caribbean families in Britain

Barrow (1982) found that mother-centred families could rely less on the support of female kin than they could in the West Indies. However, equivalent networks did build up in areas with high concentrations of West Indians.

Berthoud & Breishon (1997) identified a low emphasis on long-term partnerships, especially formal marriage. British African-Caribbean families had high rates of separation and divorce and were more likely than other groups to have children outside marriage. Nevertheless, over half of Caribbean families with children were married or cohabiting in long-term relationships.

Reynolds (2002) emphasizes the diversity of African-Caribbean families and the importance of visiting relationships, where a female head of household has a male partner but they do not cohabit.

The evidence from different ethnic communities suggests that immigrants and their descendants have adapted to fit British circumstances but still retain some distinctive features in their patterns of family life.

Chester – the British neo-conventional family

In a strong attack on the idea that fundamental changes are taking place in British family life, **Chester** (1985) argues that the changes have only been minor:

- Nearly half the population still live in **nuclear family** households.
- It is inevitable that at any one time some people will not be members of nuclear family households. However, the vast majority of people still experience the **parent-child** household at some point.
- Chester accepts that many families are no longer conventional in the sense that the husband is the sole breadwinner. He sees this type of family as '**neo-conventional**' – little different from the conventional family, apart from the increasing number of wives working for at least part of their married lives.

Since Chester was writing, there has been a slow but steady drift away from **nuclear families** in Britain. As **Rapoport & Rapoport** argued in 1982, the degree of family diversity indicates increasing acceptance of alternative households and families. However, **Somerville** (2000) believes most people still aspire to conventional family life.

Research by **Dench *et al*** (2006) in Bethnal Green found a **new individualism** promoted family diversity, as did the nature of family life in the Bangladeshi community; but there was also a move back towards valuing conventional family life amongst some residents.

CHANGING FUNCTIONS OF THE FAMILY

AQA, OCR, WJEC   Textbook pages 495-497

As well as examining the changing structure of families, sociologists have also studied the changing functions of families. Many sociologists argue that the family has lost a number of its functions in modern industrial society. Institutions such as businesses, schools and welfare organizations now specialize in functions previously performed by the family.

Functionalist views

Parsons (1955) maintains that the family still has a vital role in preparing its members to meet the requirements of the social system (see p. 27).

Fletcher (1966) disputes the claim that some of the family's functions have been lost. He argues that the family has retained its functions and that these have increased in importance. The family is no longer a **unit of production**, but the modern home-centred family is a vital economic **unit of consumption** – for washing machines, DVD players and so on.

Feminist views

Feminists disagree that the family has lost its economic function. They argue that much of the work that takes place in the family is not recognized as such because it is unpaid and usually done by women (see p. 27).

Postmodernist and difference feminist views

These sociologists reject the view that there is any single type of family that always performs certain functions. With increasing **diversity**, some individual families and some types of family may be radical forces in society – for example, **gay and lesbian** families.

CONJUGAL ROLES

AQA, OCR, WJEC   **Textbook pp. 497-501**

A major characteristic of the **symmetrical family**, which **Willmott & Young** claimed was developing when they were writing in the 1970s, was the sharing of domestic work and leisure activities between spouses (see p. 30). Relationships of this type are known as **joint conjugal roles**, as opposed to **segregated conjugal roles** (which are unequal, spouses spending a lot of time apart and having quite different roles).

Inequality within marriage

There is no generally accepted way of measuring inequality between husbands and wives. Different researchers have measured it in different ways. However, most find little evidence that inequality in marriage has been significantly reduced.

Conjugal roles, housework and childcare

Oakley (1974) argues that **Willmott & Young**'s claim of increasing **symmetry** is based on inadequate methodology. Their conclusions were based on only one interview question, which was worded in a way that could exaggerate the amount of housework done by men.

Small-scale research in the 1970s by **Oakley** (1974) and **Edgell** (1980) found little sharing of household tasks.

The *British Social Attitudes Survey* (1992) found more sharing of child-rearing than household tasks, although there was some movement towards a more egalitarian division of labour over time.

Ferri & Smith (1996) used survey data to focus on **childcare**. In almost every kind of household – even where the woman had paid employment outside the home and the man did not – the woman usually took the main responsibility for childcare.

Inequality can also be measured in terms of time use. **Willmott & Young** found that the differences between men's and women's total work time inside and outside the home were not that great.

Gershuny (1992, 1999) found that the husbands of working women continued to do less than half the total paid and unpaid work done by their spouses. However, although the '**dual burden**' of paid and domestic work remained for women, men seemed to make more effort to do housework when their wives were in paid work.

Laurie & Gershuny (2000) found that over time there had been a slow drift towards men taking on more domestic responsibilities.

Lader et al (2006) conducted time-use surveys and found that in 2005 men and women in partnerships had similar amounts of leisure and work time, though amongst all men and women females had less leisure time than males. This was largely because women were more likely to be lone parents.

Conjugal roles and power

A study by **Hardill et al** (1997) found that although males dominated decision-making in most households, this was not the case in a significant minority of households where relationships were more equal.

Power can also be measured in terms of control over money:

- **Pahl** (1989, 1993) studied how couples manage their money. Just over a quarter of the couples in her study had a system of money management in which there was a fair degree of **equality**. However, in about 60% of families the husband was in control (**husband control**) or had more say (**husband-controlled pooling**). **Wife control** was most common in poorer families where managing the budget was a burden.
- Research by **Vogler** (1994) largely confirms Pahl's findings. She found an increase in the proportion of relationships with **egalitarian** financial arrangements but this proportion remained small.

Emotion work

- **Duncombe & Marsden** (1995) identify an invisible element of women's domestic work: **emotion work** – the management of an individual's own feelings in a relationship. Many women in their study expressed dissatisfaction with their partner's emotional input into the relationship and the family. Most men did not acknowledge that emotion work needed to be done to make the relationship work. Women can end up doing a **triple shift**. Having completed their **paid employment** they not only have to do most of the **housework**, they also have to do the **emotion work**.

Inequality within marriage – conclusion

A study of lesbian households by **Dunne** (1999) suggests that an equitable domestic division of labour can be achieved. However, it is hard to achieve in a culture that still differentiates so clearly between **masculinity** and **femininity**. Overall, the evidence indicates that women are still some way from achieving equality within marriage. Husbands of wives with full-time jobs seem to be taking over some of the burden of housework and childcare, but in other respects men still have advantages over women.

CHILDHOOD

AQA, OCR, WJEC   Textbook pp. 743-746

Life cycle and life course

The different stages of life (including childhood, adolescence, parenthood, retirement, old age, dying) are sometimes described as a **life cycle**. Life cycle implies a series of inevitable stages through which you pass based upon biological ageing. Many sociologists now prefer to use the term **life course** to life cycle.

Pitcher (1995) defines the life course as 'a socially defined "timetable" of behaviours deemed as appropriate for particular stages within any one society'. This implies that the expected behaviour can vary between societies, over time and between different groups in society, for example:

- Western societies view youthfulness as having a higher status than non-western societies.
- Some minority ethnic groups are more deferent to the elderly than the white ethnic majority.
- Attitudes towards childhood have changed over time (see below).

From this viewpoint **chronological age** (the number of years lived) does not determine the nature of age groupings in society (childhood, youth, old age etc.) which are largely a social construct – their meaning is defined by society. **Postmodernists** such as **Featherstone & Hepworth** (1991) (Textbook pp. 754-755) believe that even the life course has been **deconstructed** (broken down) so there are no clear distinctions between the behaviour expected at different stages of life. For example, middle-aged people take part in youthful sports; surgery can minimize the appearance of ageing; children are less segregated from adult life than they were; elderly people are healthier than in the past and less likely to feel restricted by age. Personal age (how old you feel) is more important than how old you feel or the stage of life course reached.

Childhood across different cultures

Textbook pp. 756-764

Childhood is often seen as a natural stage of life shaped by biological age. What is expected of children, and the social roles they take, is seen as a product of the chronological age (age in years) of children. If this were true then childhood would be very similar throughout the world and throughout history. But this is not the case. In the world today some children live very different lives to those in western society. For example:

- **Wyness** (2006) notes that in Mexico, until recently, most children did paid work.
- According to **Amnesty International** (2007) there are child soldiers in more than 30 countries.
- In Samoa children are expected to perform dangerous and physically demanding tasks.
- Amongst the Tikopia in the Western Pacific children are not expected to be obedient.

The historical development of childhood

The idea of childhood as we know it today is comparatively new. Many sociologists see childhood as a **social construct** – a role which is socially defined and specific to particular societies at particular times.

Philippe Ariès (1973) believes that the whole idea of childhood is modern, and that childhood did not exist in medieval times. Children in this period were treated as little adults:

- People didn't bother to note their chronological age.
- There were few specialist clothes, toys or games for children.
- Children were not seen as innocent or kept away from the adult world.
- They were expected to help out at work as soon as they could.
- Many children died before growing up but families did not keep pictures and there was limited mourning of child deaths.

After the sixteenth century modern conceptions of childhood developed in which:

- chronological age was seen as important;
- children who died were mourned and portraits of them sometimes kept;
- specialist toys, games and clothes for children developed;
- schooling kept children away from the adult world and children came to be seen as innocent;
- families became much more **child-centred**, with children coming to be seen as more special.

Ariès gives the following reasons for this:

- The introduction of education kept children separate from adults and extended the transition to adulthood.
- The **infant mortality** rate fell. As most children survived and parents had fewer children, they were more committed to the children they had.
- By the twentieth century specialist sciences like psychology and pediatrics emphasized the need for parents to care for and nurture children.

Shorter (1976) puts forward other reasons for modern ideas of childhood developing:

- The idea of **romantic love** developed, which made children seem more important – as the product of a special relationship.
- Philosophers such as **Rousseau** emphasized that children were born good and needed careful nurturing.
- The idea of motherhood involving **sacrifice** for the benefit of children emerged.

Other factors are also suggested as having influenced modern ideas of childhood.

Postman (1982) argues that the invention of the printing press is important because it meant children had to spend many years learning to read before becoming adults.

Pilcher (1995) sees 19th-century factory legislation banning children from factories and mines as crucial.

Jenks (2005) puts more emphasis on changing attitudes, arguing the **Apollonian** image of the child as a special individual in need of careful treatment has changed the position of children.

Childhood in late modernity

Some sociologists believe that childhood is again in the process of change.

Postman (1994) puts forward a **postmodern** view of childhood. He argues that the distinction between childhood and adulthood is breaking down in postmodernity, leading to the **disappearance of childhood**. The development of the mass media exposes children to the adult world, including images of sex and violence.

Jenks (2005) disagrees that childhood is disappearing. There is concern about loss of innocence, antisocial behaviour by children and exposure to adult knowledge, but children are still very restricted and regulated; for example, they have to attend school, can't vote, drink alcohol, or have sex under 16. However, he does think adult-child relationships are changing in **late modernity**. Parents place even more emphasis on relationships with children than they do on relationships with partners. Parent-child relationships are the last **primary relationships** because rising divorce rates make marriages less permanent.

Jenks (2005) argues that all theories of childhood tend to generalize about changes in childhood and fail to take account of variations according to class, gender, ethnicity etc.

Prout (2005) agrees with Jenks but points out that Jenks himself tends to generalize. Prout emphasizes the massive differences in the experience of childhood between wealthier and poorer countries – for example, the lack of education and the requirement to work from a young age in some poorer countries.

MARRIAGE AND MARITAL BREAKDOWN

AQA, OCR, WJEC Textbook pp. 501-508

A number of threats to marriage have been identified, and this has led some commentators to express concern about the future of the family. The threats fall into two main categories:

- threats resulting from alternatives to marriage;
- threats resulting from the breakdown of marriages.

Alternatives to marriage

The rate of first marriages in England and Wales fell from 82.3 marriages per thousand single adults in 1981 from 24.7 in 2004. From one point of view, it is argued that marriage is becoming less popular. There may be a number or reasons for this:

- the greater priority women give to their careers;
- the impact of feminism, which may have made marriage seem less attractive;
- the development of what **Beck & Beck-Gernsheim** describe as **individualization** (1995). People feel they can choose whether to get married, rather than feeling they have to get married (see p. 30);

- the importance of what **Giddens** (1992) calls **confluent love**. People will only wish to marry if they can find a partner who provides them with personal fulfilment (see p. 29);
- **cohabitation** seen as a long-term alternative to marriage (see below).

However, some see the decline as due to people **delaying marriages** rather than not getting married at all. The **average age** of marriage has been steadily increasing, from around 24 in 1961 to around 30 in 2005. Nevertheless, as **Bernardes** (1997) points out, most people do get married at some point in their life. In 2003 over 90% of 45-64 year-olds in the UK had married. Cohabitation may just be a prelude rather than an alternative to marriage.

Cohabitation

Cohabitation is increasing. By 2004 nearly a quarter of non-married people in Britain were cohabiting. There are competing ways of viewing this:

- **Morgan** (2003) sees it as part of a trend in which marriage is going out of fashion. Cohabitees are much more likely to break up than married couples and cohabitation is part of a general increase in the number of sexual partners.
- **Chandler** (1993) takes a different view. She notes that the time couples spend cohabiting is lengthening, and more of them appear to be choosing cohabitation as a long-term alternative to marriage.
- The *British Social attitudes Survey* (**Barlow et al**, 2001) found that the British population has become increasingly accepting of long-term cohabitation, and suggested that marriage would become more of a **lifestyle choice** than a social obligation.

Declining fertility and birth rates

A further threat to marriage comes from declining fertility and birth rates. These are discussed in detail below (see p. 37).

Single-person households

Many **single-person households** may be formed as a result of divorce or separation but others may result from a deliberate choice to live alone. Single-person households are becoming more common in Britain.

Marital breakdown

The second type of threat to contemporary marriage is the apparent rise in marital breakdowns. Marital breakdown can be divided into three main categories:

- **divorce** – the legal termination of a marriage;
- **separation**, which refers to the physical separation of the spouses;
- so-called **empty-shell marriages**, where the spouses continue to cohabit but their marriage exists in name only.

There was a steady rise in **divorce rates** in modern societies throughout the twentieth century. The rates appeared to stabilize during the 1990s, though they are still very high. The proportion of remarriages has also been rising, standing at around 40% in 2005. Reliable figures for separation and empty-shell marriages are not available.

Explanations for marital breakdown

Functionalists such as **Parsons** (1955) and **Fletcher** (1966) argue that the rise reflects the increasing value that is now put on marriage. People expect and demand more from marriage, and are more likely to end a relationship which might have been tolerable in the past. The *British Social Attitudes Survey* (2001) has found that people still value marriage but they also see **divorce** as a legitimate alternative.

The isolation of the nuclear family from wider kin places strain on the marital relationship. **Leach** (1967) suggests that the nuclear family suffers from an **emotional overload** which increases the level of **conflict** between its members. **Allan & Crow** (2001) suggest that greater **financial independence** for women makes them less willing to accept conflict with their spouse.

Gibson (1994) claims that the development of **modernity** has put increasing emphasis on individual aspirations. The ideology of the market emphasizes **consumer choice**: if you are not satisfied with your first choice of partner you are more likely to leave and try an alternative in the hope of greater personal satisfaction.

It is generally agreed that the **stigma** attached to divorce has been considerably reduced. **Gibson** (1994) believes that **secularization** (the decline of religious beliefs and institutions) has weakened the degree to which religious beliefs can bind a couple together and make divorce less likely.

Changing attitudes to divorce have led to changes in the law which have made it easier to obtain a divorce. In Britain, before 1857, a private Act of Parliament was required to obtain a divorce. Since 1857 the costs of obtaining a divorce have gone down and the grounds for divorce have been widened. By 1996 there was no need to show that either partner was at fault in order to prove that the marriage had broken down. Instead, the partners simply had to assert that the marriage had broken down and undergo a 'period of reflection', normally a year, to consider whether a reconciliation was possible. In 2002 new legislation required spouses to pay a fixed proportion of their income towards childcare costs if they did not have custody of the child or children.

Conclusion

It is easy to exaggerate the extent to which there has been a retreat from marriage. The socialist feminists **Abbott & Wallace** (1992) recognize the increasing diversity of family forms but see the alleged decline of the family and marriage as having been exaggerated for political ends by the **New Right**. **Somerville** (2000) believes that despite 'diversification of family forms and relationships' most people still believe in the value of family life.

THE FAMILY, POLITICS AND SOCIAL POLICY

AQA, OCR   Textbook pp. 508–512

Despite the traditional belief that politicians should not interfere in the family, state policies have always had an impact on family life. Taxation, welfare, housing, education policies and divorce laws all influence the way in which people organize their domestic life.

Feminists have argued that government policies tend to favour the traditional nuclear family with a male breadwinner.

Allan (1985) argues that much state policy is based on an ideology of the 'normal' family. Such policies assume that one family member will put primary emphasis on childcare rather than work, that families will usually take care of the elderly, and that wives are economically dependent on their husbands.

Johnson (1982) argues that school hours and holidays make it difficult for single parents to work. There is little help for women to care for elderly relatives, and in England a lack of financial help for care of elderly people with savings. Despite more state provision of nursery schooling, the costs of childcare are not tax deductible for working parents.

Mothers still tend to be given custody of children in divorce cases.

Fox Harding (1996) gives some examples of state policies that favour the traditional family:

- Few council or other public-funded houses have been built to accommodate groups larger than conventional nuclear families.

- Married women can only receive **invalidity pensions** if they can show that their physical condition prevents them from doing housework – a rule that does not apply to men and single women.

- Regulations relating to **maternity leave** and pay reinforce traditional gender roles, despite the introduction of **paternity leave** in 2001.

However, not all policies reinforce traditional gender roles and nuclear families. Fox Harding points out that in 1991 the House of Lords ruled that men were no longer exempt from being charged with raping their wives.

The liberalization of divorce laws has led more families to break up, while the rights of cohabitees have been extended.

Civil partnerships between gay or lesbian couples have been allowed since 2005.

Almond (2006) believes recent changes actually undermine traditional families; for example, liberal divorce laws and tax laws discriminate against families with one breadwinner.

The New Right and the family

Abbot & Wallace (1992), critics of the **New Right**, describe the New Right approach to the family in the following way:

- The New Right support **liberal economic policies**: support for the free market and cuts in government spending.

- The New Right support **conservative social moral values**, in favour of the conventional family, against divorce, lone parenthood, cohabitation, gay/lesbian partnerships, working mothers etc. They see these values and the types of family they favour as under threat and in decline.

- The New Right are critical of any laws or aspects of the welfare state which might allow or encourage alternatives to traditional nuclear families (for example: liberal divorce laws, benefits for lone parents, civil partnerships). They object to benefit payments both because of cost to government and because they might encourage dependency on the state.

- The governments of **Margaret Thatcher** and **John Major** in Britain followed New Right thinking. They introduced some policies which followed this philosophy – for example, changing the tax system so cohabiting couples did not get the same tax breaks as married couples. Abbott & Wallace argue, however, that they largely failed to reassert traditional moral values, and some policies – such as making divorce easier – seemed to go against their stated philosophy.

Charles Murray's (1989) **underclass theory** (see p. 11), which sees welfare-dependent single parents as an underclass, is an example of a New Right perspective.

Criticisms

New Right thinking has been heavily criticized:

- **Feminists** see it as ignoring gender inequality and abuse within families.
- **Marxists** see it as ignoring the role of families in capitalism.
- **Postmodernists** celebrate the move away from traditional families rather than criticizing it.
- A lot of research contradicts underclass theory, suggesting that single parents would like jobs and would prefer to live in conventional families (see p. 31).

New Labour and the family

In general, the **Blair/Brown** government's policies have been based around strengthening traditional families, seeing marriage as still the ideal for raising children. A number of measures have been taken to help parents combine paid work with domestic responsibilities, particularly **Working Family Tax Credits**. Policies have encouraged both married and single mothers to work.

New Labour has recognized that diverse family forms are here to stay. It has also moved away from supporting traditional families and traditional morality, in allowing gay and lesbian **civil partnerships** and banning discrimination on the grounds of sexuality.

DEMOGRAPHY

AQA, OCR   **Textbook pp. 503-504**

Declining fertility and birth rates

Total fertility rate (the number of children born per woman of childbearing age) was around 2 in the 1870s, just below 2 in the 1930s, 2.94 in 1964 and just 1.77 in 2004. There has been a corresponding fall in the **birth rate** (the number of live births per thousand of the population) from 28.6 in 1900-02 to 12 in 2005. Partly, this is because women are having children later in life meaning they have less time to have further children. Between 1971 and 2004 age at first birth rose from 23.7 to 27.1.

Morgan (2003) argues that the decline is due to a rise in **cohabitation** – cohabitees have fewer children than married couples. Also, she believes that **marriage** is going out of fashion as part of a general decline in family life.

Geographers such as **Waugh** (2000) see the decline as part of the **demographic transition** – a period in the development of advanced societies when birth and death rates both fall. This results from:

- improved **contraception**, and greater access to sterilization and abortion, making family planning easier.
- increased desire for more material goods and the increasing cost of raising children as school leaving ages rise.
- the **emancipation of women** (partly due to feminism) and higher levels of labour-force participation and participation in higher education. This involves changing priorities. Research by **Sue Sharpe** (1994) (see Textbook p. 644) suggests that in the 1970s love, marriage and children were the highest priorities for women; by the 1990s careers and jobs were more important.
- a decline in the death rate of young children as a result of improvements in **medicine** and **hygiene**, meaning that there is no need to have extra children on the assumption that some might die.

From this point of view, declining birth and fertility rates are part of social change which does not necessarily reflect a decline in the family. Another important factor could be **individualization** (**Beck & Beck-Gernsheim**, 1995): people increasingly see children as restricting individual choices and reducing personal fulfilment, rather than as a source of fulfilment.

The death rate

Textbook pp. 298-299

The **mortality** or **death rate** is the number of people dying per million of the population per year. The **standardized mortality ratio** (SMR) is used to compare the death rates of different groups. 100 represents the average death rate for 16- to 65-year-olds; figures higher than 100 show a higher than average death rate and vice versa.

Death rates in Britain have fallen steadily. The death rates for males fell from 25,829 per million in 1901 to 8,477 in 2000. Over the same period it fell for women from 21,705 to 5,679.

Between 2001 and 2007 the death rate for males fell by a further 15% and for females by 11%.

Infant mortality (deaths per thousand live births) fell from 151 in 1901 to 4.8 in 2007. (All figures from www.statistics.gov.uk)

Biomedical reasons for falling death rate

The **biomedical model** (see p. 152) sees the body as a biological machine which requires proper maintenance and repair when it goes wrong. **Jewson** (1976) argues that the development of **laboratory medicine** has been crucial. Medical improvements include:

- the development of **immunization** against infectious diseases such as smallpox (the first to be introduced, in 1798) plague, TB, diphtheria, polio, measles, mumps etc.;

- the discovery of **penicillin** by **Fleming** in 1928 helping to fight infectious diseases such as pneumonia and meningitis;
- the continuing development of new **surgical techniques** to deal with conditions such as coronary heart disease and cancer, the two major killers of recent years.

From this point of view, **Unschuld** (1986) sees the **history of progress** in medicine as responsible for falling death rates.

Sociological reasons for falling death rate

Textbook pp. 298-303

McKeown (1979) argues that most of the fall in death rates from the 18th century onwards was due to improvements in nutrition and hygiene, not developments in medicine – the biggest falls in the death rate occurred before the main medical developments. This view is supported by studies which show that social factors such as class have a strong influence on the death rate.

The *Acheson Report* (1998) found that the middle class had considerably lower death rates than the working class, and that the gap was widening. This was due, in part, to **cultural factors** (for example, poor diet and smoking) but underlying these behaviours were **material factors** to do with income and class inequality.

Material factors include lack of money for a healthy diet, the dangers of manual jobs (for example: lung disease from mining, asbestosis) and stress caused by low income.

Wilkinson (1996) argues that **poverty** causes high death rates and death rates fall once income reaches an income of around $5000 per head. Once this level is reached an **epidemiological transition** takes place and death rates fall rapidly.

THE AGEING POPULATION AND SOCIETY

OCR, WJEC   **Textbook pp. 744-745**

One consequence of the reduction in the death rate is an increased **life expectancy**. Combined with a declining birth rate this has led in Britain to an **ageing population** – the proportion of the population in older age groups has increased.

By 2005 the average age in Britain was 38.8 compared to 34.1 in 1971. In 2006 16% of the population was over 65, projected to rise to 22% by 2031 (www.statistics.gov.uk). An ever increasing proportion of the population is in retirement.

An ageing population can produce problems for society, with the ageing population sometimes known as the **demographic time bomb**.

A particular problem facing Britain is the large numbers in the 'baby boom' generation, a particularly large cohort born after the Second World War. Problems include:

- increasing cost of pensions for employers and the state;
- a declining proportion of the population of working age, reducing the taxes available to pay for the cost of the elderly;

- an increased financial burden on health and social services;
- an increased burden on adult children caring for elderly relatives.

Feminists argue this burden tends to fall on women, who may have paid employment themselves.

Consequences of an ageing population

Vincent (1995, 2006) (Textbook pp. 747-750) argues that there is an exaggerated fear of the consequences of an ageing population. The problem is not the size of this group but the **unequal distribution of wealth**: it tends to be working-class individuals on low pay who cannot afford to finance their own care and have inadequate pensions.

Gannon (1999) (Textbook p. 751) argues that women are the most adversely affected by old age because the problems of **ageism, sexism** and **poverty** produce an accumulated disadvantage which contributes to difficulties in old age.

Blaikie (1999) (Textbook pp. 755-756) argues that improved health, longevity and affluence means that many people past retirement age can enjoy an active and relatively healthy **third age** as a time of fulfilment and choice, without being an undue burden on society or relatives. Only amongst the most elderly/ill does the **fourth age** of 'dependence, decrepitude and death' become a problem.

A more negative view is taken by **Hockey & James** (1993) (Textbook pp. 752-753) who argue that stereotypes of the elderly in the media and elsewhere mean that the elderly tend to be treated like children (**infantilized**), making a fulfilling old age very difficult.

DEVELOP YOUR ANALYTICAL AND EVALUATION SKILLS

Essay plans

For each of the following questions write your own essay plan before comparing it with the suggestions given here. For the final question you can write a full answer and compare it with the provided model answer.

The family is a universal, essential and beneficial social institution. Discuss.

Background

This is advocating a functionalist view of the family, which sees it as present in all societies and essential and beneficial because it performs vital functions. Murdock is a good starting point and Parsons is also important. The short section on the functions of the family is useful as well. There are many ways of criticising the statement using critics of Murdock and Parsons and perspectives which put forward very different views. Both Marxism and feminism see aspects of the family as far from beneficial.

For	Against
● Murdock (p. 26)	● Marxism (p. 28)
● Parsons (p. 27)	● Feminism (p. 28)
● Fletcher and Parsons (p. 33)	● Critics of Murdock (p. 27)
	● Critics of Parsons (p. 27)
	● Loss of family functions (p. 27)

Top Tip

The question of whether the family is universal depends on how you define 'the family'. There is lots of evidence of increased diversity in family types in Britain (p. 31), so you can discuss whether alternatives to conventional nuclear families are good for society or not.

The conventional nuclear family is dying out in Britain today. Discuss.

Background

This issue is dealt with in several parts of the chapter, particularly those on the historical development of the family, family diversity, marriage and marital breakdown. Recent studies on families and kinship, and the dispersed extended and beanpole families, suggest something like the nuclear family remains important. However, most of the research on family diversity and evidence of increased family breakdown suggests otherwise. The claim that conventional nuclear families are 'dying out' is perhaps too strong, and you might suggest they are weakening rather than about to disappear.

For	Against
● Theories of diversity (p. 31)	● McGlone, Willmott (p. 30)
● Evidence marriage may be in crisis (p. 35)	● Brannen (p. 30)
	● Chester (p. 32)

Top Tip

Postmodernism (p. 29) might be useful for suggesting that nuclear families are now just one choice among many.

The family is still patriarchal. Discuss.

Background

This is clearly a statement that feminists would tend to support. Chapter 12, on theory, is useful for defining and discussing patriarchy and for criticising the concept. Radical feminists support this view most strongly, liberal feminists more weakly, and Marxist and socialist feminists partially agree because they see families as both male-dominated and shaped by capitalism. Evidence on conjugal roles suggests some

reduction in inequality but would generally support the statement.
Postmodernists deny that generalizations such as this are useful, seeing families as
diverse and therefore considering all sweeping statements about them to be
invalid.

For	Against
● Radical feminism (p. 28) ● Liberal feminism (p. 28) ● Marxist/socialist feminism (p. 28) ● Evidence of continuing inequality in conjugal roles (p. 33)	● Functionalism (p. 33) ● Postmodernism (p. 29) ● Evidence of reductions in inequality in conjugal roles (p. 33)

Top Tip

You might consider whether different types of family are equally patriarchal. Lesbian
families would seem to be at least one exception.

Discuss reasons for the increasing divorce rate in Britain.

Background

You will need to start by explaining what the divorce rate is and giving some evidence
on how much it has increased. An initial distinction should be made between the
argument that more marriages really are breaking up and the view of some that
divorce is simply easier because of legal changes, and that in the past many people
separated or stayed in 'empty-shell marriages'. You will need to give details of some
legal changes and how they have made divorce easier. Most sociologists agree there is
increased breakdown of marriage, but they differ over the reasons for it. Your answer
can then be structured around describing and evaluating competing explanations
which can be related to different sociological perspectives. These are detailed
below.

Theory	Explanation
Functionalism	Parsons and Fletcher (p. 33) believe marriage is as highly valued as ever but people expect and demand more from it leading to divorce.
Theories of modernity	Beck & Beck-Gernsheim (p. 30) and Giddens (p. 29) see divorce as resulting from increased individualization and the pure relationship, meaning marriage is not seen as necessarily permanent. See also Gibson (p. 36).
New Right	Murray (p. 31) and Morgan (p. 37) argue that benefits to single parents, and changing social attitudes with less stigma attached to divorce, are part of an undesirable decline in family life.
Feminism	Feminists see increased divorce in a positive light as it allows women to escape from patriarchy and domestic violence, and reflects growing financial independence of women. Aspects of this view are supported by Allan & Crow (p. 36).
Postmodernism	Stacey (p. 29) emphasizes postmodern variety and choice, and more egalitarian relationships.

There is quite lot of agreement amongst sociologists that there is increased marital breakdown due to reduced stigma and greater freedom to choose lifestyle, but they disagree about whether this is good or not. Mention that there are other explanations as well; for example, Leach explains it in terms of increased conflict due to the greater isolation of the nuclear family (p. 30).

Examine reasons for changes in the position of children in the family and in society.

Background

The answer can outline the idea that childhood is a social construct (p. 34) and explain that writers such as Ariès (p. 34) see the whole idea of childhood as relatively new. Explain how Ariès sees the changes involved in a distinctive modern form of childhood and how these affect the family – for example, families becoming more child-centred. You then need to explain the different reasons put forward for these changes, drawing on the ideas of Ariès, Shorter, Pilcher, Postman and Jenks. Contrast the view of Ariès with the views of other writers to broaden the analysis and evaluation in the answer. You could conclude by discussing whether childhood is entering a new, postmodern phase.

Arguments for childhood entering a postmodern phase	Arguments against childhood entering a postmodern phase
• Featherstone & Hepworth: the deconstruction of the life course (p. 34) • Postman: mass media undermine the innocence of children (p. 35)	• Jenks: children remain very restricted and regulated (p. 35)

Top Tip

Make sure you point out that it is dangerous to generalize about childhood, as the experience of childhood will vary according to gender, class, ethnicity etc.

Model answer

Examine reasons for changes in the position of children in society and in the family.

Sociologists have identified a number of changes in the position of children in the family and society. Most sociologists agree that childhood is socially constructed. Although being a child is a biological state, the meanings given to being young vary from society to society. Sociologists largely agree about the type of changes that have taken place in the position of children in the family and in society, but they have put forward a variety of reasons for these changes.

Philippe Ariès argues that in preindustrial societies there was little difference between childhood and adulthood. Children were treated as little adults and were expected to take part in adult activities as soon as they were capable of doing so. Children dressed similarly to adults and there were few specialist children's toys and games. There was little sentimentality about children and families were not at all child-centred. Children were subject to harsh discipline and families did not see the welfare of children in the family as a primary concern.

Ariès argues that by the eighteenth and nineteenth centuries modern ideas of childhood were emerging. Childhood was now regarded as a distinct phase of life, with children separated from the adult social world and families becoming more child-centred and more concerned with the welfare of children rather than with disciplining them.

Ariès believes that this change was the result of changing religious attitudes (which thought that children needed nurturing to become religious) and the development of education. Education prolonged the period when children were separated from the adult world and, as a result, the idea of childhood innocence developed. Another factor was declining infant mortality and fertility. Women had fewer children but expected them to survive, meaning that it was more worthwhile to invest time and emotional commitment in the smaller number of children they had. This led to a more child-centred family.

Ariès believes that in the twentieth century the development of specialist sciences like psychology and pediatrics have further encouraged families to prioritise the physical and psychological well-being of children.

Other sociologists accept Ariès's description of the changes, but disagree about the reasons. Edward Shorter believes that the development of romantic love led to an idealized image of children as innocent (the Apollonian image of the child). As a result mothers developed a sacrificial role in families — the interests of children came before their own.

Postman sees the development of the printing press as more important. Because reading is a skill that develops over a long period, and literacy is an important part of being an adult, childhood became extended as a preparation for adulthood. Jane Pilcher emphasizes the importance of employment legislation which banned children first from work and later from other forms of employment.

In reality, all the above changes have probably contributed to the development of modern childhood rather than one single factor being of primary importance.

Some sociologists believe that the role of children in the family and in society is changing again as we enter postmodernity. Neil Postman argues that the distinction between adulthood and childhood is breaking down. Children are growing up quicker because they are increasingly exposed to adult knowledge, with easy access to adult media content. As a consequence, children engage in adult activities (for example: drink, drugs and sex) at a younger age. However, this view can be exaggerated. In some ways, children stay dependent on families longer than ever before. The school leaving age has been raised several times, and more children stay on to higher education than in the past. Rather than becoming independent adults at a young age, children may be experiencing an extended adolescence where they are neither children nor adults but remain partially dependent on parents/guardians.

A problem with all the theories, however, is that they assume that all children have the same position in society and the family. In reality, the position of children varies considerably from family to family, and in different ethnic, class and religious groups. For example, in Britain some Asian families place more emphasis on the maintenance of family honour than other families, so the duties of children towards the family are stressed as much as the duties of parents to children.

RESOURCES

Family diversity

```
                          Gay and lesbian ───── Chosen families          ┌─ Divorce
                          families                                       │
                                                                         ├─ Separation
                                                            Causes ──────┤
  Nuclear family ─┐                                                      ├─ Death
                  │                                                      │
  Female carer/   ├─── 'Cereal packet'                                   └─ Never married
  housewife       │    image (Leach)
                  │                                                      ┌─ Rising divorce rates
  Male breadwinner ┘                                                    │   and births outside
                                                                        │   marriage
                                                      Lone-parent       │
  Robert Chester ──── Family diversity ───── families                  ┌┤─ Greater social
                                                                        │   acceptability
  Neo-conventional                            Reasons for ─────────────┤
  family – wives work                         increase                 └─ Murray – benefits
  but nuclear family                                                       system
  still very important
                                                                        ┌─ Murray – helps
                                              Effects ─────────────────┤   create underclass
  Organizational ─┐
                  │                                                     ├─ Research on
  Cultural        │                                                     │   negative effects on
                  │                          Black British             │   children
  Class           ├─── Types of              families have higher      │
                  │    diversity             rates of lone             ├─ Effects largely due
  Life cycle      │    (Rapoports)           parenthood                │   to poverty
                  │
  Cohort         ─┘                          British Asians have       └─ Cashmore – two-
                                             strong extended              parent families can
                                             kinship networks,            be harmful
                                             low rates of divorce
                                             etc.
                          Ethnic diversity ─┤
                                             Ballard – children
                                             in Asian families
                                             have two cultures

                                             Bhatti – some
                                             changes in Asian
                                             families but izzat
                                             still important
```

Sociological perspectives on the family

	Marxism	Feminism	Functionalism	New Right
How they see nuclear families	A way of maintaining class inequality and coping with capitalism	Patriarchal, male-dominated institution	The bedrock of industrial society, needed for geographical/ social mobility	The ideal family form but under threat
Main roles of the family	Consumption, transmitting inequality, free reproduction of workers	Maintaining male power, exploiting and/or abusing females	Sexual, economic, reproductive, educational, primary socialization, stabilizing adult personalities	Raising children, producing self-reliance not reliance on welfare
Main thinkers	Engels Zaretsky	Greer Somerville Benston Delphy & Leonard Barrett Macintosh	Parsons Murdock	Thatcher Murray
View of changes in the family	Family changes as a result of changes in capitalist society	Some accept family becoming more equal and varied, most see it as remaining very unequal	Evolutionary progress; family has evolved into nuclear families meeting needs of industrial society	Welfare state and declining morals threaten well-being of family
Evidence used in support of theories/main contribution	Historical evidence, analysis of changes in capitalism	Studies of domestic violence, housework, decision-making etc.	Comparison of 250 societies; historical evidence on family change	Evidence on single parenthood, unemployment, divorce, crime etc.
Main criticisms	Ignores gender; ignores positive side of family	Ignores class and positive side of family	Ignores negative side of family; paints too 'rosy' a picture	Exaggerates family breakdown and welfare dependency etc.

Writers and their work

Writer	Perspective or approach	Concept	Study
Murdock	Functionalism	Universality of family	Comparison of 250 societies
Stacey	Postmodernism	Postmodern family variety	Pam and Dotty in California
Postman	Postmodernism	Postmodern childhood	Media and childhood
Giddens	Theories of late Modernity	Pure relationships	Changing nature of love/relationships
Featherstone & Hepworth	Postmodernism	Deconstruction of the life course	Study of the changing meanings attached to age
Young & Willmott	Progressive development of the family	Symmetrical family	Study of Bethnal Green and family in London
Calhoun	Difference feminism	Chosen families	Lesbian couples
Ariès	Social constructionism	Childhood as a social construct	Changing childhood over several centuries in Europe
Engels	Marxism	The monogamous nuclear family	The origins of the family and its purpose in class societies
Delphy & Leonard	Radical feminism	Family as economic system	Study of French farming and other families
Waugh	Geography	Demographic transition	Study of changes in birth rates
Gibson	Theories of modernity	Consumer choice	Study of divorce
Beck & Beck-Gernsheim	Theories of late modernity	Normal chaos of love/ individualization	Study of changing nature of intimacy
Parsons	Functionalism	Structural differentiation	Study of changing family functions
Murray	New Right	Underclass	Study of lone parenthood, crime and unemployment
Cooper	Marxism	Family as an ideological conditioning device	Study of how family brings up children
Rapoport & Rapoport	Theories of diversity	Organizational diversity	Study of different family forms in Britain in the 1980s

Chapter 3 | EDUCATION

SPECIFICATION COVERAGE

Specification	Details
AQA AS SCLY 2: Education, Health, Sociological Methods	This chapter covers the education option and the education component for this module. See chapter 11, *Methodology*, for the education component
OCR A2 Unit G673: Power and Control, Sociology of Education option	
WJEC Unit SY2: Understanding Culture, Option 1, Education	This chapter covers the education option

EXPANSION OF EDUCATION

AQA, OCR, WJEC   Textbook pp. 599-600

Free **state education** in Britain began in 1870. By 1918 school attendance was **compulsory** up to the age of 14, rising to 16 in 1972. Since then the government has encouraged more people to stay on in **post-compulsory** education. By 2005 76% of 16-18 year-olds were in full-time education in England and Wales. In 2007 it was announced that, from 2013, everybody would have to stay in education or training until the age of 18. In 2002 more than 13.5% of government spending was on education.

FUNCTIONALIST PERSPECTIVE

AQA, OCR, WJEC   Textbook pp. 600-602

Functionalists ask two key questions about education:

- What are the functions for **society** as a whole?
- What are the **functional relationships** between education and other parts of the social system?

Functionalists tend to focus on the positive contribution education makes to society.

Durkheim – education and solidarity

Writing at the end of the nineteenth century, Durkheim saw the major function of education as the transmission of society's **norms** and **values**.

A vital task for all societies is the welding of a mass of individuals into a united whole – in other words, the creation of **social solidarity**. Education, and in particular the teaching of history, provides this link between the individual and society.

The school is a **society in miniature**. In school the child learns to **interact** with other members of the school community and to follow a fixed set of rules. This experience prepares the child for interacting with members of society as an adult and accepting social rules.

Education teaches individuals specific skills which are necessary for their future occupations.

Criticisms

Durkheim assumes that the norms and values promoted in schools are those of society as a whole rather than those of powerful groups.

Most contemporary changes in education appear to be aimed at encouraging individual **competition**, and training pupils for particular **vocations**. It could be argued that the sort of education favoured by Durkheim is not the best preparation for future working life.

Hargreaves (1982) believes that most British schools fail to transmit shared values.

Unlike Durkheim, other functionalists see competition as a vital aspect of modern societies.

Parsons – universalistic values

Parsons (1961) argues that school performs three major functions for society:

1   Education acts as a bridge between the family and wider society.

2   Education helps to **socialize** young people into the basic values of society.

3   Education selects people for their future role in society.

The family and society

In the family **particularistic standards** apply: children are treated as individuals. In society however, **universalistic standards** predominate. The individual is judged against standards which apply equally to all members of society.

In the family, **status** is fixed by birth – it is **ascribed**. However, in society, status is **achieved** (according to occupation, for example) – that is, it is based on **meritocratic** principles.

Education helps to ease these transitions. The exam system judges all pupils on merit, and school rules such as wearing uniform are applied to all pupils equally.

Education helps to **socialize** young people into the basic values of society.

Socialization

Schools instil two major values:

- the value of **achievement**;
- the value of **equality of opportunity**.

Future role in society

The education system assesses students' abilities so that their talents can be matched to the job for which they are best suited.

Criticisms of Parsons

Parsons fails to consider the diversity of values in modern societies.

His view that education works on meritocratic principles is open to question.

Davis & Moore – education and role allocation

Like Parsons, **Davis & Moore** (1967, first published 1945) see education as a means of **role allocation**. The education system sifts people according to their abilities. The most talented gain high qualifications which lead to functionally important jobs with high rewards.

Criticisms

There is only a weak link between educational **qualifications** and **income**.

Intelligence and ability have only a limited influence on educational achievement.

The system of **social stratification** prevents the education system from grading individuals according to their ability.

CONFLICT PERSPECTIVES

AQA, OCR, WJEC   Textbook pp. 602-608

Bowles & Gintis – capitalist schooling

Bowles & Gintis (1976) argue that there is a close relationship between social relationships in the workplace and in education. This **correspondence principle** is the key to understanding the working of the education system. Work casts a 'long shadow' over the education system: education operates in the interests of those who control the workforce – the **capitalist class**.

The hidden curriculum

Capitalism requires a hard-working, obedient workforce which is too divided to challenge the authority of management. The education system helps to produce a workforce with these qualities through the '**hidden curriculum**'. The hidden curriculum consists of those things that pupils learn through the experience of attending school rather than through the stated aims of the school. It shapes the workforce in the following ways:

- It helps to produce a **subservient workforce**. Bowles & Gintis found that students who were more conformist received higher grades than those who were creative and independent.

- The hidden curriculum encourages an acceptance of **hierarchy**. Teachers give orders, pupils obey. Students have virtually no control over what and how they study. This prepares them for relationships at work where they will also need to defer to authority.

- Pupils learn to be motivated by **external rewards**. Pupils work only for the qualifications they eventually hope to achieve. There is little satisfaction from school work, as learning is based mostly on the '**jug and mug**' principle: teachers 'pour' their knowledge into students' empty 'mugs'. In a similar way, work is unsatisfying because it is organized to generate maximum **profit** rather than with the needs of the worker in mind. Workers, like pupils, are motivated only by external rewards – in their case, pay.

- School subjects are **fragmented**. Knowledge in schools is packaged into separate subjects with little connection between them. In a similar way, most jobs are broken down into specific tasks carried out by separate individuals. Workers are kept unaware of all parts of the production process, so they remain divided.

The myth of meritocracy

Bowles & Gintis reject the functionalist view that capitalist societies are meritocratic, providing genuine equality of opportunity. The children of the wealthy and powerful obtain high qualifications and well-rewarded jobs irrespective of their abilities. The education system disguises this with its **myth of meritocracy**. Those denied success blame themselves rather than the system. Inequality in society is thus **legitimated**: it is made to appear fair.

Evaluation

Bowles & Gintis have been accused of exaggerating the correspondence between work and education. **Brown et al** (1997) argue that much modern work requires teamwork. **Reynolds** (1984) claims that much of the curriculum in British schools does not teach the skills needed by employers and nor does it encourage uncritical passive behaviour.

Numerous studies, such as that of **Willis** (1977) (see below), show that many pupils do not accept the **hidden curriculum** in schools. They have little respect for teachers or school rules.

Bowles & Gintis developed their theory in 1970s America, and much has changed since then. However, some developments appear to support their theory:

- The freedom of teachers has been curtailed by the **National Curriculum**.

- Education has become more explicitly designed to meet the needs of **employers** (see p. 49).

Willis – Learning to Labour

Willis (1977) accepts the **Marxist** view that education is closely linked to the needs of capitalism, but he does not believe that there is a simple and direct relationship between education and the economy. Willis used a range of **qualitative research** methods, including **observation** and **group interviews**, to study a group of 12 working-class boys during their last year at school and first months at work.

The 12 pupils – the 'lads' – formed a friendship group with a particular attitude to school. Willis refers to this as a **counter-school culture**. It had the following features:

- The lads felt superior to teachers and **conformist** pupils, who they called 'ear 'oles'.

- They saw no value in gaining qualifications.

- Their main objectives were to avoid going to lessons and to do as little work as possible. They entertained themselves by 'having a laff'. This usually involved misbehaviour.

- The lads found school boring and tried to identify with the adult world by smoking, drinking alcohol and not wearing school uniform.

- The **counterculture** was strongly **sexist** and **racist**. Traditional **masculinity** was valued and members of ethnic minorities were regarded as inferior.

- Manual labour was seen as more worthy than 'pen-pushing'.

These pupils did not defer to authority, nor were they obedient or docile. They rejected the belief that hard work would lead to success. Willis's 'lads' have very little in common with the sort of conformist pupils described by **Bowles & Gintis**.

Shop-floor culture and counter-school culture

When Willis followed the lads into their first jobs he found important similarities between the school counterculture and the factory **shop-floor culture**:

- Both were **racist** and **sexist**.

- Both had no respect for **authority**.

- Both tried to minimize work and maximize 'having a laff'.

- Both cultures were ways of coping with **tedium** and **oppression**.

In their rejection of school the lads partly see through, or **penetrate**, the **capitalist system**. Ultimately however, rejecting school merely leads them into some of the most exploitative jobs capitalism has to offer.

Evaluation

Gordon (1984) believes that Willis's study has helped Marxists overcome a tendency to over-simplify the role of education in society.

Blackledge & Hunt (1985) put forward three criticisms of Willis:

- His **sample** is inadequate for generalizing about the role of education in society.

- Willis largely ignores the full range of **subcultures** within schools. Many pupils fall somewhere in between total conformity and total rejection.

- Willis may have misinterpreted some evidence to fit in with his own views.

With the decline in manual work since the period of Willis's research, male working-class attitudes to education may well have become more positive.

SOCIAL DEMOCRATIC PERSPECTIVES

AQA, OCR, WJEC   Textbook pp. 612-613

Social democratic perspectives argue that a democratic system can produce governments which promote the welfare of the population as a whole. However, they believe that inequalities in society prevent equality of **educational opportunity** and reduce the effectiveness of education in producing **economic growth**.

Skilled workers are more productive but some are not developing skills to their full potential because of inequality of opportunity.

Social democrats believe that a **meritocracy** is desirable, but a **market economy** gives unfair advantages to the children of middle-class parents.

Halsey (1977) (also **Halsey & Floud**, 1961) believed that middle-class children were more likely to get places at **grammar schools** which provided an **academic** education, as opposed to **secondary modern** schools which provided more **vocational** schooling. This discriminated against working-class pupils, created **class divisions** in society, and was inefficient because it wasted the potential of working-class pupils to contribute to the economy.

1970s social democrats believed that changes were needed to make education more meritocratic and promote economic growth:

- Grammar schools and secondary modern schools should be replaced with **comprehensive schools** so that pupils from all social classes would receive a similar education.

- **Inequalities** in society should be reduced through government taxation and welfare policies.

Criticisms

Despite the introduction of comprehensive schools in most areas, class inequalities in education have remained.

Social democrats might therefore exaggerate the influence of the school system on inequality of opportunity and underestimate the importance of inequalities in society.

Woolf (2002) questions the social democratic view that higher spending on education will automatically produce economic growth. She accepts that good primary and secondary education is necessary, but more and more spending does not guarantee growth. Switzerland, for example, has relatively low education spending but high economic growth. Amongst poorer countries, Egypt has very high spending but low economic growth.

Woolf believes that growth can be achieved by concentrating **higher education** expenditure on the most talented rather than trying to get as many people as possible into expensive higher education.

However, the **New Labour** perspective (see p. 50) disagrees and argues that the more skilled the workforce the better in a **global**, **competitive economy**.

MARKET LIBERAL PERSPECTIVES

AQA, OCR, WJEC   **Textbook pp. 613-616**

New Right/market liberal (or **neo-liberal**) perspectives influenced the policies introduced by governments throughout the 1980s and 1990s.

Market liberal theory

Market liberal theory is critical of the state provision of services such as education.

High government spending on education and other services is undesirable because it requires high taxes. These taxes ultimately come from company profits, and high taxation therefore makes companies less competitive.

Public choice theory (**Buchanan & Tulloch**, 1962) believes that services provided by state bureaucracies tend to be ineffective and inefficient. The **producers** (for example, teachers) have little incentive to provide a good service because there is no **competition**, and **providers** (schools) cannot go out of business.

Chubb & Moe (1997) believe that state education is unresponsive to the needs of pupils and parents and tends to have low standards. In contrast, **private education** has to please its customers in order to survive; therefore, standards are high and there is constant pressure to improve them further.

Market liberals believe that rising standards are essential if countries are going to compete in an increasingly **global economy**. Without high levels of skills, workers will lose their jobs to more skilled workers in other countries.

The New Right and educational reform

Market liberal theory had a strong influence on the educational policies of New Right governments under **Margaret Thatcher** and **John Major** in Britain from 1979 to 1997 (see Textbook pp. 616-621). A number of reforms were introduced based on the following key themes:

- education and economic growth;
- competition, choice and standards;
- testing and examining;
- curriculum content.

Education and economic growth

Education should largely be concerned with promoting economic growth rather than creating greater equality. Many school-leavers were unemployable because of their lack of skills. A whole range of changes were introduced developing **vocational education**. This policy was termed the **new vocationalism**. The policy was developed in a range of government initiatives:

- **YTS** (the Youth Training Scheme) – a two-year course aimed at combining work experience with education, aimed at unemployed young workers who were believed to lack basic skills.
- **GNVQs** (General National Vocational Qualifications) – introduced as a vocational alternative to academic subjects.
- **Training credits** – piloted in 1991, entitled school-leavers to spend a specified sum of money on training.

Competition, choice and standards

The best method of raising standards in education was to introduce **market forces** and encourage competition between educational institutions. Schools that failed to attract students would lose funding and be forced to improve or close. The **1998 Education Reform Act** introduced changes to increase choice and encourage competition.

Parents were given the right to send their children to the school of their choice. A policy of **open enrolment** compelled every school to recruit the maximum number of pupils that could be accommodated.

Existing schools were allowed to **opt out** of local authority control and instead be funded directly from central government. Opting out created a new category of **grant-maintained** schools. By 1996 these schools were educating about 20% of school pupils.

Under the system of **formula funding**, the financing of schools was based on the number of enrolments. This was intended to reward the most successful schools.

The government laid down a **National Curriculum** which all state school pupils had to follow. Its aim was to ensure that pupils concentrated on what the government saw as key subjects.

Testing and examining

Parents needed information in order to be able to make informed choices about schools. Increased testing and the publication of results were therefore necessary.

League tables were introduced to enable easy comparisons between schools to be made.

Testing and attainment targets were introduced for children aged 7, 11, 14 and 16, in the hope that standards would rise as schools competed with each other to reach targets.

Curriculum content

A more **business-oriented** curriculum was favoured by the New Right; but at the same time, according to **Ball** (1990), there was an emphasis on retaining **traditional values** and **traditional subjects** such as Latin and Greek. Social education and multicultural approaches were frowned upon. Initiatives such as **TVEI** (Technical and Vocational Education Initiative) and courses such as **GNVQs** were introduced to produce young people who had more understanding of work and the economy.

Evaluation of educational reforms

Critics have argued that that New Right policies can be harmful for schools.

Bartlett & Le Grand (1993) believe it leads to 'cream-skimming' – schools try to select the best pupils to improve their results and image.

Less popular schools may be left behind and provide an inadequate education. Research from New Zealand suggests this can particularly affect working-class pupils (**Lauder** *et al*, 1999).

Where schools are **over-subscribed** there is little genuine choice. Class differences in opportunities to go to good schools can be created – for example, better-off parents may buy houses in areas with better schools.

Ransom (1996) believes the policies create an over-emphasis on **results** at the expense of other aspects of education.

Research in the USA by **Levin & Belfield** (2006) found that the introduction of greater competition led to small improvements in overall standards. However, those from middle-class backgrounds improved more than those from working-class backgrounds, increasing inequality.

Ball et al – parental choice

Ball *et al*'s (1994) study attempted to discover the effects that **parental choice** and the encouragement of competition between schools were having on the education system, and particularly on opportunities for different social groups. The study found that the changes were having significant effects on secondary schools:

- The publication of **school league tables** meant that schools were keen to attract academically able pupils who would boost their results.
- Some schools had reintroduced **streaming** and **setting** and were directing more resources at pupils who were likely to be successful in tests.
- As schools concentrated on the more able pupils, they paid less attention to those with **special needs**.
- In an effort to attract more pupils, some schools had taken to publishing glossy brochures, and some had brought in public relations firms. More attention was devoted to the **image** of the school, particularly to making it seem to have a traditional academic focus – for example, by strictly enforcing rules about school uniform.
- Neighbouring schools had ceased to cooperate with each other, and instead there was 'suspicion and hostility'.

These changes have led to a shift from **comprehensive** to **market values** in education.

The education market

Ball *et al* argue that groups of parents can be distinguished in terms of their **ability to choose** between schools. Parents can be divided into two groups:

- **Privileged/skilled choosers** – these parents spend a lot of time finding out about different schools and evaluating the claims made in their publicity. They often have the money to make choices that will assist their children's education, such as moving house or paying for **private education**. This group is usually **middle-class**.
- **Disconnected choosers** – these parents are not inclined to get involved in the education market. They tend to consider only the two schools closest to their home, often because they do not own a car or have easy access to public transport. They put more emphasis on the happiness of their child than on the academic reputation of the school. Disconnected choosers are likely to be **working-class** and are more likely to send their children to an under-subscribed school.

Generally, the higher a person's social class, the more likely they are to benefit from the best schooling. According to Ball *et al*, the impression of choice is an illusion. In practice, people's choice is restricted by the limited number of schools available in any area and the class-based nature of the system of choosing.

Youth training schemes

Finn (1987) has strongly attacked the **new vocationalism** involved in the various youth training schemes. He believes that its real objectives were different from those stated:

- The trainees could be used as a source of cheap labour.
- The small allowances paid to trainees would depress general wage levels.
- The scheme would reduce embarrassing unemployment statistics.
- The government hoped that the scheme would reduce **crime** by taking up the free time of young people.

Finn believed that there was no truth in the claim that school-leavers were unemployable. Many school pupils had experience of work through part-time jobs. The real problem was simply lack of jobs.

NEW LABOUR AND EDUCATION

AQA, OCR, WJEC   Textbook pp. 621-624

The election of a Labour government in 1997, under the banner 'New Labour', led to some changes in the direction of educational policy. New Labour was influenced both by **social democratic** and **neoliberal/ New Right** thinking.

Social democratic-influenced policies

These policies were influenced by a desire to create greater **equality** in education, though they might also have other intended effects such as increasing **choice** and raising **standards**.

Extra resources went into **Education Action Zones**. These were established in areas of high deprivation in an attempt to boost educational achievement.

The **Excellence in Cities** programme steadily replaced EAZs as a means of improving attainment for those from low income backgrounds. It included special help for gifted children and learning centres with good IT facilities in cities.

Sure Start was an intervention aimed at children under four living in deprived areas, providing home visits to advise parents and play centres run by professionals.

Academies were introduced to replace 'failing' comprehensive schools and drive up standards. They raise money through **sponsorship** by businesses, charities, faith groups or city councils, who then appoint the majority of the governors – though central government provides most of the funds. It was planned to have 200 academies by 2010.

Further education was expanded, leading to rising participation rates – participation in further education more than doubled between 1990 and 2004.

Education Maintenance Allowances (EMAs) were introduced in 2004 to provide financial support to children from low income backgrounds staying in education after 16.

Participation in **higher education** nearly doubled between 1990 and 2004, as Labour tried to increase opportunities for people from all class backgrounds.

Market liberal-influenced policies

Labour continued to encourage the development of **specialist schools**, explicitly rejecting the 'bog-standard' 'one-size-fits-all' comprehensive. To encourage **diversity** and **choice** schools could apply to become **specialists** in one or two of ten areas, such as computing, engineering, science, sports or humanities. Specialist schools can **select** up to 10% of their intake according to aptitude in their specialism. By 2007 75% of all schools were specialist schools.

Labour continued to use **assessments**, **targets** and **league tables** to measure the performance of schools and provide information for parents. However, they also introduced a **value-added** measure alongside raw exam results to indicate how much pupils were improving at the school.

Labour followed the market liberal/New Right agenda in seeing the primary objective of education as training the **workforce**. All education was therefore seen as **vocational**. **Tomlinson** (2005) argues that 'education was subordinated to the economy'. Specific vocational policies included the following:

- The **New Deal for Young People** (from 1998) provided education, training, voluntary work or subsidized jobs for young people who had been unemployed for six months or more, with support from personal advisors.
- **Vocational GCSEs and A-levels** – in 2001 Labour rebranded NVQs (National Vocational Qualifications) in an attempt to raise their status.

Evaluation of Labour's policies

Tomlinson (2005) argues that Labour's preoccupation with standards, competition, choice and markets

have led to greatly increased **selection in education**: this has favoured the middle class who are more likely to get their children into over-subscribed schools. Successful schools increasingly 'cream-skim' the most able pupils to maintain or improve their results. The emphasis on results and league tables has led to teachers teaching 'to the tests' and neglecting broader aims of education.

McKnight *et al* (2005) conducted research showing that overall educational standards have risen under Labour with improvements in GCSE, A-level and Key Stage tests; participation in higher and further education has risen. They also found a small reduction in class differences in achievement at GCSE and A-level. However, the **class gap** in achievement was still very wide.

Strathdee (2003) believes some progress has been made in developing **Vocational Education and Training** (VET) but it still largely remains a route into lower-paid jobs.

Trowler (2003) believes that New Labour has exaggerated the power of education to change society, and underestimated the extent to which **inequality** in society continues to hold back the disadvantaged.

DIFFERENTIAL ATTAINMENT

AQA, OCR, WJEC   **Textbook pp. 625-638**

Class and achievement

The children of parents in higher social classes are more likely to stay on in post-compulsory education, more likely to achieve examination passes when at school and more likely to gain university entrance. These differences were a feature of British education throughout the twentieth century and remain significant today.

The *Youth Cohort Study* (2004) found that 33% of the children of **routine workers** but 77% of children from **higher professional** backgrounds gained five or more GCSE A*-C passes.

In 2006 57% of children from higher professional backgrounds but just 16% of those from routine backgrounds gained A/AS-level qualifications. (*Youth Cohort Study*, 2006).

Participation in **higher education** has been increasing for all social classes. The proportion of those from lower classes participating has risen faster than the proportion of those from higher classes. However, the *Youth Cohort Study* (2005) found that in 2005 59% of 19-year-olds from higher professional backgrounds but 19% of those from routine backgrounds were in higher education.

Intelligence, class and attainment

The most obvious explanation for differences in educational achievement is the **intelligence** of the individual.

In Britain, the **tripartite system** allocated an individual to one of three types of school largely on the basis of their performance in the **eleven-plus** intelligence test. There was a strong correlation between results and social class, with middle-class children gaining more places at **grammar schools**.

Culture and intelligence

Many researchers argue that intelligence tests – IQ tests – are biased in favour of the white middle class, since they are largely constructed by members of this group.

Different social groups have different **subcultures** and this affects their performance in IQ tests. This means that comparisons between such groups in terms of measured intelligence are invalid.

Genes and intelligence

There is general agreement that intelligence is due to:

- the **genes** individuals inherit from their parents;
- the **environment** in which they grow up and live.

Despite objections to their views, some social scientists still argue that **genetically based intelligence** accounts for a large part of the difference in educational attainment between social groups.

According to **Hernstein & Murray** (1994), American society is increasingly meritocratic. People's class position is increasingly determined by their intelligence.

Environment and intelligence

Research has indicated that a wide range of **environmental factors** – such as motivation, previous experience and education – can affect performance in IQ tests.

Many researchers now conclude that it is impossible to estimate the proportions of intelligence due to **heredity** and **environment**.

Gillborn & Youdell – the new IQism

Gillborn & Youdell (2001) argue that the idea of 'ability' has now replaced that of intelligence but is used in the same way. Research in two London schools suggested that teachers thought children had largely **fixed abilities**. They concentrated on children who were **borderline** for achieving 5 grade Cs in GCSEs because it affected the school's league table results (the '**A-C economy**'). **Black** and **working-class** children tended to be perceived as **low ability** and few were thought to have the potential for 5 GCSEs, so they were held back in the education system.

Class subcultures and attainment

It has been argued that the distinctive **norms** and **values** of different social classes affect their educational performance.

Douglas – The Home and the School

Douglas's longitudinal study (1964) related educational attainment to a variety of factors, but the single most important factor was **parental interest**.

In general, middle-class parents:

- visited the school more frequently to discuss their children's progress;
- wanted their children to stay at school beyond the minimum leaving age;
- gave their children greater attention and stimulus during their early years.

Douglas argued that many differences in educational performance could be traced back to **primary socialization** during the pre-school years.

Feinstein – parental support and education

Feinstein (2003), using data from the *National Child Development Study*, reached the following conclusions:

- **Nursery schooling** improved educational achievement if it was a good quality nursery school.
- In most ways the school attended made little difference, but children with average or below average ability did poorly in schools that had few children from **professional backgrounds**.
- **Financial deprivation** had some effect but this seemed to be largely related to parental interest.
- The most important factor affecting achievement was the extent to which **parents** encouraged and supported their children.

Evaluation of cultural deprivation theories

The above views have been strongly criticized. **Blackstone & Mortimore** (1994) make the following points:

- The studies are based on **teachers' assessments** of parental interest. Working-class parents may have less time to visit the school because of the demands of their jobs.
- Working-class parents may be put off visiting the school by the way teachers interact with them.
- More middle-class than working-class children attended a school where there was an established system of **parent-school contacts**.

Bernstein – speech patterns

Since speech is an important medium of communication and learning, attainment levels in schools may be related to differences in **speech patterns**. **Bernstein** (1961, 1970, 1972) distinguished two patterns of speech:

- **Restricted code** – this is a kind of **shorthand speech**, which uses short, simple and often unfinished sentences. Users of the code have so much in common that there is no need to make meanings explicit in speech. Meanings are more likely to be conveyed by gesture and tone of voice. Members of the working class are usually limited to the use of the restricted code. *Example: 'She saw it.'*
- **Elaborated code** – this code is characteristic of the middle classes. It fills in the detail and provides the explanations omitted by restricted codes. Anyone can understand elaborated code users in any situation. *Example: 'The young girl saw the ball.'*

Bernstein explained the origins of these speech codes in terms of **class differences** in the family and the work situations of the working and middle classes:

- In middle-class families and in **non-manual work**, relationships tend to be less rigid, people are treated as individuals and decisions are reached by negotiation.
- In working-class families and in **manual work**, relationships are based on a clear hierarchy and little discussion is needed.

Bernstein believed that the middle classes could switch from one code to the other but that the working classes were only able to use the restricted code. As **formal education** is conducted in terms of an **elaborated code**, working-class children are placed at a disadvantage.

Criticisms

Gaine & George (1999) attack Bernstein's arguments, arguing that:

- Bernstein's distinction between the classes is over-simplified. Even if there was a clear working class in the 1960s when Bernstein was writing, this is not the case today.
- Bernstein produces little evidence for his assertions about working-class and middle-class family life.

Compensatory education

From observations on working-class life like those of Bernstein, the theory of **cultural deprivation** was developed. This placed the blame for working-class educational failure on the culture of low-income groups.

This led to the idea of **positive discrimination** in favour of culturally deprived children: they must be given extra resources to help them compete on equal terms with other children. This policy is known as **compensatory education**.

Various schemes of compensatory education have been introduced. The most recent is the **Education Action Zones**, later replaced by **Excellence in Cities**, introduced by the Labour government. These provide extra educational resources in inner-city areas.

Criticisms

By placing the blame for failure on the child and his or her background, attention is diverted from the deficiencies of the education system and the effects of **inequality** in society as a whole on educational attainment.

Whitty (2002) believes that Education Action Zones do not redistribute sufficient resources to poor areas to make them effective, and they neglect poor areas which are not designated zones.

Bourdieu – cultural capital and attainment

The French sociologist **Bourdieu** is strongly influenced by **Marxism**. He argues that the education system is biased towards the culture of dominant social classes; it devalues the knowledge and skills of the working class.

Bourdieu (1984) refers to the dominant culture as **cultural capital** because it can be translated into wealth and power via the education system. Students with upper-class backgrounds have a built-in advantage because they have been socialized into the **dominant culture**.

The educational attainment of social groups is closely related to the amount of cultural capital they possess. Thus middle-class students have higher success rates than working-class students because middle-class culture is closer to the dominant culture.

Ball *et al* – parental choice

Ball *et al*'s study (see p. 66) is influenced by **Bourdieu**. It discusses whether the increased emphasis on **parental choice** and **market forces** has led to greater equality of opportunity.

The educational market

Ball argues that **middle-class** parents are in a better position than **working-class** parents to ensure that their children get to the school of their choice. There are a number of reasons for this:

- **Middle-class** parents possess **cultural capital**, which means they have contacts and can 'play the system' to their advantage – for example, by making multiple applications.
- Middle-class parents have the '**stamina**' to research, visit schools, make appeals and so on.
- Middle-class parents also possess **material advantages**. They can afford to pay for the transport necessary to send their children to more distant schools; they can move house if necessary to enter the catchment area of a desirable school; and they can afford extra tuition and childcare if necessary.

Ball *et al* did not find that working-class parents were any less interested in their children's education than their middle-class counterparts. However, they did lack the **cultural capital** and **material resources** needed to use the system to their advantage.

Many working-class parents preferred to send their children to the nearest school because of neighbourhood links, safety concerns and transport costs.

Some **ethnic minority** parents have limited experience of the British educational system and do not feel confident enough about their English language skills to manipulate it.

Reay *et al* – class and higher education

Reay *et al* (2005) used questionnaires and in-depth interviews in six sixth-forms to study choice of higher education institution. Two of the sixth-forms were in private schools, two in FE colleges and two attached to comprehensive schools. They examined factors influencing whether students applied and got into **elite universities** (for example, Oxford and Cambridge) or less prestigious ones.

They found that the **habitus** of the schools was different (the habitus is a term used by **Bourdieu** to describe the dispositions, tastes and lifestyles of different groups.)

When choosing universities students wanted to know what *kind of people* inhabit these institutions. Students at private schools found the habitus of elite universities meant the students in top universities were most like themselves. Progression to top universities was taken as normal and natural at their schools, but for most students at FE colleges and comprehensives such universities seemed alien and they thought they would feel out of place.

Middle-class students from private schools also had the **cultural capital** to feel confident when applying to elite universities. Working-class students lacked the confidence to apply to them.

Material factors and attainment

Although **Bourdieu** thought cultural factors were very important in explaining differential educational achievement, he also attached importance to **material factors**, particularly differences in income and wealth. Bourdieu calls this economic capital.

Smith & Noble (1995) reassert the importance of material factors in influencing class differences in educational achievement:

Marketization is likely to lead to large differences between successful, well-resourced schools in affluent areas and under-subscribed poorly resourced schools in poor areas.

Having money allows parents to provide educational toys, books, a healthy diet, more space in the home to do homework, greater opportunities for travel and private tuition.

To make ends meet, schools are increasingly charging for trips, material and equipment (technically, parents are asked for 'voluntary contributions'). Local education authorities are cutting back on free school meal provision and transport costs.

Reay et al (2005) found material factors as well as cultural factors were important in access to elite universities:

- Students from working-class backgrounds often had to do part-time work to pay for attendance at college, and this distracted from their studies.

- Working-class students worked longer hours than middle-class ones.

- Over 25% of the children at private schools received extra private tuition to help them get good A-levels.

- Most children from poorer backgrounds applied to local universities so they could live at home to cut their costs, whereas most middle-class children intended to move away from home to study.

Loans and tuition fees

In 1998 **tuition fees** were introduced for HE courses, and loans partially replaced grants which did not have to be repaid.

Callender & Jackson (2004) surveyed 2,000 prospective HE students to examine the effects of changes in higher education funding.

They found that those from poorer backgrounds were most afraid of debt and this led many to choose not to go on to higher education.

A study by **Universities UK** (2005) found students from poorer backgrounds were more likely to take paid employment during term-time, and to work long hours, than students from more affluent backgrounds.

INTERACTIONIST PERSPECTIVE

AQA, OCR, WJEC   Textbook pp. 638-642

Interactionists focus on **processes** within the education system which result in different levels of achievement, including the details of day-to-day life in schools.

Labelling and the self-fulfilling prophecy

The self-fulfilling prophecy theory argues that **predictions** made by teachers will tend to make themselves come true. The teacher defines or labels the pupil in a particular way, such as 'bright' or 'dull'. The teacher's interaction with pupils will be informed by their labelling of the pupils, and the pupils may respond accordingly, verifying the label and fulfilling the prophecy.

Rosenthal & Jacobson (1968) selected a random sample of pupils in an elementary school in the USA and informed their teachers that these pupils could be expected to show rapid intellectual growth. They tested the IQ of all pupils and re-tested one year later. The sample population showed greater gains in IQ.

Rosenthal & Jacobson claim that by altering the teachers' *expectations* they had significantly affected their pupils' *performance*. They speculate that the teachers' encouragement and positive feedback produced a **self-fulfilling prophecy**.

Criticisms

It has been suggested that the IQ tests used by Rosenthal & Jacobson were of dubious quality and were improperly administered.

Some interactionists have recognized that not all pupils will live up to their labels. **Fuller** (1984) found that black girls in a comprehensive school resented the **negative stereotypes** associated with being both black and female. They felt that people expected them to fail, but they tried to prove them wrong by devoting themselves to their work in order to achieve success. Fuller's work avoids some of the pitfalls of the **deterministic** versions of labelling theory, which suggest that failure is inevitable for those with negative labels attached to them.

Ability grouping

Labelling may affect groups of pupils if they are allocated to classes according to ability. There are several types of ability grouping:

- **Streaming** – children are placed in a class according to general ability.

- **Banding** – a more flexible form of streaming where there is some variation between subjects.

- **Setting** – pupils are placed in sets according to performance in particular subjects.

- **Mixed ability teaching** – children of different ability are educated in the same classes.

Ball – Beachside Comprehensive

Ball (1981) examined the **banding** system of a comprehensive school. Pupils were put into one of three bands according to information supplied from their primary schools. However, Ball found that, for pupils of similar measured ability, those whose fathers were **non-manual** workers had the greatest chance of being placed in the top band.

Ball identified the following effects of this banding:

- The behaviour of band two pupils deteriorated.

- Teachers had lower expectations of band two pupils. They were directed towards practical subjects and lower-level exams.

Keddie – streaming and classroom knowledge

Keddie (1973) studied the effects of **streaming** in a London comprehensive school. She found that:

- more advanced knowledge was withheld from lower streams.

- knowledge that came from pupils' own experiences was devalued. Abstract knowledge was valued more highly.

- teachers assumed that lower sets were not interested in their education and tended to interpret their contributions in class negatively.
- middle-class children fitted the image of the ideal pupil more closely than working-class pupils and therefore tended to be placed in higher streams.

Pupil subcultures and identities

Hargreaves (1967) found that children in lower streams in a secondary school were labelled as 'troublemakers'. As a result they turned against the values of the school and developed a **non-conformist delinquent subculture**.

Mac an Ghaill (1994) studied working-class students in a working-class comprehensive in the Midlands.. He found that three distinct working-class male **peer groups** developed as a result of: setting; student-teacher relationships; the position of the students in the working class; changes in the local economy. Mac an Ghaill defined these groups as follows:

- **Macho lads** were 'academic failures' who were hostile to the school and generally came from less skilled working-class backgrounds.
- **Academic achievers** were academic 'successes'; they generally came from skilled working-class backgrounds and were ambitious to gain high qualifications.
- **New enterprisers** saw the vocational curriculum, for example business studies, as their avenue to a good job.

Gillborn & Youdell (2001) studied **setting** in two London secondary schools. They found that:

- working-class and black pupils were more likely than middle-class and white pupils to be placed in lower sets even when they had been achieving similar results.
- teachers perceived working-class and black pupils to have lower ability even when they were doing well.
- once in lower sets they were not entered for higher tiers of GCSEs, making it impossible for them to get the highest grades.

Ireson *et al* (2001) examined the effects of setting on GCSE results in 45 comprehensive schools. They found no evidence that the amount of setting experienced from year 7 to year 11 had any effect on attainment.

Evaluation of interactionism

Advantages of the interactionist approach are that:

- it is based on far more detailed empirical evidence than functionalist or Marxist approaches.
- it shows that educational experiences are not just determined by home background and IQ.

Woods (1983) claims that the interactionist approach has practical applications. Its insights could help schools to improve teaching and reduce deviance in schools.

Limitations of the interactionist approach are that:

- many interactionists refer to class differences in education but fail to explain the origins of these differences.

- according to some critics, interactionists fail to take account of factors outside the school which might influence what happens within education (for example, cultural and material factors).
- many of the studies are rather dated and may not be applicable today.

GENDER AND ATTAINMENT

AQA, OCR, WJEC   Textbook pp. 642-649

By the late 1980s underachievement by females was attracting more concern than working-class underachievement. At that time girls were less likely than boys to obtain one or more A-levels and were less likely to go on to higher education.

In the mid-1990s there was a sudden reversal. Changes in achievement statistics meant that attention switched to **male underachievement**.

By 2006 45% of females but 35% of males obtained two or more A-levels.

In 2004/5 57% of people studying in higher education were female. On average, women now get better degrees than men.

There is disagreement over whether this change in emphasis due to the underachievement of males is really justified.

Explanations for female underachievement

Most of these explanations are based on the assumption that girls underachieve in school, and so are more relevant to earlier decades. However, some of the processes described may still be preventing female pupils from achieving their full potential.

Innate ability

One possible explanation for female underachievement is that there are differences in **innate ability** between girls and boys. However, girls actually out-perform boys in **IQ tests** at young ages. Some researchers have argued that this is because they mature earlier.

In a review of the available evidence, **Trowler** (1995) raises strong doubts about the usefulness of biological explanations of female underachievement. He points out that:

- there is very little difference between the IQ scores of boys and girls.
- differences in specific abilities might well be a product of social rather than biological differences.

Early socialization

Norman *et al* (1988) point out that, before children start school, **sex stereotyping** has already begun:

- Playing with dolls and other types of toys that reinforce the stereotype of women as carers may affect girls' educational aspirations.
- Boys are more likely to be given constructional toys which help develop **scientific** and **mathematical concepts**.
- Gender stereotypes are further reinforced through the **media**.

Girls may come to value education less than boys, as a consequence of early **socialization**. **Sharpe** (1976) found that the concerns of her sample of working-class girls were 'love, marriage, husbands, children, jobs, and careers, more or less in that order'. (See below for an update of this research).

Socialization in school

Abraham (1986) analysed textbooks used in a comprehensive school. He found maths textbooks to be especially male-dominated. Women tended to be shown in stereotypical roles such as shopping, while men were typically running businesses.

Classroom behaviour

Stanworth (1983) did a study of A-level classes in a further education college. She found that classroom interaction disadvantaged girls in the following ways:

- Teachers found it difficult to remember the girls in their classes.
- Teachers held stereotypical views of what their female pupils would be doing in the future.
- Pupils felt that boys received more attention than girls. They were more likely to join in classroom discussion, seek help from the teacher and be asked questions.
- Girls underestimated their ability and placed themselves below their teacher's ranking.

Criticisms of Stanworth

Randall (1987) criticizes the methods used by Stanworth. Her study was based on **interviews** rather than **direct observation**. Therefore, it cannot actually establish that teachers are giving less attention to girls. Randall's own research failed to find such a clear-cut bias.

Francis – girls and achievement

Francis (2000) makes a number of points about girls and achievement:

- Gender divisions in terms of subject choice are actually getting stronger, with fewer women going on to IT and pure science degrees than ten years earlier.
- Although female achievement may have overtaken male achievement, her own research in London found that males still dominate classrooms and get more teacher attention than girls.
- She found boys tended to be disciplined more harshly or frequently than girls, but in the process girls were getting little attention.
- Things had improved since the studies of early feminists but significant problems remained for females in education.
- Boys also faced problems in the education system.

Gender and subject choice

Although inequalities of educational achievement between males and females have declined, differences in the subjects studied remain considerable.

The **National Curriculum** limits these differences as school pupils have few options. When choices are available, however, distinct patterns arise.

At A-level:

- **males outnumber females** in business studies, economics, political science, sports and all science and technical subjects apart from biology.
- **females outnumber males** in all other subjects. English, modern languages, psychology and sociology have a particularly high proportion of female entries.

At degree level:

- males are more likely to graduate in physical and mathematical sciences, engineering and technology, and architecture, building and planning.
- in all other areas women predominate; females have overtaken males in medicine and dentistry, business and financial studies.
- men remain dominant in scientific and technical subjects and are more likely than females to obtain PhDs.

Colley – gender inequalities in subject choice

Colley (1998) reviewed the reasons why gender differences in subject choice persisted in the late 1990s. She found that:

- despite all the social changes in recent decades, traditional definitions of masculinity and femininity are still widespread.
- different subjects have different images. Computer studies, for example, involves working with machines rather than people, and this gives it a masculine image. The lack of opportunity for group activities and the rather formal way of teaching add to this.
- according to some research, girls are more comfortable with scientific and technical subjects when taught in single-sex schools or single-sex classes.

Changes in male and female attainment

Textbook pp. 646-649

The educational achievement of both males and females has been increasing over recent decades. However, the performance of females has improved faster than that of males. These changes have been interpreted in a number of ways.

Explaining girls' achievement

A number of reasons have been suggested for the improvements in girls' achievement.

Sharpe (1976, 1994) interviewed a sample of girls in the 1970s and another sample in the 1990s. She found that their priorities had changed from love and marriage in the 1970s to jobs and careers in the 1990s. A major reason for the change may therefore be increased **career ambition** by females. This in turn may be influenced by parents.

Francis & Skelton (2005) found middle-class parents were increasingly concerned about the educational success and career prospects of their daughters.

According to **Mitsos & Browne** (1998), the **women's movement** and **feminism** have raised the expectations and self-esteem of women.

The increase in **service sector** and part-time work has opened up employment opportunities for women.

There is now more incentive for women to gain educational qualifications. **Francis & Skelton** (2005) found many girls now aspire to jobs which require degree level qualifications.

Francis & Skelton (2005) use the work of **Beck** (1992) to argue that we increasingly live in a **risk society** where people face increasing uncertainty about their future (for example, there is less job security and higher divorce rates). Society has also become more **individualized** – people are increasingly self-reliant. Girls are more **risk averse** and seek greater security through being well qualified. They also see their career as an expression of their **identity** and a vehicle for future fulfilment, rather than relying upon marriage.

Explaining boys' underachievement

Francis & Skelton (2005) believe that there is an exaggerated **moral panic** about the achievement of boys. Boys' achievement has been improving over recent decades; it is just that girls' achievement has improved faster.

Francis (2000) argues that both boys and girls have problems in the education system. Her research suggests the following reasons for male underachievement:

- Boys get more classroom attention but are criticized more by teachers for their behaviour.
- Unlike in the 1970s, boys no longer believe they are more able than girls.
- Girls are more likely than boys to fit teachers' stereotypes of the **ideal pupil**.
- Boys are particularly keen not to be regarded as 'swots' or 'nerds' by being seen to be working too hard at school.

Jackson – laddish schools

A study by **Jackson** (2006) used a mixture of interviews and questionnaires to study masculinity and femininity in a total of eight schools.

The schools were dominated by a culture of **hegemonic** (or dominant) **masculinity**. This valued toughness, power and competitiveness.

Academic work was defined as too feminine to be seen as 'cool' by boys. This resulted in many boys messing about in schools and not concentrating on their work, acting out **laddish masculinity**.

However, many boys also wanted good qualifications so they tended to work harder at home than at school. Middle-class boys had more facilities than working-class boys (for example, space and computers) to succeed using this strategy.

Jackson believes that laddish masculinity is a response to **fear of failure** in an increasingly competitive education system. Laddish behaviour masks and cushions the disappointment for boys who do poorly.

The number of **unskilled** and **semi-skilled** manual jobs available to boys leaving school has rapidly declined. These jobs used to give working-class males a sense of identity. Most of the new jobs in the service sector are more feminine. Laddish behaviour is used by working-class boys to restore a sense of masculinity.

AQA, OCR, WJEC   Textbook pp. 649-661

Most studies indicate that ethnic minorities tend to do less well than other members of the population. However, this hides important variations between and within ethnic groups, with some ethnic minorities being particularly successful.

The *Youth Cohort Study* (2006) found that in England Indian pupils were most likely to gain five or more A*-C GCSEs, followed by other Asians, whites, Bangladeshi, Pakistani and black pupils.

The performance of Bangladeshis at GCSE level has improved rapidly in recent years to reach the national average, but black pupils remain some way behind the national average.

Girls are more likely than boys to get five or more higher grade GCSEs in all ethnic groups.

Asian pupils are slightly more likely than the national average to obtain one or more AS/A-level or equivalent qualifications, but black pupils are less likely than the average to get this level of qualification.

Young people from all ethnic groups are more likely to stay on in education until 18 than whites.

Overall, Chinese are the most successful ethnic group in the British education system.

In 2000/01 whites had the lowest participation rate in higher education, with all ethnic minorities having higher rates. The highest rates were for Black African ethnic groups followed by Indians, Black other, Pakistani and African Caribbean. (**Connor**, 2004). However, black undergraduates are more likely than the average to be at the less prestigious universities and are also more likely to drop out of HE than whites.

Ethnicity, social class and attainment

As we saw earlier, class is closely linked to educational attainment, with members of lower social classes gaining fewer qualifications and leaving the education system earlier than higher classes. Poor educational performance by **ethnic minorities** could be a result of the relatively high proportion who come from a working-class background.

However, research by **Modood** (2004) found that class differences in achievement at GCSE between middle-class and working-class groups were highest amongst whites and lower in ethnic minority groups.

Modood argues that some ethnic minority pupils do well despite coming from a working-class background because they possess high levels of **cultural capital** even though they are working-class. Some members of ethnic minorities, for example Indians and East African Asians, experienced **downward mobility** when migrating to Britain, and come from relatively well-educated, middle-class backgrounds. Modood's research also suggests that ethnic minority parents place a particularly high value on educational success for their children.

Racism and the education system

One ethnic group which has continued to do relatively poorly in education in Britain has been **African Caribbeans**, particularly boys and young men. African

Caribbean boys start primary school on a par with their white counterparts but by the time they take GCSEs they do much less well. Some writers have attributed this to racism.

Coard – African Caribbean underachievement

Coard (1971) argues that African Caribbean children are made to feel inferior in the British education system because:

- a disproportionate number are placed in ESN (educationally subnormal) 'special schools' when many have the ability to be educated in mainstream schools.
- the **content** of education tends to ignore black people.
- many teachers are **racist**.
- teachers tend to have low expectations of black pupils.
- attitudes in the classroom are reinforced by pupils in the playground, where racial abuse and bullying may occur.

Coard believes that this leads to black children developing low self-esteem and low expectations.

Coard's views have been criticized for being partly based on **impressionistic evidence** and for being out of date. However, his work has been recently reprinted and research shows that African Caribbean boys are between four and fifteen times more likely to be excluded than white boys (**Richardson**, 2005).

Wright – racism in primary schools

Wright (1992) conducted an **ethnographic study** of four multi-racial inner-city primary schools using **classroom observation** and **interviews** with the teachers. She found that, although the majority of staff were committed to **equality of opportunity**, there was still considerable **discrimination**:

- **Asians girls** received less attention from teachers; Asian customs and traditions were sometimes disapproved of.
- **African Caribbean boys** received much negative attention from teachers, who expected African Caribbean pupils to behave badly.

Recent studies emphasize the variety of ways in which ethnic minorities respond to racism in the education system.

Mirza – young, female and black

Mirza (1992) studied two comprehensive schools in south London using **observation**, **questionnaires** and **informal interviews**.

The black girls in Mirza's sample did better in exams than black boys and white pupils in the school. She believes that the educational achievements of black women are underestimated.

Mirza also challenges the **labelling theory** of educational underachievement. Although there was some evidence of **racism** among teachers, she denies that this undermined the self-confidence of the black girls. Most girls were concerned with academic success and prepared to work hard.

Most teachers tried to meet the girls' needs but failed to do so by, for instance, failing to push black pupils hard enough or by patronizing them.

Mac an Ghaill – ethnic minorities in the sixth form

Mac an Ghaill (1992) studied African Caribbean and Asian students in a sixth-form college in the Midlands. He used **observation** and **interviews** with students, parents and teachers. He found that the way students responded to schooling varied considerably and was influenced by their **ethnicity**, **gender** and the **class** composition of their former secondary schools.

All of the ethnic minority students experienced problems in the education system, but they experienced them differently, depending on their gender and ethnic group. Nevertheless, they had all enjoyed some success. They had achieved this through adopting a variety of 'survival strategies':

- Some of the girls had banded together They would help each other out with academic work but were less willing to conform to rules about dress, appearance and behaviour in class.
- Some of the other ethnic minority pupils were less hostile to their schools. They tried to become friendly with some teachers while avoiding others who they identified as racist.

The study is important because it shows how class, gender and ethnicity interact within the school system. Like Mirza's study, Mac an Ghaill shows that **negative labelling** does not necessarily lead to academic failure. Although such labelling creates extra barriers, some students are able to overcome them.

Gillborn et al – rationing education

Research by **Gillborn & Mirza** (2000) and **Gillborn & Youdell** (2000) suggests that racism continues to significantly disadvantage ethnic minorities in British education.

Using documents containing official statistics, Gillborn & Mirza found that in some local education authorities ethnic minorities seemed to be particularly disadvantaged, suggesting that those areas had a significant problem with racism.

Gillborn & Youdell studied two London comprehensives using **lesson observation**, **documentary research** and **interviews** with pupils and teachers. They found that a system of educational **triage** – in which education was rationed – adversely affected black pupils. Extra help was directed at those who were borderline cases for gaining five GCSEs at grade C. However, many black pupils were considered to have little chance of achieving this standard and were effectively written off, being placed in lower sets or entered for lower tiers of GCSEs.

There was a system of **racialized expectations**, in which the behaviour of black pupils was interpreted as threatening, rather than as evidence of wanting to succeed. **Unintentional racism** therefore held many black pupils back.

Sewell – black masculinities

Sewell (1997) argues that factors outside school are more important than racism in school to explain the low achievement of many African Caribbean boys. His findings are based on a study of black students in a boys' comprehensive school.

Sewell finds that a disproportionate number of African Caribbean boys are raised in **lone parent families**.

Many therefore lack a positive, **adult male role model** and they may not be well disciplined in the family, making them more vulnerable to **peer pressure**.

Some boys are drawn into gangs which emphasize an aggressive, **macho masculinity** and do not respect authority figures including teachers.

This is reinforced by the media which reports black gun crime and the culture of hip hop and gangsta rap.

The **gang culture** compensates for a sense of rejection by fathers and by society, and education which they experience as racist.

In the school Sewell found four subcultures:

- **conformists** (41% of the sample) who rejected black street culture and saw education as the route to success;

- **innovators** (35%) who wanted to succeed and kept out of trouble but rejected the way schools educated them;

- **retreatists** (6%) who were loners and kept themselves to themselves – many had **special educational needs**;

- **rebels** (18%) who rejected the norms and values of the school and were confrontational. They came into conflict with the school when they brought aspects of **street culture** into the school (for example, patterns in their hair) even when they had no intention of challenging the school. They saw this as a lack of respect and responded aggressively.

Sewell has been criticized for blaming black culture for the educational failure of African Caribbean boys and drawing attention away from the failings of the education system.

However, he does show that only a minority of African Caribbean boys are part of an **anti-school culture**.

Connolly – young children and ethnicity

Some recent studies focus more on **identity** than differential achievement but have implications for understanding achievement as well.

Connolly's study (1998) of young children in a multi-ethnic inner-city primary school emphasizes the diverse influences on gender in schools. In particular, he examines how school relationships are also shaped by ethnicity.

Teachers were more willing to criticize the behaviour of **black boys** than that of other groups. They felt that some of the black males in the school were in danger of growing up to be violent criminals, and they saw them as a threat to school discipline. However, they also took positive steps to encourage them to participate in school activities such as football.

The boys also brought their own values and attitudes to school – for example, those relating to masculinity. These also contributed to their identity.

Black girls were also perceived by teachers as potentially disruptive but likely to be good at sports, music and dancing.

Some teachers contrasted what they saw as the close and supportive Asian families with the high rates of single parenthood amongst other groups in the area. **South Asian boys** tended to be seen as immature rather than seriously deviant.

There was a tendency for other boys who wanted to assert their **masculinity** to pick on South Asian boys. The South Asian boys had difficulty in gaining **status** as males. This made it difficult for them to feel confident at school.

South Asian girls were seen to be even more obedient and hard-working than South Asian boys, although Connolly's observations showed that their attitude to work was not significantly different from that of other female groups. These girls had a relatively **low status** among their peers. They were seen as feminine in terms of their passivity and obedience, but they were not seen as potential girlfriends by black and white boys because their culture was considered too alien.

Archer – Muslim boys and education

Archer (2003) carried out research involving **group interviews** with a total of 31 14-15 year-old Muslim boys in four schools in northwest England. She studied the types of identity they developed.

The boys saw themselves primarily as **Muslim** but felt they did not truly belong in England or in the country of origin of their parents/grandparents (Pakistan or Bangladesh).

The boys drew on African Caribbean **street culture** (for example, gangsta rap); some called themselves black, but their black identity was ambiguous. Most claimed to be members of gangs.

The boys thought that teachers favoured girls and expected them to do better in exams. They responded by seeing laddish behaviour in school as part of their masculine identity.

Nevertheless, they saw themselves in a **breadwinner role** as adults, supporting other family members, and they saw education as important for getting a well-paid job. They had very positive images of family life.

Some felt that **racism** would hold them back so they looked to **family businesses** as a way of earning their living.

Evaluation of Archer

This study shows that identities are fluid and can have both a positive and a negative impact on educational achievement.

However, the validity of the data can be questioned. The interviews were conducted either by Archer herself (a white, British woman) or by a British Pakistani woman. The nature of the **audience** (the interviewer and the other Muslim boys) may well have influenced the sorts of responses they gave.

DEVELOP YOUR ANALYTICAL AND EVALUATION SKILLS

Essay plans

For each of the following questions write your own essay plan before comparing it with the suggestions given here. For the final question you can write a full answer and compare it with the provided model answer.

Cultural factors are largely responsible for working-class children underachieving in the education system. Discuss.

 Background

You might start by noting some evidence that the working class still do relatively poorly in education (see p. 51). Cultural arguments include those of Douglas, Bernstein and Feinstein, but all have been criticized. More sophisticated arguments are partly based on class culture, as in those put forward by Bourdieu, but Bourdieu also holds the education system responsible, as he sees it as biased towards the dominant culture. Alternative arguments suggest that material factors are more important or that labelling within schools is largely responsible. The different viewpoints are not mutually exclusive, and you might conclude that a combination of material and cultural factors, and factors inside and outside school, are all significant.

For	Against
● Douglas (p. 52)	● Criticisms of cultural theories (p. 52)
● Feinstein (p. 52)	● Material theories (p. 53)
● Bernstein (p. 52)	● Interactionist theory (p. 54)

For and against
● Bourdieu (p. 53)

 Top Tip

The studies by Ball *et al* (p. 53) and by Reay *et al* (p. 53) are useful for illustrating Bourdieu's approach, which suggests how cultural factors are linked to wider class inequality and the operation of the education system.

Education serves the interests of the ruling class. Discuss.

 Background

This view is a Marxist one and the clearest supporters are Bowles & Gintis. Willis agrees with this view, although he sees the relationship between education and the ruling class as complex. Finn uses something similar to a Marxist approach when discussing training schemes. Marxism is not without its direct critics (see p. 48) and other approaches take a very different view. The New Right deny there is a ruling class (see p. 49) and believe education has failed to produce a suitable workforce. Functionalists, on the other hand, see education as effectively serving the needs of society as a whole.

For	Against
● Bowles & Gintis (p. 47)	● Functionalism (p. 46)
● Willis (p. 48)	● The New Right (p. 49)
● Finn (p. 50)	

 Top Tip

Much of the research on education suggests that it serves the interests of middle-class children rather well (for example, see Ball *et al*, p. 53) and doesn't just benefit the ruling class. The working class, however, may miss out on the full benefits.

The education of boys is now more of a problem in Britain than the education of girls. Discuss.

Background

You need to explain the changes in recorded achievement, with girls overtaking boys at all levels of the education system (p. 55). This has led writers like Mitsos & Browne and Carolyn Jackson to discuss the reasons for boys doing less well than girls. Francis also suggests some problems with the education of boys, though she sees both boys and girls facing some problems. Francis & Skelton (p. 56) believe there is a 'moral panic' about male education. Colley points that there are still many prestigious subjects that females are unlikely to study.

For	**Against**
• Statistics on achievement (p. 55)	• Colley (p. 56)
• Jackson (p. 57)	

For and against
- Mitsos & Browne (p. 56)
- Francis, and Francis & Skelton (p. 56)

Top Tip

Connolly's work (p. 59) is useful for showing how gender interacts with class and ethnicity to create educational problems for particular groups of boys and girls, as are studies by Sewell (p. 58) and Archer (p. 59).

The educational underachievement of ethnic minorities in Britain is due to racism in schools. Discuss.

Background

First, you need to examine whether ethnic minorities are underachieving. The evidence shows that most ethnic groups are not, with Chinese, and Indian ethnic groups doing very well in British education and Bangladeshis having improved their results dramatically. The main focus will probably be on African Caribbeans (boys, in particular), who still perform less well than other groups.

For	**For and against**
• Coard (p. 58)	• Mirza (p. 58)
• Gillborn & Mirza (p. 58)	• Mac an Ghaill (p. 58)
• Gillborn & Youdell (p. 58)	• Sewell (p. 58)
• Wright (p. 58)	

Top Tip

The work of both Connolly (p. 59) and Archer (p. 59) shows that a range of factors shape both identity and achievement, with the experience of racism playing some, but not the major role, in the response of different ethnic groups to education.

New Labour have succeeded in greatly improving the British education system. Discuss.

Background

You will need to start with some political background, explaining that New Labour was elected in 1997 and was influenced both by New Right and social democratic thinking. You can discuss what the aims were and how they compared to those of the New Right Conservative government that preceded it.

For	**Against**
• McKnight *et al* (p. 51) • Progress by ethnic minority groups (p. 57) • Progress by girls (p. 55)	• Sally Tomlinson (p. 51) • The New Right (p. 49) • Continued class inequality (p. 49)

For and against
• Strathdee (p. 51)
• Social democrats (p. 48)

It is worth discussing higher education in this answer. Higher education has expanded, producing more opportunities under New Labour, but research by Callender & Jackson (p. 54) explains why the working class have failed to take full advantage.

Spending on education benefits the economy and therefore benefits society as a whole. Discuss.

This statement supports the functionalist view of education, but it would be supported at least partly by other perspectives as well. A number of viewpoints agree that education can, or should, benefit the economy; however, they argue that imperfections in education prevent it from being as beneficial as it might be. Recent Labour government policies have viewed education as crucial to promoting growth in a globally competitive world, but the New Right don't think more spending itself will necessarily create more growth.

For	**Against**
• Functionalism (p. 46) • New Labour (p. 50)	• Marxists and neo-Marxists (p. 48) • Feminists (p. 65) • The New Right (p. 49)

For and against
• Social democrats (p. 48)

Alison Woolf (p. 49) is one of the few people who directly questions whether more spending on education will lead to greater economic growth.

Model answer

Spending on education benefits the economy and therefore benefits society as a whole. Discuss.

Education is one of the most costly areas of government spending, accounting for more than 13.5% of government spending in 2003/4. Spending on education has steadily risen since free state education was introduced in 1870. The percentages staying on in education until 18 and progressing to higher education have also risen.

From the viewpoint of the current Labour government, the increased participation is good news and the extra investment is money well spent. When Tony Blair was elected in 1997 he claimed that his priorities were 'Education, education, education'. Blair, and his successor Gordon Brown, both believe that we live in an increasingly globalized economy, with Britain having to compete with every other country in the world. Employment in Britain is relatively expensive, so the only way to compete successfully is to have an increasingly skilled workforce whose labour can produce more value than the labour of competitor countries.

Although the emphasis on globalization is new, the idea that education spending can benefit the economy is not. Early functionalists such as Davis & Moore, believed that education had a vital economic role. For them, education had the function of role allocation, sifting and sorting the most able to ensure that they were placed in the most functionally important jobs. For Parsons, education encouraged an emphasis on individual achievement, providing the motivation to work hard and contribute to economic growth. Functionalists supported the human capital theory, arguing that investing in education was like investing in new machinery: it increased productivity and therefore increased wealth creation.

These views were partially accepted by social democrats such as AH Halsey, who influenced Labour governments of the 1960s and 1970s. They agreed with human capital theory in principle, but argued that much talent was being wasted in an education system which held back the working class.

A very different view was put forward by New Right thinkers such as Chubb & Moe and the Conservative government of Margaret Thatcher. The New Right agreed that a high quality education was important for the economy, but did not think that more spending on education was the way to achieve it. Indeed, the New Right thought that too much government spending on education or other state services reduced the profitability of companies and held back economic growth. Instead, they advocated and introduced market forces, through formula funding and increased competition between schools. The aim was to force up standards without spending more, and they attached no importance to the social democratic aim of creating greater class equality.

From the Marxist point of view, exemplified by Bowles & Gintis, education is closely tied to the economy, but its main purpose is not to create economic growth as such. Instead, it aims to create a docile, easily exploitable workforce unwilling to challenge ruling-class power. While it allows the ruling class to make profits, it largely benefits them rather than society as a whole. Neo-Marxists such as Paul Willis agree that education reproduces inequality and helps to maintain ruling-class power. However, Willis believes that it only does so indirectly, through the rejection of school by working-class boys, which prepares them for mundane manual jobs. Feminists, too, do not see education as benefiting society as a whole. For example, Michelle Stanworth believes that education is deeply sexist and benefits girls much less than boys, thereby preventing girls from contributing as much as they could to the economy.

Alison Woolf is directly critical of the view that education spending always benefits the economy. She accepts that good primary and secondary education is necessary, but more and more spending does not guarantee growth. For example, Switzerland has relatively low education spending but high economic growth. Amongst poorer countries Egypt has very high spending but low economic growth. She believes that growth can be achieved by concentrating resources on higher education expenditure for the most talented students rather than trying to get as many people as possible into a very expensive higher education system. For Woolf, continuing to expand higher education can lead to a surplus of over-qualified graduates, many of whom have developed skills for which there is no demand in the economy.

Woolf shows that we should not simply accept the argument that all education spending is good for the economy. However, even she accepts a fair amount of government spending is needed. Perhaps, a balance needs to be struck between excessive spending and an inadequate educational system. However much is spent, some of the money may be wasted if the class and gender inequalities which waste talent are not addressed. Education still tends to benefit some groups more than others.

RESOURCES

Class and educational achievement

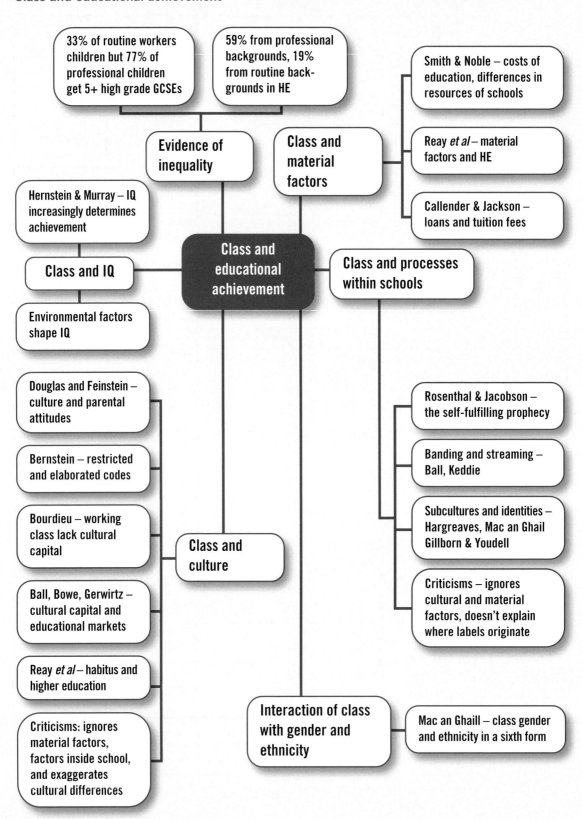

33% of routine workers children but 77% of professional children get 5+ high grade GCSEs

59% from professional backgrounds, 19% from routine backgrounds in HE

Smith & Noble – costs of education, differences in resources of schools

Reay *et al* – material factors and HE

Callender & Jackson – loans and tuition fees

Evidence of inequality

Class and material factors

Hernstein & Murray – IQ increasingly determines achievement

Class and IQ

Environmental factors shape IQ

Class and educational achievement

Class and processes within schools

Douglas and Feinstein – culture and parental attitudes

Bernstein – restricted and elaborated codes

Bourdieu – working class lack cultural capital

Ball, Bowe, Gerwirtz – cultural capital and educational markets

Reay *et al* – habitus and higher education

Criticisms: ignores material factors, factors inside school, and exaggerates cultural differences

Class and culture

Rosenthal & Jacobson – the self-fulfilling prophecy

Banding and streaming – Ball, Keddie

Subcultures and identities – Hargreaves, Mac an Ghail Gillborn & Youdell

Criticisms – ignores cultural and material factors, doesn't explain where labels originate

Interaction of class with gender and ethnicity

Mac an Ghaill – class gender and ethnicity in a sixth form

Sociological perspectives on education

	Functionalism	Marxism	Feminism	Social democratic	New Right/ neo-liberal
What role of education should be	To provide equal opportunities, promote growth, create social solidarity	Not clear – it can serve useful functions in capitalism	To provide opportunities for women who are disadvantaged	To create greater equality between classes and train workers	To provide efficient, good value education to make country competitive
What education actually does	As above	Reproduces class inequality, produces docile workers	Patriarchal – reproduces gender inequality	Gives unfair advantages to middle class, reinforces class divisions	Wastes money, inefficient; standards are too low
What needs to be changed in education	Nothing much	Society needs to change, ie. communism introduced	Get rid of sexism, more opportunities for women	Mixed ability teaching, help and opportunities for working class	More competition, choice and specialization
View of inequalities in education	It is meritocratic so there are no unfair inequalities	They reproduce existing class inequalities	Unfair gender inequalities exist	Unfair class inequalities exist	Concerned with standards not inequalities
View on education and economy	Vital for successful economy	Controlled by dominant economic class	Not relevant	Equal opportunities vital to economic success	Raised standards vital to economic success
How influential and when	Very influential in 1940s and 1950s	Popular in 1970s, but little influence on policies	Most popular in 1980s, has led to less sexist education	Most popular in 1960s and 1970s, has had some influence on New Labour	Most influential in 1980s and 1990s, has had some influence on New Labour
Main criticisms	Ignores evidence of lack of meritocracy and other problems	Ignores gender, ignores problems with communism	Males do better now than females	Weaknesses of comprehensive schools, failed to create equal opportunities	Creates unequal opportunities; may not raise standards much

Research methods in the sociology of education

Author: Willis (1977) **Research:** Working-class 'lads' at school and work (Textbook pp. 605-608)
Research methods: Qualitative observation and group interviews
Strengths: High validity, close to actual social life in schools
Weaknesses/problems: Small, all-male sample. May have influenced behaviour of subjects. Researcher couldn't be full participant as too old

Author: Ball *et al* (1995) **Research:** Study of 15 schools and education market (Textbook pp. 618-619)
Research methods: Observation of meetings; interviews with teachers and 150 parents; LEA documents
Strengths: Triangulation of data. Mixed primary and secondary sources. Large-scale study. Able to look at link between policies and parental decision-making
Weaknesses/problems: Didn't interview pupils. Didn't directly observe effects of markets in schools

Author: McKnight *et al* (2005) **Research:** New Labour education policies (Textbook p. 624)
Research methods: Examined official statistics on Key Stage tests and GCSE results
Strengths: Able to do statistical analysis using reliable government statistics
Weaknesses/problems: Validity of data could be questioned, e.g. have standards required to pass GCSEs changed over time?

Author: Gillborn & Youdell (2001) **Research:** 'Intelligence' and 'ability' in two London secondary schools (Textbook p. 628)
Research methods: Qualitative research using observation and interviews
Strengths: In-depth study provides detailed picture of two schools – should be high in validity
Weaknesses/problems: Small, unrepresentative sample of schools. Hard to generalize from findings. Hard to know how honest and open teachers would be when interviewed

Author: Douglas (1964, 1970) **Research:** Home influence on educational attainment (Textbook pp. 629-630)
Research methods: Longitudinal study used IQ tests, statistics on attainment, data on parents' evenings attendance to measure parental interest in education
Strengths: Able to track changes without asking respondents to remember past events. Large sample (5,362), used fairly reliable quantitative data
Weaknesses/problems: Sample declined over time. Attendance at parents' evenings may not be a valid measure of interest in education. Didn't study working-class and middle-class culture himself but relied on other studies

Author: Bernstein (1961, 1970, 1972) **Research:** Influence of speech patterns on education (Textbook pp. 630-632)
Research methods: Interviews with young children where they described pictures to evaluate their linguistic skills
Strengths: Interviews allowed a fairly large sample of children to be studied
Weaknesses/problems: Interviewer bias? William Labov found black children only showed their true skills when interviewed by black interviewers in an informal setting

Author: Reay *et al* (2005) **Research** Class influence on higher education choice (Textbook pp. 625-626)
Research methods: Questionnaire to a sample of 502 students, 120 in-depth interviews, focus groups with students at six schools or colleges around London
Strengths: Triangulation allowed results to be checked for greater reliability. Good-sized sample. Qualitative and quantitative data collected
Weaknesses/problems: Sample entirely based on London area so may not have been representative. Possibility of interviewer bias

Author: Universities UK (2005) **Research:** Class and attitudes to higher education (Textbook pp. 637-638)
Research methods: Sample of nearly 2,000 postal questionnaires to 1,500 final-year undergraduates
Strengths: Large, geographically dispersed sample increases ability to generalize. No problem of interviewer bias. Easy to replicate to increase reliability
Weaknesses/problems: Problem of non-response. Lack of in-depth explanation of attitudes which might be revealed in an interview

Author: Rosenthal & Jacobson (1968) **Research:** Labelling and the self-fulfilling prophecy (Textbook p. 639)
Research methods: Field experiment: teachers were given incorrect information about IQ
Strengths: Looks at effects in real social situation (high ecological validity). Pupils and teachers unaware of experiment so high validity
Weaknesses/problems: Ethical problems of lying and of harming some pupils deemed to have a low IQ. No observation of effects in the classroom

Author: Hargreaves (1967) **Research:** Development of classroom subcultures (Textbook p. 641)
Research methods: Classroom observation
Strengths: High ecological validity as observed actual classroom interactions
Weaknesses/problems: Observer's presence affected behaviour of teachers and pupils. Relied very much on observer's interpretations so low on reliability

Author: Lobban (1974), Best (1992)
Research: Gender bias in reading schemes (Textbook pp. 644-645)
Research methods: Content analysis
Strengths: Systematic analysis for high reliability
Weaknesses/problems: Lack of qualitative research to find how pupils interpreted stories. Studies now dated

Author: Sharpe (1976, 1994) **Research:** Girls' priorities (Textbook p. 644)
Research methods: Structured interviews
Strengths: Allowed comparisons to be made over time
Weaknesses/problems: Possibility of interviewer bias. Small sample size

Author: Stanworth (1983) **Research:** Gender bias in sixth form (Textbook p. 645)
Research methods: Structured interviews
Strengths: Method allowed wide-ranging questions on gender issues
Weaknesses/problems: Lack of classroom observation to show actual classroom interaction

Author: Modood (2004) **Research:** Ethnic minorities in education (Textbook pp. 650-652)
Research methods: Official statistics from DfES and Youth Cohort Study
Strengths: High reliability, large sample size, statistics easy to access and no ethical issues
Weaknesses/problems: Secondary sources don't provide exact information required by researcher, e.g. no figures on social class available so data on free school meals used to infer income inequality. Schools may manipulate results, e.g. by using exclusions

Author: Wright (1992) **Research:** Racism in primary schools (Textbook p. 652)
Research methods: Classroom observation with 970 pupils and 57 staff, observation in staff room, informal interviews with teachers, support staff and head teachers, examination of test results
Strengths: Advantages of triangulation. Large numbers of observations and interviews increasing reliability. High validity due to observation. Revealed racism that teachers might not admit in interviews
Weaknesses/problems: Only three schools studied so difficult to generalize

Author: Sewell (1997) **Research:** Black masculinities and schooling (Textbook pp. 657-658)
Research methods: Observation and unstructured interviews of pupils in one school. Use of official statistics on family structure
Strengths: In-depth data on a small sample of pupils. Interviews allowed exploration of factors outside school
Weaknesses/problems: Lack of direct research on family life. Hard to generalize as all pupils attended a single school

Author: Archer (2003) **Research:** Muslim boys and education (Textbook pp. 660-661)
Research methods: Discussion groups led by three different interviewers (two British Pakistanis, one white British) with 31 boys in four schools in northwest England
Strengths: Interviews gathered in-depth qualitative information about a wide-range of issues
Weaknesses/problems: Possibility of interview bias varying depending upon interviewer. Small sample in one geographical area makes generalization problematic

| # RELIGION AND BELIEFS

SPECIFICATION COVERAGE

Specification	Details
AQA A2 Unit 3 SCLY 3: Beliefs in Society	All the essential notes are relevant for the AQA specification in this topic
OCR AS Unit C672: Sociology of Religion	Religion is an AS option for OCR. Material which is relevant to the specification is indicated in the text
WJEC SY2: Understanding Culture – Religion	This is an AS option so less depth is required than is included in some sections

DEFINITIONS OF RELIGION

AQA, OCR, WJEC   Textbook pp. 395-396

Religious beliefs of some sort are present in every known human society, but the nature of those beliefs varies considerably. Any definition of those beliefs must encompass this variety. Two main approaches have been taken to defining religion:

* **Substantive definitions** – these are concerned with the content of religion. For example, **Yinger** (1981) defined religion as 'a system of beliefs and practices by means of which a group of people struggles with the ultimate problems of human life' (quoted in **Hamilton**, 1995).

* **Functional definitions** – these define religion in terms of the functions it performs for society and for individuals. **Durkheim** (1961) defined religion in terms of a distinction between the **sacred** and the **profane**. Sacred objects produce a sense of awe and respect, whereas profane objects do not.

All definitions emphasize certain aspects of religion and ignore others. Functional definitions tend to be too inclusive (it is too easy to qualify as a religion); while substantive ones tend to be too exclusive (it is difficult to qualify as a religion).

FUNCTIONALIST PERSPECTIVES

AQA, OCR, WJEC   Textbook pp. 396-399

Functionalist analysis is concerned with the contribution religion makes to meeting society's needs, such as social solidarity, value consensus, harmony and integration between its parts.

Emile Durkheim

Durkheim (1912) argued that, in worshipping God, people are in fact worshipping society. Society is more important and more powerful than the individual, just as God is.

Religion reinforces the shared values and moral beliefs – what Durkheim called the **collective conscience** – that hold society together. By defining these shared values as **sacred**, religion endows them with greater power.

In worshipping society, people are, in effect, recognizing the importance of the social group and their dependence on it. In this way religion strengthens the unity of the group: it promotes **social solidarity**.

Through acts of **collective worship**, members of society express, communicate and understand the moral bonds which unite them (for example through singing or chanting).

Criticisms

Durkheim only studied a small number of Aboriginal tribes. It may be misleading to generalize from this small sample.

Most sociologists would not go as far as Durkheim in arguing that religion is, in fact, the worship of society. **Hamilton** (1995) points out that Durkheim's theory may only be applicable to small non-literate societies. Modern societies are characterized by diversity. Hamilton also argues that Durkheim overstates the degree to which common values influence individual behaviour. Often religious beliefs will conflict with dominant values.

Bronislaw Malinowski

Like Durkheim, **Malinowski** (1954) uses data from small-scale, non-literate societies to support his ideas. He focuses on the role of religion in dealing with situations of **emotional stress** that threaten social solidarity. He identifies two sorts of events that may create this kind of stress:

1 Anxiety and tension tend to disrupt social life. Situations that produce these emotions include **life crises** such as birth, puberty, marriage and death. Malinowski notes that in all societies these life crises are surrounded by **religious ritual**. At a funeral ceremony, for example, the social group unites to support the bereaved. The expression of **social solidarity** reintegrates society.

2 Actions that cannot be fully controlled or predicted also produce tension and anxiety. From his observations in the Trobriand Islands, Malinowski noted that such events were surrounded by ritual. Rituals reduce anxiety by providing confidence and a feeling of **control**. For example, religious rituals are performed before the islanders go fishing in their canoes in the dangerous and unpredictable deep sea waters, but not in the calm and relatively safe waters of the inland lagoons in the islands.

Criticisms

Malinowski has been criticized for exaggerating the importance of religious ritual in helping people to cope with situations of stress and uncertainty.

Talcott Parsons

Parsons (1965a) argues that religious beliefs provide guidelines for human action and standards against which people's conduct can be evaluated. The Ten Commandments, for example, provide the basis for many social norms. In the USA Christian religious beliefs underpin the **value consensus** even for those who are not Christians because laws and norms have their origin in Christianity.

Like Malinowski, Parsons sees religion as dealing with problems that disrupt social life – problems such as unforeseen, unpredictable events and situations of uncertainty.

Another main function of religion for Parsons is to make sense of all experiences, no matter how meaningless or contradictory they appear. Religion

provides a range of answers to questions about suffering, evil and so on.

Criticisms of functionalism

The functionalist perspective emphasizes the positive contributions of religion to society and ignores its **dysfunctional** aspects. Functionalism neglects the instances where religion can be seen as a divisive and disruptive force – for example, in the Middle East conflicts between Palestinian Muslims and Israeli Jews; in Northern Ireland, between Catholics and Protestants; in India, between Hindus and Muslims.

MARXIST PERSPECTIVES

AQA, OCR, WJEC   Textbook pp. 399–401

For Marx (1964, first published 1842), religion is an illusion which eases the pain produced by exploitation and oppression. It is a series of myths that justify and legitimate the domination of the ruling class. As such it forms the basis of much ruling-class ideology. Marx famously described religion as the '**opium of the people**'. Like a drug, it dulls pain and creates a dream world rather than bringing true happiness. Religions, for Marx:

- promise a paradise of eternal bliss in life after death, making life bearable by giving people something to look forward to.

- make a virtue out of the suffering produced by oppression. In particular, those who suffer poverty with dignity and humility will be rewarded in the afterlife. Religion thus makes poverty more tolerable.

- offer the hope of **supernatural solutions** to problems in earthly life. Anticipation of this future can make the present more acceptable.

- often justify the **social order** and a person's position within it. In this way social arrangements appear inevitable, and those at the bottom can accept and come to terms with their situation. In the same way, poverty and misfortune can be seen as a punishment for sin.

Religion and social control

For Marxists, religion does not simply cushion the effects of oppression. It also acts as a mechanism of **social control**, keeping people in their place:

- By making unsatisfactory lives bearable, it discourages people from attempting to change their situation.

- By offering an illusion of hope in a hopeless situation, it prevents thoughts of overthrowing the system.

- By providing justifications for society, religion distorts reality and helps to produce **false class consciousness**. This blinds members of the oppressed class to their true situation.

Ruling classes also adopt religious beliefs to justify their dominance, to themselves and others.

Marx thought religion was a form of **alienation** – humans create an imaginary alien being which then controls them. However, religion would die out under **communism** because there would be no exploitation and therefore no need for religion.

Evidence to support Marxism

There are many examples from history where ruling groups have used religion to justify their dominance. The **caste system** in traditional India was justified by Hindu religious beliefs; whilst in medieval Europe, kings and queens ruled by '**Divine Right**'.

Bruce (1988) points out that conservative Protestants in the USA – the **New Christian Right** – consistently support right-wing political candidates. Although they have had a limited influence on American politics, they have tended to defend the interests of the rich and powerful at the expense of other groups in the population. George W. Bush (President from 2001-2009) consistently supported right-wing views, for example low taxes for the rich, and was a supporter of the New Christian Right.

The limitations of Marxism

Some evidence suggests that religion does not always legitimate power and that it can sometimes provide an impetus for change (see p. 71).

The fact that religion sometimes acts as an ideological force in the way suggested by Marx does not explain its existence.

Maduro – the relative autonomy of religion

Some neo-Marxists argue that religion is not always a conservative force. **Maduro** (1982) claims that religion can be **revolutionary**. Members of the clergy can develop revolutionary potential when oppressed members of the population have no other outlet for their grievances.

This has occurred in Latin America, where some Catholic priests have criticized ruling groups and helped to organize resistance. Their political activism is driven by a concept known as **liberation theology**.

GENDER, FEMINISM AND RELIGION

AQA OCR WJEC   **Textbook pp. 401-405**

Feminist theories follow Marxist theories in arguing that religion can be an instrument of domination and oppression. However, unlike Marxism, they see religion as a product of patriarchy (see p. 84) rather than capitalism.

Armstrong (1993) points out that women occupy a **marginal** position in most major religions. Although they have made gains in many areas of life, their gains in most religions have been very limited.

Women continue to be excluded from key roles in many religions (although the Church of England finally allowed the **ordination of women priests** in 1992). This is despite the fact that women often participate more than men in organized religion.

Holm (1994) argues that in many religions men dominate the powerful positions of the **public sphere**, while women do most of the 'behind the scenes' work in the **private sphere**. For example:

- In Orthodox **Judaism** only men take part in public ceremonies.
- Women still cannot be priests in the **Roman Catholic** religion.

- In some **Islamic** cultures women are not allowed to pray in mosques and men make the legal rulings.
- In **Hinduism** only men can become Brahmanic priests.

Holm (1994) notes that women's second-class status is often related to female biology and sexuality. For example, **Islamic** women cannot touch the Qu'ran when menstruating and **Hindu** women can't approach family shrines when pregnant.

Armstrong (1993) argues that the lower status of women is associated with the development of **monotheism** – the triumph of religions that believe in a single, male god, such as Christianity and Islam. Before these religions became dominant there was widespread worship of **goddesses**.

Simone de Beauvoir – religion and patriarchy

De Beauvoir (1949) sees religion as an instrument of male domination.

Men usually control religious organizations and claim that their authority comes from God; for example, kings used to rule by 'Divine Right'.

Religion gives women a false belief that their suffering will be rewarded in heaven. It deceives women into thinking they are equal to men whilst in reality they are disadvantaged as the '**second sex**'.

Some religions portray women as being closer to God, but only if they are passive and do not question male authority. Religion therefore gives women a form of **false consciousness** which keeps them in their place.

De Beauvoir is criticized by **El Saadawi** (1980). She accepts that women are exploited through religion; for example, Islamic men in some countries use religion to justify barbaric practices such as '**female circumcision**' (where part of the clitoris is removed). However, El Saadawi believes it is not religion itself which is to blame, because Islam does not actually support practices which oppress women. The real problem is the manipulation and misinterpretation of religious teachings by men for their own benefit.

Women and resistance to religious oppression

Sociologists have come to acknowledge that women cannot always be seen as passive victims of religious oppression, and that religious practices are open to interpretation.

Badawi (1994) notes that aspects of Islam are positive for women. For example, Islamic women keep their own family name when they get married.

Watson (1994) examines the **veiling** of Islamic women. This practice is seen by many non-Muslim writers as a form of **social control**. However, Watson argues that veiling can have advantages for women in that it can reduce, or allow them to cope with, male oppression. For example, it reduces the possibility of **sexual harassment** and allows Muslim women to be judged for who they are rather than what they look like.

Holm (1994) notes that **Quakerism** is one religion that has always had relative equality between men and women. Holm also argues that women are starting to resist patriarchal religion and gain some rights, so religion is not as male-dominated as it once was.

Wright (1994) notes that **reform Judaism** allows women to become rabbis.

Evaluation

Marxists see religion as an instrument of class oppression rather than an instrument of patriarchy.

Functionalists see religion as creating a value consensus which is beneficial to society rather than being used to oppress women.

Some feminists (notably, **de Beauvoir**) generalize about religion always being oppressive and ignore the differences between religions.

Feminists focus on one aspect of religion at the expense of all others.

Most religions do still give more power to men. (For more discussion of the role of women in religion see p. 76)

RELIGION AND SOCIAL CHANGE

AQA OCR WJEC   **Textbook pp. 405–410**

Religion as a conservative social force

Functionalists and **Marxists** have generally dismissed the possibility that religion can cause changes in society. They believe that religion acts as a conservative force and that it is changes in society that shape religion and not *vice versa*. Religion can be seen as a conservative force in two senses:

- **Functionalists** have claimed that it acts in this way because it promotes **integration** and **social solidarity**. In this way it facilitates the continued existence of society in its present form. **Marx** had similar views, although he saw religion as maintaining the status quo in the interests of the ruling class rather than those of society as a whole.

- 'Conservative' can also refer to traditional beliefs and customs. In some circumstances, religion can support social change while at the same time promoting **traditional values**. This often occurs when there is a revival in **fundamentalist** religious beliefs.

Fundamentalism

Recent years have seen the rise of fundamentalist religious beliefs in different parts of the world. **Taylor** (1987) defines **fundamentalism** as following a distinctive pattern:

1 A group perceives a challenge to an ultimate authority, usually a god, in which they believe.

2 The group decides that the challenge cannot be tolerated.

3 They reaffirm their belief in the authority that is being challenged.

4 They oppose those who have challenged the established beliefs and often use political means to further their cause.

If fundamentalists are successful, they succeed in defending traditional values, but they also change society by **reversing innovation** that has already taken place. A dramatic example of this process took place in **Iran**. During the 1960s and 1970s, Iran underwent a process of **liberalization**. Attitudes to women changed and there were good relations with the West.

In 1979 the Iranian revolution took place, partly inspired by **fundamentalism**, and these changes were reversed. In this case, religious beliefs contributed to producing **revolutionary** change. In the case of Iran, religion did not act as a **conservative** force in the political sense, but in terms of supporting traditional values it was conservative.

Social impacts on religion

Most sociologists agree that changes in society lead to changes in religion.

Parsons (1937, 1964, 1965a), believed that, as society developed, religion lost some of its functions (see p. 78).

Marx argued that changes in the economic base of society would lead to changes in the superstructure of society, including religion.

Supporters of **secularization theory** think industrialization has led to changes which have reduced the importance of religion in society (see p. 77).

Some sociologists have claimed that **globalization** and the advent of the **postmodern** world have produced changes in religion (see p. 82).

Max Weber

Both functionalists and Marxists emphasize the role of religion in promoting social integration and impeding social change. However, **Weber** argued that in some circumstances religion can lead to **social change**. In his most famous book, *The Protestant Ethic and the Spirit of Capitalism* (1958), Weber examines the relationship between the rise of a certain form of Protestantism, known as **Calvinism**, and the development of Western industrial capitalism.

Calvinist Protestantism originated in the seventeenth century. Calvin thought that there was a distinct group of the **elect** - those chosen to go to heaven – and that they had been chosen by God even before they were born. Those who were not among the elect could never gain a place in heaven.

This produced a **psychological problem** for Calvinists. They did not know whether they were among the elect, and suffered from uncertainty about their status. Virtuous behaviour helped them convince themselves, and others, that they had been chosen to go to heaven.

The Protestant ethic

The **Protestant ethic** was **ascetic**, encouraging abstinence from life's pleasures, a simple lifestyle and rigorous self-discipline. It produced individuals who worked hard in their careers or callings. Making money was a concrete indication of success in one's calling, and success meant that the individual had not lost grace in God's sight.

The spirit of capitalism

Weber argued that capitalism is grounded in a set of ideas, ethics and values that he termed the **spirit of capitalism**. He claimed that ascetic Protestantism was a vital current within this, because the methodical and single-minded pursuit of a calling encourages the creation of wealth and a frugal approach to spending. This **accumulation of capital** produced the early businesses that expanded to create capitalist society.

Evaluation

Weber's book has received both criticism and support. It has been argued that Calvinism was strong in some parts of the world where capitalism did not develop until much later, such as Switzerland and Scotland. However, **Marshall** (1982) counters this by pointing out that Weber did not claim that Calvinism was the *only* factor necessary for the development of capitalism.

Kautsky (1953) argues from a Marxist perspective that early capitalism preceded and largely determined Protestantism. In his view, Protestantism became the **ideology** capitalists used to legitimate their position.

Other writers question the view that it was the religious beliefs of Calvinists that led to them becoming business people. Instead, they devoted themselves to business because they were excluded by law from holding public office and joining certain professions.

Religion as a force for change

Many sociologists now accept that religion can be a force for change. **Nelson** (1986) points to a number of instances where religion has undermined stability or promoted change:

- In **Northern Ireland**, Roman Catholicism has long been associated with Irish Republicanism.
- In the USA, in the 1960s, the **Reverend Martin Luther King** played a leading role in the campaign for civil rights.
- From the 1960s onwards, a number of radical groups emerged within the Roman Catholic Church in Latin America. They preached **liberation theology**, arguing that it was the duty of church members to fight against unjust and oppressive right-wing dictatorships.
- In Iran, **Islamic fundamentalism** played a part in the 1979 revolution.
- The Roman Catholic Church in Poland opposed the Communist state and supported the free trade union **Solidarity**.
- In South Africa, **Archbishop Desmond Tutu** was a prominent opponent of **apartheid**.

Conservative or radical religion?

AQA

The capacity of religion to effect social change may be determined by:

- **culture** – in societies where religious beliefs are central to the culture, anyone wishing to produce change tends to use a religious legitimation for their actions. In Britain, religion plays a less central role, so it is less significant in justifying social change.
- **social location** – where an established church or other religious organization plays a major role in political and economic life, there is considerable scope for religion to have an impact on processes of change.
- **internal organization** – religions with a strong, centralized source of authority have more chance of affecting events.

RELIGIOUS ORGANIZATIONS

AQA OCR WJEC   Textbook pp. 410-423

The table on p. 73 illustrates some of the key differences between the main kinds of religious organizations. Some sociologists have suggested, however, that these categorizations may be over-simplified when applied to contemporary societies.

Conservative and radical churches

McGuire (1981) examines the factors that influence the role that religion plays in society. For example, religions that emphasize adherence to **strong moral codes** are more likely to produce members who are critical of society and seek to change it.

Bruce (1996) argues that the concept of a **church** is primarily useful in describing premodern Christian societies. The development of **religious pluralism** (many different religious groups) in modern societies makes it difficult for the state to lend exclusive support to one religion because a single set of religious beliefs is no longer taken for granted and reinforced by all groups in society.

Robertson (1987) argues that there has been an increase in **church-state tensions** throughout the world. There is little room for religious concerns in the world of international trade and diplomacy, so governments may come into conflict with the moral concerns of domestic churches.

Denominations

Stark & Bainbridge (1985) are critical of the concept of a **denomination**. They claim that the division of religious organizations into separate types obscures rather than clarifies the differences between them.

Sects

Bruce (1996) acknowledges that **sects** may prosper in modern societies where people have more opportunity to form **subcultures**. Even with the greater toleration that exists within contemporary societies, however, some sects may come into serious conflict with the wider society. In the 1990s there were a number of instances involving the deaths of sect followers – for example, the deaths of more than 80 Branch Davidians in the siege at **Waco** in Texas.

Wilson (1982) argues that **Troeltsch's** description of sects (see p. 73) does not account for the increase in **new religious movements** and sects in Europe and the USA in recent decades. Some of these are examined below.

Cults

Cults tend to be more **individualistic** than other organized forms of religion because they often lack a fixed set of beliefs. They tolerate other beliefs, and their own beliefs are often vague. They often have **customers** rather than members, and customers may have relatively little involvement with the organization once they have learned the basics. Many aspects of the **New Age** movement (see p. 75) are based around cults.

Comparing religious organizations

	Church	Denomination	Sect
Example	**Roman Catholic Church**	**Methodism**	**Jehovah's Witnesses**
Sociological study	Troeltsch (1931)	Niebuhr (1929)	Troeltsch (1931)
Social background of members	Members are drawn from all classes in society, though particularly associated with higher socioeconomic classes	Does not have universal appeal; not associated with highest socioeconomic classes	Associated with lower socioeconomic classes
Relationship to state	Sometimes closely related to the state	Does not identify with the state and approves the separation of church and state	Unconnected to the state and may be in conflict with it
Relationship to society	Churches accept and affirm life in this world	Members generally accept the norms and values of society	Members reject the values of the world that surrounds them
Demands on members	Members do not have to demonstrate their faith to become members of a church	Some minor restrictions may be placed on members – for example, Methodists are discouraged from drinking and gambling	Members may be expected to withdraw from life outside the sect. Deep commitment demanded from members
Toleration	Churches will often jealously guard their monopoly of religious truth	Denominations do not claim a monopoly of religious truth and are tolerant of other religions	Sects tend to believe that they possess a monopoly of religious truth
Type of organization	A formal organization with a hierarchy of paid officials	Usually smaller than a church but still a formal organization with a hierarchy of paid officials	Central authority often rests with a charismatic male leader whose special qualities persuade others to follow him

Roy Wallis – new religious movements

Roy Wallis has developed two typologies of religion, one of religious organizations in general and one of **new religious movements**. **Wallis** (1976) distinguishes churches, sects, denominations and cults in terms of whether they are seen as **respectable** or **deviant**, and whether they accept the **legitimacy** of other religions or not. His typology is summarized in the table below.

A typology of religious organizations

	Respectable	Deviant
Uniquely legitimate	Church	Sect
Pluralistically legitimate	Denomination	Cult

The development of a range of new religions in the 1970s led **Wallis** (1984) to categorize these differently, as new religious movements. He divides new religious movements into three main groups based on their relationship to the outside world. He distinguishes between them according to whether the movement and its members reject, accommodate or affirm the world.

World-rejecting new religious movements

World-rejecting new religious movements have most of the characteristics of a **sect** described by **Troeltsch**. Their ideology is highly critical of the outside world, and the movement expects or seeks change.

In order to achieve salvation, members are expected to make a sharp break with conventional life when they join the movement. Organizations of this type act as **total institutions**, controlling all aspects of their members' lives. As a result, they often develop a reputation for 'brainwashing' their members, since families and friends find it hard to understand the change in their behaviour.

Most are based around a **communal lifestyle**, and, as such, develop unconventional ways of living. The ill-fated Branch Davidians in Waco, Texas, are a case in point.

World-accommodating new religious movements

World-accommodating new religious movements are usually offshoots of an existing major church or denomination. For example, Pentecostalist groups are variants of Protestant religions.

Typically these groups neither accept nor reject the world as it is, they simply live with it. They are concerned with religious rather than worldly questions.

World-accommodating sects seek to restore the **spiritual purity** to a religion that they believe has been lost in more conventional churches and denominations. Pentecostalists, for example, hold that belief in the Holy Spirit has been lost in other Christian religions.

World-affirming new religious movements

World-affirming new religious movements are very different from all other religious groups and may lack some of the features normally associated with a religion. However, these groups do claim to be able to provide access to **supernatural** or **spiritual powers**, and in that sense can be regarded as religions.

Rather than rejecting existing society or existing religions, world-affirming groups accept the world as it is. They offer the follower the potential to be successful in terms of the dominant values of society by unlocking spiritual powers within the individual. Followers of world-affirming movements carry on normal lives, and there is little social control over the members or customers.

An example of a world-affirming new religious movement is **Transcendental Meditation** or **TM**. TM is based on the Hindu religion and was first introduced to the West in the late 1950s, achieving prominence when adopted by the Beatles in 1968. Adherents claim that the meditation technique can provide 'unbounded awareness' which can have beneficial effects for individuals and society.

To Wallis, most world-affirming movements are cults, since, unlike sects, they tolerate the existence of other religions, have a rapid turnover of membership and are relatively undemanding on their followers.

Criticism of Wallis

Wallis realizes that no religious group will conform exactly to his categories. He recognizes that some groups occupy the middle ground, incorporating elements of all three categories.

Beckford (1985) offers some criticisms of Wallis. He argues that Wallis's categories are difficult to apply. It is not clear whether it is the teachings of the movement or the beliefs and outlooks of individual members that distinguish the different attitudes to the world.

According to Beckford, Wallis pays insufficient attention to the **diversity of views** that exists within a sect or cult. Beckford also questions the value of defining some groups as 'world-rejecting'. In his view, no group is able to reject the world altogether.

Stark & Bainbridge's religious categories

Stark & Bainbridge (1985) are critical of all **typologies**, arguing there are always overlaps between categories. Instead they categorize organizations in terms of a **continuum**, ranging from organizations least in tension with society (**churches**) to those most in tension (**sects** and **cults**). **Denominations** are in the middle.

They see **sects** as based upon an **existing religion** (for example, People's Temple) and **cults** as novel or based upon a religion from another society. Stark & Bainbridge distinguish three types of cult:

- **Audience cults** have minimal contact with followers – for example, astrology.
- **Client cults** offer services to followers and have more contact – for example, Scientology.
- **Cult movements** involve members more comprehensively – for example, the Unification Church (known derogatorily as the 'Moonies') and the Heaven's Gate Cult.

GROWTH OF RELIGIOUS GROUPS

AQA OCR WJEC   Textbook pp. 416-420

Religious sects and cults have existed for centuries, but the 1960s saw the growth of many new examples of these religious groups. This growth can be explained in terms of why individuals choose to join, or in terms of wider social changes. In fact the two explanations are linked, because social changes affect the number of people available as potential recruits.

Marginality

Weber provided one of the earliest explanations for the growth of **sects**. He argued that they were likely to arise within groups that were **marginal** in society. Members of groups outside the mainstream of social life often feel that they are not receiving the rewards they deserve.

Some sects offer explanations for the **disprivilege** of members, and promise them a better future either on earth or in the afterlife.

In part, the growth of sects such as the **Black Muslims** in the USA in the 1960s was accomplished through recruitment from disadvantaged groups. However, most of the members of world-rejecting sects in the 1960s and 1970s came from young, white, middle-class backgrounds.

Wallis (1984) does not believe that this contradicts the marginality theory. Many of the recruits had become marginal in society because they were 'hippies, drop-outs, surfers, LSD and marijuana users'.

Relative deprivation

Relative deprivation refers to subjectively perceived deprivation. In objective terms the poor are more deprived than the middle class, but in subjective terms certain members of the middle class may feel more deprived than the poor. They do not lack material wealth, but they feel **spiritually deprived** in a world they see as too materialistic, lonely and impersonal. They seek salvation in the sense of community offered by the sect.

Social change

Wilson (1970) argues that sects arise during periods of rapid **social change**, when traditional norms are disrupted. He uses the example of the early **Methodist** movement, which had the characteristics of a sect. This grew up as a response by the urban working class to **industrialization**. In a situation of change and uncertainty, it offered the support of a close-knit community, clear norms and values, and a promise of salvation.

Bruce (1995, 1996) believes that the weakness of conventional religions has encouraged some people to consider less traditional alternatives. As modern societies developed, faith in traditional forms of authority declined and denominations became popular. In contemporary secular societies, cults have become more popular because they require fewer sacrifices and less commitment than churches and sects.

The growth of new religious movements

Wallis (1984) argues that new religious movements were attractive to young people in the 1960s because they offered a more spiritual and caring way of life.

Bruce (1995) sees the particular appeal of world-rejecting new religious movements as deriving from the failure of the youth '**counterculture**' to radically change the world. Disillusioned young people sought their path to salvation through religion instead of peace and love.

Bruce believes that world-affirming movements have grown because people find it difficult to gain satisfaction and a **sense of identity** from their work in contemporary societies. They no longer have a sense of 'calling' about their work and may not identify strongly with their workmates. World-affirming movements offer a solution – they offer people both success and a spiritual element to their lives.

The development of sects

AQA

Niebuhr (1929) argues that sects are inevitably short-lived, and eventually either disappear or become denominations. This is because:

- **children** born inside the sect do not have the same level of commitment as their parents. The beliefs of the sect become watered down and it turns into a denomination.

- the **charismatic leader** may die and the sect loses support.

- sects with an **ascetic creed** work hard and spend little money. As the members become better off they are no longer willing to accept the restrictions of sect membership and the ideology is relaxed.

Some sects have also disappeared because of mass suicide – for example, the People's Temple.

Long-lived sects

Wilson (1969) points out that some sects survive for long periods. Long-lived sects tend to have **adventist** beliefs (for example, Seventh Day Adventists): they believe that a judgement day is coming and only a few will get into heaven. This prevents them growing large enough to become denominations.

Evangelical sects, which try to recruit as many people as possible, may become denominations if they are successful.

Wallis (1984) takes a more complex view, arguing that **new religious movements** can change type rather than disappearing or becoming denominations. For example, they can move from being **world-rejecting** to being more **world-affirming** if members enjoy success.

THE NEW AGE

AQA, OCR, WJEC   Textbook pp. 420-423

The term **New Age** has been applied to a range of ideas that started to become prominent in the 1980s. Although some of these beliefs became embodied in new religious movements, in many cases they were not attached to any organization. Examples of New Age beliefs and practices include:

- interest in clairvoyance, contacting extra-terrestrials, types of meditation and therapy;

- beliefs in magic, crystals, tarot cards, feng shui, astrology and witchcraft;

- participation in self-healing and natural or traditional remedies such as yoga and aromatherapy.

New Age themes

Heelas (1996) believes the key features of the New Age are:

- a belief in **self-spirituality**: people have turned away from traditional religious organizations in their search for the spiritual, and have begun to look inside themselves;

- **detraditionalization**: valuing personal experience above the authority that comes from traditional sources;

- the belief that you can become responsible for your own actions. It emphasizes freedom to discover your own truth.

Heelas uses Wallis's typology of new religious movements to distinguish between different aspects of the New Age:

- **World-affirming** aspects can help you experience the best of the **outer world** – for example, to be more successful in business.

- **World-rejecting** aspects stress how to experience the best of the **inner world**, how to achieve spirituality and turn away from any concern with worldly success.

- Most New Age beliefs offer the best of both worlds, claiming you can be successful *and* spiritually fulfilled.

The appeal of the New Age

Drane (1999) argues that the appeal of the New Age comes from the failure of the modern world to deliver personal satisfaction. He believes people in Western societies no longer trust institutions such as the medical professions, and are disillusioned with the inability of churches to satisfy their craving for spirituality. Drane sees the popularity of the New Age as part of a move towards **postmodernity**.

However, **Bruce** and **Heelas** both argue that the New Age can best be explained as a product of the latest stage of modernity, which emphasizes individual freedom and choice.

Bruce claims that the New Age appeals to the middle classes working in '**expressive professions**' who have an interest in **human potential**. Many aspects of the New Age are based on 'watered down' versions of Eastern religions such as Buddhism. However, unlike many of these, they emphasize the individual. The New Age is popular because of the decline of mainstream religion, but it has much less influence on people and society than traditional religion had.

Heelas examines four ways in which **modernity** might explain the appeal of the New Age:

1 People have many roles but there is little overlap between those roles. They end up with a **fragmented identity** – the New Age offers ways of finding a **single identity**.

2 **Consumer culture** creates dissatisfaction, as people fail to achieve the perfection portrayed by advertisers. The New Age offers different ways of achieving perfection.

3 Following Wilson, Heelas argues that periods of rapid social change disrupt traditional norms and values, so people seek certainty and security in spiritual beliefs.

4 The decline of conventional religion leaves people without strong alternatives to New Age beliefs.

SOCIAL GROUPS AND RELIGIOSITY

AQA, OCR, WJEC   Textbook pp. 423-429

Religiosity varies by social group, and sociologists have examined and explained these variations.

Social class

Marxist theory suggests that religion develops in response to class exploitation. It develops first amongst **exploited classes** but is adopted by higher classes to legitimate their position.

Neo-Marxists such as **Maduro** (1982) see radical religions such as **liberation theology** as a response to exploitation, as a group develops class consciousness (see p. 70).

Different types of religion, spirituality and religious organization appeal to different classes – for example, the **New Age** to middle-class professionals in expressive professions; **world-rejecting new religious movements** to lower socioeconomic classes or marginal groups; **world-affirming movements** to higher socioeconomic classes, and so on (see p. 74).

Class interacts with **gender**, **ethnicity** and **age** in shaping participation (see below).

Gender and religious participation

Evidence suggests women are more religiously active than men. In 2005, 57% of those attending one of the main churches or denominations were women (**Brierley**, 2006a).

Opinion polls suggest women are more likely to believe in God, and research by **Modood** *et al* (1997) found

that Muslim women were more likely than Muslim men to see religion as 'very important'.

A large majority of **New Age** followers are women.

Miller & Hoffman (1995) identify two main explanations for female religiosity:

● **Differential socialization** – women are socialized to be more submissive, passive and obedient than men, and these characteristics fit well with being religious.

● Women have a different **structural location** to men – being less likely to do paid work than men they have more time for religion. Religion gives women a sense of identity whereas men get their sense of identity from their job. Women also socialize children through taking them to church, which increases their own attendance.

Miller & Hoffman argue that even taking the above into account, women are still more religious than men. This is because women, according to survey research, are less willing to take **risks**. Not believing in religion can be seen as risky behaviour.

Bruce (1996) provides the following explanations for the gender difference:

● Female religiosity links to **femininity**, which is less aggressive and goal-orientated than masculinity and therefore fits well with 'healing' and 'channeling' in New Age beliefs. Male 'New Agers' are more interested in parapsychology.

● **Secularization** has increasingly restricted religion to the **private sphere**, which is more a female sphere. Men in the **public sphere** (for example, at work) have lost religiosity because of secularization.

● **Working-class women** have retained stronger religious beliefs than middle-class women; lack of control over their lives makes them identify more than middle-class women with an all-powerful God.

Woodhead (2005) links gender differences in religion to a **spiritual revolution** in which traditional religions are declining (**congregational domain**), while the New Age (in the **holistic milieu**) is growing.

Secularization of traditional religion has affected the **rationalized public sphere**. Traditional religion has become the preserve of women, who emphasize the feminine caring and compassionate aspects of religion. However, as women have increasingly taken paid work they too have been affected by secularization, leading to a decline of the **congregational domain**. Nonetheless, congregational religions remain feminized and more attractive to women than men.

Women are also more attracted to **New Age** beliefs as a way of establishing an identity which can be discovered within the self. This overcomes the contradiction in identity which comes from women's dual role as workers (where identity come from position) and carers (where identity comes from relationships).

Religion and ethnicity

Degrees of religiosity vary by **ethnic group**. The **2001 Census** found that more than half of British Chinese had no religion, as did 15% of White British, 11% of Afro-Caribbeans but only 0.43% of Bangladeshis. Religions of ethnic minority groups largely reflect place of origin, for example:

- over 90% of Pakistanis and Bangladeshis said they were **Muslim**;
- 25% of those of Caribbean origin belonged to **New Protestant Churches** such as Seventh Day Adventists.

Modood et al (1997) found 62% of Muslims attended a service/prayer meeting weekly, compared to:

- 57% of Caribbean members of New Protestant churches;
- 39% of Sikhs;
- 29% of White Roman Catholics;
- 27% of Hindus;
- 9% of white Church of England members.

Bird (1999) finds that the greater religiosity of ethnic minorities reflects the stronger religious beliefs of their originating countries. Religion acts as a basis for **community solidarity** following migration to an unfamiliar country, and serves to maintain **cultural identity** for minorities. **Socialization** maintains religiosity across generations.

Religion can also help disadvantaged minority groups cope with **oppression** and **injustice** – for example, Pentecostalist and Rastafarian religions in the Afro-Caribbean community in Bristol (**Pryce**, 1979).

Bruce (1996) argues that ethnic minority religions are popular largely for social reasons rather than as an expression of strong religious commitment (see p. 79). Religion enables:

- **cultural defence** – the maintenance of a sense of identity and pride;
- **cultural transition** – coping with the upheaval of migration.

Bruce believes that ethnic minority religions are now declining as a result of being exposed to **secularization** in Britain.

Chryssides (1994) argues that ethnic minority religions have followed one of three paths:

1 **apostasy** – where religion is abandoned in the face of hostility;

2 **accommodation** – where practices are modified to take account of the changed environment;

3 **renewed vigour** – where the religion is asserted strongly in response to hostility.

On the whole, ethnic minority religions have not followed apostasy but have remained vigorous, and have even attracted some converts.

Kepel (1994) argues that Muslims throughout the world, including Britain, have been affected by a **worldwide revival** of Islam.

The English Church Census (2006) found that attendance by ethnic minorities at Christian churches rose between 1998 and 2005, but **Modood et al** (1997) found that younger members of ethnic minorities were a little less religious than older members.

Age and religiosity

AQA

Research suggests that in all ethnic groups younger **people** tend to be less religious than older people. For example, the average age of churchgoers has risen from 37 in 1979 to 45 in 2005 (**Brierley**, 2006a).

Heelas et al (2005) have found that most people involved in the New Age are middle-aged or older. **Voass & Crocket** (2005) identify three possible reasons for this age profile:

- People get more religious as they get closer to death, and experience life events such as having children.
- It could be a **period effect**: those born in a particular period (a **cohort**) could be more religious. **Brierley** (2006a) argues that **Generation Y** (born in the 1980s) are a cohort with little interest in spirituality.
- The differences could be due to the **progressive decline of religion**.

Using data from the *British Social Attitudes Survey*, Voass & Crocket found little evidence for people overall getting more religious as they age, or for a cohort effect. They concluded that the decline of religion was responsible. Each generation was less likely to socialize children into their religion than the previous one.

Some critics have attacked the theory of **secularization** (see below). **Heelas et al** (2005) claim that spiritual beliefs are actually growing – each generation reaching middle age is showing more interest than the previous one.

SECULARIZATION

AQA, OCR, WJEC   Textbook pp. 429-445

Many classical sociologists have argued that industrialization and the growth of **scientific knowledge** would lead to **secularization**, which can broadly be defined as the process of religious decline. For example:

- **Marx** thought religion would come to an end with the advent of communism;
- **Durkheim** thought religion would decline as a source of values, as the **division of labour** in society became more complex;
- **Weber** thought the modern world would undergo a process of **rationalization**, where rational planning left little room for faith.

Many contemporary sociologists have followed in their footsteps, arguing that modern societies are not compatible with the retention of a central role for religion. For example, **Wilson** (1966) defines secularization as 'the process whereby religious thinking, practice and institutions lose social significance'.

The concept of secularization is, however, given different meanings by different sociologists. **Bruce** (2002) points out: 'there is no one secularization theory. Rather there are clusters of descriptions and explanations that cohere reasonably well.'

Participation

Some researchers have measured the importance of religion in society in terms of **institutional factors** such as church attendance, membership, and participation in religious ceremonies. Some of this evidence does point towards secularization; however:

- patterns vary between countries;
- the **reliability** and **validity** of the statistics are open to question.

Church attendance in Britain

Church attendance figures show a continuing drop in attendance throughout the twentieth century, particularly in Anglican, Baptist, Catholic and United Reformed churches. In 1851 the *Census of Religion* found just under 40% of the population attending church. In 2005 it is estimated that only 6.8% of the adult population regularly attended church (**Brierley**, 2005).

Attendance at special Christian ceremonies such as **baptisms** and **marriages** has also declined. In 1900, 73% of children were baptized; by 2000 the figure had dropped to 35%.

Church membership in Britain

Overall, there has been a decline in membership of religious organizations in the UK. Institutional Christian religions have declined most, while many non-Christian and smaller religions have gained members. Overall, the proportion of the population belonging to non-Christian religions doubled between 1975 and 2000 (**Brierley**, 2001).

World religious participation

Rates of religious participation in the USA are much higher than those in Britain.

Barrett (discussed in **Brierley**, 2001) estimates that 34.5% of the world population was Christian in 1990, declining only slightly to 33% by 2000. Christianity has declined in Europe but increased in Africa, Latin America and Asia.

Globally, there has been a big increase in the proportion of **Muslims** in the world and, overall, a decline in the proportion who are not religious.

Interpreting the evidence

Most of the long-term evidence on membership and attendance in Britain seems to support the secularization theory. Although recent years have seen a growth in smaller religious organizations, there is little doubt that fewer people attend a place of worship or belong to a religious organization. In the USA, however, the evidence seems to support those who question the secularization theory. In both cases, the **reliability** and **validity** of the statistics are open to question:

- Nineteenth-century statistics pose problems because the methods of data collection do not meet today's standards of **reliability**.
- Different criteria are used to record membership in different religions.
- US statistics are based on **survey evidence**, and it has been suggested that more people claim to attend a place of worship than actually do.

The decline in church attendance in Britain can be interpreted in a number of different ways. **Martin** (1969) claims that in the nineteenth century church-going was a sign of middle-class respectability, to a greater extent than it is today.

Religion today may be expressed in other ways. It may have become **privatized**; people develop their own beliefs and see religious institutions as less important.

Belief, churchgoing and atheism

Opinion poll data generally find that many more people retain religious beliefs than are members of religious organizations or regular attenders at places of worship. In 2000, 70% of people retained some sort of belief, while only 15% rejected the idea of a God or life force altogether.

However, **Bruce** (2001) points out that the results of a number of surveys show a strong weakening of religious beliefs. Nevertheless, in the **2001 Census**, 71.6% of people stated they were Christian (though the number of people who claimed to be 'Jedi' – 0.7% – suggests that not everybody took the religion question entirely seriously).

Religious belief and participation may be the obvious place to look for evidence of secularization, but some theorists, such as **Casanova** (1994), argue that that the role of religion in society is more significant in assessing whether secularization is occurring.

Religion and society

Disengagement

Some sociologists have seen the truly religious society as one in which the church as an institution is very powerful in every aspect of society. A **disengagement**, or withdrawing of the church from wider society, is seen as secularization.

Martin (1969) sees this view as concerned with decline in the power, wealth, prestige and influence of the church. In medieval Europe, the church and state were very close; today the church is hardly represented in government.

However, **Martin** points out that the church's contemporary concern with purely spiritual matters represents a purer form of religion, unblemished by secular concerns such as politics.

Casanova (1994) believes that religion is still important in public life. During the 1980s, religion was linked to political conflicts such as the conflict between Jews and Muslim Arabs in the Middle East, and between Protestants and Catholics in Northern Ireland. Casanova does not reject the secularization theory, but he does argue that there has been a **deprivatization** of religion.

Structural and social differentiation

An alternative to the view that disengagement equals secularization is provided by **Parsons** (1951, 1960, 1965a). Parsons agrees that the church has lost many of its former functions. He argues that the evolution of society involves a process of **structural differentiation**: parts of the social system become more specialized and so perform fewer functions.

However, this process does not necessarily lessen the importance of social institutions. Parsons argues that religious beliefs still give meaning and significance to life (p. 69).

Bruce (1995) discusses what is essentially the same process, but he refers to it as **social differentiation**. He argues that social life in modern societies is dominated by the logic of capitalist production, with its emphasis on efficiency and profit. Religious faith is not significant.

Societalization

Bruce (1995, 2002) uses the term **societalization** to refer to a process in which social life becomes **fragmented** and ceases to be locally based. The decline of communities in modern societies undermines religion in three ways:

1 Churches can no longer serve as the focal point for communities.

2 People's greater involvement with the broader society leads them to look more widely for services. They are less likely to turn to the local vicar or priest for support.

3 The cultural diversity of the society in which people live leads them to hold beliefs with less certainty.

Religious pluralism

Some researchers imply that the truly religious society has **one faith** and one church. This picture is influenced by accounts of some small-scale societies, such as the Australian Aboriginals, described by **Durkheim** (p. 68).

Modernization and **industrialization** tend to create a plurality of cultural and religious groups. This reminds individuals that their beliefs are a matter of **personal choice** and no longer part and parcel of their membership of society.

Strong religion, which dominates people's lives, cannot be widespread in a fragmented society (**Bruce**, 2002).

Weak religion, which is more a matter of personal choice and does not claim to be the only legitimate religion, is more suited to fragmented societies.

Some sociologists argue that **religious pluralism** is not incompatible with a society in which religion thrives. It is not necessary for everyone to share the same beliefs for religion to be important. Northern Ireland is a case in point.

Pluralism in modern societies stems from two main sources:

● the existence of different **ethnic groups**;

● the growth of **sects** and **cults**.

Ethnicity and religious diversity

Bruce (1996) acknowledges that certain ethnic groups retain strong religious beliefs. However, he does not see this as an argument against the secularization theory. He believes that religion remains strong because of its social importance rather than because of any deep religious convictions among members of the groups. Bruce argues that religion tends to serve one of two main purposes for ethnic groups:

● **cultural defence**: where two communities are in conflict and are of different religions, their religious identity becomes a way of asserting their ethnic pride. Bruce gives the example of Ian Paisley's Democratic Unionist Party in Northern Ireland. Only a tiny percentage of the population of Northern Ireland is a member of the religious group associated with the party, but many more support the party. This is because, according to Bruce, ethnic Protestants identify

with the party's opposition to a united Ireland, not because of the religious convictions of the party's leaders.

● **cultural transition**: religion is used as a resource for dealing with situations where people have to adjust their identity. For example, Asian and African-Caribbean migrants to Britain can use mosques, temples and churches as centres for their communities, and they can use their religion as a way of coping with the difficulties of being Asian, or black, and British.

Bruce believes that these processes keep religion relevant but do not create a religious society. **Brown** (1992) disagrees and sees '**ethnic defence**' as a key function of religion in the modern world.

There is certainly plenty of evidence that religion remains strong among many ethnic minorities. **Chryssides** (1994) (see p. 77) finds a general pattern of **accommodation** and **renewed vigour**, with buildings being converted into mosques and religious practices being maintained or adapted.

Sects, cults and secularization

The apparent vitality of sects (see p. 74) seems to provide evidence against the theory of secularization. **Greeley** (1972) believes that the growth of new religious movements represents a process of **resacrilization**, meaning that interest and belief in the sacred are being revived.

Since the 1980s, interest has grown in **New Age** ideas (see p. 75). **Heelas** (1996) points to opinion poll evidence suggesting substantial belief in reincarnation, horoscopes and flying saucers. Other sociologists see the growth of sects and new religious movements as evidence of **secularization**.

Wilson (1982) believes that sects are the last outpost of religion in societies where religious beliefs and values are of little significance.

Bruce (1995, 1996, 2002) argues that **new religious movements** (see p. 73) recruit very small numbers compared to the decline in mainstream Christian denominations. **World-rejecting** sects have affected the smallest number of people, while **world-accommodating** groups – who have the least influence on people's lives – have recruited the most.

Secularization and the New Age

Bruce sees the growth of the New Age as posing little threat to the validity of the theory of secularization. He believes that New Age beliefs are weak and often temporary.

However, in a study of Kendal in Cumbria (**The Kendal Project**) **Heelas** *et al* (2005) (see p. 77) found New Age beliefs to be quite significant in the lives of many people. They found that more people took part in some sort of spiritually inclined New Age activities than attended Anglican churches. They argue that a **spiritual revolution** is underway in which the **congregational domain** (consisting of worship by congregations in conventional churches) is declining and the **holistic milieu** (the informal networks through which people take part in New Age activities) is growing.

Based on current trends, they estimate that the New Age may replace conventional churches in popularity around 2020.

Secularization in the USA

According to **Herberg** (1960), the main evidence for secularization in the USA is to be found in the decline of the religiosity of churches and denominations themselves. These organizations have compromised their religious beliefs to fit in with the wider society.

Herberg claims that the major denominations in America have undergone a process of secularization. They increasingly reflect the '**American way of life**' rather than the **word of God**.

Herberg's general view has been supported by **Heelas & Seel** (2003). They claim that there has been a move away from traditional religions in the USA and a growth in the more **subjective religions** which allow considerable freedom to believers.

The New Christian Right

Herberg's argument has been challenged using the example of the **New Christian Right** in the USA. **Roof & McKinney** (1987) note the growth of conservative forms of Protestantism, which combine serious commitment to religious teachings with a refusal to compromise religious beliefs.

Bruce (1988) argues that the New Christian Right has had very little impact. For example, very few of its members who have stood for national office have won their elections. The only reason it gets so much attention, Bruce argues, is because its members are unusual for holding strong religious convictions in a secular world.

Desacrilization

A number of sociologists have argued that society has been undergoing a process of **desacrilization**, in which supernatural forces are no longer seen as controlling the world, and action is no longer directed by religious belief.

Weber (1963) provided one of the earliest statements of the desacrilization theory. He believed that modern societies are characterized by **disenchantment**: they are no longer charged with mystery and magic; the supernatural has been banished from society. Instead they are based on **rational action**, the product of deliberate and precise calculation and logic.

Following the ideas of **Weber**, **Bruce** (2002) stresses the importance of rationalization in undermining religious beliefs. Technological advances have given individuals a greater sense of control over the natural world and less need to resort to supernatural explanations. There are some things, such as life and death, which science and rationality cannot deal with. However, when people turn to God they do so as individuals and as a last resort, after all the rational and scientific possibilities have been exhausted.

The theory of **postmodernism** suggests that societies have begun to move beyond the scientific rationality of modernity, partly because of a growing distrust of

science. People are increasingly aware of the failures of science (such as the failure to find a cure for AIDS) and the damaging side effects of science and technology (such as environmental damage). Some postmodernists believe that this is promoting a move back towards stronger religious beliefs, although in line with **consumer culture** – people choose for themselves what to believe (see p. 82).

International comparisons

By concentrating on Britain and the USA, sociologists have taken a rather narrow view of social change and religion. **Davie** (2002, 2006) argues that the strength of religion varies enormously between countries:

- In Europe many countries have low participation rates, but Poland and the Republic of Ireland have very high rates.
- Religion is also thriving in the USA, South Korea, and much of the Islamic world; in Latin America and Africa Pentecostalism is rapidly gaining support.

Bruce (2002) argues that secularization applies only to pluralistic, democratic Western societies such as those found in Europe and North America. Such societies are fragmented and lack the strong communities needed to sustain religion as an important force in society.

Religious revival

Kepel (1994) claims that any trend towards secularization was reversed from 1975 onwards. Since then, religious revivals have taken place around the world, often aimed at changing whole societies. Examples include Christianity in the USA and Europe, Judaism in Israel, and Islam throughout the world. However, **Bruce** (2001) believes that even Islamic fundamentalism is susceptible to the influence of modernization.

Casanova's types of secularization

Casanova (1994) distinguishes three aspects of secularization:

1. **differentiation**: non-religious spheres of life become separate from religion;
2. **decline** of religious beliefs and participation in religious activity;
3. **privatization**: religion stops playing a part in public life and does not try to influence people's lives.

For Casanova, it is only in the first sense that secularization has taken place. Religion no longer has a central position in modern societies but neither is it fading away.

Secularization – conclusion

As the views of sociologists such as **Martin** and **Kepel** illustrate, the theory of secularization has not been definitely proved or disproved. This is partly because different writers have used the term in different ways. This has led to confusion, since writers discussing the process of secularization are often arguing about different things. **Glock & Stark** (1969) argue that researchers have not paid sufficient attention to defining religion and religiosity.

Contemporary theorists do pay more attention to the different aspects of secularization. **Steve Bruce** (2001), a strong supporter of the theory of secularization, accepts that religion can remain an important part of individual beliefs, but he believes religion has lost its social and political significance.

FUNDAMENTALISM

AQA, OCR, WJEC   **Textbook pp. 445-451**

Almond *et al* (2003) define fundamentalism as a 'pattern of religious militancy by which self-styled "true believers" attempt to arrest the erosion of religious identity ... and create alternatives to secular institutions and behaviors'.

Bruce (2000) sees fundamentalism as a religion which calls for a return to the 'Fundamentals of the Faith', claiming authority for a sacred text as the basis for regulating a society.

Almond *et al* (2003) note that fundamentalism is widespread and growing – for example, amongst some Jews in Israel; Muslims in Pakistan, Palestine, Afghanistan; Sikhs and Hindus in India; Christians in the USA; Buddhists in Sri Lanka.

The existence of fundamentalism seems to undermine the theory of **secularization**, as it involves a return to strong religious beliefs.

The causes of fundamentalism

Bruce (2000) believes that fundamentalism is caused by a group feeling their traditions are under threat from changes associated with **modernization** and **secularization**.

Societalization, **differentiation** and **rationalization** (see p. 78) are all seen as threats by fundamentalists.

According to Bruce, fundamentalism is more likely to develop when the following circumstances apply:

1   The religion has a **single sacred text** (such as the Bible or Qur'an).
2   There is a **common enemy** for believers (for example, the USA for many Muslims).
3   The religion does *not* have a central source of **religious authority** (like, for example, the Pope in Roman Catholicism).
4   There is a supply of potential recruits who feel threatened, dispossessed or **relatively deprived** (for example, Palestine).

This fundamentalism can turn violent in circumstances where democratic politics cannot be used to express grievances.

Bruce sees Islam as being more prone to violent forms of fundamentalism than Christianity, because it places more emphasis on being religious through one's actions (**ortho-praxis**) than through one's beliefs (**orthodoxy**).

Almond *et al* (2003) identify similar factors to Bruce, but think the following are also important in encouraging the development of fundamentalism:

- low levels of **education**;
- high levels of social **inequality**;
- high levels of recent **migration** and the displacement of people by war;
- **economic** problems;
- **Western imperialism** resulting in an anti-imperialist movement – for example, Iranian opposition to US involvement in the region (see also **Armstrong**, below).

They also point to **contingency** and **chance** – events such as poor harvests – as important, along with **leadership** to mobilize potential recruits.

RELIGION AND CONFLICT

Huntingdon (1993) argues that sources of identity that are not religious have declined in significance. The world is now divided between **civilizations** which are Western, Confucian, Japanese, Islamic, Hindu, Slavic-Orthodox, Latin American, and African. Religion is very important in differentiating most of these civilizations.

Where these civilizations come into contact, conflict tends to break out – for example, in clashes between Muslims and the West; Muslims and Hindus in the Indian sub-continent; Orthodox Serbs, Catholics and Muslims in the former Yugoslavia. Religion is therefore a key cause of conflict in the world today.

Armstrong (2001) argues that economic and political factors are more important in causing conflict than religion itself. Fundamentalist interpretations of Islam have become popular because of the failure of **modernization** to bring prosperity to most ordinary Muslims, and the constant interference of **Western countries** in the Islamic world – in ways which are seen to damage Muslims but support Western interests.

Bruce (2000) believes that the importance of religion in causing conflict varies. Sometimes religious factors are of paramount importance, sometimes other factors are more important, and often factors are intertwined:

1   Religion can be used to justify conflict which really concerns **national or ethnic disputes** – for example, the First World War and the Bosnia conflict in the 1990s.
2   Religion can be a central cause of conflict – for example, Osama Bin Laden and Al Qaeda have largely religious motives.
3   Religious and secular issues overlap so conflict may be over ethnicity, nationality and ethnicity simultaneously – for example, Israel and Palestine.

RELIGION AND POSTMODERNITY

AQA, OCR, WJEC   **Textbook pp. 451-456**

Bauman – religion and postmodernity

Bauman (1992) believes that in **modernity** people search for **universal truths** – theories that are always true.

Postmodernity rejects the idea of universal truths and denies that other people have authority over you. Instead people have an almost unlimited **choice** as to what to believe and how to behave.

However, without the rules found in modernity and the idea that a **rational plan** can be devised to perfect society, people have to make their own **ethical choices**. Without agreed ethics in society as a whole **morality** is **privatized** as a personal choice.

People continue to want guidance in what rules to follow, and they turn to experts for advice. Religious leaders are **experts in morality**, so some people look to them for help. Unlike the modern era, people can turn to any religious leaders, not just the ones they were brought up to respect.

This leads to more interest in religion and much greater **religious pluralism**; people can also change their religious beliefs if they wish. Whatever beliefs they follow, however, they take them less seriously than they did in the modern era.

Criticisms

Beckford (1996) argues that:

4 Bauman exaggerates changes in religion. Rather than declining in modernity and reviving in postmodernity, religion has been continuously important throughout history.

5 Bauman contradicts himself by arguing both that people make their own choices and that they turn to religious experts for guidance.

David Lyon – Jesus in Disneyland

Lyon (2000) believes that postmodern elements are developing in society with **globalization**, the development of **information technology** and the growth of **consumer society**. These lead to people having greater choices including **choice of gods**.

Because of these changes, religion is relocating to the **sphere of consumption**. People are unwilling to be *forced* to accept the authority of Christian church religion, but they are willing to *choose* a religious narrative (story) that appeals to them. For example, in Canada 75% of people do not attend church regularly, but 80% of non-attenders are still influenced by religious beliefs.

Religion is no longer a **social institution** but rather a **cultural resource** on which people can draw if they wish. For example, a religious event, the Harvest Day Crusade, has been held at Disneyland in California, showing how religion is becoming another part of consumer culture and mixing with the postmodern fantasy world of Disney.

Dedifferentiation is taking place – a blurring of the boundaries and differences between different parts of social life. In this case the distinction between religion and **popular culture** is being affected.

Criticisms

Bruce (2000) sees the changes described by Lyon as evidence of the **secularization** of society rather than of a revival of religion in a postmodern world. Today only **weak religion** is left – religion which has little real influence on people's lives – unlike the **strong religion** of the past.

Postmodernity and the New Age

AQA

Heelas (1996) does not see the **New Age** as part of postmodernity, but admits there are a number of ways it could be interpreted as postmodern:

- Postmodernity is often seen as involving a decline of traditional beliefs and authority or **detraditionalization**. Traditional church and denominational religions are declining while the New Age is becoming more popular, so this could be seen as evidence of **religious postmodernism**.

- Postmodernity is often seen as involving **dedifferentiation** (see above). As the boundary between religion and popular culture blurs, this could be seen as evidence of postmodernity.

- Postmodernity is usually seen as involving **relativism** – knowledge is seen as a matter of personal opinion rather than of facts. The New Age fits this description, as individuals can pick and choose what aspects of the New Age they wish to follow.

- The New Age has **consumers** of its different 'products', unlike the **believers** in traditional religion. **Consumer culture** is an aspect of postmodernity.

- The New Age emphasizes the importance of **experience** rather than of achieving particular goals. This again is typical of postmodernity whereas modernity is based upon the **rational pursuit of objectives**.

- Both postmodernity and the New Age imply we are entering a **new era**.

However, Heelas argues the New Age is not postmodern but part of the latest stage of **modernity**. This is because:

- the New Age is ultimately based upon a **metanarrative** – that you should use personal experience to plan your life.

- some New Agers take their beliefs as seriously as followers of traditional religions, not as throwaway parts of consumer culture.

- the New Age is based upon an extreme version of **individualism**, which is a key feature of modernity.

- many aspects of the New Age – for example, spiritualism – are not really new, but have a long history. Their origins predate the time (roughly the 1970s) when postmodernity is supposed to have started.

Heelas concludes that there is no clear dividing line between a modern and a postmodern era, and the changes in religion such as the **spiritual revolution** (see p. 79) can be seen as a continuation and development of trends in modernity.

Giddens – high modernity and religion

Giddens (1990, 1991) also sees changes in religion as part of the latest stage in development, which he calls **high modernity**, rather than part of **postmodernity**.

The central feature of late modernity is increased **reflexivity** – constant monitoring of and reflection on social life in order to improve it. Reflexivity can produce a questioning of religion but it also undermines individuals' **sense of self**.

People no longer blindly follow tradition but have to make **conscious choices** about who they are and what they want to become. This can lead to a sense of personal meaninglessness; religion can fill the vacuum left by the decline of tradition. However, unlike earlier stages of history, people have to choose what, if any, religious beliefs to follow, rather than adopting the same beliefs as their parents.

Fundamentalism is the response to a society in which there is no certainty and tradition has lost its influence (**detraditionalization**). In a **globalized world** in which competing religions exist side by side, some people react against the uncertainty, and seek definite answers about how to live their lives, by adopting a rigid interpretation of their particular religion.

Criticisms of Giddens

Beckford (1996) sees the strengths of Giddens's theory as offering an account of diverse phenomena, such as fundamentalism and the New Age. It also explains how religion can survive and even prosper in the modern world.

Beckford sees as a weakness of Giddens's theories the claim that religion is based upon **reflexivity**, which could just as easily lead to people choosing **atheism** as turning to religion.

Postmodernism – conclusion

Although they disagree about whether we have entered a postmodern era, all the above writers agree that significant changes are taking place in society, which are leading to changes in religion. They also agree that traditional religion is declining and there is greater choice of religious belief for individuals.

Some see this as evidence of religious decline and **secularization** (for example, **Steve Bruce**); others see it as part of the revival of some types of religion/spirituality (for example, **Paul Heelas**).

IDEOLOGY

AQA   **Textbook p. 851**

Objectivities, values and ideology

Religious beliefs represent only one type of **belief system** in society. Other belief systems include **political** and **scientific** beliefs. Although followers of these different belief systems might see them as **objective** (unbiased and true) others might see them as being **value-laden**.

Bierstedt (1963) defines **objectivity** as meaning that 'the conclusions arrived at as the result of enquiry or investigation are independent of the race, colour, creed, occupation, nationality, religion, moral preference, and political predisposition of the investigator'.

Value-laden beliefs, on the other hand, are influenced by the political or moral preferences of a person, and are therefore at least partly **subjective** (a matter of personal opinion) rather than **objective.**

Sociologists refer to a whole set of value-laden beliefs as an **ideology**. An ideology can be defined as a set of beliefs supporting the interests of a social group – for

example: the rich, men or the ethnic majority. Ideologies may be used to maintain the power of a social group.

Marxism and ideology

Marxists (Textbook pp. 10-11) argue that capitalist and other class-based societies are dominated by a **ruling-class ideology**: a set of beliefs that supports the interests of the dominant economic class in society. In capitalism the dominant class is the **bourgeoisie** – the owners of the means of production, in the form of capital used to finance production. They are able to control the **superstructure** of society, including its beliefs and values.

In *The German Ideology* (1846) (Textbook p. 668) **Marx & Engels** argued that 'The ideas of the ruling class, are, in every age, the ruling ideas ... The dominant ideas are nothing more than the ideal expression of the dominant material relationships expressed as ideas'.

Marxists believe that in capitalist societies the dominant ideology, reproduced partly through the mass media (Textbook pp. 713-718), encourages:

- acceptance of capitalism as the best or only viable economic system;
- acceptance of the power of the **capitalist state** (Textbook pp. 535-539);
- a **consumer culture**, to consume the products of capitalism, making **profits** for companies;
- a passive and dedicated workforce which does not question the low wages they receive (see **Bowles & Gintis** (1976) on the role of education, p. 47 and Textbook pp. 602-604).

Neo-Marxism and ideology

Some **neo-Marxists** believe that the classical Marxist view of ideology is too deterministic: it sees the beliefs of all members of society as directly determined by the economic system.

Some of Marx's writings suggest that the **economic base** of society influences the values and beliefs of a society but does not directly determine them. Neo-Marxists have therefore developed less deterministic views of ideology.

Gramsci (1971) (Textbook pp. 539-540) believes members of society possess **dual consciousness**. They are partly influenced by **ruling-class ideology** because of the media, education system and religion which promote it. However, they also have direct experience of **exploitation**, for example from poor working conditions and low wages. The working class are therefore unlikely to fully accept the capitalist system.

Williams (1961, 1965, 1978) (Textbook pp. 672-673) argues that class cultures and beliefs are much more varied and creative than crude Marxist views imply. Different classes tend to develop different views of the world. For example, the ruling class tends to have a more **individualistic culture** (you succeed by pursuing your own individual interests) whilst working-class culture tends to be more **collective** (you succeed through group action – for example, by going on strike through a trade union).

Ruling-class ideology may be further challenged by:

- **residual cultures** (the ideology of a declining class – for example, landowners in Britain);
- **emergent ideologies** (the ideology of a new class which is developing – for example, rich celebrities).

Residual and emergent ideologies may be **oppositional** (opposed to the dominant culture) or **alternative** (they coexist with the dominant culture).

Criticisms of neo-Marxism

Postmodernists such as **Pakulski & Waters** (1996) (Textbook pp. 84-85) argue that neo-Marxists exaggerate the influence of class on culture and ideology. They deny there is a ruling class, and argue that classes are no longer significant. Society is too **fragmented** and based on **lifestyle choices** to have ideologies – widespread beliefs that support the interests of particular groups.

Other sociologists, including **feminists** and **anti-racists**, argue that ideology can reflect other social divisions apart from class.

Feminism and ideology

Feminists (Textbook pp. 100-104) see society as dominated by **patriarchal ideology** rather than ruling-class ideology. Patriarchal ideology assumes that men are and should be dominant in society.

Radical feminists are most emphatic about the dominance of patriarchal ideology. **Millett** (1970) (Textbook pp. 109-110) sees ideological factors as important in maintaining male dominance. Males are socialized into having a dominant temperament, and the society's culture sees it as natural for men to have dominant roles. **Myth and religion** – for example, the story of Adam and Eve – reinforce patriarchal ideology. However, Millett believes non-ideological factors, such as the use of violence, are also important in maintaining men's dominance.

Greer (2000) (Textbook pp. 135-136) sees patriarchal culture as deeply entrenched in society. It is reflected in:

- **sexuality**: women are expected to meet men's needs;
- **fashion and body image**: women are expected to be obsessive about their physical appearance;
- **fear of men**: women are afraid of men and are restricted in their movements by fear of attack by men.

Alternative feminist views of ideology

The radical feminist view of ideology is not accepted by some feminists.

Bryson (1999) (Textbook p. 101) criticizes the idea of patriarchy, arguing that it merely describes rather than explaining gender inequality and ignores variations in the beliefs of women according to **class** and **ethnic** background.

Marxist and **socialist feminists** (Textbook pp. 101-102) believe society is shaped by a combination of ruling-class and patriarchal ideology. For example, **Benston** (1972) (Textbook p. 111) believes that male power and capitalist

interests are both served by an ideology which sees women as **secondary wage earners**.

Black feminists (Textbook pp. 103-104) believe other feminists ignore the role of **racist ideology** in defining the position of women. For example, **Mirza** (1997) (Textbook p. 104) believes black British women can challenge racist, patriarchal and class ideology which sees them as the passive victims of discrimination.

Ideology, discourse and ethnicity

Black feminists take account of racist ideologies as they affect black women, but they do not discuss ideologies which devalue other ethnic groups – for example: people of Asian, Chinese or Arabic origin.

Feminist and **Marxist** theories see ideology as grounded in inequalities in society.

Discourse analysis sees beliefs as playing an important role in creating those inequalities. A discourse is a way of thinking and talking about something that involves the exercise of power.

Orientalism

Said (1995, 1997) (Textbook pp. 183-184), is concerned with ideologies which affect people of 'Oriental' origin. Orientalism is created by **discourse**, embodied in Western descriptions of the East or Orient.

Orientalism sees non-Westerners as the **other** or others: people who are alien to the West and very different. Politicians, popular culture and the mass media tend to portray Orientals as being belligerent, violent, primitive, cunning and untrustworthy.

Recently, Orientalist ideology has been directed specifically against Islam, and has helped to create **Islamophobia** (Textbook pp. 186-188).

Said does not believe there is any truth in Orientalist ideology, seeing it as a way of justifying American intervention in Islamic countries.

Criticism of Said and discourse analysis

Marxists dispute the discourse analysis approach to ideology, which sees language as creating power inequalities; Marxists argue that it is power inequalities that create the discourse or ideology.

Like many theorists of ideology, Said exaggerates the dominance of a particular ideology. For example, there are many critics of American foreign policy, and sympathetic views of Palestinians and other 'Oriental' groups, in parts of the Western media.

Postmodernism and ideology

Postmodernists do not generally use the term ideology. However, **Lyotard's** (1979) (Textbook pp. 563-564 and 891-893) concept of **metanarrative** has a similar meaning.

By metanarrative, Lyotard means a 'big story' about how the world works and how it should be improved. Lyotard believes that in postmodern society people no longer believe in metanarratives such as communism, fascism or scientific rationalism.

In modernity, metanarratives which aimed to improve the world have ended in disaster – for example: the

Holocaust; mass deaths under Stalin in the Soviet Union; global warming.

Lyotard sees postmodernity as involving **incredulity towards metanarratives** and, by implication, the decline of ideology.

Postmodernists argue that all viewpoints are valid, and if nobody tries to impose their metanarrative (or ideology) on others then society will be the better for it.

Criticism of postmodernism

Philo & Miller (2001) (Textbook p. 894) argue that postmodernism itself is value-laden and therefore a form of **ideology**. It celebrates the apparent choice of consumer culture without acknowledging that the poor cannot afford to consume like richer members of society. Philo & Miller see postmodernism as an ideology which supports capitalist societies, with their inherent large inequalities.

SCIENCE AND IDEOLOGY

AQA   **Textbook pp. 847-851**

Karl Popper and positivism

One belief system which is often seen as **objective** and therefore not ideological is **science**.

Positivists believe that social facts can be objectively observed and measured. **Scientific methods** can be directly applied to the study of society. Sociologists should look for correlations between different social facts to try to discover **causal relationships** and **laws** of human behaviour.

Popper (1959) also argues that sociology can be objective if it makes precise predictions that can be **falsified**. Although it is always possible that a theory will not be proved wrong in the future, any theory that can be falsified is a scientific theory.

Popper does not regard **Marxism** as scientific because Marx did not produce precise predictions about when a **proletarian revolution** would take place.

Science in the social context

Some sociologists argue that science is not objective and is at least partly shaped by the **social context** in which it is practised.

Gomm (1982) argues that Darwin's theory of **evolution** was accepted in the 19th century, despite gaps in the evidence, because it made gradual evolutionary social change seem natural and desirable. This fitted the preferences of political leaders of the time. The idea of **competition** and **natural selection** could be used to support **free market capitalism** and legitimate a view of the poor as 'undeserving'.

Thomas Kuhn's scientific revolutions

Kuhn (1962) questions the idea that science is objective. He argues that science operates through **paradigms**: general theories or sets of beliefs held by groups of scientists.

Each scientific paradigm has a **social base**, the scientists who have dedicated their careers to working within it. Scientists tend to work within a single paradigm, ignoring evidence which contradicts or fails to fit within the paradigm.

Only when many inexplicable anomalies are found does a **scientific revolution** take place, when the paradigm is replaced by a new one. (For more discussion of sociology and science see p. 206)

Postmodernism and science

Some of the most extreme views of science are put forward by **postmodernists** (Textbook pp. 890-894).

Lyotard (1984) believes that science is just another **metanarrative** or 'big story' about the world, with no more validity than other metanarratives. Science involves a metanarrative of **progress**, suggesting that humans can control and perfect the world. The metanarrative of progress has shaped Western thought for centuries, but in postmodern societies it has broken down.

Science consists of **denotative language games**, which are based upon whether statements are true or not. However, science has failed to solve old problems or prevent new ones arising, so people have turned against the claim that science can provide truthful, objective knowledge.

Denotative language games have been replaced by **technical language games**, concerned with whether things are useful rather than whether they are true.

Science and ideology – conclusion

Most sociologists agree that scientific knowledge is influenced by social factors. However, many sociologists believe that science is more than ideology. For example, the **realist view of science** suggests that both natural and social sciences can produce valid knowledge (Textbook pp. 850-851).

The postmodern view that **scientific rationalism** has been replaced could be supported by the increasing belief in the **New Age** (see p. 75). However, it is both a generalization and an exaggeration to claim that scientific rationalism has lost its influence. For example, the **biomedical model of health** (Textbook pp. 288-291; this book p. 152) is still dominant.

DEVELOP YOUR ANALYTICAL AND EVALUATION SKILLS

Essay plans

For each of the following questions write your own essay plan before comparing it with the suggestions given here. For the final question you can write a full answer and compare it with the model answer provided.

Church membership and attendance statistics indicate a clear decline in religiosity Discuss.

Background

This statement represents one aspect of the secularization debate – the view that religion is losing its social significance. The view expressed does not indicate any particular church or country, and the evidence does vary across the world and between religions.

For	Against
<ul><li>Decline in church attendance in UK (Brierley) (p. 77)</li><li>Decline in church membership in UK (Brierley) (p. 77)</li><li>Bruce – surveys show clear decline in religious beliefs (p. 78)</li></ul>	<ul><li>Increase in non-Christian and smaller religions (p. 78)</li><li>Growth of New Age beliefs (p. 75)</li><li>Doubts about reliability and validity of figures (p. 77)</li><li>Religion in Victorian Britain (Martin) (p. 78)</li><li>Rates of attendance and membership much higher in USA (p. 78)</li><li>Christianity increasing in some countries (Barrett) (p 78)</li><li>Rise of Islam (p. 77)</li></ul>

Top Tip

A key issue here is the extent to which participation in formal religious organizations is a valid indicator of religiosity. It may be possible to go to church but not have strong religious feelings, while it is equally possible that people may have deep religious beliefs but do not attend church.

The growth of new religious movements and 'New Age' beliefs since the 1960s indicates a revival of religion. Discuss.

Background

A variety of explanations have been put forward to explain the increase in these organizations and beliefs. This statement focuses on the social significance of this growth rather than the reasons for it.

For	Against
<ul><li>Greeley – resacrilization (p. 79)</li><li>Heelas – significance of New Age beliefs (p. 75)</li></ul>	<ul><li>Bruce – small numbers in new religious movements (p. 79)</li><li>Wilson – religious pluralism indicates insignificance of religion (p. 79)</li><li>Drane: New Age reflects move to postmodernity (p. 75)</li></ul>

Top Tip

A key point is that although the numbers involved in these groups have grown, they are still very small. Although it is important to explain the terms 'new religious movements' and 'New Age', try not to spend too much time doing so, as this is not the main point of the question.

The main role of ideology in society is to maintain the power of dominant groups. Discuss.

Background

An ideology is a set of value-laden beliefs, often one which supports the interests of a dominant group in society. This suggests that the role of ideology is to maintain the power of those who already have it, but this view is questioned by some sociologists.

<table>
<tr><td>

For
- Marx and Engels who believe that all class-based societies are dominated by ruling-class ideology (p. 83)
- Feminists: particularly radical feminists like Kate Millett and Germaine Greer, who think that society is dominated by patriarchal ideology (p. 84)
- Discourse theorists such as Edward Said, who believes that Orientalism helps to keep the West dominant (p. 84)

</td><td>

Against
- Postmodernists who believe that no ideology is dominant, and that people no longer believe in metanarratives (p. 82)

</td></tr>
</table>

Partially in favour
- A number of conflict theorists argue that society has competing ideologies, including some ideologies which oppose the dominant ideology
- Gramsci (p. 83) believes that the working class have a dual consciousness which is partly critical of dominant ideology
- Raymond Williams (p. 83) believes residual and emergent ideologies can be oppositional or alternative to the dominant ideology

Top Tip

Remember you can use examples from religion or politics to illustrate these competing viewpoints.

Religion is usually a cause of conflict rather than of harmony in society. Discuss.

Background

Conflict can take many forms including war, civil war, civil unrest, struggles for power. Many theories of religion suggest that religion is a cause of harmony, but there are many conflicts both in the world today and in the past which show a link between religion and conflict. Conflict may be within or between religions.

For

- Huntingdon sees clashes between civilizations with different religious traditions as inevitable (p. 81)
- Sects and cults can be in tension with society (p. 74)
- There is evidence of conflict over gender issues within religion (p. 70)
- Fundamentalist religions are often in conflict with modernity (p. 71)
- There are many examples of conflicts involving religion (p. 81)
- Neo-Marxists such as Maduro think religion can become revolutionary, causing conflict with the state (p. 70)

Against

- Functionalists believe religion creates solidarity and harmony (p. 68)
- Marxists believe religion prevents conflict by fostering false class consciousness (p. 69)
- Feminists like de Beauvoir believe that religion prevents conflict by supporting patriarchy (p. 70)
- Karen Armstrong believes that political and economic factors are more important in causing conflict than religion (p. 81).
- Secularization theory suggests that as the influence of religion weakens it is playing a lesser role in society and therefore lesser role in causing conflict (p. 77)

Top Tip

The best way to conclude is by using Bruce's ideas (p. 81), which suggest that the role of religion and other factors in causing conflict varies, but religious and social factors are often intertwined.

Discuss the relationship between religion and social change.

Background

Functionalists and Marxists share the view that religion is essentially a force acting for stability and against change in societies. Weber's classic study *The Protestant Ethic and The Spirit of Capitalism* is the starting point for arguments that religion can promote social change. Many theories claim that changes in society will shape religion – for example, theories of secularization and globalization.

For religion causing change

- Weber (p. 71)
- Maduro (p. 70)

Against religion causing change

- Durkheim (p. 68)
- Malinowski (p. 69)
- Parsons (p. 78)
- de Beauvoir (p. 70)
- Marx (p. 69)

Top Tip

McGuire (p. 72) is useful in evaluating this debate in so far as she identifies specific factors that affect the role of religion in society, and avoids large-scale generalizations.

Model answer

Discuss the relationship between religion and social change.

There is no single definition of religion, but it can be generally defined as a belief system that involves some claims to answer ultimate questions, or a belief in supernatural power or forces. There are several possible relationships between religious beliefs and organizations, and social change. Firstly, religion might impede changes in society, acting as a conservative force. Secondly, religion might encourage social change, acting as a radical force. Thirdly, changes in society could shape religion and lead to changes in religious organizations or beliefs. Although different theories tend to support particular viewpoints, it is of course possible that the relationship acts in different ways at different times.

Both Marxists and functionalists believe that the predominant effect of religion is to act as a conservative force. Durkheim used the example of the worship of Totems, which symbolized aboriginal tribal groupings, to suggest that religion was actually the worship of society. He believed that religious ceremonies strengthened social groups by providing a sense of social solidarity. Malinowski's studies of the Trobriand Islands suggested that religion was a way of coping with stressful or dangerous tasks essential to society (such as deep sea fishing), thus helping to maintain social stability. Parsons believed that religious beliefs underpin the value consensus by providing divine support for social values — for example, the Ten Commandments — which provide the basis for the norms and values of society. He also believed that ceremonies such as funerals help individuals to overcome personal crises so they can carry on with their socially important roles.

The functionalist view that religion helps to preserve and reinforce existing values, and therefore prevents change, has been widely criticized. Durkheim never visited Australia, and recent researchers doubt whether Totemism was actually a religion. Furthermore, functionalists tend to see religion in a very one-sided way, ignoring the conflict that religion can cause — which in turn can lead to social change. Religion may help to unite those who share the same religious beliefs, but schisms within religion and differences between competing religions often disrupt society. Examples include the Arab-Israeli (Jewish-Muslim) conflict in the Middle East, the Northern Irish conflict between Loyalist Protestants and Republican Catholics; the war between Catholic Croats, Orthodox Serbs and Muslims in Bosnia-Herzegovina in the 1990s. Such conflicts usually end with some sort of political solution in which society changes, although no resolution has yet been achieved in the Middle East.

Despite the many differences between functionalism and Marxism, Marxists too see religion as generally preventing change. When Marx described religion as being like opium he was suggesting both that it dulled pain and allowed subject classes to cope with oppression, thus postponing any ultimate revolution and the social change that went with it. There are certainly examples of religion acting in this way — for example, conservative Christianity in Latin America. Marx also believed that religion could legitimate the position of a ruling class, a view which can be supported by the example of the influential New Christian Right in the USA. In this case though, Christians are also on the side of social change, calling for a return to traditional moral values — for example, in campaigns against abortion.

Both Engels and neo-Marxists such as Otto Maduro have, however, pointed out that religion can as be used to legitimate radical beliefs which see change in society as desirable and actively campaign for it. An example is the Catholic liberation theology movement in Latin America, the opposition of Buddhist priests in Burma to the military government and even (somewhat paradoxically) the opposition of the Catholic Church in Poland to the Communist regime in the 1980s.

Neo-Marxists are right to recognize that religion can be a force for change, but Weber was the first to develop this theoretical point. In The Protestant Ethic and the Spirit of Capitalism, he claimed that the belief in predestination amongst Calvinists encouraged them to lead austere ascetic lifestyles while accumulating wealth, because they believed that work was godly. Weber did not believe that religion was the only factor that caused the advent of capitalism — the right economic circumstances had to be in place as well — but it did mark a fundamental difference between Europe and countries such as China and India, which had the preconditions for industrialization but lacked a religion that encouraged the reinvestment of wealth.

Weber's thesis is controversial — for example, Marxists such as Kautsky see the advent of capitalism as causing the birth of Protestantism (rather than the other way round) — but Weber is undoubtedly right that social change can sometimes result from religion. For example, the anti-Western Islamic revolution which propelled Ayatollah Khomeini to power in Iran in 1979 was based upon religious beliefs. However, religion is clearly only one a series of factors in any situation.

All the main sociological perspectives argue that changes in society can lead to changes in religion. Parsons believed that religion lost functions with the structural differentiation of society. Marxists believe that a change in the economic base or mode of production changed the superstructure, which includes religion. Marx was clearly wrong in predicting the demise of religion with the advent of communism. Numerous sociologists including Bryan Wilson, Max Weber and Steve Bruce have claimed that modernity and scientific rationalism would lead to secularization. Postmodernists have claimed that postmodern societies are undergoing resacrilization, as individuals rediscover spirituality through the ability to 'pick and mix' New Age beliefs which fit with their changing identities. Feminists have discussed both how the advent of patriarchy led to the abandonment of goddesses and the adoption of patriarchal monotheism, and how women's liberation has helped to improve the position of women in religion (for example, the ordination of female Anglican vicars). It has also been suggested, for example by Steve Bruce, that the processes of globalization and modernization have led to fundamentalism (in Islam, for example, in the case of Al Quaeda).

To conclude, there is therefore no doubt that changes in individual societies, or globally, can lead to changes in religion, but that religion itself can help to shape the wider social changes that take place. The one-sided materialism of Marxism (which sees religion as determined by the economic base) is less credible than Weber's partial idealism, which acknowledges that ideas can sometimes shape society. Most sociologists now accept that religion can be either a radical or conservative force and, as Meredith Maguire suggests, a variety of factors influence whether religion helps to change society, or helps to maintain the status quo. Religion is most likely to play a role in social change when a religion has a strong belief system and a centralized organizational structure, in societies where religion is central to economic and social life and the culture of society.

RESOURCES

Writers and their work

Writer	Perspective or approach	Concept	Study or area of research
Heelas & Woodhead	New Age as part of modernity	The Spiritual Revolution	The Kendal Project
Weber	Weberian	The elect	*The Protestant Ethic and the Spirit of Capitalism*
Steve Bruce	Pro-secularization	Cultural defence	Study of ethnicity and secularization
Zygmundt Bauman	Postmodernism	Privatized morality	Postmodern ethics
David Lyon	Postmodernism	Religion as a cultural resource	*Jesus in Disneyland*
Anthony Giddens	High modernity	Reflexivity	The development of modernity and consequences of globalization
Maduro	Neo-Marxism	Relative autonomy	Liberation theology and other radical religions
Durkheim	Functionalism	Collective conscience	Aborigine religion
Parsons	Functionalism	Structural differentiation	Evolution of religion in the USA
Malinowski	Functionalism	Life crises and religious rituals	Trobriand Islands
Roy Wallis	Typologies of organization	World-affirming, world-rejecting, world-accommodating	New religious movements
Troeltsch/Niebuhr	Typologies of religious organizations	Churches, denominations, cults	Types of Christian religious group
de Beauvoir	Feminism	False consciousness of women	Women in Christianity
Marx	Marxism	'Opium of the Masses'	Class and religious belief
El Saadawi	Feminism	Patriarchal misinterpretation of religion	Islam and gender
Greeley	Anti-secularization theory	Resacrilization	Growth of new religious movements
Kautsky	Marxism	Protestantism as a capitalist ideology	Study of the development of capitalism

| # CULTURE AND IDENTITY

SPECIFICATION COVERAGE

Specification	Details
AQA AS SCLY 1: Culture and Identity	All sections are relevant
OCR AS G671: Explaining Socialization, Culture and Identity AS G672: Sociology of Youth	G671 sections on culture and identity (Textbook pp. 662-666) and socialization (Textbook pp. 686-692) are relevant. See also G672, on youth subcultures (Textbook pp. 771-782). A study of sociological methods is also required in this unit
WJEB AS SCY1: Acquiring Culture, Introductory Core; SCY2 Understanding Culture, Option 2: Youth Culture	Sections on defining culture and identity (Textbook pp. 662-666) and socialization (Textbook pp. 686-692) are relevant. See also Option 2, on youth subcultures (Textbook pp. 771-782)

THE DEFINITION OF CULTURE

AQA, OCR, WJEC   Textbook pp. 663-664

The word 'culture' has been used in different ways. **Jencks** (1993) distinguishes four main senses in which the word is now used. Culture is:

1 a **quality** possessed by **individuals** who are able to gain the learning and achieve the qualities that are seen as desirable in a 'cultured' human being. This definition is **elitist** as it sees some aspects of human activity and attainment as superior to others.

2 a **quality** possessed by some societies, seen as more civilized and superior to others. This definition is linked to evolutionary ideas and is also elitist.

3 the collective body of all the **arts and intellectual work** in a society. This is a common definition; culture in this sense is sometimes called **high culture**.

4 the **whole way of life** of a people. As **Linton** (1945) puts it: 'The culture of a society is the way of life of its members; the collection of ideas and habits which they learn, share and transmit from generation to generation.'

Most contemporary sociologists use the fourth definition. Culture in this sense includes virtually all of the subject matter of sociology.

When the third definition is used it is easier to identify a distinct area of study, which includes the sociology of art, music and literature.

Types of culture

These definitions of culture can be developed by examining the different types of culture identified by sociologists:

● **High culture** – usually refers to cultural creations that have a particularly high status – for example, the products of long-established art forms such as opera, classical music and literature. For many who use the term, high culture is seen as superior to lesser forms of culture.

● **Folk culture** – refers to the culture of ordinary people, particularly those living in preindustrial societies. Examples include traditional folk songs and stories that have been handed down from generation to generation.

- **Mass culture** – for its critics, mass culture is seen as less worthy than high culture or folk culture. It is a product of the mass media and includes popular feature films, TV soap operas and pop music. Critics of mass culture (see p. 95) see it as debasing for individuals and destructive to the fabric of society.

- **Popular culture** – often used with a meaning similar to 'mass culture'. Popular culture includes any cultural products appreciated by large numbers of ordinary people: for example, TV programmes, mass-market films, and popular fiction such as detective stories. While mass culture is usually used as a term of abuse, this is not the case with popular culture. While some do see popular culture as shallow and harmful, others, including some postmodernists, argue that it is just as valid and worthwhile as high culture.

- **Subculture** – the term has been applied to a wide range of groups, including: those who live close together and have a shared lifestyle; youth groups who share common musical tastes and enjoy the same leisure activities; ethnic groups; people who share the same religious beliefs; members of the same gang.

- **Global culture** – implies an all-embracing culture common to people all over the world. **Featherstone** (1990) argues it does not exist because people do not share a common lifestyle; however, some cultural products cross national boundaries.

Some theorists, particularly functionalists, emphasize the degree to which culture is shared by members of a society. Many other theorists emphasize **cultural pluralism** or subcultural variety in society.

SOCIALIZATION

AQA, OCR, WJEC   **Textbook pp. 664-665**

Giddens (2006) defines socialization as the process through which culture is passed from generation to generation. It initially takes place in the family; later education, religion, the media and peer groups are important.

The culture of society is always changing so the process of socialization is never complete.

Handel (2006) argues that individuals gain their own unique identity during socialization.

IDENTITY

AQA, OCR, WJEC   **Textbook pp. 665-666**

The definition of identity

Identity refers to the sense that someone has of who they are, and of what is most important about them. Important sources of identity are likely to include: nationality, ethnicity, sexuality, gender and class. Sociologists define two types of identity:

- **Personal identity** refers to how a person thinks about themselves.

- **Social identity** refers to how they are perceived by others.

Personal and social identity do not necessarily match – for example, a person perceived by others to be male may see themselves as a woman trapped in a man's body.

The importance of identity

The concept of identity has become increasingly important in sociology. In the past people's identities were seen as fairly stable, widely shared and based on one or two key variables such as class and nationality. More recent postmodern theories of identity have suggested that people's identities can frequently change and may contain considerable contradictions. For example, the meaning of 'masculine' and 'feminine' has become much less clear-cut.

According to **postmodernists**:

- people actively create their own identities.

- people have a great deal of choice about what social groups to join.

- through shopping and other forms of consumption people can shape and change their identities.

For some writers, individuals no longer have a stable sense of identity at all – their identities are **fragmented** (see p. 101).

Identity and culture

The concept of identity is closely related to the concept of culture. Identities can be formed through the cultures and subcultures to which people belong. However, different theories see the relationship between culture and identity in rather different ways:

- Theories influenced by **functionalism** and **Marxism** see identity as originating in a fairly straightforward way from involvement in particular cultures and subcultures – for example, people living in Britain would be expected to have a strong sense of British identity.

- **Postmodernist** theories stress the diversity of factors influencing identity – for example, British people from different ethnic or national origins interpret British identity in different ways.

CULTURE

AQA, WJEC   **Textbook p. 666**

Durkheim – culture and conformity

Durkheim (1963) believed that a **shared culture** is necessary if a society is to run smoothly. This shared culture is passed down from generation to generation and exists outside of the wishes and choices of individuals. People must **conform** to the culture of their society if they are to avoid the risk of punishment.

In order to develop culture humans must develop a system of classifying things. The categories come from society, so a simple society with two social groups will classify everything in twos whilst more complex societies have more complex categories.

Religion is based on the classification of objects as **sacred** or **profane** and is the basis of the **collective conscience** in simple societies. This is weaker in more complex societies, but a common culture is necessary for societies to run smoothly.

Evaluation

Durkheim's work has been criticized for using evidence selectively and exaggerating the extent to which the social structure determines culture. However, his work paved the way for later work on the way social factors might shape culture.

Marxist theories of culture and identity

AQA, WJEC   Textbook p. 667

Marx claimed that in class-stratified societies culture can be seen as little more than **ruling-class ideology**. It is simply an expression of the distorted view of the world advanced by the dominant class. Contemporary Marxists have developed theories of cultural forces, such as the mass media, along these lines (see p. 96).

One interpretation of Marx sees the working class as suffering from **false class consciousness** – its beliefs and culture are shaped by the ruling class.

Other interpretations see working-class culture and other cultural forms as possessing some independence from ruling-class domination.

Neo-Marxist theories

Neo-Marxist approaches (Textbook pp. 672-673) have been significantly influenced by Marxism, but all tend to argue that culture has considerable independence from economic influences, and that there is no straightforward correspondence between class and culture.

Williams (1961, 1965, 1978) criticizes Marxist theorists for being too **deterministic**. He argues that they underestimate the creativity of different groups within the culture and have too narrow a focus on art and literature.

The basis of working-class culture is **collective action** in response to lack of opportunity. Working-class culture and **bourgeois individualistic** culture interact and overlap.

Evaluation

Williams encouraged others to take working-class culture seriously, but postmodernists deny its relevance today.

YOUTH SUBCULTURES

AQA, OCR, WJEC   Textbook pp. 771-772

For the **CCCS** (Birmingham Centre for Contemporary Cultural Studies), youth subcultures often represent creative attempts to win space from dominant cultures. Youth cultures create their own distinctive styles of dress and music and these represent an attempt to 'solve', in an imaginary way, the problems faced by youth. The example of Teddy boys can illustrate these arguments.

Jefferson – Teddy boys

Jefferson (1976) argues that the youth culture of **Teddy boys** (or 'Teds') represented an attempt to recreate a sense of working-class community which came under threat in the post-war period from urban redevelopment and growing affluence (wealth) in some sections of the working class.

Some unskilled working-class youth responded by forming groups in which members had a strong sense of loyalty and were willing to fight over their territory.

Their style of dress incorporated Edwardian-style jackets, bootlace ties and suede shoes.

Jefferson sees aspects of this style as part of an attempt to buy status. Edwardian-style jackets were originally worn by upper-class 'dandies', and by wearing them the Teds hoped that some of the status of this group would rub off on them. Bootlace ties appeared to come from Western films where they were worn by the 'slick city gambler' who was forced to live by his wits. Like their counterparts in the Westerns, the Teddy boys felt themselves to be outsiders who needed to live by their wits.

By adopting these styles, working-class youth could feel that they were doing something to protect their territory, gain status and recreate community.

Evaluation

Neo-Marxist theories such as those of the CCCS tend to fall between two stools:

- For conventional Marxists, they fail to fully acknowledge the importance of the economy in shaping culture.

- For postmodernists, they fail to fully accept the freedom that people have to invent cultures.

Hebdige – The Meaning of Style

Hebdige (1988) uses some Marxist ideas in his analysis of youth subcultures but is also influenced by semiotics – the study of the meaning of symbols and signs (also known as semiology, see p. 96). Each subculture develops its own style by taking everyday objects and transforming their meaning. This new 'secret' meaning expresses, in code, a form of resistance to subordination. **Punks**, for instance, transformed the meaning of safety pins and ripped jeans.

Each subculture is **spectacular**: it creates a spectacle and intends to get noticed.

Hebdige contrasts **mod** and **skinhead** subcultures. Skinheads' appearance was a kind of exaggerated version of the working-class manual labourer and expressed the image of the 'hard' working-class man. Mods, on the other hand, adopted a more respectable appearance which reflected aspirations to be upwardly mobile and join the middle class. However, despite their respectable suits, their style reflected a love of 'cellar clubs, discotheques, boutiques and record shops' which was outside the conventional middle-class world.

Hebdige also analyses **black British** subcultures. First-generation migrants adopted smart and conventional dress which reflected their aspirations to succeed in Britain. By the 1970s, the disappointments that stemmed from racism and high levels of unemployment began to be expressed in the style of **Rastafarians**. British Rastafarians expressed their alienation from British culture by adopting simple clothes with an African feel. The key themes of Rastafarian style were resistance to the dominance of white culture and the expression of black identity.

Criticisms

There is no evidence that members of the youth subcultures Hebdige writes about saw their own subculture in the same way as Hebdige. This lack of empirical evidence could be seen as a limitation of his work.

For **postmodernists**, Hebdige is wrong to assume that it is possible to attribute any one meaning to a subculture. Rather, it is open to a variety of interpretations, each of which is equally valid.

Bennett & Kahn-Harris (2004) criticize Hebdige for assuming that the subcultures had a class basis, for exaggerating their oppositional nature and for ignoring other factors such as ethnicity and gender.

Postmodernists have questioned whether well-defined subcultures really existed.

GENDER IN SUBCULTURES

AQA, OCR, WJEC   Textbook pp. 774-782

McRobbie (1976) argues that girls were marginalized or largely absent from earlier work. This is because young women had a structurally different position to young men. Girls faced a restricted future and adopted a **culture of femininity** based on a close relationship with their best friend and the ideology of romance. Girls were trapped materially and ideologically into marriage. The culture of femininity exists mainly in private space so could be seen as **bedroom culture**.

Lincoln (2004) found bedroom culture continuing in the 1990s with significant modifications. Girls entertained both male and female friends in their bedrooms; television and, increasingly, the internet were important elements of this culture.

Reddington (2003) argues that females were central to the music and fashion of punk, but their contribution has been unfairly reduced to a '**subculturette**'.

The evidence suggests that the neglect of females in the study of youth subcultures may be partly due to their lower participation and partly due to their neglect by male researchers.

Thornton (1995) carried out an ethnographic study of clubbers. She does not see club cultures as oppositional or class-based. Clubbers come together in loose-knit groups at specific dance events. Using the ideas of **Bourdieu** she argues that **subcultural capital** provides status to the clubber. It is expressed through haircuts, record collections, being 'in the know', and keeping up with the latest trends.

Thornton sees dance club cultures as **taste cultures** where demonstration of good taste brings status. Subcultural capital also provides escape from **parental control** – the most avid clubbers are 15-19 years old. Thornton describes how subcultures relate to the transition from childhood to adulthood.

Girls are more likely to go clubbing because boys have a wider range of out-of-home activities, including sport. Club culture looks down on the relatively powerless: working-class girls with the least valued musical taste. It is not therefore a form of rebellion against the ruling class. Club culture requires the media to communicate the degrees of subcultural capital associated with different clubs, DJs or musical styles, so the media are integral to the production of club cultures.

Bennett (1999) argues that youth groups are not distinct subcultures but **neo-tribes** – loose groupings of young people who come together in a particular setting to express particular tastes. They are not a coherent group and will adopt different identities in different settings. Bennett believes **traditional identities** based on locality, occupation and gender are breaking down, so people move between neo-tribes and express different identities in each.

Muggleton (2000) studied young people in a pub setting looking for evidence of a shift to postmodern subcultures. He argues that **individuality** is more important than **subculture**. The majority of his respondents were **liminal** – on the fringe of subcultures or with mixed or ill-defined social identities. The subcultures were hostile to the mainstream but, apart from supporting freedom of expression, were not interested in politics or challenging the ruling class.

Muggleton rejects the CCCS description of homogeneous oppositional subcultures and believes the concept of **neo-tribe** is useful. His respondents used subculture as an important part of identity, but these subcultures were not distinct, and they believed individuality was also important.

Neither Bennett nor Muggleton found well-defined, distinct subcultures sharing a common lifestyle. However, rather than studying a way of life, their studies were based on weekend leisure activities.

Hodkinson (2004) used ethnographic methods to study **goths**. He found considerable **subcultural substance**. The subculture had distinct **values**, a **shared identity** and practical **commitment** among its participants. Members were distinguished by their sombre music, black clothing and distinctive makeup. They had a shared sense of identity with other goths and a shared dislike of 'trendies'. Goths came from a variety of backgrounds but were mainly middle-class. Hodkinson rejects the concept of neo-tribes: his respondents were not liminal – they were part of a distinct and committed group. He also rejects the CCCS notion that subculture reflects class difference.

Hodkinson's conclusions may reflect the subculture he studied and the way he conducted his research. Goths are a very distinct group and he was able to immerse himself in the scene. Muggleton interviewed people in pubs and was unlikely to discover similar levels of commitment. Neither Hodkinson or Muggleton support the CCCS claim that subculture is an expression of class position.

MASS CULTURE

AQA, OCR, WJEC   Textbook pp. 673-674

In 1950s America there was considerable concern about the impact of what was called **mass culture**. As individuals had increasing leisure, the mass media stepped in to fill people's spare time with undemanding entertainment such as soap operas, popular films and magazines.

Macdonald (1957) saw no merit in mass culture. He believed it had nothing of significance to say and was designed to appeal to the lowest common denominator. He argued that mass culture was actually undermining the fabric of society because people were losing their involvement in social groups and becoming isolated individuals.

Gans (1974) argued that America has a large number of equally worthwhile but differing taste cultures including:

- **high culture** – serious music and literature for small audiences.

- **upper-middle culture** – the culture of well-educated professionals and managers. It rejects both the over-abstraction of high culture and the vulgarity of low culture.

- **lower-middle culture** – the dominant culture in the USA, based around cultural products which are enjoyable and understandable.

- **low culture** – transmitted by the mass media, this culture stresses substance, action and stories with a moral. It is the culture of factory workers and semi-skilled white-collar workers.

- **quasi-folk, low culture** – a simpler version of low culture with an emphasis on melodrama, action comedies and morality plays. It is the culture of some blue-collar workers and the rural poor.

Gans also describes cultures based on age and ethnicity, and speaks of a **hierarchy** of tastes which, he argues, is not based on merit. He believes each culture meets the needs of its audience.

Evaluation

Gans's work is a major advance on mass culture theory because it describes a **plurality** of cultures and shows how differing cultures meet differing audience needs.

Strinati – critique of mass culture theory

Strinati (1995) attacks mass culture theory on a number of grounds:

- The consumers of mass culture are not a **passive** mass of people. They are discriminating, and reject many products which they find insufficiently interesting or entertaining.

- It is not the case that all popular culture is **homogeneous** (the same). In reality, there is a wide variety of styles. Popular music, for example, includes rap, jazz, heavy metal and so on.

- It is not possible to distinguish a superior 'folk culture' from an inferior 'mass culture'. Folk, blues and country music, for example, have all been influenced by a range of musical traditions.

- There is no clear distinction between mass culture and high culture. Strinati gives the examples of jazz music, the films of Alfred Hitchcock, and rock'n'roll records which have attained the status of classics.

GLOBAL CULTURE

AQA, OCR, WJEC Textbook pp. 677-678

Global culture has some similarities with mass culture – it is shared by many people and spread through the mass media. However, global culture is not necessarily seen as morally inferior in the way mass culture has often been presented.

Storey (2003) argues that in the past cultures were separated by time and space, but increasing tourist travel, migration, satellite communications and the internet have increased contact between different cultures.

One dominant view of global culture is of **homogenization** and **Americanization** destroying local cultures.

Storey argues that commodities such as hip hop are consumed in a local context and adapted to fit. The result is **hybridization** – a mixture of the global and the local – and an increasing **cultural diversity**. Thus local culture may be undermined but not completely destroyed. The process does not result in a single global culture. Storey does not agree that American culture is superior but he does see it as powerful.

Criticisms

Sklair (1993, 1995, 2003) disagrees with Storey and believes the ideology of consumerism has become very influential.

STRUCTURALISM

AQA Textbook pp. 678-680

Structural approaches see social life conducted and shaped through **language**.

Saussure (1857-1913) was the founder of **semiology** – the science of signs. People experience the world through signs because language organizes and constructs their access to reality. Signs are social phenomena shared by social groups and passed down to children through language.

Saussure also founded the study of **linguistics**, showing the underlying structures of language.

Evaluation

Saussure has been criticized for exaggerating the extent of shared language and ignoring the fact that the powerful may try to define their language as superior, which may cause conflict.

POSTSTRUCTURALISM

AQA Textbook pp. 681-682

Poststructuralists reject the idea of structure. However, their work builds on the work of semiologists and structuralists. Language, for poststructuralists, does not describe some underlying structure, rather it **creates reality**; meaning is always related to a particular context. The thought and emotions of individuals are shaped through involvement with the **discourses** that surround them. As these change constantly, individual identities have no fixed meaning. Thus, for example, people's understanding of motherhood will depend on contested discourses of femininity.

Poststructuralists argue that some discourses are particularly influential. **Foucault** believed power is not based on structure; rather it is linked to the way people talk about things and create particular discourses.

Evaluation

Poststructuralists have been criticized for ignoring material reality and for relativism. In a world with no truth there is no reason to believe poststructuralism above any other perspective.

MODERNITY AND POSTMODERNITY

AQA, OCR, WJEC   Textbook pp. 682-686

Crook *et al* (1992) argue that societies are moving from modernity to postmodernity through a process of **postmodernization**.

Modern culture is:

- **differentiated into spheres** such as political, economic and social. Each sphere develops its own specialist institutions and occupations and is judged by different criteria. Over time culture evolves into the **high culture** of those trained in specialist institutions such as art colleges, and the **folk culture** found amongst ordinary people.

- **rationalized** – technology is increasingly used to make culture available to a wider audience. This reinforces the status of high culture.

- **commodified** – culture is turned into products that can be bought and sold. Taste develops when the whole population have sufficient resources to choose the cultural products they consume.

In modern societies culture is differentiated from other areas of social life and high culture is differentiated from popular culture.

However, in **postmodernization**:

- **commodification** invades all areas of social life. Members of the same family can consume different cultural products, make differing lifestyle choices and select differing styles to show others their individuality.

- the use of **technology** has spread cultural products more widely, removed the constraints of time and place and given consumers more lifestyle choices. Public cultural events become less important as the **media** dominate society. Media images begin to replace the reality they represent.

- culture **fragments** into a 'fantastic variety' of cultural forms with no dominant type. High culture is absorbed into other cultural forms – for example, classical music used in advertising – and the distinctions between the different types of culture break down.

The result is **post-culture**, characterized by variety and choice. Lifestyle choice replaces the hierarchy of tastes based on social class and other social differences. The process is ongoing.

Strinati – postmodernism and popular culture

Strinati (1995) describes how theories of postmodernism explain popular culture. The main features of postmodernism are:

- the breakdown of the distinction between culture and society. Society has become '**media-saturated**' and this means that the media are extremely powerful. They become so all-consuming that they actually create our sense of reality.

- 'an emphasis on **style** at the expense of substance'. Products become popular because they have designer labels rather than because they are useful. Surface qualities assume more importance than anything deeper.

- a 'breakdown of the distinction between art and popular culture'. Elements of what used to be thought of as 'high culture' become incorporated into popular culture – the pop artist **Andy Warhol**, for example, produced a print consisting of thirty representations of the Mona Lisa. Unlike the critics of mass culture (see p. 95), postmodernists see no reason to be unhappy about this: they welcome the fun and variety of postmodern culture.

- '**confusions over time and space**' caused by rapid travel and instantaneous communications. The media make it possible to witness events on the other side of the globe almost as if you were there. Theme parks recreate the past and try to create the future; some films and novels avoid following a chronological storyline from start to finish.

Finally, postmodern culture involves 'the decline of **metanarratives**'. People no longer have faith in any absolute claim to knowledge, such as religion, science or Marxism. Postmodern culture denies that there is any sense of progress in history. Everything is equally valid and the search for truth is pointless and dangerous.

The emergence of postmodernism

Strinati (1995) identifies three main reasons for the emergence of postmodernism:

- Advanced capitalist societies emphasize **consumerism**. A more affluent population with more leisure time needs to be entertained and persuaded to spend money. The media is central to these processes and so media images come to dominate society.

- New **middle-class occupations**, such as design, marketing and advertising, involve persuading people about the importance of taste. Once persuaded, people seek guidance on taste issues from the media. Other occupations – such as teaching and therapy – promote the idea that lifestyle is important, and so people are encouraged to consume the goods and services required for their favoured lifestyle.

- There has been a gradual disappearance of identities based on such things as class, local communities and religion. People's identities become more personal and individual and are constructed by the media.

Evaluation of postmodernism

Strinati raises a number of problems with postmodern theories of culture:

- Postmodernists exaggerate the importance of the mass media. There is no reason to think that people cannot distinguish between image and reality. Few people actually believe that characters in soap operas are real, for example.

- People do not buy products just because of their image or the designer label attached to them; they also buy them because they are useful. What is more, not all members of society have a culture that attaches importance to the image of products.

- Postmodernism is itself a 'metanarrative', so this undermines the claim that metanarratives are in decline.

- Some people have less opportunity than others to experience changes in concepts of time and space. Poorer people do not have access to computer or satellite technology or jet travel. What is more, there are no studies that show that people actually are confused about space and time.

- Most people still find it possible to distinguish between what they consider art and what they see as popular culture. Strinati believes that postmodernists simply create their own hierarchy of taste, placing their own favourite cultural products at the top.

- Postmodernism's impact on popular culture is exaggerated. Strinati focuses on films and points out that many of the supposed postmodern aspects of contemporary cinema are nothing new. Also, many films regarded as postmodern still have strong narratives (storylines).

SOCIALIZATION

AQA, OCR, WJEC   **Textbook pp. 686-692**

Through socialization individuals learn the culture of their society and become self-aware.

Functionalist perspective

Parsons (1937, 1951 ,1955 ,1959) argued that societies require certain features, or **functional prerequisites**, in order to survive. One of these is **pattern maintenance** – the passing on of society's norms, values and culture to the next generation. These are passed on initially by the family (**primary socialization**). Within the family children are treated as individuals (**particularistic values**) and learn common goals, appropriate behaviour and **gender roles**.

Secondary socialization takes place outside the home, mainly in schools. Here, children learn to treat each other by general rules (**universalistic values**) and to conform to abstract, general rules.

Criticisms

Parsons has been criticized for:

- ignoring the conflict involved in socialization;

- seeing children as passive recipients of society's rules;

- thinking socialization is always successful and ignoring deviance – an 'over-socialized' view of humanity.

Marxism and socialization

Marxism sees socialization as an **ideological conditioning** device ensuring children accept exploitation in later life.

In the family they learn conformity, obedience and gender roles, and their creativity and development of self is constricted.

The process continues in school where the '**hidden curriculum**' teaches children to be subservient, obedient and motivated by external rewards. They also learn to see inequality as legitimate.

Neo-Marxism and socialization

Neo-Marxists emphasize that socialization can be full of **conflict** and is not necessarily successful.

Willis (1977) showed how school pupils – 'lads' – developed a **counterculture** to oppose the school. They socialized each other, but not to passively obey their teachers. In doing so they unintentionally prepared themselves for their role in the workplace.

Gramsci (1971) argues that humans have **dual consciousness**. They are indoctrinated during socialization to see society as legitimate – a state of false consciousness – yet their daily experience of exploitation contradicts this. Thus they do not fully accept capitalist ideology.

Bourdieu (1984) argues that socialization involves the transmission of **cultural capital** (the cultural knowledge necessary for success) from one generation to the next. This ensures inequality is maintained.

Evaluation of Marxism and Neo-Marxism

Marxists have been accused of exaggerating the success of socialization.

Neo-Marxists have been criticized for assuming class is the only basis of inequality.

Postmodernists argue we are free to construct our identities outside our class backgrounds.

Feminists believe that socialization indoctrinates patriarchy rather than ruling-class ideology.

Symbolic interactionist perspective

Socialization is an active process based on interactions between adults and children.

Handel (2006) describes how a newborn infant is unable to take part in society due to physical immaturity and lack of socialization. During socialization children develop three capacities:

- **empathy** – picturing themselves in the place of others and understanding how others feel;

- **communication** – the use of language;

- **sense of self** – this allows children to distinguish themselves from others and to regulate their own behaviour.

Socialization agents – parents and teachers – have the responsibility for preparing children for adult society, but differences in the background of these adults means children are not all raised with identical norms and values. Children are also socialized in **peer groups**. Here children take part in making rules, which may conflict with adult norms and values.

Socialization involves considerable conflict, but in most societies there are at least some widely shared norms and values.

Evaluation

Handel has been criticized for concentrating on day-to-day interaction and making little reference to the impact of social structure.

Feminist perspectives

Feminist writers highlight the way socialization contributes to gender inequality (Textbook pp. 100-104).

Oakley (1974) argues that distinct gender roles come from culture not biology. Parents **canalize** their children by offering differing objects and activities to boys and girls.

Other sociologists point to gender stereotyping in children's books, reading schemes and the media.

Criticisms

Feminists have been criticized for over-simplifying the situation. Some children are brought up in feminist households, and children do not necessarily accept the gender stereotypes presented to them by the media.

Thorne – gender in school

Thorne (1993) argues the social construction of gender roles is an active and ongoing process, but notes many variations in the roles themselves.

She examined **gender segregation** in two US elementary schools, and found that:

- gender segregation is more likely in crowded spaces like school playgrounds, and that boys dominate the space. Public choosing of groups and teams makes gender segregation more likely.

- lack of adults accentuates gender-based choosing. Often adults can intervene to allow mixed sex games

- segregation can be reinforced by **border-work** – the making of boundaries between groups. Activities here include **cross-gender chasing** (for example, 'kiss chase') and **invasion**, where boys disrupt girls' games.

These processes reinforce both gender difference and male power. However, segregation is not total. Some girls may join in with football and boys may join in the girls' activities – though they may face teasing for doing so.

Thorne argues that schools reinforce gender divisions but it is a very complex process.

IDENTITY

AQA, OCR, WJEC **Textbook pp. 692-706**

Jenkins (1996) argues that social identity is 'our understanding of who we are and of who other people are; and, reciprocally, other people's understanding of themselves and of others'. Identity involves making comparisons between people and establishing similarities and differences between them. Those who are believed to be similar share aspects of their identity.

Woodward – formation of identities

Woodward (2000) discusses three central questions about the formation of identities, as described below.

To what extent do we shape our own identities?

Identity is partly subjective but also partly external and dependent on the judgement of others. You may choose to support a football team but it is more difficult to make a personal decision about your gender identity. You may regard yourself as a man but everybody else might see you as a woman. Thus identity is formed through a combination of **individual agency** and **structural constraints**.

How are identities formed?

Woodward draws on the work of three key writers:

- **Mead** argued that human development involves imagining the way others see us. Thus our identity is linked to the external identity others give us.

- **Goffman** saw the social world as rather like a play. Individuals put on a performance for others to convince them about who they are. Through presenting themselves in particular roles individuals develop identities.

- **Freud** believed that childhood experiences, often unconscious, were vital for the development of identities in adulthood, particularly gender and sexual identities.

Are there particular uncertainties about identity in contemporary Britain?

Woodward believes that there is evidence of greater uncertainty over identities. She suggests a number of reasons:

- Heavy manufacturing industry has declined, undermining **traditional masculine identities** based on being the family breadwinner with a job for life.

- The increased employment of married women has created uncertainty about gender roles, particularly the role of housewife.

- **Family roles** are an important source of identity. However, family life has undergone radical change and the old certainties have gone. The increase in divorce and single parenthood and new reproductive technologies are threatening old biological 'certainties'.

- **New social movements** have developed and have encouraged positive identification with new groups – for example, the women's movement, movements for gay and lesbian rights and environmental movements.

- **National identity** has become more uncertain. Britain is increasingly **multicultural** and there is an increasing emphasis on local and regional identities.

- The growth of **consumer culture** increases people's choices about identity. People can express identity through what they buy – for example, their clothes and jewellery. They can alter their bodies through cosmetic surgery or visiting the gym.

Stuart Hall – fractured identities

According to **Hall** (1992), contemporary societies are increasingly characterized by the existence of **fractured identities**. People no longer possess a single, unified concept of who they are. This fragmentation of identity has a number of sources:

- **Modernity and change** – the pace of change has increased in **late modern** societies and this makes it difficult for people to retain a unified identity.

- **New social movements** – in the past, social class provided a '**master identity**'. However, in the 1960s and 1970s people began to organize around issues other than class. New social movements developed, based around issues such as gender, ethnicity and the environment; and identity itself became a political issue. Identity politics emphasizes the importance of hearing the voices of oppressed groups such as gays and lesbians, black women, disabled people.

- **Globalization** – the ease with which people move around the world, improvements in communications, and the global marketing of styles and images, can lead to a '**cultural supermarket**' effect. People can choose from a wide range of identities, adopting the values and lifestyles of any group they choose. On the other hand, global consumerism can also lead to increased similarity, as products such as Coca-Cola can be found anywhere.

Globalization and identity

In modern societies nationality was an important source of identity. National identity was used to create a sense of solidarity among citizens of different classes, ethnic origins and so on. With globalization this is not so easy. **Hall** (1992) identifies three responses:

- In some places people have tried to reaffirm national identity as a **defensive mechanism**. They have perceived a threat to their national identity from immigration, for example.

- The defensive mechanism is characteristic of **ethnic majorities**. But **ethnic minorities** sometimes react in defensive ways as well. In response to racism and exclusion, ethnic minorities have sometimes placed a renewed emphasis on their **ethnic identities** and culture.

- A third reaction is the construction of **new identities**. A British example is the construction of a '**black**' identity, embracing British African Caribbeans and Asians. In this case identity becomes hybrid, mixing more than one existing identity into a new identity.

The first two responses to globalization have had the effect of reviving ethnicity as a source of identity, often in opposition to existing nationalism. In several parts of the world ethnic groups have demanded their own nation-states as bigger nation-states (such as the USSR and Yugoslavia) have broken up. This has led to considerable violence and even civil war. Hall argues that the idea of **ethnic purity** is largely a myth, as nearly all populations come from a variety of ethnic backgrounds.

NATIONALISM AND IDENTITY

AQA, OCR, WJEC   Textbook pp. 192-198

Cohen – nationality and identity

Robin Cohen (1994) discusses **British nationality** and identity. He argues that there is no clear dividing line between being British and not being British. For example, the Scottish and Welsh and people in former colonies may, to different degrees, identify themselves as British or distance themselves from being British.

There is also some overlap between European and American identities and being British, which means that defining who is alien – i.e. non-British – is not clear cut.

Pilkington – the global age

Pilkington (2002) argues that national identities are **socially constructed** and always subject to change. Globalization has resulted in two contradictory processes – **cultural homogenization** and **fascination with difference**. In response 'Little Englanders' adopt a culturally racist view of Britishness as white English-speaking culture, whilst others embrace multiple identities. Pilkington argues there is considerable evidence of new **hybrid identities** in British Caribbean and British Asian youth.

Hall – new ethnicities

The complexity of national identity is reflected in the emergence of **new ethnicities**.

Stuart Hall (1996) sees new ethnicities in terms of the development of new identities in black cultural politics in Britain.

These new identities stress the great variety of differences between people. People see themselves, and are seen by others, not just in terms of ethnicity but also in terms of age, religion, sexuality, class and gender.

Hall also argues that there is increasing **hybridization**, with the merging and overlapping of different identities. Globalization and migration have led to increasingly diverse populations living in the same areas, with different cultures influencing one another.

In some areas the response has been **ethnic absolutism**, based on trying to maintain ethnic purity and hostility to members of other groups – for example, **ethnic cleansing** in the former Yugoslavia. Hall sees ethnic absolutism and nationalism as major threats in a globalizing world.

Modood – new ethnic identities

Some evidence of changing ethnic identities in Britain is provided by survey research carried out by **Modood et al** (1997). This found that by the mid-1990s most British Caribbeans and South Asians thought of themselves *both* as British and as members of ethnic minorities.

Older Caribbeans and South Asians born outside the UK identified more with their country of origin than younger generations born in Britain.

There were considerable variations in people's sense of identity in all ethnic groups.

Back – urban ethnicities

Research by **Les Back** (1996) on two London council estates found both racism and the development of **new ethnicities**. On one estate a number of white youths adopted elements of black youth culture and felt they had as much in common with some black people as with white people.

Some young black people had a strong sense of British citizenship.

Bauman – From Pilgrim to Tourist

Bauman (1996) argues identity no longer has a stable base; it is merely the result of ongoing choices. In the modern world people were pilgrims heading for known goals, but in the postmodern world change is so rapid that this is no longer possible. So people adopt lifestyle choices, such as:

- the **stroller** – wanders aimlessly through the shopping mall, sampling products at will, constructing fleeting identities through the products they consume.
- the **vagabond** – wanders from place to place and identity to identity, never settling down. They are unpredictable, always strangers, and have no settled place in the world.
- the **tourist** – travels from place to place always looking for new experiences. The equivalent postmodern life strategy involves trying out new identities, always looking for something new to sample.
- the **player** – treats life as a game which they play to win. Once the game is over they play another. In postmodern societies people play the game of having one identity but will change identity when they think the game is over.

There are no lasting identities so the main aim of the postmodern citizen is to enjoy life.

Evaluation

Hall and Bauman both agree there has been movement away from stable identities based on social factors such as class. Other sociologists disagree.

Marshall et al (1988) and **McDonough** (1997) argue that class remains an important part of identity.

Radical feminists stress that gender issues continue to impact on women's lives.

Jenkins (1996) believes identity remains rooted in social experiences.

Jenkins – identity as a social product

Jenkins (1996) uses **interactionist** concepts to argue that identity is both social and individual, a mixture of **collectively shared** and **personal elements**. During socialization children take on parts of their identity which remain relatively stable, and in trying to manage the impressions they make on others they construct their identities (see Textbook pp. 881-882). Thus identity is not fluid in the way **Bauman** describes, it is closely linked to social position. Interactions lead to the construction of **boundaries** between different groups which carry different identities – for example, male and female. When some groups have more power than others to claim identities, struggles take place.

Bradley – levels of identity

Bradley (1997) attempts to pull together classical and postmodern sociological approaches to understand the relationship between identity and inequality. She describes identity as working at three levels:

- **Passive identities** – these are identities which have the potential to become important but largely lie dormant. Bradley sees class identity in this way. Most British people accept that class inequalities exist but do not see themselves as a member of a class most of the time. However, circumstances can change.
- **Active identities** – these are identities which individuals are conscious of and which provide a basis for their actions.
- **Politicized identities** – these are formed through campaigns highlighting the importance of a particular identity and using it as a basis for organizing collective action. For example, feminists succeeded in turning gender into a politicized identity in the 1970s and 1980s.

Bradley accepts the point made by postmodernists that there is a good deal of choice over identity, and that identities are becoming more fragmented. However, she sees identities as rooted in membership of social groups.

Bradley examines four aspects of inequality: class, gender, race/ethnicity and age, although she does recognize other important social divisions such as those relating to sexuality and disability.

Class and identity

Class is no longer the strongest source of identity in contemporary Britain. Bradley sees it as a **passive** form of identity, partly because it is less visible in the everyday world than age, race/ethnicity and gender. However, she notes that inequality is increasing and that this creates the potential for class to be an increasingly important source of identity.

Gender and identity

Bradley notes the move away from theories such as radical feminism, which saw women as a single group, towards theories which see women (and men) as being **fragmented** into different groups. She believes that both types of theory are important, and that the common experience of **sexism** provides a basis for a shared identity for women.

However, not all women experience disadvantage to the same extent or in the same ways. **Black feminists**, for example, have suggested that the family is experienced differently by white and black women.

For Bradley, gender is a very important source of identity in contemporary Britain. It is also an **active**, **politicized identity** for women as a result of feminism.

Race/ethnicity and identity

Like gender, race/ethnicity has become a more important source of identity in Britain than class, and is more likely to produce **active** and **politicized identities**. Sometimes this is due to the visibility of skin colour but this is not always the case. The violence in the former Yugoslavia occurred between white ethnic groups, for example.

The importance of race/ethnicity depends on how it is used politically to mobilize groups and provide them with a sense of belonging. **British Muslim identity** has assumed more importance than other potential identities as a result of the revival of Islam as a world religion.

For dominant ethnic groups, ethnic identity is rather less politicized but can become more politicized in certain situations. In Britain, Scottish and Welsh ethnic identities are more active and politicized than English identity, but an English identity can become important in some contexts (such as sporting events).

Age and identity

Age is an important source of identity for individuals but it is not usually a politicized identity. This is because people move through different age groups and know they will not stay in one group for ever. Also, the most disadvantaged groups are the young and the old, and they have little in common.

Some aspects of **youth culture** express a sense of conflict with adults and have helped age to become a more active identity. There are also some examples of age becoming a politicized identity, such as the coalition of youth groups that opposed the **Criminal Justice Bill** in the 1990s, and the activities of the **Grey Panthers** in America who have campaigned for the rights of the elderly.

Conclusion

Bradley concludes that stratification systems and identities are becoming both polarized and fragmented:

- **Polarization** – there are increasing differences between the rich and poor and young and old. There is also some polarization between ethnic groups, particularly with the re-emergence of nationalist and fascist organizations.
- **Fragmentation** – there is fragmentation and division in each of the categories above. As a result, people in contemporary societies tend to have fractured identities. They lack an identity that overrides all others.

Identity, leisure and consumerism

Postmodern theory suggests that people construct their identity from leisure and consumption rather than class, gender and ethnicity.

Rojek (1995) argues that leisure in the modern world is associated with freedom from people's main social roles and identity. In the postmodern world the boundaries between leisure and other areas of social life are broken down and leisure becomes an end in itself, a way of constructing identity.

Scraton et al (1995) describe how in modern society leisure for the masses was a result of organizing work within specific hours. The more diverse structure of postmodern work has led to changes in leisure culture:

- Modern leisure was **disciplined**; postmodern leisure is **self-indulgent**.
- Modern leisure was a search for **self-improvement** and relaxation; postmodern leisure is the expression of a **particular lifestyle**.
- Modern leisure was concerned with **bodily health**; postmodern leisure is concerned with lifestyle, appearance and **image**.

Leisure activities may be restricted by income, gender and ethnicity.

Rojek and Scraton believe leisure is becoming increasingly important in shaping identity.

CONSUMERISM AND IDENTITY

AQA, WJEC   Textbook pp. 706-709

As consumers, people can purchase a wide range of products which they can use to construct their identities.

Katz (2005) notes how mobile phones have become fashion statements associated with **aspirations** and **identity**. They are personalized by accessories and ring tones.

For **Ling** (2000), mobile phones are increasingly part of teenage fashion. When most teenagers did not own mobile phones those using them in public were thought to be pompous and vulgar. Today they are expressions of group identity – the age, price and style is important and phones must be changed regularly to remain fashionable. Some groups remain deliberately anti-fashion, but this too is a response to fashion.

Craik (1994) argues that clothing, which is predominantly designed by men, is an important part of gender identity. Fashion expresses **male ideals of femininity** and body shape and there is a conflict between couture and practical clothing. Women diet and struggle in the search for a fashionable body shape. Thus fashion reproduces gender inequality. Some women challenge the fashion industry and deliberately wear 'non-feminine' clothing.

Craik makes a strong case for the influence of **inequality** on identity.

Criticisms of Craik

McRobbie (1994) argues that **class** has as much influence as gender in the development of fashion. Clothing may be used in oppositional styles, but these eventually become absorbed into designer clothing. In McRobbie's opinion, Craik underestimates the complexity of the relationship between identity, consumers, fashion and gender.

DEVELOP YOUR ANALYTICAL AND EVALUATION SKILLS

Essay plans

For each of the following questions write your own essay plan before comparing it with the suggestions given here. For the final question you can write a full answer and compare it with the provided model answer.

Culture is shared by members of a society. Discuss.

This view is central to functionalist approaches. Functionalists believe that society is not possible without some sort of consensus over values. Marxists see this consensus as an illusion, providing a smokescreen for continuing class inequality and exploitation. Postmodernists emphasize the diversity of cultures and identities in contemporary Britain.

For	Against
● Durkheim (p. 93)	● Marx (p. 94)
● Parsons (p. 98)	● Neo-Marxist subcultural approaches (p. 94)
	● Postmodern approaches (p. 97)

Culture has been defined in a number of ways (see p. 92), and a brief discussion of these differences will be useful. Examples of cultural diversity in Britain (see chapter 4, p. 79) will also assist evaluation.

Mass culture has a dangerous effect on society. Discuss.

A definition of mass culture can be found on p. 95. Note its similarity to the term 'popular culture'. Negative views, such as those of Macdonald, were particularly popular during the 1950s when there was considerable concern about the impact of the mass media on society. Postmodernists tend to celebrate popular culture and deny any distinction between high and popular culture.

For	Against
● Macdonald (p. 95)	● Strinati (p. 96)
	● Postmodernism (p. 93)

Be careful to discuss the definition of 'mass culture'. Make sure you identify the views of writers such as Macdonald as dating from some time ago, although bear in mind that there is still concern today about popular culture 'dumbing down' British culture.

Do sociologists agree that a person's identity is shaped by their social position?

In the past sociologists have thought of identity as based on social structures such as social class. However, postmodernists believe identity is derived from leisure and consumption (p. 97). Hall and Bradley speak of 'fractured identities'.

For	Against
● Jenkins (p. 101)	● Rojek (p. 102)
● Bradley (p. 101)	● Scraton (p. 102)
● Craik (p. 102)	

Top Tip →

The argument here is about the degree to which consumption has replaced social position as a source of identity. Be clear about all the factors that shape identity and evaluate each theory carefully.

Postmodernism provides a good explanation of popular culture. Discuss.

Background →

Postmodernism describes a world with no structure and endless choice. Image is all important, style is emphasized over substance. There is no truth or progress. Link these ideas to the characteristics of popular culture.

For	For and against
● Crook (p. 97)	● Strinati (p. 97)

Top Tip →

Think about the differentiation of popular culture from other forms of culture in modern societies. Have all those distinctions disappeared? Consider whether postmodern culture has really arrived.

Assess the view that socialization is an ideological conditioning device which leads children to accept exploitation.

Background →

Socialization is the process of learning culture. Marxists see socialization as a process of ideological conditioning, teaching children to accept inequality and exploitation. Functionalists stress its importance in pattern maintenance; children must learn what is expected of them if society is to continue. Interactionists see children as active participants in the process.

For	Against
● Marxists (p. 94)	● Functionalists (p. 98)
● Neo-Marxists (p. 94)	● Parsons (p. 98)
● Willis (p. 98)	● Interactionists (p. 98)
● Gramsci (p. 98)	● Handel (p. 98)

Top Tip →

Look for areas where Marxists and functionalists agree – both are structural theories. Some of these theories are quite old, so consider Neo-Marxists also.

Model answer

Assess the view that socialization is an ideological conditioning device which leads children to accept exploitation.

Socialization is the process through which children learn the language, skills and information required for them to survive in adult society. A newborn baby has very few survival skills and communicates through crying. During childhood they mature and learn a wide range of skills so they can take part in society. This essay will consider the Marxist view stated in the question, together with opposing views.

Marxism is a structural theory which argues that children of the subordinate class are socialized during childhood to accept their inferior place in society. Their parents are 'wage slaves' with little choice about their work and no power over the payment they receive. Capitalism needs workers who have been trained to accept long hours of work, to accept the authority of their bosses, and to accept the level of wages they are paid. Marxists believe the family is a key part of this process. The mother bears the children and both parents socialize them into respecting parental authority and being obedient. Girls learn to accept the role of motherhood and boys learn to be breadwinners. All this ensures that girls will grow up to produce workers at no cost to the capitalist system and boys will become passive and obedient.

Marxists believe the process continues at school. Through the 'hidden curriculum' children learn to accept the authority of teachers, to work hard, to be polite, smartly dressed and punctual. They also learn to be motivated by external rewards. This experience prepares them for the workplace where they will become a placid docile workforce, exploited by capitalism. For Marxists, society's values are the values of capitalism, which children are ideologically conditioned to accept.

Neo-Marxists see the process of socialization as less passive, with conflicts between parents and children, and between school pupils and teachers. Willis's 'lads' were neither passive nor docile. Gramsci argues that children are taught during socialization to accept society as legitimate, but in their daily lives they recognize the unfairness of the capitalist system and their own exploitation within it.

Other sociologists would argue that socialization is important both for society and for the children concerned. Functionalists such as Parsons believe that by understanding and internalizing society's norms and values children learn their place, they learn how to behave, and they learn to strive and to achieve. This is both in the children's interests and in the interests of society.

Interactionists such as Handel believe that children learn three capacities during socialization. They learn: to communicate; to understand themselves as separate from other people; to moderate their behaviour and understand how other people feel. These capacities ensure children develop a sense of self and an awareness of the people around them. Handel argues the process is organized by parents and teachers and later by peer groups. Differences in parental background mean children do not share an identical experience nor do they share identical norms and values. Thus they become individuals, not a mass of exploited people.

Sociologists agree that children learn about society during their childhood from their parents, their school and their peers. The disagreement between structural theorists and interactionists is about whether they are all learning the same thing. The disagreement between Marxists and functionalists is about whether children are learning to accept exploitation or whether they are learning agreed norms and values.

RESOURCES

Culture, socialization and identity

Perspective	Culture	Socialization	Identity
Functionalism	Society needs a shared culture to run effectively. The collective conscience reflects society's values	Children are socialized into society's shared norms and values	Identity is based on social position, knowing your place, understanding your duty to society
Marxism	Culture is merely ruling-class ideology, a way of subduing the masses	Children are brainwashed into conformity. They learn to accept exploitation	Identity is based on social class
Neo-Marxism	Culture is not just a reflection of social class. Working-class culture is based on collective action	Socialization can be full of conflict. It involves the transfer of cultural capital from one generation to the next	Identity may be broadly based on economic factors, but other factors such as media are also important
Interactionism	Culture is based on shared interactions and is always subject to change	Children interact with the adults around them and are active partners in socialization	Identity is a mixture of collectively shared and personal elements
Postmodernism	Culture has fragmented into a 'fantastic variety' of forms based on individual choice. The media dominate society	Individualization has led to extensive choice in family practices	Identity has no stable base. It is the result of ongoing choices

Writers and their work

Writer	Perspective	Concept	Study
Durkheim	Functionalist	Collective conscience	*Primitive Classification*
Marx	Marxist	False class consciousness	*Das Kapital* (Capital)
Gans	Influenced by Neo-Marxism	Taste cultures	Popular culture and high culture
Strinati	Critic of cultural theories	Mass culture threatens the hierarchy of taste by allowing everybody choice	Introduction to theories of popular culture
Storey	Globalization theorist	Hybridization	Global culture and popular culture
Saussure	Structuralist	Semiology	Study of signs and linguistics
Crook	Postmodernist	Post-culture	Lifestyle choice replaces social difference
Parsons	Functionalist	Pattern maintenance	Functional pre-requisites – things societies need to survive
Willis	Neo-Marxist	Counterculture	*Learning to Labour*
Bourdieu	Neo-Marxist	Cultural capital	Structures, habitus and practices
Handel	Interactionist	Empathy, communication and self-awareness	Childhood socialization
Oakley	Feminist	Canalizing through toys and books	*Housewife; Women Confined; Gender on Planet Earth*
Thorne	Feminist	Gender segregation	Gender in school
Woodward	Sociologist studying the sources of identity	Identity comes from individual agency and structural constraints	*Questioning Identity*
Hall	Marxist	Fragmented identities	*Questions of Cultural Identity*
Bauman	Postmodernist	Lifestyle choices	*From Pilgrim to Tourist*
Jenkins	Interactionist	Identity is mix of collectively shared and personal elements	Social identity
Bradley	Combination of classical and postmodern approaches	Passive identities	Fractured identities
Scraton	Evaluation of postmodern theories of leisure	Self-indulgent leisure	Leisure, postmodernity and identity
Craik	Feminist	Male concepts of femininity	Study of women's fashion

Chapter 6

WEALTH, WELFARE & POVERTY

SPECIFICATION COVERAGE

Specification	Details
AQA AS Unit 1, SCLY1: Wealth, Welfare and Poverty	The essential notes for this chapter are an exact match for AQA AS Unit 1

WEALTH AND INCOME

AQA   Textbook pp. 19-20

There are a number of sources of inequality in society, and inequalities in **wealth** and **income** are amongst the most important. These inequalities can lead to **stratification systems**, where people are divided into distinct groups in society.

Social class systems are an example of a stratification system – for example, the division between the upper class, middle class and working class.

Inequalities in wealth and income affect people's **life chances** – that is, their chances of obtaining those things defined as desirable by society and of avoiding those things defined as undesirable.

Inequalities in wealth and income largely determine whether an individual suffers **poverty** or not, and affect their chances of succeeding in the **education** system.

INCOME

AQA   Textbook pp. 35-38

Measurement and distribution of income

Income can be defined as the money being received by a person or institution. Government statistics for 2003-4 have estimated the proportion of personal income from different sources (*Social Trends*, 2005):

- 74% came from wages and salaries
- 10% from self-employment
- 7% from state benefits

- 3% from pensions
- 2% from investments
- 1% from tax credits

The importance of different sources of income varies by **social group**. For example, 71% of the income of the long-term unemployed comes from benefits.

Official statistics measure income in a variety of ways:

- **Original income** refers to all income apart from state benefits.
- **Gross income** includes state benefits.
- **Disposable income** deducts tax and national insurance.
- **Final income** includes the value of benefits such as healthcare, which are not given in cash.

However income is defined there are problems in measuring it. Some individuals fail to declare income – for example, by working for cash in the **black economy** and not declaring it to the Inland Revenue. Rich people may be able change income into **capital** (for example, using share options) in order to avoid income tax. They may also transfer income overseas to low tax areas to avoid paying tax. Overall, this probably leads to the income of the rich being significantly underestimated.

The changing distribution of income

A **Royal Commission** in 1979 found that income became more equally distributed between 1949 and 1979. This was partly through the use of **progressive taxes**, such as income tax, which take a bigger proportion of the earnings of high earners than low earners. The expansion of the **welfare state** also led to some money being redistributed to lower earners.

Between 1979 and 1997, during the years of **Conservative** government, income distribution became more **unequal**. Income tax was cut and **indirect taxes** such as VAT were raised. Lower income groups tend to pay a higher proportion of their income in indirect tax than higher income groups. Rising **unemployment** also led to growing income inequality.

Webb (1997) found that in 1993 the poorest 10% of the population received just 2.9% of national income whilst the 10% with the highest income received 26.2%.

The **Institute for Fiscal Studies (IFS)** (2006) found that income inequality carried on rising for several years after **New Labour** came to power in 1997. This was partly because the incomes of the richest rose very rapidly during the economic boom: the highest-paid company directors can earn several million pounds per year, and very high salaries and bonuses in the City of London added to the inequality.

However, the IFS found that after 2001 income inequality started falling due to factors such as falling unemployment, the use of **tax credits** to boost the pay of low earners, the **minimum wage**, and increased spending on welfare.

Government figures show that the poorest 20% of the population receives less than half the average final income, while the richest 20% receives nearly twice the average. Nevertheless, taxes and benefits do equalize and redistribute income to some extent.

WEALTH

AQA   Textbook p. 19

The definition of wealth

Wealth refers to material possessions defined as valuable in particular societies. It can include:

- land;
- livestock;
- bank or building society deposits;
- cash;
- buildings;
- shares or bonds;
- valuable possessions such as paintings, antiques or jewellery.

Marxists (Textbook pp. 39-41) believe that a particular form of wealth – the **means of production** – is crucial in determining the distribution of power in society and creating class differences.

Wealth is also important in **Weberian** theories, though these see income as important as well.

Wealth can be defined in different ways. Official statistics distinguish between **marketable** and **non-marketable** wealth:

- **Marketable wealth** consists of assets that can be sold.
- **Non-marketable wealth** includes assets such as non-transferable pensions.

Official figures fail to distinguish between wealth used to finance **production** and wealth used for **consumption** (for example, the ownership of a valuable home).

Marxists see wealth used for production as much more important in shaping society than wealth used for consumption.

Wealth used for consumption does, however, affect **life chances** and gives some indication of **lifestyle**.

Measuring wealth

The Government does not collect information on wealth on a regular basis. Wealth is only taxed when people die and the value of estates is assessed to calculate **inheritance tax.**

These figures can give a distorted view of the distribution of wealth because:

- individuals may transfer some of their wealth before they die to avoid tax;
- they only measure the distribution of wealth amongst those who have died, and the distribution amongst the living (who are less likely to be elderly) may be quite different;
- beneficiaries of estates may hide some of the wealth to avoid tax.

Figures on wealth distribution are sometimes produced using **survey research**, but this type of data also has problems, because:

- some people refuse to take part in surveys and this distorts the findings;
- participants may lie, and the rich in particular may underestimate, or understate, their wealth.

Trends in wealth distribution

Westergaard & Resler (1976) found that inequalities of wealth reduced between 1911 and 1960, but in 1960 the richest 10% of the UK population still owned 83% of the wealth.

Government statistics suggest that reductions in inequalities in wealth distribution continued until the early 1990s, after which the distribution became increasingly unequal (*Social Trends*, 2002 and 2006).

In 2002 Government estimates suggested that the wealthiest 1% of the British population owned 23% of **marketable wealth** and the richest 10% owned 75% of marketable wealth.

Westergaard & Resler attribute the trend towards greater equality for most of the twentieth century to transfers within wealthier groups to relatives rather than real redistribution from the rich to the poor. However, the development of the **welfare state**, **progressive taxation** and the growth of **home ownership** all played a part.

More recently the growth in inequality may be caused by:

- growth in house prices;
- rises in the value of shares and bonds;
- the growth of a new group of the super-wealthy (**Lansley**, 2006) as a result of cuts in taxation, high city bonuses and big profits made by successful companies in the global economy.

Although statistics are not yet available, the **credit crunch** in 2008 and resulting falls in share values, company profits, house prices and city bonuses may have had a bigger impact on the wealthy than on the rest of the population, resulting in some reduction in inequality.

Theories of distribution of income and wealth

A number of general sociological theories explain the unequal distribution of income and wealth.

Davis & Moore – role allocation and performance

Davis & Moore (1967, first published 1945) (Textbook pp. 22-23) hold that the unequal distribution of income and wealth is justified because it is beneficial to society. They argue that all societies share certain **functional prerequisites**. One of these is **role allocation**: ensuring that roles are filled and performed effectively and conscientiously by properly trained people.

Some jobs are more **functionally important** and some people have more **ability** than others. To match the most able to the most important jobs, and to ensure that tedious, unpleasant or dangerous jobs are filled, a rewards system is needed. This inevitably means that some will get higher rewards than others.

The better-rewarded will form a **higher stratum**. This process is **inevitable**, **universal** (found in all societies) and **beneficial** because it helps society to function better.

Criticisms of Davis & Moore

Tumin (1967) argues that:

- many low-paid and even unskilled jobs are just as vital as higher-paid or more skilled jobs;
- there is a greater pool of talent than Davis & Moore assume;
- training is a pleasant experience and does not require extra rewards to persuade people to undertake it;
- **stratification systems** can demotivate those at the bottom;
- stratification systems do not provide equality of opportunity and tend to prevent those from lower strata achieving their potential;
- stratification systems encourage 'hostility, suspicion and distrust';
- unequal rewards and incomes are not inevitable and can do more harm than good.

Marxist perspective

Karl Marx (1978, 1974) (Textbook pp. 26-29) sees the distribution of one type of wealth – the means of production – as the key to understanding inequalities in society. Marx argues as follows:

- All stratified societies have two major classes: a **ruling class** and a **subject class**.
- The ruling class owns the **means of production** (land, capital, machinery etc.), and the subject class does not.
- The ruling class **exploits** the subject class.
- The ruling class uses the **superstructure** (for example, the legal and political systems) to **legitimate** (justify) its position and prevent protests by the subject class.

- In capitalist societies the main classes are the **bourgeoisie** (the capitalist class that owns the main means of production – capital) and the **proletariat** (the working class that has to sell its labour to survive).
- The bourgeoisie exploits the working class through the system of **wage labour**. Capitalists pay wages to workers, but make a profit (**surplus value**) because they pay workers less than the value of what they produce.
- The working class will tend to get poorer and the ruling class richer, and inequality will grow. **Capitalism** is the newest type of class society but it will also be the last. Eventually it will be replaced by a **communist society** in which the means of production (land, capital, factories, machinery etc.) will be **communally owned** and there will be little inequality of income or wealth.

Criticisms

The living standards of the working class in many capitalist countries have improved rather than getting worse.

Communism in countries such as the Soviet Union still produced considerable inequality, though less than in capitalist countries.

Marx does not explain the big differences in the income of different groups of workers – for example, doctors and unskilled labourers.

Weberian perspective

Max Weber (1864-1920) (Textbook pp. 29-31) accepted some of Marx's ideas but rejected others. He tried to explain why some groups of workers got paid more than others. Weber argued that classes develop from people's market situation (their situation in relation to buying and selling things, including their labour power) in market economies.

Weber differs from Marx in a number of ways:

- Like Marx he saw a basic division between those who have considerable property (and can live off the proceeds) and those who do not – the **propertyless** – who have to sell their labour. However, there are also significant differences within the two groups as well as between them.
- Within the property-less group there are some who can sell their labour for a higher price (those with scarce but sought-after skills such as professionals and managers). They have an advantaged **market situation** compared to other groups of workers. Unlike Marx, Weber believed that different occupational groupings could form **classes**.
- Weber saw no evidence of a **polarization** of classes. Instead he thought that the **middle class** of white-collar workers in **bureaucracies** would expand.
- Weber did not believe that a **revolution** led by the proletariat was likely.
- He thought that some, but not all, **power** came from wealth.

He argued that class was not the only basis for group formation nor the only source of inequality. **Status groups** (groups of people who enjoy similar levels of status or respect in society) could also be formed. Status groups might be based on ethnicity, age, nationality, gender etc., and tended to share similar lifestyles. Class and status could be closely linked (for example, ethnic minorities might be excluded from highly-paid jobs in a society), but this was not always the case. Status groups often cut across class divisions (for example, members of the gay community in today's society).

POVERTY

AQA Textbook pp. 213-226

Definition and measurement

Since studies of poverty began, researchers have been trying to establish a fixed standard against which to measure it. There are three main areas of controversy:

- absolute and relative poverty;
- material and multiple deprivation and social exclusion;
- inequality and poverty.

Absolute and relative poverty

Some writers argue that a common minimum standard of subsistence can be applied to all societies. Individuals without the resources to maintain a healthy life can be said to be in poverty.

Supporters of the concept of **relative poverty** dismiss this idea. They believe that definitions of poverty must relate to the standards of a particular society at a particular time. The poverty line will vary according to the wealth of a society.

Multiple deprivation and social exclusion

Some sociologists assume that poverty consists simply of a lack of material resources, a shortage of the money required to maintain an acceptable standard of living.

Others argue that poverty involves more than material deprivation. They see poverty as a form of multiple deprivation, involving additional factors such as inadequate educational opportunities, unpleasant working conditions and powerlessness. Today many writers prefer to use the term **social exclusion** to describe a situation where **multiple deprivation** prevents individuals from participating in social activities such as paid employment.

Inequality and poverty

From one point of view, any society in which there is inequality is bound to have poverty. Those at the bottom will always be 'poor' and poverty could only be eliminated by abolishing all inequality.

Most sociologists accept that some reduction in **inequality** is needed in order to abolish poverty but believe that it is possible to establish a **poverty line** – a minimum standard below which it is not possible to maintain an acceptable standard of living. Thus it would be possible to have a society with some inequality but where poverty no longer existed.

Absolute poverty

The concept of absolute poverty involves a judgement of **basic human needs**. Most measures of absolute poverty are concerned with establishing the quality and amount of **food**, **clothing** and **shelter** deemed necessary for a healthy life.

Absolute poverty is also known as **subsistence poverty**, since it is based on assessments of minimum subsistence requirements. This definition limits poverty to material deprivation.

The **United Nations** (1995) defines absolute poverty as 'severe deprivation of basic human needs, including food, safe drinking water, sanitation facilities, health, shelter education and information'.

Absolute poverty is usually **operationalized** (put into a form which can be measured) by pricing the basic necessities of life and defining as poor those whose income falls below this line.

Criticisms of 'absolute poverty'

The concept of absolute poverty has been widely criticized. It is based on the assumption that there are basic minimum needs for all people in all societies. The problem is that needs vary both within and between societies:

- **Within a society** – the nutritional needs of a bank clerk sitting at a desk all day are very different from those of a labourer working on a building site.
- **Between societies** – the Bushmen of the Kalahari desert, for example, have very different nutritional needs from those of office workers in London.

The concept of absolute poverty is even more difficult to defend when it includes needs other than food, shelter and water. These needs vary from time to time and place to place, so that any attempt to establish a fixed standard is bound to fail. The level of healthcare, life expectancy, education or information that is regarded as an absolute minimum varies by time and place.

Budget standards and poverty

The **budget standards** approach to measuring poverty calculates the cost of those purchases that are considered necessary to raise an individual or family out of poverty.

Seebohm Rowntree (1901, 1941, 1951) conducted three studies of poverty in York using this approach. **Rowntree** drew a poverty line in terms of a **minimum weekly sum** of money needed to live a healthy life. In the later studies he included extra items which were not strictly necessary for survival, such as newspapers and presents. He found that the percentage of the population in poverty dropped rapidly between 1899 and 1950.

Rowntree believed that increased welfare benefits would eventually eliminate poverty.

Criticisms of Rowntree

Rowntree's selection of necessities was based on **expert views** and ignored the customs of ordinary people.

Rowntree's view that poverty was declining was challenged by later writers who adopted a **relative definition** of poverty.

Budget standards in practice

The work of the **Family Budget Unit** (FBU) represents one attempt to develop the budget standards approach. On the basis of information provided by experts and consumer groups the FBU worked out the cost of a 'low-cost but acceptable' (LCA) standard of living and a 'modest but adequate' (MDA) standard.

Howard et al (2001) compared the cost of these budgets with Income Support levels. Although the situation had improved since 1998, in 2001 a family on Income Support with two children under 11 were still only receiving 93% of the LCA standard.

Spicker (1993) points out that people's **quality of life** is not solely determined by how they spend money. For example, living standards can be improved by the unpaid labour of family members. However, Spicker does support the collection of data on what people actually spend, rather than what experts say they should spend.

Townsend – poverty as relative deprivation

Peter Townsend (1979, 1993, 1997) has carried out a number of studies on poverty and has played a major part in highlighting the continuing existence of poverty. He has also been a leading supporter of defining poverty in terms of **relative deprivation**.

Townsend believes that society determines people's needs – for example, tea is not essential for survival, but in British culture people are expected to be able to offer visitors a cup of tea.

Townsend (1979) argues that relative deprivation needs to be thought of in terms of the **resources** available to individuals and households, and the way in which these resources affect **participation** in the community. Poverty involves an **inability to participate** in social activities that are seen as normal, such as visiting friends or relatives, having birthday parties for children and going on holiday.

Townsend used his definition of poverty to measure the extent of poverty in Britain. He used a **deprivation index** that included 12 items he believed to be relevant for the whole population, and he calculated the percentage of the population deprived of these items. The items included:

- not having had a week's holiday in the previous year;
- children not having had a friend over to play in the previous month;
- not having a refrigerator;
- having gone through one or more days in the past fortnight without a cooked meal;
- not usually having a Sunday joint.

On the basis of these calculations Townsend found that 22.9% of the population (12.46 million people) were living in poverty in 1968-9.

Criticisms of Townsend

Piachaud (1981, 1987) claims that the index on which Townsend's statistics are based is inadequate. Going without a Sunday joint or eating salads may reflect cultural preferences rather than deprivation.

Townsend claims that he has identified a '**poverty line**' – deprivation increases rapidly when income drops below a particular level. Piachaud rejects this view, arguing that this line is arbitrary.

Piachaud argues that the implications of Townsend's definition of poverty are that poverty will remain so long as people behave in different ways – choosing to be vegetarian or not to go on holiday, for example.

Mack & Lansley – poor Britain

Joanna Mack and **Stewart Lansley** (1985) took note of many of the criticisms of Townsend's work in their study of poverty in Britain. Their deprivation index included a question asking respondents whether they lacked a particular item through **choice** or **necessity**.

They selected the items in their **deprivation index** on the basis of a social survey in which they asked respondents what they considered to be necessities in modern Britain. Where 50% or more saw it as a necessity it was included in the index.

Mack & Lansley found poverty to be widespread, although on a lesser scale than Townsend. However, in a follow-up study (1992), they found that the numbers in poverty had risen significantly. Mack & Lansley argue that this increase was due to changes in the **benefits system**.

David Gordon – poverty and social exclusion

Gordon et al (2000) adopted a similar approach to Mack & Lansley. They considered:

- whether people lacked a broad range of items because of low income;
- the extent to which people were excluded from essential social activities.

They found that the percentage of households experiencing poverty had increased from 14% in 1983 to 24% in 1999. This was despite a big increase in living standards over this period. Gordon et al provide two main explanations:

- Despite the rise in average income, the income of the poorest households actually decreased over the period, after allowing for inflation and housing costs. The incomes of the rich, however, grew rapidly, creating growing income inequality and a rise in relative poverty.
- The public's **perceptions of necessities** had changed. In 1999 possession of a telephone and 'friends or family round for a meal' were both considered 'necessities' by over 50% of the sample for the first time.

Criticisms

The deprivation index was constructed by the public but the list they chose from reflected the researchers' values rather than a general **consensus**.

The researchers defined poverty as the lack of three or more items from their list in the case of Mack & Lansley, two in the case of Gordon *et al.* A different definition would have produced very different results.

Walker (1987) points out that Mack & Lansley's method does not take into account the **quality** of items, only whether or not they are owned.

Using a 50% cut-off point to decide whether something is considered a necessity is **arbitrary**.

OFFICIAL STATISTICS ON POVERTY

AQA   **Textbook pp. 223-226**

British governments have used different measures of poverty, and for a time had no official poverty line. Before 1995 figures on low income families were sometimes taken as a measure of poverty.

Low income families

Between 1972 and 1985 the Government published figures on **low income families**: those living at or just above the main **means-tested state benefit** level.

However, critics felt that the numbers in poverty depended on the political decisions of the government of the day: increasing benefits would actually create more poverty! By this measure, poverty rose from 8% of the population in 1979 to 15% in 1993.

Households below average income

In 1988 these figures replaced those for **low income families**. Official statistics measure the number of households receiving **60% of average income** before and after housing costs. Figures are adjusted to take into account the number of children and household size. This is now the official poverty line in Britain and is based technically on the **median** income (the income in the middle of the income distribution) rather than the average. In 2004/5, a couple with children required a weekly income of £268 to avoid poverty and a single person required £100.

Criticisms of official poverty line

Giles & Webb (1993) argue that the figures simply measure income distribution rather than poverty.

There is a lack of agreement about whether figures before or after **housing costs** should be used.

The 60% of median income cut-off point for defining poverty is **arbitrary** – why not 50% or 70%?

Despite these criticisms, the official poverty line draws on the most comprehensive official figures available and allows comparisons between countries and over time.

Trends in households below average income

According to the **Child Poverty Action Group** (CPAG, 2006) there has been a significant increase in poverty since 1979. Poverty increased from 9% of the population in 1979 to around 23% in 1999/2000 and then fell back a little to 20% in 2005/2006. The overall increase is partly explained by increases in income inequality over this period.

One of the **Labour Government**'s stated aims is to reduce and eventually eradicate child poverty. In its first five years in office poverty fell quite quickly. Despite this the Labour governments have failed to reduce poverty as quickly as their own targets demand.

Using the government's definition of poverty, the British poverty rate was about 3% above the **European average** in 2000 (EU, 2005).

Using a **United Nations** measure of poverty – based upon income, unemployment, mortality and literacy – the UK had the 15th lowest rate of poverty in the world, with the lowest rates being found in Sweden, Norway and the Netherlands (UN, 2005).

SOCIAL EXCLUSION

AQA   **Textbook, pp. 226-232**

In recent years some commentators have tried to broaden the issues around deprivation by using the term social exclusion rather than poverty. The Labour Government set up a Social Exclusion Unit in 1997. This aimed to encourage social inclusion by tackling social problems such as truancy and unemployment.

Defining social exclusion

There is no agreed definition of social exclusion. **Burchardt** *et al* (2002) describe it as a 'contested term'.

Byrne (1999) differentiates between the terms '**social exclusion**' and '**underclass**'. He argues that social exclusion draws attention to the relationship between those who are excluded and those who are doing the excluding. The socially excluded cannot be seen as an underclass.

Poverty refers to a lack of **material resources**, whereas all definitions of **social exclusion** include a broader range of ways in which people may be **disadvantaged** or unable to participate in society. The socially excluded may include the unemployed, those who do not register to vote and isolated elderly individuals.

Views on social exclusion

The shift from the discussion of poverty to social exclusion has been seen as both a **regressive** and a **progressive** step.

Nolan & Whelan (1996) see it as a **regressive** step, a way of avoiding the issue of poverty and therefore avoiding any possibility of tackling income inequality.

Lawson (1995) sees it as a **progressive** step: tackling the problems of social exclusion would involve measures to deal with racism, to encourage a stronger sense of community and to combat sex discrimination.

Byrne (1999) supports what he calls '**strong**' definitions of social exclusion. These emphasize the importance of both material inequalities and inequalities of power. Tackling social exclusion would therefore require redistribution of income and radical changes in the structure of society. '**Weak**' definitions do not require any great increase in equality to tackle social exclusion.

The different definitions of social exclusion tend to reflect the political preferences of those who produce the definitions.

Official statistics on social exclusion

The **Department for Work and Pensions (DWP)** produces an annual report (*Opportunity for all*) to monitor progress on tackling poverty and social exclusion. In 2002 the fourth annual report identified the following factors which reinforce social exclusion:

- lack of **resources**;
- lack of opportunities to **work**;
- lack of opportunities to **learn**;
- experience of **health inequalities**;
- lack of decent **housing**;
- disruption of **family life**;
- living in a disadvantaged **neighbourhood**.

The report uses 52 indicators to monitor social exclusion. Compared with 1996, the 2002 report found a worsening trend in only one indicator (the level of suicide and 'undetermined injury'). In 31 areas there had been improvements, in 11 there had been no significant change, and in 9 there was insufficient data to determine a trend.

Problems with the DWP reports

Sinclair (2003) points out that the **reliability** of some of the findings can be questioned.

The report produces no overall figures for individuals experiencing poverty and social exclusion.

The **selection of indicators** changes between reports, and there is no clear indication as to why some are included and others excluded.

Alternative measurements of social exclusion tend to produce a less rosy picture of changes. However, the reports do show that **Labour** governments since 1997 have taken issues of poverty and social exclusion seriously (see p. 119).

Monitoring poverty and social exclusion

An alternative source on the extent of, and trends in, poverty and social exclusion is provided in the annual report *Monitoring Poverty and Social Exclusion*. It differs from the DWP reports in the following ways:

- It uses a broader range of indicators.
- It is more critical of government policy.
- There is more data on which groups are experiencing what types of social exclusion.

The 2005 report found that:

- 12 million people were below the threshold of 60% of median income, a fall of 2,000,000 from the peak year in the 1970s but still nearly double the number of the late 1970s;
- useful progress had been made towards the Government's target of cutting **child poverty**, though the report questioned whether progress could be maintained at the same rate;
- **low wages** continued to be a major cause of poverty and social exclusion;

- **educational outcomes** were improving and deprived areas were sharing in that improvement;
- **health inequalities** were found to be deep and persistent;
- there was some progress on **crime** figures, with a decline in the number of burglaries and violent crime, but poorest areas were still worst affected;
- there was a mixed picture on **housing**, with more central heating for low income households but a 20% rise in homelessness.

Evaluation

The research is independent and not tied to government priorities. Careful justifications are given for choice of indicators.

The report is still tied to indicators for which government statistics exist.

SOCIAL DISTRIBUTION OF POVERTY

AQA   Textbook pp. 232-237

The chances of experiencing poverty are not equally distributed. Some groups are much more prone to poverty than others.

Economic and family status

Being in **paid employment** on a full-time basis greatly reduces the risk of poverty.

Retirement and **unemployment** are both strongly associated with poverty because of inadequate state and other retirement pensions. Over a quarter of pensioner couples are poor, although some evidence suggests that the elderly are becoming less prone to poverty.

Lone parenthood leads to a high risk of poverty. **Flaherty *et al*** (2004) explain this in terms of:

- lack of labour market participation;
- lone parenting: lone parents who have never been married are least likely to work due to lack of experience and qualifications;
- childcare responsibilities and the lack of affordable childcare: these are major obstacles for lone parents trying to earn a good living.

Because of the above, the work found by lone parents is often part-time and/or temporary and/or low paid.

Flaherty *et al* found that the effects of **deprivation**, such as poor diet and ill health make it more difficult to escape poverty.

Divorced, separated or widowed lone parents face similar problems and also tend to have low living standards, but they may have more experience and resources than never-married lone parents.

Levitas *et al* (2006) found that lone mothers are more likely than other people to have damp homes, long-standing illness, cramped accommodation and inadequate heating. They also tend to experience **social exclusion** – for example, not socializing with friends or going on holiday.

Some sociologists, such as **Charles Murray** (1989, see p. 116), blame poverty on the **underclass culture** of lone parents. **Levitas** *et al*, by contrast, explain it in terms of practical problems, widening inequality and the lack of employment opportunities. Even when lone parents find work it is often so low paid it does not raise them out of poverty.

Gender and poverty

Government figures for 2001/2 showed 18% of men and 21% of women in poverty. Women are more likely than men to be poor in every European country apart from Sweden.

Lister (2004) argues that there is a trend towards greater female poverty, a trend she calls the **feminization** of poverty. Lister also believes the official figures underestimate female poverty due to **hidden poverty**. Hidden poverty occurs when women do not get a fair share of the total income of a household.

Flaherty *et al* (2004) identify the following reasons for higher female poverty rates:

- Women are more likely than men to be **lone parents**, and lone parenthood is associated with poverty.
- Women are less likely than men to be in paid employment because they have more **childcare** responsibilities and more responsibility for **caring** for the sick and elderly.
- When women do have paid work it is often part-time.
- Because of the above, women are more likely to earn low wages. Two thirds of workers paid less than the **minimum wage** are women.
- **Benefits** for carers, most of whom are female, are very low.
- On average, women live longer than men but they tend to have lower **pension entitlements** because of their employment histories.

Lister (1995) argues that women are affected by **structural factors** such as their position in the labour market, and **agency** – for example, they choose to make sacrifices for the benefits of others, especially children. She also argues that women are likely to have more responsibility for dealing with the **effects of poverty** because of their continued responsibility for most **domestic labour**.

Feminist theories also offer explanations as to how male power of patriarchy can contribute to female poverty (see p. 124).

Ethnicity and poverty

Minority ethnic groups are more likely to experience poverty than other groups. **Flaherty** *et al* (2004) suggest the following reasons for this:

- Minority ethnic groups have higher rates of unemployment than whites.
- Apart from Chinese and Indian men, minority ethnic groups are more likely to have unskilled/semi-skilled jobs and less likely to have professional or managerial jobs than whites.
- Partly because of the above, most minority ethnic groups have below average pay.

- Some minority ethnic groups (for example, Pakistanis) have lower than average educational qualifications.
- Minority ethnic groups tend to live in more deprived areas where there are few opportunities to escape from poverty.
- Poor housing and poor living conditions can create health problems, including mental illness, which increase the risks of falling into poverty.
- The benefits system denies full benefits to recent immigrants. Some ethnic minority individuals, for example those for whom English is a second language, may find it difficult to understand the complexity of the system. As a result they may not succeed in claiming the full benefits to which they are entitled.
- **Asylum seekers** and **refugees** face the biggest problems of all because of severe restrictions on work and benefits entitlement.

Alcock (1997) believes that the **social exclusion** of ethnic minorities makes it difficult for them to get out of poverty and the exclusion is partly caused by **racism**.

Poverty and disability

It has been estimated that nearly half of all disabled people live in poverty. The figure is high because:

- most households containing a disabled person receive no income from employment so they are likely to rely on state benefits;
- disabled people tend to have high spending costs.

Alcock (1997) argues that **social exclusion** is particularly great for the disabled – for example, problems of wheelchair access.

The **2005 Disability Discrimination Act** may improve the situation slowly but is unlikely to abolish high rates of poverty.

CULTURAL THEORIES OF POVERTY

AQA   Textbook pp. 237-247

Herbert Spencer – dissolute living

The earliest theories of poverty placed the blame for poverty on the poor themselves. For example, the 19th-century English **functionalist** sociologist **Herbert Spencer** (1971) blamed the **dissolute living** of the poor for their situation and believed the poor would be forced to work harder if they received no welfare. Although most sociologists reject these views, they are still popular with a minority of the general public.

The New Right – culture of dependency

The politics of Conservative governments (1979-97) were influenced by the ideas of the New Right. A central plank of their policies was the claim that the welfare state was leading to a **culture of dependency**. Writers such as **David Marsland** have used this concept to help explain poverty.

Marsland (1996) claims that much research on poverty has exaggerated the extent of poverty in Britain, because **relative definitions** of poverty have confused poverty with **inequality**. In fact, steadily **rising living standards** have largely eradicated poverty.

In Marsland's theory, low income for most people results from the generosity of the welfare state. Marsland argues that **universal welfare provision** (the provision of benefits such as education and health services to all members of society regardless of whether they are on low or high incomes) has created a **culture of dependency**: an expectation that, ultimately, the state will look after people's problems.

Criticisms of Marsland

Marsland ignores some important evidence such as the fact that the **real incomes** of the poorest have been falling.

Jordan (1989) claims that societies relying on **means-tested benefits** (welfare benefits that only go to the most needy) tend to develop a large **underclass**. These cause poverty, rather than universal benefits, because if members of the underclass take low-paid jobs they lose benefits and end up worse off.

Dean & Taylor-Gooby (1992) interviewed social security claimants and found that their attitudes and ambitions were little different from those of other members of society. They wanted to earn their own living and would prefer not to have to rely on benefits. The study found little evidence of a **dependency culture**.

The culture of poverty

Many researchers have noted that the lifestyle of the poor differs from that of other members of society. This observation has led to the concept of a **culture of poverty** (or, more correctly, a subculture of poverty), with its own norms and values.

The idea of a culture of poverty was first introduced by **Oscar Lewis** (1959, 1961, 1966) in the late 1950s. His fieldwork in Mexico led him to identify a particular design for living which had the following elements:

- Individuals feel **marginalized** and helpless.
- There is a high rate of **family breakdown**.
- There is **lack of participation** in social institutions.

These attitudes and behaviours are passed on to the next generation through **socialization**, making it very difficult to break out of poverty, as members of the subculture are not able to take advantage of opportunities that may be offered.

Criticisms

A great deal of research in both the developed and developing worlds has failed to identify a clear culture of poverty.

Recent qualitative research conducted by the **Joseph Rowntree Foundation** and summarized by **Kempson** (1996) provides support for the argument that no more than a small proportion of those on low income are part of a culture of poverty.

The studies found that many people looked very hard for work but encountered considerable barriers in their search for a job. Age, lack of skills, poor health and disability, for example, were all problems.

These kinds of barriers (known as **situational constraints**) may well be a more significant factor in keeping individuals on low incomes than a culture of poverty.

THE UNDERCLASS AND POVERTY

AQA   Textbook pp. 242-247

In recent years the concept of an underclass has become widely used and increasingly controversial.

Murray – the underclass in Britain

Charles Murray (1989, 1994) is an American sociologist who visited Britain in 1989 and 1993. He claimed that, like the USA, Britain was developing an **underclass**. This underclass did not just consist of the poorest members of society. It consisted of those whose lifestyles involve a type of poverty characterized by what Murray calls '**deplorable behaviour**', such as refusal to accept jobs, delinquency and having illegitimate children.

Murray puts forward evidence in three areas to support his claim:

- **Illegitimacy** – Murray argues that illegitimacy is rapidly increasing, particularly among women from the lower **socioeconomic** classes. The absence of a father means that illegitimate children will tend to 'run wild'. According to Murray, cohabitation does not provide the same stability as marriage.
- **Crime** – Murray associates the development of an underclass with rising crime. He argues that crime is damaging because it fragments communities. People become suspicious of each other and, as crime becomes more common, young boys start to imitate older males and take up criminal activities themselves.
- **Unemployment** – Murray does not see unemployment itself as a problem; instead it is the unwillingness of young men to take jobs that creates difficulties. Young men without jobs cannot support a family, so they are unlikely to get married when they father children, and the illegitimacy rate rises. In the absence of family responsibilities they find other, more damaging, ways to prove themselves – for example, through violent crime.

Murray argues that the **benefits system** needs to be changed to get rid of disincentives to marriage and to discourage single parenthood. Single mothers can now afford to live on benefits and so males who father children are often isolated from the responsibilities of family life. To force pregnant women to marry, Murray advocates cutting benefits for unmarried women entirely.

Criticisms

Murray's views have come under serious attack. **Walker** (1990) argues that:

- lone parenthood is often short-lived – most lone parents find a new partner in a relatively short time;
- most of the so-called underclass have conventional attitudes. They want stable relationships and paid employment. It is not their values that prevent them from achieving their aims, but lack of opportunities.

Heath (1992) collected data to test the claim that the attitudes of the underclass are different. Most of the evidence suggests that the majority of the underclass have conventional aspirations. They want jobs and happy marriages, though they are slightly less likely than other members of society to believe that people should get married before having children.

Alcock (1994) points out that Murray's sweeping generalizations about the negative effects of lone parenthood are unjustified. Two-parent families can also produce poorly socialized children.

Blackman (1997) conducted an ethnographic study of the young homeless in Brighton. He argues against Murray's view that the underclass rejects society's values. What the young homeless needed was jobs and homes, not a change of culture. Blackman sees members of the so-called 'underclass' as victims of society whose behaviour changes when they are given genuine opportunities to improve their situation.

CONFLICT THEORIES OF POVERTY

AQA   Textbook pp. 247-254

The sociology of poverty has increasingly been studied within a **conflict perspective**. Conflict theorists argue that poverty continues to exist because society fails to allocate its resources fairly. Poverty is explained in terms of the structure of society (**structural explanations**) rather than the attitudes or behaviour of individuals or groups.

To some extent, conflict theorists disagree about the reasons why society has failed to eradicate poverty. Some regard poverty as the result of the failings of the **welfare state**. Others place more emphasis on the disadvantages faced by the poor in the **labour market**.

Marxists believe that poverty is an inevitable consequence of **capitalism**.

Poverty and the welfare state

Recent studies of relative poverty have found that those who rely on state benefits for their income are among the largest groups of the poor. However, it is widely assumed that the **welfare state** makes a major contribution to reducing poverty, and that it **redistributes** resources from the rich to the poor.

Many sociologists have challenged this view.

Taxation and redistribution

Giles & Johnson (1994) show that tax changes between 1985 and 1995 made the richest better off and the poorest worse off.

From 1997 the **Labour Government** introduced **tax credits** for those on lower incomes. **Clark & Goodman** (2002) calculate that the changes between 1997 and 2001 led to a gain of about 12% of net income for the poorest fifth of families, but just one percent for the highest paid tenth of families. However, **McKnight** (2002) sees tax credits as a subsidy to employers which might have led them to reduce wages for the low paid.

There is little evidence that government policies up to 1997 redistributed resources to the poor, and income inequality was only slightly reduced under Tony Blair's premiership. However, according to **Hills et al** (2002), Labour governments since 1997 have done more to tackle poverty and inequality than previous administrations.

Provision of welfare

The provision of welfare is one of the principal means governments have of tackling poverty and social exclusion. However, some conflict theorists have questioned the effectiveness of state welfare. **Le Grand** (1982) suggests that better-off people had benefited more from the British welfare state than poor people. For example, the children of the middle classes were more likely to stay on at school and were more likely to go to university.

Means-tested benefits

Piachaud & Sutherland (2001) calculated that basic Income Support levels are not high enough to allow recipients to escape poverty.

Tax avoidance

The rich can avoid taxes by living overseas, using tax-free accounts, contributing to their pension, and by paying themselves dividends from companies rather than a salary.

Education

Better-off groups are more likely to benefit from **higher education** than poorer groups.

Critics of Labour education policy have argued that their policies lead to those from richer backgrounds securing places in the most successful state schools (see p. 50).

McKnight et al (2005) accept that Labour has tried to improve the education of the poor (for example, through initiatives in inner-city areas such as **Excellence in Cities**) but believe it is too little to compensate for the better schools usually enjoyed by the middle and higher classes.

Housing

Ginsburg (1997) notes that recent housing policy has been aimed at encouraging home ownership, while spending on new council houses has been restricted.

Health

Benzeval (1997) has found a growing **health gap** between the rich and poor in Britain.

Poverty and the labour market

Not all of those who experience poverty rely on state benefits for their income. A considerable proportion of the poor are employed, but receive wages that are too low to meet their needs. **Weberian** theories emphasize the concept of **market situation**: the ability of individuals to influence the labour market in their favour. Sociologists have put forward explanations to explain the market situation of the low paid:

● There is increasing demand for **specialist skills** in advanced industrial societies. However, the unemployed tend to be unskilled, with low educational qualifications.

- With increasing mechanization and **automation**, the demand for unskilled labour is contracting.
- Competition from **developing world** manufacturers tends to force wages in Britain down.
- Many low-paid workers are employed in **declining industries**. The narrow profit margins in these industries drive wages down.

Post-Fordism and globalization

Enzo Mingione (1996) argues that increases in international poverty are linked to a shift from **Fordist** to **post-Fordist** production in the world economy. This involves a decline in **heavy industry** and **mass production**, and an increase in the **service sector** coupled with more **flexible production**. This results in an increase in casual, insecure and temporary employment.

Globalization means that companies can move investment from country to country in search of cheap labour and freer trade. This makes more people vulnerable to poverty as jobs are less secure, and the increasing numbers of women in work means that more families rely on two earners.

The 'reserve army' of labour

Byrne (1999) argues that poverty has been increased as a deliberate policy. Trade union legislation has made it difficult for workers to go on strike and organize to improve their ages. This has create a '**reserve army of labour**' – workers with few rights who are paid low wages and can be easily hired and fired.

Marxist theories of poverty

Marxists argue that the poor are not a separate group in society but simply the most disadvantaged section of the working class. Marxists believe that poverty exists because it benefits the ruling class, allowing them to maintain the capitalist system and maximize their profits.

Those whose services are not required by the economy, such as the **aged** and **unemployed**, must receive a lower income than wage earners – if this were not the case there would be little motivation to work.

Low benefits and high unemployment help to reduce **wage demands**, as workers tend to assess their incomes in terms of the baseline provided by the low-paid.

Evaluation

With the increased emphasis on market forces, **Westergaard** (1995) argues that Marxist views are more relevant than ever. However, they are less successful than other conflict approaches in explaining why particular groups and individuals become poor. Nor do they explain variations in poverty rates between different capitalist countries and over time.

Burchardt et al – social exclusion

Burchardt *et al* (2002) offer a 'framework for understanding social exclusion'. They argue that economic factors, behaviour and government policies all play a role in causing social exclusion.

Barry – social and individual factors

Barry (2002) develops aspects of the approach outlined by Burchardt *et al*:

- Money, or **financial capital**, is very important in determining whether or not people can participate in social activities.
- Wider factors, such as the provision of **public services** (for example, public transport) are also important.
- Choices made by individuals are influenced by circumstances. For example, lack of job opportunities in an area may depress motivation in education.
- The rich exclude themselves through choice, for example by sending their children to private schools.
- The wealthy also gain advantage through social contacts with other rich and influential people.

Barry sees social exclusion as influenced by individual choices, but these are shaped by **constraints** and wider social factors. He concludes that social exclusion cannot be tackled just by trying to deal with individual examples of the problem such as truancy. Some **redistribution** of income is necessary.

GOVERNMENT POLICIES

AQA   Textbook pp. 255-259

New Right solutions

The post-1979 Conservative governments of Margaret Thatcher and John Major were inspired by New Right ideas. They aimed to:

- reduce **welfare** expenditure so that a more dynamic economy could be created. As the economy grew and living standards rose, wealth would '**trickle down**' to those on low incomes.
- move away from **universal benefits** in order to reduce the **dependency culture** which made people rely on state benefits.
- **target** resources to the poor so that benefits would only go to those in genuine need.

Criticism of Conservative policies

Most of the evidence cited earlier in this chapter suggests that poverty actually worsened during this period. **Hills** (1995) argues that many of the tax changes, such as increasing VAT, made those on low incomes much worse off. **Oppenheim** (1997) finds no evidence of a 'trickle down' effect, although the government claimed that its policies had increased the income of the poorest 20% of the population.

Welfare and redistribution

Some sociologists believe that the solution to poverty lies in improving welfare provision. **Townsend** (1997) argues for a national plan to eliminate poverty. The plan might ultimately require the development of a kind of **international welfare state**. This might enable governments to:

- introduce **limits on wealth and earnings** and ensure adequate benefits for the unemployed;

- maintain a link between benefits and average earnings;
- make sure that taxation is **progressive**;
- implement policies of **job creation**.

Alcock (1997) argues that state policies can help to avoid the need for redistribution of income and wealth by preventing individuals from falling into poverty or suffering from social exclusion. He calls for a comprehensive and generous welfare system.

Marxist solutions to poverty

Because **Marxists** see poverty as simply one aspect of inequality, eliminating it involves a radical change in the structure of society.

Westergaard & Resler (1976) maintain that no substantial redistribution of wealth can occur until **capitalism** is replaced by **socialism**.

However, there is little prospect of an imminent socialist revolution in any part of the world, and there is no evidence that the few remaining communist countries have eliminated poverty.

New Labour – 'a hand up, not a hand-out'

The Labour Government, which took power in Britain in 1997 under the banner of 'New Labour', claimed it had policies that would reduce poverty and social exclusion: what the poor needed was a 'hand up, not a hand-out'. In other words, they needed to be given the support they needed to help themselves rather than simply depending on state benefits – the poor had **rights** to some state help, but they also had **responsibilities**, such as trying to find work. Another important aspect of the Government's approach was to combine a concern with **poverty** with wider issues of **social exclusion**.

In general, the Labour Government's policies have contained a novel mix of contradictory ideologies, influenced by both left-wing sociologists such as **Peter Townsend** and **New Right** thinkers such as **Charles Murray**.

Labour policies

Policies introduced after 1997 included:

- the launch of a **Social Exclusion Unit** to help the socially excluded reintegrate into society.
- a strategy to reduce and eventually eradicate **child poverty**, involving changes to the tax and benefits systems to raise the incomes of low income households. A **minimum wage** was introduced in 1999 and new **tax credits** were introduced to boost the incomes of working parents.
- measures to encourage people back to work and cut unemployment, including **Welfare to Work** schemes focused on young people and lone parents.
- measures to tackle social exclusion, such as **Education Action Zones**, **literacy** and **numeracy hours** and after-school **homework clubs**. The **New Deal for Communities** provided extra resources for the most disadvantaged areas.

Evaluation of Labour policies

Sinclair (2003) believes the Labour Party is moving away from its traditional concern with the redistribution of wealth and income. Most of the benefits that have been increased above the level of inflation have been those targeted at groups such as children and disabled people who are unable to work.

Levitas (1998) detects a shift in the dominant values of the Labour Party from a concern with poverty to a concern with social exclusion. Social exclusion is seen as involving greater social integration and social solidarity. This view owes much to the work of **Emile Durkheim** (see p. 68). Levitas argues for a more radical, egalitarian approach.

Page (2005) is more supportive of Labour's approach. He argues that Government policies have brought significant improvements to people's lives. He points to successes in reducing child poverty and to educational reforms which have reduced exclusions and improved literacy and numeracy.

THE WELFARE STATE

AQA   Textbook pp. 259-277

Definitions and types of welfare

Welfare is concerned with meeting human needs for such things as food, shelter and clean water, preventing absolute or relative poverty and providing health, education and other services. **Pete Alcock** (2003) divides welfare provision into four sectors:

- the informal sector;
- the voluntary sector;
- the private sector;
- the state sector.

The informal sector

Informal care is provided by friends, relatives or neighbours helping somebody out without payment. Alcock points out it is not organized or regulated and relies upon goodwill.

Informal care is of vital importance, providing much day-to-day care. It limits the amount of provision needed from other sectors, which supplement provision when informal care is insufficient to meet needs.

Some informal providers are supported by the state – for example, carers of the elderly through **Attendance Allowance**. However, allowances are small, many carers do not receive them, and most of the cost is borne by the individual.

One advantage of informal care is that it is free and therefore saves money for the state (reducing dependence on the state sector), the recipient (who may otherwise turn to the private sector for some services), or charities (reducing dependence on voluntary sector funds). Another advantage is that the care is personal, and may therefore be tailored to meet the needs of the individual.

However, there are many disadvantages of informal care. There is no **regulation** of the competence or training of providers. Because it is not organized, provision is haphazard and may not meet the recipient's needs. There is no vetting of providers, which makes **abuse** of recipients more likely. The provision of informal care can also place a significant burden on providers.

Feminists (see p. 124) criticize informal care as disadvantaging women – since women do most of the care – and contributing to **patriarchy** by limiting women's opportunities.

Social democrats (see p. 121) criticize reliance on informal care because the lack of organization or regulation means there is no guarantee of comprehensive, fair or high quality provision.

Market liberals and **New Right** theorists (see p. 122) favour the informal sector as a provider because it saves money for the state – they are hostile to state expenditure – and because they see the family as the cornerstone of society.

The voluntary sector

This sector consists of organizations, usually **charities**, which provide welfare and are set up to deal with social problems such as old age, poverty, homelessness or child abuse. Examples include Shelter, the NSPCC, Help the Aged. In 2002 voluntary sector organizations spent some £15.6 billion in the UK.

Advantages of the voluntary sector are that:

- it employs trained staff as well as volunteers;
- it is professionally organized;
- it reduces dependence on state funding, as the sector's income does not come primarily from the state;
- it encourages individuals to support welfare provision, and provides additional services to those which the state offers;
- because it is largely independent of the state, many organizations within the voluntary sector can also act as **pressure groups**, providing expertise to government, pressurizing the state to improve provision and raising **public awareness** about welfare issues.

One problem with the voluntary sector is that its funding is often not guaranteed, and so it cannot always provide **continuity** of service.

Writers and policy-makers from all perspectives see the voluntary sector as useful, but some are more supportive than others:

- **Market liberals** support this type of provision because it reduces reliance on state funding and encourages individual responsibility and community involvement.
- **Social democrats** are less supportive because the voluntary sector cannot always guarantee services and relies partially on unpaid volunteers who do not offer a professional service.

The private sector

The private sector consists of welfare services provided by **private companies** or organizations which charge for their services and usually make a **profit**. Examples include private hospitals, schools and nursing homes.

Advantages of private provision are that they can provide trained staff and continuity of service, and may offer services in addition to, or of higher quality than, state provision.

Some of the **disadvantages** of the private sector are that:

- the services have to be paid for and many people cannot afford them;
- it tends only to provide services which are profitable;
- it gives some people an unfair advantage over others – for example, allowing some medical patients to 'jump the queue';
- it may be more expensive than other forms of provision because the private sector has to make a profit for investors as well as meeting its running costs.

Market liberals are particularly keen on private provision because they see it as more **efficient** than state provision. The lack of **competition** in state welfare provision means that providers have little incentive to improve quality or lower costs. They believe that private provision offers more **consumer choice**.

Social democrats and **Marxists** are the most critical of private provision. They see it as favouring the better-off and thereby promoting and perpetuating class inequality in society. Private medical care, for example, is based on ability to pay rather than exclusively on medical need. Private education is seen as perpetuating the class system by providing elite education (for example, at public schools such as Eton) which offers a route to elite positions in society. For social democrats and Marxists, private provision violates principles of **social justice**.

The state sector

The **state sector** consists of the benefits and services provided by the state. Unlike the private sector it is generally supported by **social democrats** and criticized by **market liberals**.

The state sector:

- is the only sector which aims to provide a comprehensive, organized, continuous and professional service based more on need than on the ability of the recipient to pay;
- does not rely upon the availability of volunteers or the generosity of donors;
- may redistribute wealth and income, encourage social justice and greatly reduce poverty.

To **market liberals**, the state sector is inefficient and expensive for taxpayers, and it encourages a **culture of dependency**.

To **social democrats**, it helps to reduce poverty, and promotes **social justice** and **social cohesion**.

ORIGINS OF THE WELFARE STATE

Michael Hill (2003) traces the origins of the welfare state back to the Elizabethan **Poor Law** of 1601, which made parishes responsible for helping the poor.

The 19th century saw an expansion of the welfare state, following:

- the **Poor Law Amendment Act** of 1834 which set up workhouses for the destitute;
- the introduction of **public health officials**;
- the introduction of **compulsory state education** in 1870.

The foundations of the modern **welfare state** were laid in the early years of the twentieth century. Liberal governments introduced means-tested benefits (for those with low or no income): **old age pensions** in 1906 and **National Insurance** schemes in 1911 to help sick or unemployed workers.

Until the Second World War state welfare remained a patchy rather than comprehensive service.

THE MODERN WELFARE STATE

The Beveridge Report

During the **Second World War**, the Government took on responsibility for many areas of social and economic life as part of the war effort. The success of central planning prompted a review of welfare provision, and a civil servant, Sir William Beveridge, was asked to produce a report on the establishment of a peace-time state welfare system. The Beveridge Report was published in 1942.

The aim was to produce a **safety net** to look after people's needs '**from the cradle to the grave**', whilst it anticipated people would need welfare less as they became healthier and better off.

The report described how state provision could conquer 'five giants':

1 **Want** – state would provide **child allowances**, **unemployment benefit** and a **means-tested safety net** (now Income Support)

2 **Disease** – report called for the establishment of a **national health service**

3 **Ignorance** – tackled through **state education**

4 **Squalor** – report called for building of affordable **council houses**

5 **Idleness** – state **economic policies** would be structured to prevent mass unemployment

George & Wilding (1994) describe Beveridge as a 'reluctant collectivist', who (like market liberals) believed in the **free market** but (like social democrats) believed the state should intervene when markets failed to meet people's needs.

The implementation of Beveridge

Most of Beveridge's proposals were introduced, particularly by the post-war Labour Government of Clement **Atlee**:

- The **Education Act** of 1944 introduced universal state education up to 15.
- **National Insurance** schemes were introduced to pay for state pensions and unemployment benefit.
- The **National Health Service (NHS)** was set up in 1948.
- There was a national programme of house building.
- Government expenditure was used to limit unemployment.

Criticisms of Beveridge

The Beveridge Report provided the framework for the modern welfare state, and its basic principles were largely accepted by Labour and Conservative governments after the war – this is called the **post-war consensus**.

However, the type of welfare state based on Beveridge's ideas has been criticized:

- **Market liberals** (or the **New Right**) such as **Marsland** (1992) attack it for discouraging individual responsibility, encouraging a **culture of dependency** and for being too expensive (see p. 121).
- **Social democrats** and **Marxists** criticize it for failing to redistribute wealth from rich to poor and thereby failing to create a fairer society.
- **George & Wilding** (1994) note that **feminists** criticize it for its assumption that women would be the main child-carers and men the main breadwinners.
- **Page** (2005) argues that **New Labour** from 1997 attacked the welfare state for failing to modernize and provide **consumer choice**, the low quality of some services, and a failure to encourage people to become self-reliant.

Despite the criticism, and later modifications, many of the basic principles and mechanisms outlined by Beveridge have been retained – for example: the NHS, state education, and a means-tested 'safety net' benefit.

SOCIAL DEMOCRATIC VIEWS OF WELFARE

The post-war consensus based on Beveridge's report was challenged by some **social democrats** both inside and outside the Labour Party. They wanted more left-wing policies.

According to **Pierson** (2006), social democratic views are based on three principles:

1 Capitalist societies are based upon the exploitation of workers, but this can be addressed by **reform** without the need for revolution.

2 The class structure has become less polarized with the growth of a **middle class** between workers and capitalists.

3 It is possible for capitalism to grow at the same time as **redistributing wealth** to make society more equal.

The social researcher **Richard Titmuss** (2000, first published 1968) believed the aims of the welfare state should include:

- giving people a shared sense of **citizenship** through universal benefits and services which everybody was entitled to as a citizen;
- ensuring that everybody shared in the benefits of economic growth;
- the creation of greater **social justice** with equal opportunities and equal treatment for all citizens;
- the creation of greater **equality**, with redistribution through the welfare state and **positive discrimination** to give extra help to the disadvantaged.

Titmuss was generally opposed to means-tested benefits because:

- there is a **stigma** attached to claiming such benefits (for example, claimants may be seen as scroungers);
- means-tested benefits are therefore **socially divisive** (claimants resent having to claim them, non-claimants having to pay for them);
- they are expensive to administer;

- many people who are entitled to help do not claim them;
- means-tested services tend to deteriorate and become low quality services because they are not used by higher socioeconomic classes, who are better placed to pressurize governments to maintain standards.

Social democrats and government policy

Social democratic writers and campaigners had some influence on the **Labour** governments of 1964-70 and 1974-79.

They supported the introduction of **comprehensive schools** in which all pupils went to the same type of school. This gradually replaced the **tripartite system** in most areas. In the tripartite system pupils attended **grammar**, **secondary modern** or **technical schools** based partly upon performance in an examination, the **eleven-plus**. Social democrats saw this as socially divisive, creating inequality of opportunity and reinforcing the class system.

Social democrats also influenced the introduction of higher tax rates for the better-off and extra help for disadvantaged areas – leading to initiatives such as **Education Action Zones**.

Evaluation

Pierson (2006) argues the social democratic perspective shows more awareness than other perspectives of the role of working-class movements (for example, trade unions) in developing welfare, and he agrees that expanding citizenship rights through universal benefits increases social cohesion. Pierson notes, however, that Sweden has adopted social democratic policies but without solving all problems – for example, unemployment is still high.

Fraser (1984) argues that by the late 1970s the social democratic model in Britain was felt to be failing because state expenditure had increased but unemployment and inflation were very high, and there was a great deal of industrial unrest.

Market liberals attack social democratic policies for leading to excessively high taxation, giving too much power to trade unions, creating a **dependency culture** and undermining economic efficiency.

Marxists criticize social democratic policies for failing to redistribute wealth and income sufficiently to create a more equal society.

Some **feminists** see the social democratic perspective as defending the rights of male workers at the expense of women.

Nevertheless, some social democratic principles – such as a universal health service free at the point of delivery – retain strong political and popular support.

MARXIST VIEWS ON WELFARE

The welfare state and capitalism

Marxists are more critical of the welfare state than social democrats. They believe that in capitalist societies the welfare state will ultimately benefit capitalism.

Some Marxists see the state as directly controlled by the ruling class – for example, **Marx & Engels** (1950a, first published in the 19th century) described it as a 'committee for managing the common affairs of the whole bourgeoisie'.

Others, like **Poulantzas** (1976), see it as having some independence or relative autonomy from the demands of particular capitalists, in favour of the long-term interests of the capitalist system as a whole.

Ginsburg (1979) see the welfare state as having four functions:

1 It creates the **myth** that society is fair by appearing to help the working class and thus reduces the chance of revolution.

2 It maintains a **reserve army of labour** on benefits, which reduces wages and provides workers during booms.

3 Social security maintains the **patriarchal family** through the benefits system which encourages male breadwinners.

4 It smoothes out the problems created by **booms** and **slumps** to prevent instability.

Other Marxists argue that the welfare state helps to control the working class:

- Social workers, health visitors and teachers monitor and control working-class behaviour.
- Workers become dependent on state welfare rather than developing their own organizations (for example, Friendly Societies).
- Working class radicalism is bought off cheaply with benefits.

Evaluation

Pierson (2006) identifies evidence which supports Marxist theories:

- The receipt of state benefits is increasingly dependent on a record of regular work and willingness to work, thereby ensuring people contribute to the capitalist economy.
- A lot of evidence shows that reformers introduced welfare measures to create a healthier, harder-working and more docile workforce.

Pierson also identifies evidence which undermines Marxist theories:

- Some governments have gone much further than capitalists would like in helping the working class and redistributing wealth. Ultimately, this money comes from ruling-class profits.
- Benefits discourage some people from taking paid work in the capitalist economy.

Pierson concludes that the welfare state benefits capitalism to some degree, but Marxists exaggerate the extent which it does; the welfare state does redistribute to some extent from rich to poor.

MARKET LIBERAL VIEWS ON WELFARE

Market liberal perspectives are also sometimes known as **New Right** (when applied to the Conservative governments of 1979-97) or **neo-liberal**.

Market liberals see the **free market** as the best way to allocate resources, and believe state expenditure is inefficient and destroys incentives to work hard; it should therefore be kept to a minimum.

Too large a welfare state is seen as leading to:

- an excessive tax burden on private industry;
- perverse incentives (for example, adults may choose to have children in order to claim benefits);
- a dependency culture, with individuals falling into a **poverty trap** – there is no incentive to take work because of lost benefits;
- lack of **productivity** and **welfare expansion** – public sector workers have no incentive to become more efficient and they encourage the continued expansion of welfare to improve their own job opportunities.

Market liberals therefore want a **minimal welfare state** that avoids universal benefits but does provide a means-tested safety net (such as Income Support) which prevents extreme poverty. Some market liberals are hostile to state-provided universal services such as the NHS.

Bartholomew – The Welfare State We're In

James Bartholomew (2004) is a radical market liberal who believes the welfare state has harmed Britain. He argues that the welfare state:

- encourages unemployment by providing an income for those who don't work; there is also hidden unemployment amongst those claiming incapacity benefit who are in reality fit for work.
- creates incentives for fraud by claimants.
- creates family instability by making lone parenthood affordable.
- creates pensioner poverty by discouraging saving for retirement while paying an inadequate state pension.
- has resulted in a woefully inadequate National Health Service with long waiting lists, poor hygiene (leading to hospital infections such as MRSA), poor service and a poor record of improving public health; the NHS is run by a very expensive bureaucracy and has little incentive to improve without the competition found in the private sector.

State education, according to Bartholomew, has led to a fall in educational standards and performs much worse than private education – thanks to high administrative costs, lack of competition, and the power of trade unions.

Council housing has created run-down estates with high crime levels. Council tenants don't have the same choice as private buyers so market forces cannot drive standards up.

High taxation to pay for welfare stifles **entrepreneurship**, and even the poor have to pay tax to finance the huge costs.

Criticisms of market liberal views

Much research criticizes the **dependency culture** theory.

There is evidence of some reduction in inequality because of the tax and welfare policies of some governments, and welfare measures do lift many people out of poverty.

Research suggests government expenditure can sometimes boost economic growth, and **Hill** (2003) argues that benefits do not increase unemployment.

Bartholomew and other market liberals do not explain how basic needs could be met and **essential services** provided without the welfare state. **Alcock** (2003) points out that voluntary and informal care do not provide comprehensive or reliable services and many people cannot afford private provision.

Market liberals and social policies

An extreme version of market liberal theory has never been implemented in Britain but Conservative governments did introduce some reforms along market liberal lines. These included cuts in some welfare payments, and increased competition within the education system and the NHS while retaining state funding.

Quasi-markets have been introduced where institutions like schools and hospitals compete to attract 'customers' such as pupils and patients.

Quasi-markets have been criticized as:

- frequently failing to provide genuine choice – for example, parents often cannot get their children into their first-choice school.
- allowing the better-off to manipulate the system – for example, parents buying houses in the catchment areas of the best state schools.

Pierson (2006) argues that the Conservatives failed in their objectives to cut welfare expenditure, as NHS spending rose and education spending did not fall. Although welfare professionals such as teachers were monitored more, spending on bureaucracy rose.

NEW LABOUR AND THE THIRD WAY

In 1997 a **Labour government**, under the banner of 'New Labour', was elected with Tony Blair as leader. Its philosophy was to follow a '**Third Way**' between **socialist** and **capitalist** (or social democratic and market liberal) approaches.

Anthony Giddens (2000), a sociologist and architect of the Third Way, argued that people had **responsibilities** in return for the **rights** given to them by the welfare state. For example, the right to unemployment benefit went with a responsibility to look for work. In Giddens's vision:

- **passive welfare** (receiving hand-outs) should be replaced by **active welfare** – people actively trying to escape dependency;
- individuals should be offered opportunities to improve their lives – '**a hand-up not a hand-out**';
- equality of **opportunity** was more important than equality of **outcome**.

The welfare state could improve competitiveness in a **global economy** by creating a more skilled workforce.

Giddens criticizes **market liberal** policies for failing to ensure opportunities for those from disadvantaged backgrounds. He criticizes **social democratic** perspectives for undermining individual initiative, creating a **culture of dependency** and encouraging fraud.

New Labour and the welfare state

Robert Page (2005) identifies the following Third Way policies introduced by Labour governments after 1997:

- **Welfare to Work** programmes were introduced to get claimants back into work, while **tax credits** made it worthwhile for people to get off benefits.

- **Targets** and closer **monitoring** of welfare professionals were used to ensure the interests of service users were met rather than those of welfare professionals.

- Competition between schools (**quasi-markets**) was retained.

- More choice was introduced for service users – for example, more specialist schools and city academies.

- **Tax credits** (which boost the pay packets of workers) were introduced for all but high-earning families, to avoid the **stigma** of means-tested benefits whilst not giving money to the very well-off (as is the case with universal benefits). It was hoped this would increase **social solidarity** without wasting money.

Some policies have followed a more social democratic approach, including:

- targets to reduce **child poverty**;
- schemes aimed at the disadvantaged, such as **Sure Start**;
- the **national minimum wage**.

Evaluation of New Labour policies

From a **social democratic** perspective, New Labour has been criticized for:

- failing to reduce income inequalities;
- using the private sector to build new schools and hospitals (through the Private Finance Initiative) – the government has to repay the money with interest, creating high costs over the long term;
- creating greater inequality through the use of markets in public services;
- creating social divisions by allowing faith schools;
- introducing tuition fees in higher education which might discourage those from poorer backgrounds from going to university.

Market liberals have criticized New Labour for:

- increasing government expenditure and some taxes;
- expanding costly and inefficient state bureaucracies;
- introducing means-tested tax credits.

Feminists have criticized New Labour for:

- trying to get as many people as possible into paid work, and thereby devaluing the unpaid caring work of women.

New Labour policies have been supported by **Hills & Stewart** (2005), who believe they prevented greater inequality, reduced poverty to some degree and improved the quality of public services.

FEMINIST VIEWS ON WELFARE

Pierson (2006) finds consensus among feminists that other perspectives on welfare:

- neglect gender issues;
- pay too little attention to the amount of informal caring done by women;
- ignore the fact that the welfare state is used by women more than men, and that most of its employees are women.

Marxist feminists criticize the welfare state for assuming that women will continue to do most of the unpaid work – including raising the next generation of workers – while men remain the main breadwinners. (Even today Child Allowance is still normally paid to women). Women are used as a **reserve army of labour**, resulting in their having fewer entitlements to benefits and pensions than men.

Recent feminists have criticized the welfare state for exploiting women as low-paid employees – for example, cleaners and secretaries – whilst men have most of the powerful and well-paid welfare jobs.

Some feminists have criticized the welfare state for failing to provide adequate services for women, such as high quality childcare.

Recent feminists have criticized the welfare state for failing to deal with a **crisis of care**. As most women work, and state care for the elderly is limited, many elderly people, especially women, have inadequate care.

Some contemporary feminists see the welfare state today as still based on the idea that paid work gives you **citizenship rights**, thereby excluding those women whose main role is as carers or mothers.

Evaluation

Pierson (2006) argues that feminist arguments are supported by the fact that women are more likely to suffer poverty than men. However, he criticizes feminists for failing to acknowledge that the rights of women within the welfare system have gradually improved.

DEVELOP YOUR ANALYSIS AND EVALUATION SKILLS

Essay plans

For each of the following questions write your own essay plan before comparing it with the suggestions given here. For the final question you can write a full answer and compare it with the provided model answer.

Social exclusion is an important term in understanding deprivation in Britain. Discuss.

Background

The term 'social exclusion' broadens the issues around deprivation to include more than simply lack of material resources. Social exclusion may be used to refer to those who are not in employment, do not have educational opportunities, access to public transport and so on.

For	Against
● Byrne supports 'strong' definition of social exclusion (p. 113) ● Lawson (p. 113)	● Byrne opposes 'weak' definition of social exclusion (p. 113) ● Nolan & Whelan (p. 113)

Top Tip

Contemporary studies of deprivation, such as the DWP reports and *Monitoring Poverty and Social Exclusion* (see p. 114), include data on social exclusion as well as poverty. More recent theoretical accounts, including those of Burchardt, Le Grand, Piachaud and Barry (see p. 118), emphasize the importance of understanding the complex links between poverty and social exclusion.

The existence of an underclass is crucial in understanding poverty in Britain today. Discuss.

Background

The term 'underclass' has been used in a number of ways but is most strongly associated with the American writer, Charles Murray. His views have been very influential in the creation of New Right ideas and policies. The underclass idea is also linked to the view that the welfare state has created a culture of dependency.

For	Against
● Murray (p. 116) ● Marsland (p. 115)	● Walker (p. 116) ● Heath (p. 117) ● Alcock (p. 119) ● Blackman (p. 117)

Top Tip

A key issue here is the extent to which those at the bottom of society have developed distinctive norms and values. Conflict theorists tend to see the poor as simply the most disadvantaged section of the working class.

Poverty cannot be abolished without major changes to social and economic structures. Discuss.

Background

This view represents a conflict approach to poverty. Conflict perspectives see the causes of poverty as lying in the way society is organized: poverty can be solved only if social resources are distributed more fairly. The most extreme version of this view comes from Marxists, who see poverty as benefiting capitalism. Its elimination is dependent on the replacement of capitalism by socialism.

For	Against
• Marxists (p. 122)	• New Right policies (p. 122)
• Alcock (p. 119)	• Lewis – the culture of poverty (p. 116)
• Westergaard & Resler (p. 109)	• Murray (p. 116)
• Barry (p. 118)	

Top Tip

Many recent writers would have some sympathy with the view expressed in the title, whilst acknowledging that progress towards eliminating poverty can be made within existing social and economic structures (see Townsend, p. 112, for example). See p. 119 for discussion of the limited progress made by Labour governments after 1997.

The distribution of wealth and income in Britain reflects the contribution of individuals to society. Discuss.

Background

This view is supported by the functionalists Davis & Moore, who argue that functional importance determines the pay for jobs. However, there is much more to explaining the distribution of income and wealth than this.

For	Against
• Davis & Moore (p. 110)	• Tumin (p. 110)
	• Marx (p. 110)
	• Weber (p. 110)
	• Feminist views on poverty (p. 124)

Top Tip

You could also discuss how factors such as taxation, economic policy and welfare policy affect income and wealth distribution.

Only the state can provide adequately for the welfare of the population. Discuss.

Background

This statement is clearly strongly in support of the welfare state. As such it reflects the views of social democrats and, in part, Marxists. (To Marxists, the welfare state can never be effective until capitalism is abolished). However, the statement denies the importance of other sectors (voluntary, private and informal), each of which also have an important role to play.

For	Against
• Social democrats (p. 121)	• Market liberals (p. 122)
• Marxists (p. 122)	

For and Against
• New Labour (p. 119)

Top Tip

You could include some discussion of poverty to show the limitations and advantages of the welfare state. Without it, there might be a great deal more poverty, though it has failed to eradicate relative poverty.

The welfare state has not eliminated poverty in Britain because it fails to redistribute wealth and income sufficiently to solve the problem. Discuss.

Background

This statement would be supported both by Marxists and social democrats. They tend to think in terms of relative poverty and therefore see the reduction of inequality as an important part of ending poverty. Market liberals see the welfare state as *creating* poverty rather than as a way to end it. However, both sides can lose sight of the variety of factors that cause poverty (see model answer, below).

For	**Against**
• Marxists (p. 122)	• Poverty viewed in absolute terms (p. 111)
• Social democrats (p. 121)	• Market liberals (p. 122)
• Townsend (p. 112)	

For and Against
- New Labour (p. 119)
- Conflict theorists emphasizing labour markets over welfare state (p. 117)

Top Tip

For this question you need to draw on all sections of this chapter.

Model answer

The welfare state has not eliminated poverty in Britain because it fails to redistribute wealth and income sufficiently to solve the problem. Discuss.

Poverty can be defined in two main ways: absolute poverty and relative poverty. The United Nations defines absolute poverty as 'severe deprivation of basic human needs including food, safe drinking water, sanitation facilities, health, shelter, education and information'. Research by Seebohm Rowntree, using a budget standards approach, showed that by 1950 very few people in Britain could not afford the basics needed to avoid absolute poverty. A combination of economic growth, rising living standards and the welfare state established following the Beveridge Report, has largely eliminated absolute poverty in Britain. However, a few individuals may still fall through the net – for example, those who fail to claim benefits and asylum seekers who are not allowed to claim them.

From the 1960s onwards, sociologists began increasingly to focus on relative definitions of poverty, partly as a result of the work of Peter Townsend who saw poverty as a form of relative deprivation. To Townsend, it involved an inability to participate in social activities that are seen as normal. Measuring poverty in this way is difficult because of the complications of choosing items to include in an index. Mack & Lansley and Gordon et al refined the method by using opinion polls to decide on the items to include, but researchers still have to choose what items to include in the opinion poll. A simpler method is to use the government statistic of 60% of median income as a cut-off point between the poor and the non-poor.

Whatever measure of relative poverty is used, there is no doubt that poverty has not been eliminated. Government figures put poverty at around 20% in 2005/2006, a big increase from 9% in 1979. Furthermore, income inequality has increased over the same period. A Royal Commission found that between 1949 and 1979 income inequality fell (as did poverty); but after 1979, according to the Institute for Fiscal Studies (IFS), income inequality increased. This trend might have been reversed in the very recent past but overall there appears to be a statistical link between income inequality and rising poverty.

Although relative poverty is not exactly the same as income inequality, the two are linked. With greater inequality, it is less likely that some people will be able to afford the sort of lifestyle that others consider normal. Furthermore, social democrats believe that the welfare state should do much more than provide a safety net; it should also create a more equal society in which differences in income and therefore relative deprivation are reduced.

Social democratic theorists such as Titmuss, and Marxists such as Westergaard, agree that the welfare state has failed to redistribute income sufficiently to eradicate poverty. Julian Le Grand argues that this is partly because the middle classes actually take more out of the welfare state than the working classes (for example, their children stay longer in education). Piachaud and Sutherland point out that basic Income Support payments are not sufficient to keep people out of poverty. These sociologists argue that there are many ways for the rich to avoid paying tax, and that income tax rates for high earners are, at 40%, relatively low.

New Right/market liberal theorists such as Murray and Bartholomew, by contrast, see the welfare state as part of the problem, not part of the solution, to poverty. Both believe that it creates a poverty trap, in that it does not pay to come off benefits to find work, and a dependency culture. To Murray, it creates an underclass whose attitudes create social problems such as illegitimacy, teenage pregnancies, crime and unemployment. From his point of view cutting benefits not increasing them would help to reduce poverty.

It is not only market liberals, however, who would disagree that poverty is caused by a failure of the welfare state to redistribute wealth. For some theorists, the causes of poverty are to be found not in the failures of the welfare state or the culture of poor communities, but in the labour market and global economy. Mingione argues that poverty is linked to the casual work patterns created by globalization and post-Fordism; Byrne believes it is caused by the development of a new reserve army of labour; Weberian theorists see the poor market situation of the unskilled as responsible.

Poverty cannot therefore be seen as the product of an inadequate welfare state alone. Cultural factors might affect some individuals but wider structural factors such as the labour market are more significant. Feminists would also point to the feminization of poverty, the product of a patriarchal society in which women still do most of the childcare and other caring work.

The Labour Government has recognized, in its recent policies, that a combination of factors cause poverty and a variety of policies are needed to reduce it. The Government has increased some welfare payments and introduced tax credits and the minimum wage, but has also encouraged active welfare – giving people a 'hand up not a hand-out'. These policies have led to some reduction in child poverty but they have certainly not eliminated it. Perhaps poverty can be reduced without redistributing wealth and income, but it is only likely to be eliminated altogether if governments make a more serious attempt to tax the rich and spend the money on providing greater opportunities to people who are still in poverty.

RESOURCES

Defining and measuring proverty

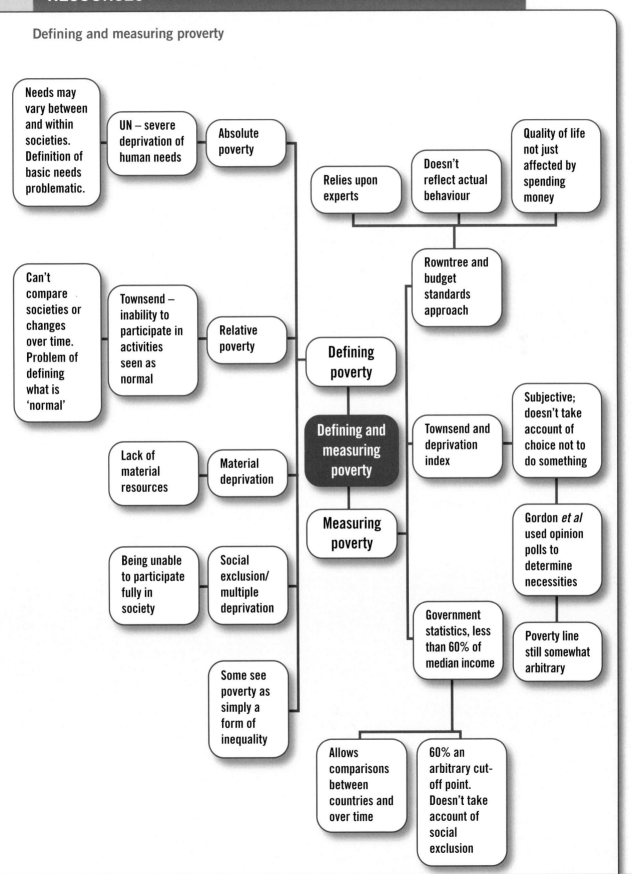

Perspectives on the welfare state

	Beveridge	Social democratic	Marxist	Market liberal	New Labour
Purpose of Welfare State	To conquer 'five giants': Want, Disease, Ignorance, Squalor, Idleness	To provide a sense of citizenship, create a more equal society, provide comprehensive services and produce social justice	To benefit capitalism and the ruling class; create myth of fairness, maintain a reserve army of labour, smooth out booms and slumps	To provide a basic safety net for those who cannot look after themselves through work	To provide active welfare, helping people to look after themselves where possible; to provide high quality universal services; to tackle poverty
Preferred type of benefits/ services	Mixture of universal and means-tested	Universal where possible	Not relevant – communism would create wealth for all	Means-tested	Mixture but with tax credits to avoid poverty trap
Attitude to different types of provision	All types seen as useful; welfare state offers 'cradle to grave' provision	Preference for the state sector to provide universal, socially just service without the stigma of claiming	State should guarantee high living standards for all	Hostile to state sector; sees private sector as most efficient, with informal and voluntary sectors also useful	Private and state sectors should work together; informal and voluntary sectors also need support
Political views	Centrist	Left of centre	Extreme left	Right of centre	Mixture of right and left
View of poverty	Absolute poverty can be eradicated through welfare state	Redistribution through welfare state can eliminate relative poverty	Capitalism needs replacing by communism to eradicate relative poverty	Relative poverty is not really poverty but a kind of inequality; absolute poverty has been eradicated	Relative poverty still a problem but can be reduced by welfare state
Influence on policy	Very influential in post-war period; still has some influence	Influential during Labour governments of 1960s and 1970s	Little influence on British governments	The main influence on Conservative governments 1979-1997	Main influence on Labour governments 1997 onwards
Main criticisms	Costs of welfare have risen rapidly without conquering the 'giants'	Led to rapid rise in state spending; created the poverty trap and culture of dependency; failed to produce equal opportunities and delivered low quality services	Unrealistic to expect a revolution; ignores rises in living standards for workers under capitalism; neglects gender issues	Led to increases in poverty and unemployment; benefited the rich while disadvantaging others; blames the victims for society's problems	Fails to deliver greater equality; state expenditure has risen; failed to meet targets for poverty reduction

Writers and their work

Writer	Perspective or approach	Concept	Study
Marx	Marxist	Ownership of the means of production	Study of the development of capitalism
Mingione	Conflict theory of poverty	Post-Fordism	Study of how changes in work increase poverty
Max Weber	Weberian	Market situation	Study of class and status
Herbert Spencer	Functionalist	Dissolute living	19th-century study of the causes of poverty
Marsland	Market liberal	Culture of dependency	Study of damaging effects of British welfare state
Oscar Lewis	Cultural theory of poverty	Culture of poverty	Study of poverty in Mexico
Davis & Moore	Functionalist	Role allocation	Study of the functions of inequality
Beveridge	Welfare reform	'Five giants'	Report for British government into the future of welfare
Ginsburg	Marxist	Reserve army of labour	Study of the role of welfare in society
Walker	Critic of Charles Murray	Blaming the victims	Study of underclass attitudes and lives
Rowntree	Defining and measuring absolute poverty	Absolute poverty and budget standards	Study of poverty in York
Bartholomew	Market liberal	Hidden employment	Study of the effectiveness of the British welfare state
Giddens	New Labour supporter	Third Way	Study of how to develop left-of-centre British politics
Townsend	Poverty as relative deprivation (social democratic)	Deprivation index	Study of poverty in Britain as a whole
Titmuss	Social democrat	Means-tests as socially divisive	Study of welfare state
Byrne	Conflict theory of poverty	Reserve army of labour	Study of poverty and the changing capitalist economy
Palmer *et al*	Critique of government policy	Indicators of poverty and social exclusion	Review of effectiveness of government policies on poverty and social exclusion
Murray	New Right	Underclass	Study of illegitimacy, unemployment and crime
Lister	Feminist	Feminization of poverty	Study of gender and poverty
Gordon	Measuring relative poverty	Public perception of necessities	Study of poverty in Britain in the 1980s

Chapter 7 | POWER AND POLITICS

SPECIFICATION COVERAGE

Specification	Details
AQA A2: Power and Politics	
OCR A2 Unit G 673: Power and Control	All sections are relevant
WJEC A2 Unit SCY3: Understanding Power and Control	

DEFINING POWER

AQA, OCR, WJEC   Textbook pp. 521-522

A distinction can be made between two types of power:

- **Authority** is power that is accepted as legitimate – for example, the power of Parliament to pass laws in a society where citizens accept the political system.
- **Coercion** is based upon the imposition of power using force, or the threat of force, against people who do not accept it as legitimate.

Weber – power and authority

Textbook p. 522

Max Weber defines power as the ability of people to get their own way despite the opposition of others. He distinguishes three different types of authority:

- **Charismatic authority** is based upon what are believed to be the special qualities of an individual.
- **Traditional authority** is based upon a belief in the rightness of accepted customs.

- **Rational-legal authority** is based on the acceptance of an impersonal set of rules – for example, a legal system.

These are ideal types (idealized, pure forms) of authority, which in reality will tend to be mixed together.

Lukes – a radical view of power

Steven Lukes (1974) provides an alternative, radical view. He sees Weber's theories as being largely based upon decision-making. For Lukes, power has three 'faces':

- The **first face** of power is **decision-making**, as described by Weber.
- The **second face** of power is **non-decision-making**, where some issues are prevented from reaching the point where decisions are made.
- The **third face** of power is **ideological power**, which shapes desires and beliefs. People are persuaded to accept the exercise of power over them even when it is against their interests – for example, women accepting patriarchal power.

A problem with this definition is determining what is for or against somebody's interests if it is not based on the opinion of the person concerned.

THE STATE

Definitions

Weber defines the state as a body that successfully claims a monopoly on the legitimate use of force in a given territory.

Most sociologists see the state as embracing institutions such as state-run **welfare services** as well as the **criminal justice** system, the **military** and state **bureaucracies**.

By the twentieth century the world was dominated by nation-states, but in some premodern societies, such as among the Nuer in Africa, there was no state.

FUNCTIONALIST PERSPECTIVE

AQA, OCR, WJEC　　　　　　Textbook p. 524

Talcott Parsons (1969) argued that all societies require a value consensus based on shared goals.

For Parsons, power is used to achieve **collective goals** such as material prosperity. Everybody therefore benefits from the exercise of power (a **variable sum** view of power). In more conventional views of power, some benefit at the expense of others (a **constant sum** view of power).

Authority in society is usually accepted as **legitimate** because it helps to achieve collective goals.

Criticisms

Critics argue that Parsons is wrong to see the exercise of power as benefiting everyone rather than being used to further sectional interests.

PLURALIST PERSPECTIVES

AQA, OCR, WJEC　　　　　Textbook pp. 525-530

Classical pluralism

Classical pluralists accept a **Weberian** (constant sum) definition of power and, unlike Parsons, do not see society as having a value consensus. They accept that there is some agreement in countries such as the USA about the basic features of the democratic system, but they believe that industrial society is **differentiated** into a plurality of social groups and **sectional interests**.

Divisions are based not only on class, occupation, age, gender, religion and ethnicity, but also on many other specific interests – for example, whether you own a car, pay a mortgage, use public libraries or have children.

Societies need to prevent a **tyranny of the majority**, in which a single large interest group always outvotes minorities.

The state is seen as an **honest broker** mediating between different interests and ensuring that no one group becomes dominant. It makes decisions which favour different groups at different times, balancing their interests over extended periods.

Political parties are seen as broadly representative since they need to attract sufficient support to be elected. If the existing parties do not represent public interests, new ones emerge. **Garnett** (2005) shows that membership of political parties is falling.

However, **interest** or **pressure groups** are needed:

- to influence governments in the periods between elections.
- to represent minority interests and ensure that governments take account of all groups in society, not just their own supporters.
- to increase participation in politics.
- to represent views on new issues that arise.
- to respond to changing circumstances.

There are two different types of pressure group:

- **Protective groups** defend the interests of a particular group in the population – for example, the British Medical Association (BMA) for doctors.
- **Promotional groups** are based on causes or issues rather than social groups – for example, environmental groups. They may have more diverse membership than protective groups.

Garnett (2005) shows membership of pressure groups is rising.

Pressure groups can try to influence the government in a variety of ways:

- by contributing to party funds – for example, union contributions to the Labour Party.
- by appealing to public opinion – for example, rock musicians campaigning for the cancellation of Third World debt.
- by providing expert opinion to the government – for example, by having seats on government committees or inquiries.
- through civil disobedience or direct action – for example, hunt saboteurs.
- through payments – for example, Mohammed Al Fayed paying cash to MPs to ask questions in the House of Commons.

A number of studies have been used to support pluralist views. They have compared government decisions with the wishes of different interest groups. Classic studies by **Dahl** (1961) in the USA, **Hewitt** (1974) and **Grant & Marsh** (1977) in the UK, appear to show that no one sectional interest gets its own way all the time.

The **New Labour** government of Tony Blair can be seen as balancing business interests (for example, allowing private involvement in public services) and worker/union interests (for example, minimum wage legislation).

Criticisms

Marxists argue that pluralists fail to take account of the **second face of power**. Radical questions such as redistribution of wealth never reach the point of decision-making.

Westergaard & Resler (1976) argue that power should be measured in terms of the consequences of decisions. Despite lots of legislation designed to help the poor, there has been little real redistribution of wealth in Britain. Indeed, Westergaard & Resler see class inequalities hardening whilst the power of private business has grown.

Grant (2003) argues that economic policy is influenced more by international financial institutions than by pressure groups

Some promotional groups have, it could be argued, very little influence – for example, anti-nuclear campaigners. The largest public demonstration in British history did not stop the invasion of Iraq. Amnesty International and the Refugee Council have not, it appears, impacted on government policy on asylum seekers. Some small pressure groups have been successful in promoting their causes – for example, ASH (Action on Smoking and Health).

Some interests may be unrepresented – for example, the unemployed lack a protective pressure group.

Pluralists ignore Lukes's **third face of power**.

Some classical pluralists now admit that power may not be as equally distributed as the model originally suggested.

Elite pluralism

Marsh (1983) argues that elite pluralists sees Western societies as basically **democratic**, government as a process of **compromise**, and power as widely **dispersed**. However, they believe that there are some inequalities in power – that, for example, leaders of interest groups are more powerful than members. Elite pluralists acknowledge that there are other faces of power.

Grant (1999) believes that, despite changes in pressure group politics, Britain remains largely democratic. Changes include:

- the decline of the influence of the Trade Union Congress (TUC) and Confederation of British Industry (CBI).
- an increase in the number of pressure groups so that most interests are now represented.
- increased campaigning directed away from Westminster – for example: consumer boycotts to put pressure on companies.
- the increased importance of the European Union and devolved governments.
- increased use of **direct action** – for example, by anti-roads protestors.
- more government consultation of pressure groups (though the insider/outsider distinction remains valid).

Although more realistic than classical pluralism, elite pluralism still ignores the **third face of power** and may underestimate the **inequality of power** in society, and the possible use of power by elites to further their own interests.

ELITE THEORY

AQA, OCR, WJEC   Textbook pp. 530–535

Elite theory divides society into a ruling minority and the majority who are ruled. There are different versions of elite theory.

Classical elite theory

Classical elite theory was developed by nineteenth-century Italian theorists such as **Pareto**, in opposition to Marxist theory. Pareto emphasized the importance of the **psychological characteristics** of elites which made them superior to the mass and which allowed them to gain and retain power. **Lions**, for example, achieve power through incisive action and the use of force; **foxes** rule by cunning.

Pareto's elites tend to circulate, with lions being replaced by foxes, and foxes then being replaced by lions, and so on.

Pareto can be criticized for simply assuming that elites are superior to the mass, ignoring the differences between political systems, ignoring the importance of wealth, and so on.

Modern elite theories

Modern elite theories offer more plausible views.

The American sociologist **C Wright Mills** (1956) argued that there was a **power elite** which had power through holding key positions (**command posts**) in three institutions:

- major corporations;
- the military;
- the federal government.

The three elites were connected through intermarriage, movement of individuals between elites, similar educational background, and membership of the same prestige clubs.

As a **unified group** they were able to exercise power over a divided and passive mass of the population who took little interest in most political issues.

Elite self-recruitment in Britain

A number of studies have found high levels of elite self-recruitment in Britain – i.e. most people recruited into elites tend to come from elite backgrounds themselves. There is evidence of **cohesion**, with people having positions in more than one elite, and elite members having shared educational backgrounds.

Williams (2006) describes the development of three distinct, but overlapping, power elites in Britain since the 1990s:

- The **political elite** consists of the upper echelons of political parties and the civil service. The power of this group has been reduced by privatization but it continues to provide 'conduits of power'. Members of the political elite have strong links with the professional, and financial and business, elites.
- The **professional elite** is more numerous than the political elite and has thrived since the 1970s. Non-elite professional expertise is no longer treated with deference; professionals have become servants of the state to be managed by these new professionals who regulate their work and earn substantially more money.
- The **financial and business elite** is the most powerful. The City of London generates more wealth than manufacturing and its elite members earn much more than the other elites. Political parties rely on this group for donations whilst businesses benefit from government contracts. The PFI initiative allows the government to spend private money and the business elite to make healthy profits.

Whilst there is a lack of systematic evidence to support Williams, a number of researchers have found that the elites in Britain are largely recruited from a minority of privileged backgrounds.

Evidence from the **Sutton Trust** (2005) found 75% of Law Lords and 81% of barristers had been privately educated, whilst over 80% of these groups had attended Oxford or Cambridge University.

The London Chamber of Commerce showed that the financial elite come from a less privileged background; only one third had attended one of Britain's top 13 universities.

Criddle (2005) showed 18% of Labour MPs and 60% of Conservative MPs had been to private schools, whilst **Cracknell et al** (2007) showed that over half of Brown's first cabinet had attended Oxford or Cambridge universities.

Evaluation

Although many top positions in Britain and the USA are held by people from elite backgrounds, that does not actually prove that they act to further elite interests rather than those of the mass of the population. Some would argue that elites have raised prosperity and increased the quality of public services in Britain. There has been little attempt to measure power.

Marxists argue that elite theory neglects the importance of **economic power** as opposed to power based on positions held.

MARXIST PERSPECTIVES

AQA, OCR, WJEC   Textbook pp. 535-539

Like elite theory, Marxist theories see power as concentrated in the hands of a minority.

Unlike elite theory, they see it as concentrated in the hands of a **ruling class** which derives its power from ownership of the means of production.

Marx and **Engels** argued that the ruling class used their power to exploit subordinate classes. It was in the interests of the subject classes to overthrow ruling-class power, but the ruling class used the **superstructure** to try to prevent this. The **state**, as part of the superstructure, was used to promote ruling-class interests.

Engels argued that the first societies were **primitive communist** ones, with no state. In primitive communism no **surplus** was produced, so class power could not develop through the accumulation of a surplus, and therefore no state was needed. As surplus was produced wealth was **accumulated**; classes developed and states were born.

Early states were **oppressive** (for example, Ancient Greece and Rome were slave-owning societies), but democratic states appear to be based on the will of the population. Engels believed that in democratic states power stays with the ruling class; such states create only the **illusion of democracy**.

Corruption and the financial power of capitalists are used to shape state policies in capitalist democracies, ensuring that the state continues to further ruling-class interests.

In future **communist societies**, based on **communal ownership** of the **means of production**, the **proletariat** would temporarily take control of the state to defeat the ruling class. Once this was completed, classes would disappear and the state would 'wither away'.

Marx and Engels describe the state as 'but a committee for managing the affairs of the whole bourgeoisie'. However, Engels accepted that the state could act independently – for example, when two classes were competing for domination in a society. In some studies Marx showed an awareness of divisions within states – for example, between industrial capitalists and financiers.

Modern Marxist perspectives

Modern Marxists have interpreted the state in different ways. **Miliband** (1969) believes the state is often the direct tool of the ruling class. He argues that:

- many of those who occupy top positions in the state come from ruling-class backgrounds and are therefore likely to act to support ruling-class interests.

- even those from other backgrounds have to accept ruling-class values to gain positions in the state.

- the protection of **private property** (which serves ruling-class interests) is assumed to be a central role of the state.

- the way in which the state supports private enterprise is **legitimated** through advertising which celebrates the activities of large corporations.

Poulantzas (1969, 1976) criticizes Miliband, arguing that it is not direct interference from the ruling class that makes the state serve ruling-class interests, but the structure of society. Using a **structuralist approach**, Poulantzas makes the following argument:

- As part of the **superstructure**, the state will automatically act to favour the ruling class.

- The state has **relative autonomy** – it has some independence from individual members of the ruling class. This allows the state to act in the overall interests of the ruling class rather than being dominated by a single capitalist **faction** – such as bankers, for example.

- The state's relative autonomy also allows it to make some **concessions** to the working class to defuse their protests and prevent an eventual revolution, and to promote the myth that it is acting in the interests of society as a whole.

Miliband (1972) criticizes Poulantzas for assuming that the state would act in ruling-class interests without showing how and why. The theory of relative autonomy makes it impossible to prove Poulantzas's theory wrong – whatever the state does can be taken as evidence of ruling-class domination or of relative autonomy.

Evidence to support Marxism

Westergaard & Resler (1976) argue that power can be measured in terms of effects rather than decision-making. Thus, the continued concentration of wealth in the hands of capitalists provides evidence of this group's power.

Westergaard & Resler argue that reforms such as the introduction of the **welfare state**, which appear to benefit the working class, have left the basic structures of inequality unchanged.

Sociologists such as **Urry & Wakeford** (1973) put forward evidence of **non-decision making** – for example, the way in which issues such as replacing capitalism are never considered.

Marxists find evidence that **ruling-class ideology** makes use of the third (ideological) face of power to support its position.

Criticisms

Marxist views can be criticized:

- for failing to explain why the state did not wither away in communist societies such as the Soviet Union.
- for exaggerating the importance of economic power.
- for failing to consider other possible sources of power.

NEO-MARXIST PERSPECTIVES

AQA, OCR, WJEC   Textbook pp. 539-542

Neo-Marxist views retain elements of Marxist theory but diverge from orthodox Marxism in a number of ways.

Gramsci – hegemony and the state

Antonio Gramsci, writing in the early twentieth century, argued against **economic determinism** (the theory that the economy determined other aspects of society). He believed that the **superstructure** could influence the **economic infrastructure** as well as vice versa.

Gramsci divided the superstructure into **political society** (essentially the state) and **civil society** (private institutions). To keep control over civil society, the ruling class needed to achieve **hegemony**, or domination, by gaining the consent of the mass of the population.

To legitimate their rule, the ruling class might need to make concessions to win the support of other classes or class factions. Different sections of the capitalist class needed to be united.

Ruling-class hegemony was never complete or total. A continuing process was needed to develop and maintain support and legitimate their position. An alliance of groups which dominated society was called a **historic bloc**.

Opposition was always likely because people possessed **dual consciousness**. The experience of exploitation and oppression – for example, at work – tended to make people radical, whereas the ideology promoted by the ruling class tended to make them more conservative.

Control over ideas was as important in maintaining or overthrowing ruling-class hegemony as was control over the economy.

Jessop – capitalism and control

Jessop (2002) argues that capitalism cannot secure all it requires through market forces. It needs non-capitalist institutions such as the family and education, some of which are provided by the state. The state is institutionally separate from capitalism and has **operational autonomy**.

Capitalism exercises **ecological dominance** by threatening to remove capital from states which threaten capitalism's interests and by introducing market forces into new areas of economic and social life.

State policies have moved away from controlling the economy to provide work and benefits for all, and towards creating the conditions for innovative business to thrive in a more **knowledge-based** and **globalized** economy.

The **workfare state** requires the unemployed to acquire skills and become employable.

The regime is **post-national** – focused on international competition.

The state retains considerable power but has moved from direct to indirect government, providing the framework for the interests of capitalism.

Evaluation

Jessop avoids being **over-deterministic** and takes account of changes in the nature and policies of states. Some writers believe he underestimates the power of the state.

STATE-CENTRED THEORIES

AQA, OCR, WJEC   Textbook pp. 543-545

All the previous theories can be seen as **society-centred**: they examine the way in which society shapes the actions of the state. State-centred theories see the state as an independent actor, able to exercise power in its own right and pursue its own interests.

Skocpol (1985) argues that states have considerable **autonomy**, and their primary aim may be to increase their own power. They have **administrative control** over a territory, the ability to raise taxes, and the ability to recruit talented people to work for them.

States such as the Communist regimes in China and Russia, and the Napoleonic regime in France, demonstrate the considerable power that states can possess.

Evaluation

Critics argue that such approaches may exaggerate state power. They also point out that some supposedly society-centred approaches recognize that the state has some independent power (for example, Poulantzas's theory of relative autonomy).

NOAM CHOMSKY

AQA, OCR, WJEC   Textbook pp. 545-548

Noam Chomsky (1996, 1999, 2003, 2006) has emphasized the power of the **US state** and the **economic elites** which he believes dominate US government policy. He believes these elites have used the economic power of corporations and the military power of the US state to promote the interests of US capitalism, with no regard for democratic or human rights. Examples include the invasions of Afghanistan and Iraq in the '**War on Terror**'; the Vietnam War; support for violent, repressive or undemocratic regimes in Russia, Turkey, Israel, Indonesia and elsewhere.

Chomsky believes that media **propaganda** helps to sustain US power.

Evaluation

Chomsky may exaggerate the power of American capitalism and the US state, though he does recognize that other countries and opponents of US capitalism exercise some power.

GLOBALIZATION

AQA, OCR, WJEC　　　　**Textbook pp. 548-557**

The idea of globalization suggests that national boundaries are becoming less important, and that events throughout the world influence what happens in particular societies.

To some theorists of globalization this means that the nation-state is losing its power to non-governmental organizations.

Ohmae – The Borderless World

Ohmae (1994) argues that there is one giant interlinked economy covering developed and rapidly developing societies. This interlinked economy is dominated by giant corporations and is made possible by a rapid growth in world trade.

Improved communications make national boundaries unimportant and allow individuals to buy products from anywhere in the world. Governments can no longer control economies within national boundaries because of the extent of trade across nations.

Corporations can move production easily to cheaper countries; financiers can move money at will around the world. Corporations and consumers now have more power than governments.

Criticisms

Ohmae can be criticized for greatly exaggerating the loss of state power.

States still have considerable control over access to their **domestic markets** from outside their immediate trading bloc (for example, from outside the EU).

States still largely monopolize **military power**.

Sklair – Sociology of the Global System

Sklair (1993, 1995, 2003) believes that states retain some power, but most power now rests with **transnational corporations** (TNCs).

Globalization can be understood in terms of the following spheres and their corresponding transnational practices:

Sphere	Transnational practice
Economic	Transnational corporation
Political	Transnational capitalist class
Cultural-ideological	Culture-ideology of consumption

Transnational corporations have much more power than consumers because of their control over global capital and resources.

The transnational capitalist class rules either directly by holding office or uses economic power to prevent states acting against its interests.

Most consumers are effectively indoctrinated by TNCs into consuming the products produced by them.

However, the global capitalist system creates two crises:

● the crisis of **class polarization** between rich and poor within and between nations;

● the crisis of **ecological unsustainability**, in which finite resources are used up and the environment is damaged or destroyed.

Globalization is opposed by **anti-global social movements** but Sklair is pessimistic about their chances of challenging the power of TNCs.

Criticisms

Sklair can be criticized for exaggerating the power of TNCs and neglecting the influence of finance capital – for example, banking.

Hirst & Thompson – questioning globalization

Hirst & Thompson (1996) are more critical of the theory of globalization. They argue that most corporations are still largely based around their home nations and regions, generating most of their profits from the domestic market or the immediate region.

They admit that states have lost some power, but the fact that states still control territory and regulate populations ensures that they retain much of their power.

Most individuals still feel part of a particular state and this gives the state some power over them.

Giddens – globalization and high modernity

Giddens (1990) takes a more balanced view of globalization than **Ohmae** or **Hirst & Thompson**. He sees globalization in terms of worldwide social relationships linking distant localities and shaping local events. Interaction is stretched across space and time in a process of **time-space distanciation**. You can interact with someone without being physically near to them or present at the same time – via the internet, for example.

There is increasing global competition in business and a world financial market, resulting in a **global economy**. This restricts nation-state power since nations have to compete to attract inward investment from corporations.

However, nation-states do not lose all their power. They can sometimes mobilize nationalist sentiments and exercise cultural influence over citizens, and they retain some economic power; but nations need to cooperate to maintain power against transnational corporations and other groups.

Held & McGrew – transnational issues

Held & McGrew (2002) argue that globalization is not a new process, and that countries retain strong **national identities** and **local cultures**. Consuming global products does not destroy the local culture; it may even strengthen it.

Politics is becoming globalized and global political institutions such as the UN and EU are increasingly important. 'Economic connectedness' and **transnational** problems are increasing. As a result of these changes people's lives are less subject to democratic control.

Held & McGrew see increasing the accountability of international institutions as the solution.

Held has been criticized as idealistic.

MANN – SOURCES OF SOCIAL POWER

AQA, OCR, WJEC   Textbook pp. 557-559

Michael Mann (1986, 1993) incorporates elements from different theories of power in his general theory.

He stresses that power has always operated across national boundaries through **networks of power**. Power cannot therefore be analysed in terms of its distribution within a particular society.

Mann argues that there are four main sources of power:

1 **Economic power** – which is important but is not the only source of power, as some Marxists believe

2 **Ideological power** – power over ideas and beliefs

3 **Military power** – based on physical coercion

4 **Political power** – exercised by states over citizens

Power is never monopolized entirely by one group, and changes in society – for example, technological changes – make the distribution of power unstable.

Evaluation

Mann's insights point up the dangers of assuming that all power comes from one source, and that power relationships are relatively fixed or stable.

POSTMODERNIST PERSPECTIVES

AQA, OCR, WJEC   Textbook p. 562

Postmodern approaches tend to broaden the definition of politics well beyond the activities of the state and pressure groups.

Baudrillard – the end of politics

Jean Baudrillard (1983) argues that politics has become detached from reality. Rather than being concerned with the substance of policy, politics is more concerned with **image**.

For Baudrillard, there is no real difference between the main parties, and voters have little real choice. Politicians have no real power and simply try to maintain the illusion that they do.

Politics is simply concerned with **simulacra** – signs that have no relationship to reality.

Criticisms

Critics argue that politicians do make decisions that affect people's lives. Wars, for example, are real, and lead to real people being killed.

Lyotard – decline of metanarratives

Jean-François Lyotard (1984) argues that in the postmodern era **metanarratives** (big stories such as political ideologies) have declined in importance. People no longer believe in **political ideologies**.

Politics becomes less about principles and more about **local issues** and the practicality of achieving things.

Politics simply becomes a series of **language games** about specialist topics.

Power is more to do with **knowledge** than state activities.

Evaluation

Lyotard's approach ignores military power and may underestimate the continuing power of nation-states.

Fraser – public and private spheres

Nancy Fraser (1995) sees politics shifting away from the **public sphere** of the economy and the state, and moving more into the **private sphere**. Politics becomes more concerned with debate within groups rather than engaging with issues on a national level. This gives the relatively powerless (such as black women or lesbians) more involvement in politics.

Politics is increasingly concerned with the definitions of **issues** rather than control over **resources** such as money. Issues such as gender, sexuality and ethnicity are increasingly important, and a greater **plurality** of groups now has a political voice.

Evaluation

Fraser may exaggerate the degree to which some of the issues she mentions are new on the political agenda. A plurality of groups and issues has had some role in politics for a considerable time.

NEW SOCIAL MOVEMENTS

AQA, OCR, WJEC   Textbook pp. 566-575

Many commentators argue that, as conventional party politics has declined in importance, new social movements have become more important.

Hallsworth – challenging power

Hallsworth (1994) sees new social movements as political movements that have emerged since the 1960s and that challenge the **established order** of capitalist society.

Examples include feminism, environmentalism, anti-racism and anti-nuclear movements.

They are based around two types of issue:

- the defence of the **natural and social environment** (for example, animal rights and environmental movements);
- furthering the rights of **marginal groups** (for example, gay liberation).

New social movements have a number of novel features:

- They try to extend the definition of what is political to include the **private sphere** (for example, domestic violence and sexuality).
- They tend not to develop **bureaucratic organizations**.
- They tend to be **diverse** and **fragmented** (for example, feminist groups).
- They do not seek to hold political office themselves.
- Unlike conventional pressure groups, they are more likely to engage in **direct action**.
- They are more concerned with **culture** than with material issues such as living standards.
- They tend to be supported by the young, students and those who work in public services (or whose parents do).

For Hallsworth, they are mainly concerned with **post-materialist values**, in societies where most people have already attained a reasonable basic standard of living.

Todd & Taylor (2004) argue that political parties have declined due to increased cynicism and disillusionment with '**spin doctors**'. The electorate no longer see clear divisions between the parties and the left-of-centre parties no longer focus on the needs of poorer groups. Class identities are less important; new social movements focus on social identity, lifestyle and human rights. Major decisions are influenced by international institutions such as the EU. Power is **diffused**, and democracy is **fragmented**.

Cohen & Rai – global social movements

Cohen & Rai (2000) question whether there is a clear-cut distinction between old and new social movements. However, they do believe there have been changes with the use of new tactics, more use of modern **technology** and a shift towards organizing on a **global scale**.

There are more **global social movements** because:

- there are more international organizations.
- communication has become easier and cheaper.
- TNCs have grown in power.
- environmental problems have become global in scope.
- universal human rights issues have become more prominent.
- key values have spread globally.

Crook *et al* – postmodernization

Crook *et al* (1992) associate the emergence of new social movements with a new politics of **postmodernizing** societies.

Old politics was **class-based** and dominated by elites. It was focused on the state and seen as separate from everyday life.

New politics involves a **volatile electorate** without strong class identities. There is a greater concern with moral issues than with sectional interests, a suspicion of leaders and elites, a move away from concentration on state activities, and a politicization of culture and lifestyle.

The move to the new politics is a result of **class decomposition** (members of the same class become increasingly dissimilar to one another) and **social differentiation** (those with similar backgrounds develop different lifestyles).

The penetration of the **media** into all aspects of life results in a greater focus on the politics of words and images.

Evaluation

Crook *et al* identify some important trends, but they may exaggerate them – for example, many sociologists deny that there has been a decomposition of classes.

Giddens – high modernity

Giddens (1990) examines the relationship between social movements and **high modernity** (he does not believe that we have entered a postmodern age).

Giddens sees modernity as characterized by four **institutional dimensions**, each of which has corresponding social movements:

1. **Capitalism** produces **labour movements** such as unionism.
2. **Military power** produces **peace movements** opposed to destructive, industrialized warfare.
3. **Surveillance** (the control of information and monitoring of populations) produces **free speech/ democratic** movements.
4. **Industrialism** produces **ecological** movements.

Globalization produces increased **risks** in terms of ecological damage and military confrontation, and this leads to ecological and peace movements assuming a greater prominence.

The emphasis in politics changes, but all these types of movement have existed throughout modernity.

Anti-capitalism and anti-globalization

A recent development in social movements is the development of the **anti-capitalist**, or **anti-globalization**, movement. There were major demonstrations against Western capitalist countries in Seattle in 1999 and Genoa in 2001. The movement has wide-ranging aims and involves many different groups.

Callinicos (2003) sees the anti-capitalist movement as united in opposing problems caused by global capitalism.

The movement developed after the collapse of communism left free-market (or **neo-liberal**) capitalism dominant.

Anti-capitalism is opposed to the neo-Liberal **Washington consensus** which has tried to spread

US style capitalism throughout the world. The movement is a response to the increased power of **TNCs**.

Specific campaigns – for example, Jubilee 2000 opposed to Third World debt and poverty – have helped its development.

The **financial crisis** in East Asia 1997-8 raised questions about the stability of capitalism.

Opposition to US capitalism in underdeveloped countries – shown, for example, in the peasant uprising in Mexico in 1994 – has highlighted the problems caused by capitalist policies.

In richer countries neo-Liberal governments have been opposed by workers – for example, public sector strikes in France in 1995.

Naomi Klein (2000) has charted the development of anti-capitalism in opposition to corporations who rely upon **branding** of products. The logos of companies have become a target of **culture jamming**, in which advertisements or **logos** are changed to reveal the negative effects of companies' products and activities.

The Nike swoosh has been dubbed the 'Swooshsticka' and campaigners have highlighted poor pay in Third World factories producing Nike products.

Culture jamming does not challenge capitalist consumer culture as a whole, but a wider movement against capitalist companies, repressive regimes and poor working conditions is now developing.

VOTING BEHAVIOUR

AQA, OCR, WJEC   **Textbook pp. 575-577**

Patterns of voting 1945-1974

From 1945 to the 1970s there were well-established and fairly predictable voting patterns. There was a fairly clear-cut division between two main parties and two types of policy:

- The **Labour Party** was seen as left-wing. It was more likely to support: the redistribution of income and wealth from rich to poor through taxation; high levels of spending on welfare; state intervention in the economy (for example, through the nationalization of industries).

- The **Conservative Party** was seen as right-wing. It was more likely to: support low taxation and lower levels of spending on welfare; accept inequality; oppose nationalization of industries.

Butler & Stokes (1974) characterize voting patterns in this era in the following way:

- Class, as measured by a person's occupation, exercised a key influence on voting.

- Most voters had a strongly **partisan self-image**, thinking of themselves as Labour or Conservative.

- There were few **floating voters**; most voted consistently for the same party.

- There was a **two-party system**, with most of the working class voting Labour and most of the middle class voting Conservative.

- People were **socialized** by parents, and the sorts of schools they attended, into supporting particular parties.

- Third or minor parties attracted few votes.

Throughout the period there were a small number of **deviant voters** who failed to vote for the party associated with their class. This group influenced election outcomes.

Butler & Rose (1960) put forward a variety of explanations for this deviant voting – for example, the experience of social mobility, having a partner from a different class background, or having parents who voted for different parties.

Many argue that the Labour Party was in decline, due to a shrinking proportion of the population in working-class, manual jobs.

THEORIES OF DEALIGNMENT

AQA, OCR, WJEC   **Textbook pp. 577-578**

Sarlvik & Crewe – partisan dealignment

Sarlvik & Crewe (1983) are leading advocates of the view that major changes affecting voting patterns were taking place in the 1970s and 1980s. They argue that:

- **partisan dealignment** was taking place – people's sense of attachment to a particular party was weakening rapidly.

- **class dealignment** was taking place – class was exercising less influence on voting.

- these changes were produced by factors such as the working class buying their own houses and leaving trade unions, which weakened their working-class attachments.

Sarlvik & Crewe believe that voting in this period was increasingly shaped by **policy preferences** – people were voting for the parties whose policies they liked rather than the parties they had been brought up to support.

Critics of Sarlvik & Crewe argue that they exaggerate their case.

Heath *et al* – five-class model

Heath *et al* (1985) argue that, during the 1970s and 1980s, class continued to exercise a strong influence on voting. They support their claims by adopting a sophisticated **five-class model**, instead of what they see as an over-simplified two-class model (working class and middle class).

They argue that voters chose more on the basis of the **ideological image** of the party than on specific policies. The Labour Party was losing support because its ideological image was too left-wing for many voters, rather than because of changes in society.

The Liberal/SDP Alliance was gaining support because its image (right-wing on economic issues but liberal on social issues) was close to the ideology supported by increasing numbers of voters.

Competing theories of voting

The Labour Party won the 1997, 2001 and 2005 elections with comfortable majorities. The various theories of voting which developed in the debates discussed above can be examined in the light of these results.

Dealignment

Crewe & Thompson (1999) find evidence of continued **dealignment**, with just 16% of voters having strong party identification in 1997. Labour failed to attract a new core of loyal voters from particular social groups. Instead it gained support from people without strong party loyalty through:

● **ideological convergence** – moving from left-wing policies to moderate policies; and

● short-term political effects, such as a buoyant economy.

However, **Whiteley et al** (2005) found that only 9% of respondents identified strongly with a political party and 40% fairly strongly. 41% of the electorate were not sufficiently partisan to vote at all.

Class and voting

Heath & Evans (1999) accept that that there is a long-term decline in the relationship between class and voting, evident in the 1997 election. They attribute this to Labour shifting to the ideological middle ground in order to appeal both to working-class and middle-class voters. However, they believe that class might become more important again if big ideological divisions between the parties return.

Norris (2001) believes evidence from the 2001 election shows that the influence of class is continuing to decline.

Clarke et al (2004) finds that the influence of class halved between 1964 and 2001.

Kavanagh & Butler (2005) use opinion poll data to show that New Labour captured a large part of the core Conservative vote in the 2005 election whilst the Conservatives captured up to 25% of the votes of semi-skilled and unskilled workers.

However, **Norris & Wlezien** (2005) find that class differences became more marked in response to messages put out by the parties.

Non-class divisions and voting

Research suggests that, as well as class, other factors are important in shaping recent voting patterns.

Sarlvick & Crewe (1983) argue that **non-class factors** such as trade union membership, housing tenure, public/private sector employment and region were increasingly important in shaping voting. There was little research on issues other than region in the 1997 and 2001 elections, but other non-class factors have been researched.

Region

Curtice & Park (1999) find that in 1997 the influence of region on voting declined, with Labour gaining more votes in the south than the north, and more tactical voting.

Clarke et al (2004) find that home ownership made people less likely to vote Labour.

Johnstone et al (2005) find the **type of constituency** more important than the region. Labour does well in regions with manufacturing industry whilst the Conservatives do well in rural and white-collar areas. However, since 1997 Labour has won more 'middle Britain' constituencies.

Ethnicity

Saggar & Heath (1999) find that between 1994 and 1997 there were no major changes in the relationship between voting and ethnicity, with Labour continuing to win a big majority of ethnic minority votes.

Russell (2002) believes similar patterns were repeated in 2001.

Fieldhouse & Cutts (2005) find that the British **Muslim** population moved away from Labour to the Liberal Democrats in the 2005 general election. This may be due to opposition to the Iraq War.

Gender

In the 1960s and 1970s women were more likely than men to vote **Conservative**.

Norris (1999) has found that in Britain and elsewhere the gender differences in voting have declined, with younger women less likely to vote for right-wing parties such as the Conservatives. This may be due to the influence of **feminism**.

Campbell & Lovenduski (2005) found that women under the age of 54 are more likely to vote Labour. This could be due to measures taken by the Labour party to attract women.

Policy, ideology and economics

Policy preference

Sarlvick & Crewe (1983) thought policy preference would become increasingly important in voting.

Denver (2002) argues that in 2001 policy preference had a big influence on the outcome, with more voters preferring Labour policies (such as increased spending on public services) than Conservative ones. However, Denver admits overall party image might be more important than specific policies.

Whiteley et al (2005) argue that policy preference was more important than ideology in the 2005 election. There was no longer a strong difference between left and right, so people voted for the party they thought best able to deliver effective services.

Bartle & Laycock (2006) finds that voters in the 2005 election did not think Labour were handling anything well except the economy. The main reason for the Labour success was the poor image of the Conservative Party.

Ideology and voting

Budge (1999) finds ideological shifts that might explain the recent successes of the Labour Party. Studying election manifestos he finds that Labour had shifted substantially to the right between 1945 and 1997 to occupy the middle ground, while the Conservatives retained distinctly right-wing policies in 1997.

Bara & Budge (2001) find that in 2001 the Conservative manifesto remained more right-wing than the views of most electors.

Whiteley et al (2005) argue there was little change in ideological stance between the parties between 2001 and 2005. **Lynch** (2006) comments on the change in Conservative policies following the change in party leadership in 2005.

The economy and voting

Crewe (1987a) argues that people vote for the party that will do most for their own prosperity (**pocketbook voting**).

Sanders *et al* (2001) argue that an image of economic competence is important if a party is to win elections. In 1997 the Conservatives lost power even though the economy was doing well, and in 1992 the Conservatives retained power despite an economic recession. The Conservatives lost the 1997 election despite a strong economy because they had lost their reputation for economic competence (in 1992, when Britain was forced to withdraw from the Exchange Rate Mechanism). They were successful in the 1992 election because voters saw Labour as economically incompetent.

Opinion poll evidence supports the view that voters' subjective view of a party's economic competence shapes voting.

Conclusion

The evidence suggests that a variety of social factors influence how people vote, but do not determine voting. Voters make their own judgements about the merits of different parties, and parties continually adapt their policies and ideology to try to attract votes.

The decline of politics?

Some social scientists have suggested that the nature of politics is changing, with the population becoming disillusioned with politicians.

The **Power Inquiry** (2006) found a turnout of around 60% at the 2001 and 2005 general elections and turnouts of around 25% in local elections. Membership of political parties has fallen below 2% of the population and the majority of those are not active members.

However, the inquiry found the population interested in current affairs and political issues and there were large increases in support for campaigning organizations such as Greenpeace.

Reasons given for declining interest included: unhappiness with the political parties; the electoral system; difficulties with the process of voting.

In recent elections the parties have concentrated on marginal constituencies without engaging most of the population.

The Power Inquiry found similar patterns in many advanced industrial societies and think this may be a reflection of a move to a **postindustrial society**.

The Power Inquiry's suggested solutions include: constituency changes, citizenship education; increased powers for local government.

Stoker (2006) argues there is a growing disenchantment with party politics, and that people's involvement is temporary and issue-based. He dismisses the idea that the disenchantment is caused by political corruption, globalization or lack of commitment to community organizations, arguing instead that **individualism** and **consumerism** are key factors.

As a result of this disenchantment, some types of political activism – such as joining political parties – are decreasing whilst other types – such as boycotting goods – have grown. Stoker believes party politics can be revived if there are changes in the voting system and an increased emphasis on local politics.

Crouch (2005) argues that although the number of democracies is rising, the established democracies are moving into an era of **post-democracy**. The underlying cause of this is globalization. According to Crouch:

- the most important institutions are **global firms**, which are primarily concerned with image.
- **public administration** has become commercialized, leaving only the most disadvantaged using state provision. As a result, public services are largely provided by the private sector and politics becomes less important.
- power has shifted away from democratic control to the **corporate elite**. Their power increases as they provide services and expertise for the government and funds for political parties.
- Labour has become a **post-democratic** party that has lost touch with the traditional working class.
- the **Third Way** – funding public services through the state but allowing service provision by private companies – has blurred responsibility for the public services and their failure.

Crouch believes that the move to post-democracy can be reversed if the corporate elite is controlled, the focus becomes public service rather than private profit, and local democracy increases in power.

DEVELOP YOUR ANALYTICAL AND EVALUATION SKILLS

Essay plans

For each of the following questions write your own essay plan before comparing it with the suggestions given here. For the final question you can write a full answer and compare it with the provided model answer.

Britain is governed by a ruling class. Discuss.

 Background

This is clearly stating a Marxist position and you would need to define 'ruling class' and outline the Marxist view. Some Marxists, such as Poulantzas, would agree that the British state serves ruling-class interests, but not that the ruling class governs directly. Sklair would tend to agree with the statement, but sees the ruling class as a transnational capitalist class rather than a class within Britain. Most of the other views in the chapter disagree with the statement: elite theory denies that the rulers form a class; pluralists reject the idea that any one group monopolizes power; postmodernists do not believe that a ruling class exists. Some theorists of globalization believe the power to control societies comes largely from outside the society, so a ruling class could not govern Britain.

For	Against
● Marx and Engels (p. 135)	● Elite theory (p. 134)
● Miliband (p. 135)	● Postmodernists (p. 138)
● Westergaard & Resler (p. 135)	● Pluralists (p. 133)
	● Ohmae and Giddens (p. 137)

For and against
● Poulantzas (p. 135)
● Sklair (p. 137)

 Top Tip

Chapter 1 (*Stratification*) is also useful for this question.

Social factors now have little influence on voting behaviour in Britain. Discuss.

 Background

Early theories of voting (for example, Butler & Stokes) saw social factors, particularly class, as the key to understanding voting in Britain. The importance of class has long been debated, with many putting an increasing emphasis on other social factors such as region, gender, age and ethnicity. Ivor Crewe has consistently challenged the importance of class, but he has seen other social factors (such as union membership, housing tenure) as increasingly important. Theories emphasizing policy preference, party ideology and images of economic competence all see political factors as more important than social ones.

For	Against
● Crewe (p. 140)	● Butler & Stokes (p. 140)
● Curtice & Park (p. 141)	● Heath *et al* (p. 140)
● Denver (p. 141)	● Saggar & Heath (p. 141)
● Clarke (p. 141)	● Norris & Wlezien (p. 141)
● Kavanagh & Butler (p. 141)	● Fieldhouse & Cutts (p. 141)

 Top Tip

You could use postmodern arguments that social divisions are declining in importance to support this statement (see p. 138).

The nation-state is becoming much less important in the arenas of politics and power. Discuss.

Background

Most of the older theories of power and the state have tended to focus on power exercised by the state, although Marxists have always seen economic power exercised outside the state as crucial. This view has been increasingly challenged by advocates of globalization, by those who see new social movements and global social movements as more important than parliamentary politics, and by postmodernists (such as Fraser and Crook *et al*) who see politics as shifting away from the public sphere. On the other hand, state-centred theories emphasize the continuing power of the state, and Chomsky's work shows the enormous power of the US state.

For	Against
● Postmodernism (p. 138) ● New and global social movements (p. 138) ● Marxist views that emphasize economic power (p. 135) ● Theories of globalization (p. 137)	● Pluralism (p. 133) ● Elite theory (p. 134) ● State-centred theories (p. 136) ● Chomsky (p. 136)

Top Tip

Anthony Giddens (p. 137) provides a balanced view that the state retains significant power although it has been reduced by globalization.

Assess the importance of new social movements in modern Britain.

Background

Whilst political parties have declining membership and less than 70% of the electorate vote in general elections, new social movements have increased in number. Crook *et al* believe they reflect the new politics of postmodern society. Giddens relates the type of social movement to the institutional dimensions of society. Some new social movements are global. Marxists and Neo-Marxists still believe that power rests with the ruling class whilst elite theorists see power resting with a small group of the population.

New social movements are new and powerful	New social movements are not new or powerful
● Hallsworth (p. 138) ● Cohen & Rai (p. 139) ● Crook, Pakulski & Waters (p. 139) ● Callinicos (p. 139)	● Marxists (p. 135) ● Elite theorists (p. 134) ● Williams (p. 134) ● Giddens (p. 137)

Top Tip

Consider whether new social movements are really new. How do they differ from interest groups? Use examples to clarify your answer. Remember the international dimension.

The population is becoming increasingly disillusioned with politics and politicians. Discuss.

Background

Much has been written about falling membership of political parties and falling turnout in national and local elections. Some writers believe this is a reflection of uninterest or disillusionment among the electorate, whilst others believe the population has become more interested in single-issue and local politics. The Power Inquiry found the population were interested in current affairs and politics, but were unhappy with political parties and the electoral system. Stoker believes consumerism and individualism are more important factors than disillusionment with politicians. Crouch blames globalization.

For

- Postmodernists (p. 138)
- Crouch (p. 142)
- The Power Inquiry (p. 142)

For and against

- The Power Inquiry (p. 142)
- Stoker (p. 142)

  Top Tip

There are two separate questions here: Are the public becoming disillusioned with politicians? Are the public becoming disillusioned with politics? It is also possible that the nature of politics is changing; Crouch suggests we live in a post-democracy.

Wright-Mills argued that there was a power elite in America in the 1950s. To what extent is this concept relevant in modern Britain?

 Background

Wright-Mills argued that small and powerful elites dominate power partly because of their status, but partly also because of their links with each other. To be a member of one group ensured strong connections with the others. Williams sees a similar situation in Britain, Marxists disagree and see a ruling class. Grant believes Britain is basically democratic.

For

- Williams (p. 134)
- Sutton Trust (p. 135)

Against

- Miliband (p. 135)
- Westergaard (p. 135)
- Grant (p. 134)

 Top Tip

Think about whether groups having social connections and similar backgrounds means they use their power to their own advantage.

Model answer

Wright-Mills argued that there was a power elite in America in the 1950s. To what extent is this concept relevant in modern Britain?

Wright-Mills argued that America was controlled by three powerful groups of the population who occupied positions in three important institutions – the major corporations, the military and the federal government. He showed how top members of these groups met and knew each other and shared a similar lifestyle. He pointed out that the power elite attended the same schools and belonged to the same high prestige clubs. This allowed them to mingle, to intermarry, and to obtain opportunities for themselves and their families to move between the groups.

Wright-Mills argued that the power elite were a unified group who could exercise power because the general population was divided and passive and showed little interest in politics.

More recently Williams has argued that a similar power elite exists in modern Britain. He identifies three main groups in this elite. The first group, the political elite, consists of top politicians and civil servants who hold political power. This group still provides 'conduits of power' despite the onset of privatization. The second group is the professional elite, who have thrived since the 1970s and are managed by the new professionals. The final group is the business and financial elite, whose members hold the greatest power.

Williams suggests that the groups are interlinked in many ways. Members of the professional elite and the political elite share similar educational background, most coming from private education and Oxford or Cambridge universities. They send their children into these educational institutions and ensure their future elite positions. The business elite fund political parties and PFI initiatives, enabling government to spend money without taxation and business to make substantial profits. Williams also suggests there is evidence of cohesion, with individuals belonging to more than one of these elite groups and moving between them — for example, politicians taking up highly paid directorships in private companies.

There is some evidence to support Williams's view. The Sutton Trust found that the top legal professionals were largely recruited from elite educational backgrounds, whilst Criddle showed that 60% of Conservative MPs had been to private schools. Whilst the background of Labour MPs was much less privileged, Cracknell showed that over half of Gordon Brown's first cabinet had attended Oxford or Cambridge universities.

Evidence from the London Chamber of Commerce shows the financial elite come from less privileged backgrounds, with less than a third attending one of the top thirteen universities. However, their financial strength can still lead to close contacts with the political and professional elites.

Marxists argue that power rests with the ruling class rather than in the hands of an elite. Miliband argues that the state is a direct tool of the ruling class and always acts to promote its interests. Those who occupy top positions in government come from ruling-class backgrounds and the state acts to protect their position. Westergaard points out that, despite years of concern for the redistribution of resources, wealth remains concentrated in the hands of capitalists — a clear sign of ruling-class power.

Grant argues that modern Britain is largely democratic, with a wide range of interests represented by pressure groups, and these groups being consulted by government. He does recognize that group leaders have more power than group members. However, power is being devolved to local assemblies such as those in Scotland, and some power rests with the European Union. If Grant is right, these changes would make it more difficult for a power elite to exercise power.

In conclusion, there is considerable agreement amongst sociologists that power is not equally distributed in society. Marxists propose a ruling class which dominates all sections of society whilst elite theorists see powerful, overlapping groups. These views have some similarities. Both see the powerful coming from a small section of the population and benefiting from privileged educational opportunities. However, Marxists see this group as a class which reproduces itself whilst elite theorists see power coming from command posts in important institutions, which operate on a principle of elite self-recruitment. Grant, an elite pluralist, sees leaders of interest groups as having some power.

There is some evidence of a powerful, self-perpetuating group in modern Britain, but whether or not it is a power elite is debateable.

RESOURCES

Power, politics and the state

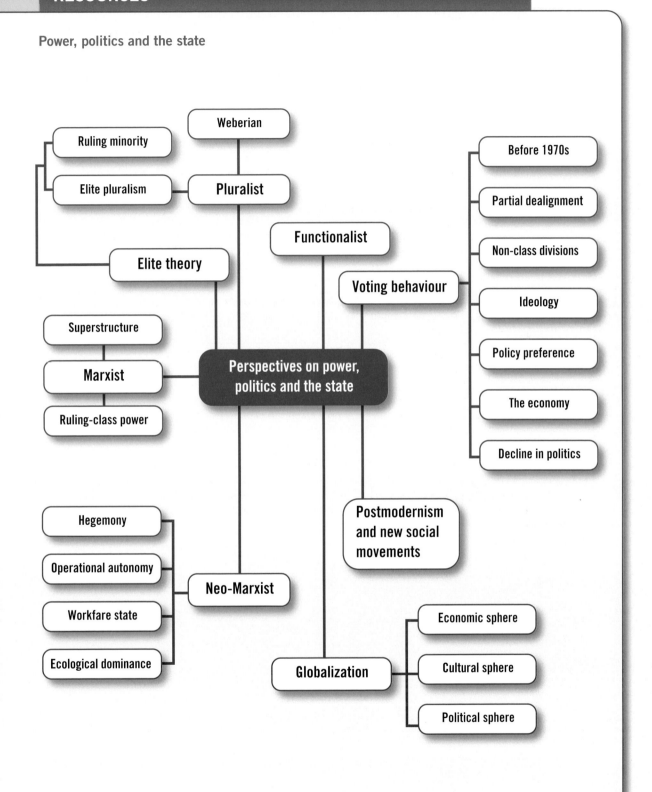

The state and power

Perspective	Source of power	Legitimation	Role of the state
Functionalists	Value consensus	Politicians are given power temporarily. If they act outside society's interests they can be removed	To use power to achieve collective goals
Marxists	Ownership of means of production	Media indoctrinate public into accumulating material possessions	To promote ruling-class interests
Neo-Marxists	Ruling-class dominance	Hegemony achieved through ruling-class ideology and concessions to the masses	Provides framework for the continuation of capitalism
Pluralists (Weberian)	Power derives from population as a whole	Over time every group will have its interests represented	Honest broker mediating between competing interest groups
Elite theory	Power elite exercises power over passive majority	The elites use the language of national interest to maintain power	Major decisions reflect elite interests
Postmodernists	Power comes from knowledge	New social movements arise to reflect the concerns of the public	State has no power. Politics fragmented into local issues
Globalization theorists	Transnational capitalist class and the TNCs who control global capital	Focus on ideology of consumerism; ownership of goods is most important	To preserve global capital in their own country

Writers and their work

Writer	Perspective or approach	Concept	Study
Weber	Pluralist (Weberian)	Types of authority	Essays in sociology
Parsons	Functionalist	Variable sum view of power	*Sociological Theory and Modern Society*
Grant & Marsh	Pluralist	No sectional interest is paramount	Study of British politics
Grant	Pluralist	Changing pressure group politics	Study of British politics
Pareto	Elite theorist	Circulating elites	Importance of psychological characteristics of the elite
Wright-Mills	Elite theorist	The power elite	Three overlapping elites exercise power over passive masses
Williams	Elite theorist	Power elite in Britain	Study of UK since 1990
Marx and Engels	Marxist	Ruling-class power	Study of all societies throughout history
Miliband	Marxist	State as tool of the ruling class	Study of the way the state supports private enterprise
Gramsci	Neo-Marxist	Hegemony	Study of the way the ruling class wins the support of other classes
Jessop	Neo-Marxist	Ecological dominance; the workfare state	Study of the way the state provides a framework for capitalism
Ohmae	Globalization theorist	One giant interlinked world economy	Study of the way giant corporations dominate world trade
Sklair	Marxist	Transnational capitalist class	Study of globalization and the international ruling class
Baudrillard	Postmodernist	Simulacra	Study of the importance of image without substance
Cohen & Rai	Globalization theorists	Global social movements	Social movements use modern technology and act globally
Giddens	Theorist of high modernity	Labour movements, peace movements, democratic movements, ecological movements	Study of the institutional dimensions of social movements
Crook, Pakulski & Waters	Postmodernist	New politics and postmodernization	Study of politicization of culture and lifestyle
Crewe & Thompson	Political scientist	Dealignment	Study of the declining impact of social class on voting behaviour
Sarlvick & Crewe	Political scientists	Non-class divisions and voting	Study showing trade union membership, housing tenure and public/private sector employment influence voting
Denver	Political scientist	Policy preference	Study showing influence of policy on election result
Crouch	Political scientist	Post-democracy	Study of the impact of globalization on established democracies

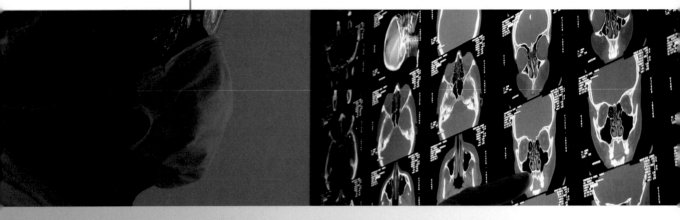

SPECIFICATION COVERAGE

Specification	Details
AQA AS SCLY2	All sections are relevant. You will also need to apply sociological research methods to the study of health
OCR AS Unit G672: Socialization, Culture and Identity	
WJEC A2: Understanding Power and Control; Option 3: Understanding health and Disability	All sections are relevant

DEFINING HEALTH AND ILLNESS

AQA, OCR, WJEC   **Textbook pp. 279–319**

The traditional medical model of health sees it as an absence of disease. **Disease** is present when the body diverges from objective, scientific definitions of the **normal functioning** of the human body. **Good health** is defined as the absence of such problems.

However, the World Health Organization (WHO) uses a much broader definition, defining health as 'not merely an absence of disease, but a state of complete physical, mental, spiritual and social well-being'. This approach uses a more positive definition which emphasizes the **positive qualities** which must be present for good health.

Research into self-defined health amongst the population suggests that many people also use a functional definition of health which involves the ability to carry out normal, everyday activities.

Blaxter (1983, 1990) found that different social groups defined health in different ways, with younger males emphasizing the positive aspects of strength and fitness while younger females used a more functional definition.

Howlett et al (1992) found Asian ethnic groups favoured functional definitions of health while African Caribbeans placed more emphasis on energy and strength.

DISEASE AND ILLNESS

Blaxter and **Howlett et al**'s research suggests that the definition of health varies between social groups and is therefore relative. However, sociologists accept that there are objective medical conditions. **Eisenberg** (1977) distinguishes between:

- **illness** – a physical state which is experienced as having an unpleasant impact; and,
- **disease** – abnormal and harmful physical changes in the body.

The examples below illustrate the **relative nature** of illness:

- **Ackernecht** (1982) showed how a skin disease – spirochetosis – was so common amongst some indigenous South Americans that those without the disease were considered abnormal and the unaffected men were prohibited from marrying.

- **L'Esperance** (1977) showed how nineteenth-century women could be defined as suffering from hysteria if they laughed or cried 'for no reason'. Hysteria is not an actual disease – women were 'hysterical' if they tried to engage in non-traditional female roles outside the domestic sphere.

- The history of the **NHS** in Britain suggests that over time people have come to expect higher standards of health and demand treatment for a wider range of illnesses. **Sen** (2002) argued that the higher the educational level of the population the higher the demand for health care.

THEORETICAL APPROACHES TO ILLNESS

AQA, OCR, WJEC   Textbook pp. 282-288

Functionalist perspective

Talcott Parsons (1951) argues that illness is socially defined in terms of the **sick role**. This is based upon two **rights** and two **obligations**.

The sick person's rights are:

- to be exempted from normal **social obligations** such as work;
- to be absolved from **blame** for their illness.

The sick person's obligations are:

- to try to get **well**;
- to seek **medical help** for their condition.

The sick role is a type of **deviance** which can disrupt the smooth functioning of society. However, because of the obligations involved, it is likely to be a temporary state with the normal functioning of the individual and society being resumed as soon as possible.

Criticisms

This approach is only useful for looking at **acute illness** and not **chronic illness** which has no short-term cure (for example, asthma or diabetes). However, Parsons argued that with chronic illness people are expected to manage their illness so that they can carry on with normal social roles.

Friedson (1970) argues that there are alternative roles to the sick role described by Parsons. Where a person is not expected to get better and faces death, people are given unconditional access to the sick role. Where the illness is **stigmatized** (for example, sexually transmitted diseases) the sickness is seen as being illegitimate – it is the person's own fault and they are not given the rights associated with the sick role.

Many people who are ill do not consult doctors. **Scambler et al** (1981) show that people are more likely to consult friends and relatives about illness than doctors.

Turner (1995) argues that Parsons ignores the fact that medical consultations may be a **site of conflict** between the different interests of doctors and patients.

Waitzkin (1971) supports Parsons's general theory but argues that the sick role can be used to allow some **deviance** – which avoids greater conflict that could seriously harm society. During the Vietnam War many better-educated men were able to avoid conscription to the US army, on the grounds of physical or mental unsuitability which reduced political opposition to the war from higher social classes.

Political economy perspective

This approach is influenced by **Marxism**, and argues that medicine serves the interests of the powerful.

Navarro (1986) sees medicine as benefiting capitalism. It maintains a workforce that is healthy enough to work, to help capitalists make profits. Illness is defined as an inability to work.

Illness has an **ideological function** of masking differences in health caused by inequality, as it portrays illness as the result of bad luck or irresponsible behaviour. According to **Doyal & Pennell** (1979) much ill health is the result of capitalism – for example, it is caused by tobacco companies, pollution and work-related accidents and diseases.

For Navarro, **biomedical** explanations of illness predominate, and emphasize the use of advanced drugs and technology. This produces large profits for capitalist drug and medical companies, and disguises the real causes of illness in inequality and exploitation. Treatments based on the biomedical approach fail to tackle the **social causes** of illness.

Annandale (1998) points out how profitable breast implants have continued to be used despite well-documented negative effects on health.

Criticisms

Hart (1985) points out that capitalist societies have experienced large rises in **life expectancy**. Hart argues that the criticisms of health care are more applicable to the USA than to some European countries with free health care and strong laws to restrict the harmful activities of companies and protect workers.

Navarro accepts that there have been some health gains under capitalism, but argues that the gap in health between rich and poor has increased.

Postmodern perspectives

Bury (1997) argues that improvements in health have led to the expectation of long and healthy lives in which people can plan their future. However, this is threatened by **chronic illness**. In a study of those diagnosed as suffering from rheumatoid arthritis he found that the diagnosis threatened people's identity, causing a **biographical disruption** and leading them to review their lives. It also disrupted relationships with others because of the likelihood of increased dependence on others. The greater people's physical, economic and relationship resources the more they could retain a positive self-image.

Williams (1984) argues that over time the biographical disruption can be overcome with a **narrative reconstruction** which makes sense of how and why they got the disease, often blaming it on negative social experiences. This helps to repair the disruption and can 'realign present and past, self and society'.

Criticisms

Carricaburu & Pierret (1995) criticize the postmodern approach, arguing that the response to disease reflects membership of particular social groups rather than individual biography. In a study of HIV-positive men, the gay men experienced a process of disruption more than the heterosexual men, as the diagnosis reinforced the gay men's perception of themselves as ill.

Similarly, **Pound et al** (1998) found that working-class men in the East End of London experienced strokes as just another crisis in their difficult lives and not as a biographical disruption.

Interactionist perspectives

Symbolic interactionists tend to see illness as a form of **socially defined deviance** rather than as a disease.

Tesh (1988) studied RSI (Repetitive Strain Injury) amongst typists. He found that views on whether it constituted a disease varied:

- **Employers** denied that it was a disease, blaming it on bad posture.
- **Psychiatrists** argued that it was a psychological problem resulting from dislike of the work.
- **Unions** claimed it was a common and serious real disease.

Scambler *et al* (1981) studied 79 women aged 16-44 and found that only one in 18 women who experienced symptoms of illness visited a doctor. **Freund & McGuire** (1991) use the phrase the '**illness iceberg**' to indicate that there is much more illness than is reported to doctors.

Becker *et al* (1977) developed the **health belief model** to explain what influenced people to visit the doctor and to follow the advice provided by the doctor. They found that **social factors** are as important as **medical factors**. Interaction between the individual and their doctor, and the individual's perceptions of health and illness and the medical profession, shape the process of consultation and treatment.

Criticisms

Day & Day (1977) argue that interactionists ignore social factors – such as inequality, pollution and stress – which may cause ill health.

Feminist approaches to health

Liberal feminism

Liberal feminism explains inequalities in health between males and females in terms of the different **social roles** and **economic positions** of men and women. Liberal feminists have tended to see the medical professions as dominated by men, who occupy most of the senior positions.

The radical feminist **Ellen Annandale** (1998) criticizes liberal feminism for believing that minor changes can challenge **patriarchal domination** of medicine. She sees liberal feminism as wanting women to overcome the 'handicaps' of the female body and emotionality. Radical feminists see these as central to the very nature of being a woman.

Socialist feminism

Socialist feminists believe **capitalist patriarchal** society must be fundamentally changed to achieve equality between the sexes.

For **Doyal** (1995), capitalism defines female health in terms of the ability to:

- **reproduce** the next generation of workers;
- undertake **domestic tasks**; and
- act as a **reserve army of labour**.

Doyal sees women's health as undermined by the **dual burden** of doing paid work as well as most of the housework. Women do more caring than men, suffer physical and emotional damage from **sexual abuse**, and risk cervical cancer through sexual activity. They suffer more stress than men and can become dependent on prescribed drugs and tobacco to cope, harming their health in the long term.

In these ways health care reproduces the class, gender and ethnic **hierarchies** of patriarchal capitalism.

Radical feminism

Radical feminists argue that *all* women are exploited in a **patriarchal** society.

Ehrenreich & English (1978) believe medicine is used to control women. In the nineteenth century it was believed that women were naturally more frail than men and they needed to save their energy for reproduction. This justified the exclusion of women from a range of activities including higher education and sport.

Graham & Oakley (1986) argue that the frames of reference of male doctors lead them to view pregnancy as an entirely medical and potentially problematic event, whereas women see it as a normal part of their lives and social relationships. Doctors control pregnant women by putting women in a position of **passivity** (for example, having women lie down to be examined) and by demanding information from them. Doctors reaffirm their **superior status** by using medical terminology and denying women information which might give them more control over the management of their pregnancy.

Radical feminism has been criticized for **essentialism** – seeing all women as essentially the same and ignoring differences between groups of women.

MODELS OF HEALTH

AQA, OCR, WJEC   Textbook pp. 288-291

Traditional medicine

Sociologists take the view that health and illness are social constructs and must be understood in the context of social, political and historical circumstances. In traditional societies models of health saw people as unique beings and took account of both their mind and their body. These wide-ranging therapies dominated until the 19th century and since then the biomedical model has taken over.

The biomedical model

This became the dominant model in the early nineteenth century. It has four key elements.

1 The **mind-body dualism** sees social factors as irrelevant in explaining illness. Illness is viewed as resulting from malfunction of part of the body.

2 **Specific aetiology** looks for precise causes of illness such as bacteria and viruses.

3 The **mechanical metaphor** sees the body in terms of the role of each body part in the overall functioning of the organism, and categorizes diseases accordingly. Illnesses are diagnosed through symptoms which indicate the malfunctioning of part of the body, and are treated by trying to return particular body parts to normal functioning. Individual systems are emphasized rather than the totality.

4 Medicine is seen as an **objective science** based on established scientific methods.

The biomedical model continues to dominate contemporary health care to the exclusion of alternative models.

Criticisms

McKeown (1979) argues that improvements in health in England and Wales from the early eighteenth century onwards were very largely the result of improved **nutrition** and **hygiene**. Developments in medicine, such as the introduction of immunization and improved medical techniques, have played a much smaller part in raising life expectancy.

Most people do not see their own health exclusively in terms of the biomedical model. For example, **Blaxter** (1983) found that working-class women understood that factors such as **stress**, **poverty** and **poor environment** were important as specific biological causes of illness.

Medicalization

Some critics of the biomedical model and the medical profession believe that medicine exercises **social control** by extending what counts as illness.

Ivan Illich (1976) argues that the medical profession actually harms people in a process known as **iatrogenesis**, in which there is an increase in illness and social problems as a result of medical intervention. Iatrogenesis takes three forms:

1 **Clinical iatrogenesis** involves serious side effects of medical intervention, which are often worse than the condition they were used to treat.

2 **Social iatrogenesis** does harm by creating a passive and docile population who become reliant on the medical profession, which prescribes drugs to help them cope with their life in society

3 **Structural iatrogenesis** refers to the way that the medical profession reduces the ability of the population to face sickness, pain and death. These things are normal parts of life and ageing but people become unable to cope with them because of the claims and activities of medicine.

Marxists such as **Navarro** (1980) link medicalization to the operation of an oppressive capitalist system. Medicine disguises the **underlying causes** of disease such as **class inequality** and **poverty**. Instead people see health as an individual problem.

Ehrenreich & English (1978) believe that women's bodies have been medicalized. Menstruation and pregnancy have come to be seen as medical problems requiring intervention such as hysterectomies.

Conrad & Schneider (1980) show how even **gambling** has been defined as an illness by the medical profession.

Moynihan & Smith (2002) argue that the population demand certain conditions – such as Gulf War Syndrome – be defined as illnesses, but the medical profession resist.

PROFESSIONS AND POWER IN MEDICINE

AQA, OCR, WJEC   Textbook pp. 292-295

This section concerns the status and power of doctors in society.

Millerson (1964) follows the functionalist view of the profession in seeing professions as having certain traits which justify their high rewards and power in society. Medical professionals:

- are in possession of theoretical knowledge;
- have undergone specialized education;
- have passed examinations in order to practise;
- have an independent professional body which regulates behaviour;

- are subject to a professional code of behaviour;
- serve the public good rather than personal interests.

Parsons (1951) argues that the medical profession serves society by treating the sick to the highest professional standards. Their specialist skill and knowledge combined with professional neutrality merits high rewards.

Critics of the functionalist approach, such as **Turner** (1995), argue that this view is simply an idealized image of doctors, which is promoted by the profession and ignores the way in which professional bodies manipulate clients to obtain high rewards.

Friedson (1970) offers a **Weberian** perspective. He argues that doctors obtain high rewards by using **social closure**. Entry to the profession is restricted by the professional body which limits the supply of qualified doctors and thus pushes up wages. The profession regulates itself, excludes other health care professionals from doing its work, and justifies high wages by promoting the view that doctors are serving the public good.

Jamous & Peloille (1970, discussed in **Turner**, 1995) argues that the medical profession maintains its position by ensuring **social distance** between itself and its clients. Prestige is maintained by mystifying the knowledge possessed by the professionals. Jamus & Peloille refer to this as the **indeterminacy/technicality ratio**.

Turner (1995) argues that doctors dominate other medical professionals by using **indeterminacy**, as well as the following processes:

- **Subordination** involves forcing other professionals (such as midwives and occupational therapists) to carry out tasks delegated to them by doctors.
- **Occupational limitation** limits the range of activities other professionals are allowed to carry out.
- **Exclusion** prevents competing occupations from practising medicine – for example, homeopaths.

From a **feminist** point of view, **Anne Witz** (1992) points out that most subordinate or excluded health care providers (for example, nurses or homeopaths) are women. This is because men use a **gendered exclusionary** strategy which blocks entry to the profession for women and a **gendered demarcatory** strategy to confine women to subordinate roles in health care.

According to Witz, men established the medical specialism of obstetrics in order to gain control of the female midwifery profession. However, midwives resisted the domination of obstetricians and managed to retain control over 'normal' births.

Increasingly, in recent years, the power of doctors has been challenged:

- **Haug** (1973) believes that **de-professionalization** has taken place, as a better-educated population makes it own choices – for example, preferring herbal remedies to conventional medicine.
- **McKinlay & Arches** (1985) believe that **proletarianization** has taken place in the medical profession, as the work of NHS doctors has become tightly controlled and regulated.
- **Carpenter** (1993) believes that other medical professions (such as nursing) have tried to

professionalize themselves and increase their power in relation to doctors. For example, nurses are now allowed to prescribe a limited range of drugs.

COMPLEMENTARY MEDICINE

AQA, OCR, WJEC   Textbook pp. 295-298

Complementary or **alternative** medicine refers to a wide range therapies which often pre-date the biomedical model.

Ernst & White (2000) concluded that 20% of the population use complementary medicine, spending £1.6 billion each year.

In a US study, **Eisenberg** *et al* (2001) found people using conventional and complementary medicine together, and believing this to be the most effective treatment.

Sharma (1992) showed people use complementary therapies when conventional ones have been unsuccessful. Their perception is that the therapies have fewer side effects, and that they are treated better by the practitioner than by their doctor. Most do not tell their doctor that they are using complementary therapy.

The resurgence of complementary medicine

Postmodern explanations

Postmodernists believe the resurgence of alternative therapies is a reflection of the move to a postmodern society, characterized by plurality and choice.

Saks (1998) believes the biomedical model is a feature of **modernity**, when scientific explanations were paramount, and other therapies dismissed as superstitious or irrational.

Bakx (1991) links the decline of biomedicine to its failure to treat the chronic (long-term) illnesses which affect a growing number of people. People seek relief from their symptoms and greater choice in their treatment.

Neo-Weberian approaches

Friedson (1994) attributes the dominance of biomedicine to the successful occupational strategy of marginalizing competing therapies.

Saks (1998) argues the dominance of biomedicine comes from '**interest-based politics**'. The BMA has succeeded in ensuring that only scientific treatments can be regarded as medicine. However, the fall in the number of children being immunized with the MMR vaccination (following a study which alleged a link between the vaccination and autism) shows that people do not always accept biomedical advice.

Cant & Sharma (1999) suggests that complementary medicine has continued to treat people in all societies – only in the UK and USA has biomedicine become dominant.

Bakx (1991) distinguishes three types of medicine:

- **popular medicine** – informal caring done by women in the home;
- **folk medicine** – a wide range of complementary therapies;
- **biomedicine**.

Most health care happens through **popular** and **folk medicine**. State provision and insurance schemes are based on biomedicine.

Conclusion

The biomedical model remains dominant, but increasingly people choose to use this in conjunction with complementary medicine.

INEQUALITIES IN HEALTH

AQA, OCR, WJEC   Textbook pp. 298-306

Health inequalities can be measured in different ways:

- **Mortality rates** are the number of people dying over a period of one year per 100,000 of the population.
- **Standardized mortality rates** measure the relative chances of dying compared to the average mortality rate amongst 16-65 year-olds, which is represented by a figure of 100.
- **Morbidity** rates measure rates of illness and disease.

Studies of health inequality

The **Black Report** (1980) was the first major British study of social class and rates of morbidity and mortality. It found that higher social classes tended to show lower rates of mortality and morbidity.

The **Acheson Report** (1998) showed continuing class inequality and a widening of class inequalities in health when comparing the highest and lowest socioeconomic classes.

In the 1970s the **mortality rate** amongst men of working age in the lowest socioeconomic class was twice that of those in the highest class. By the 1990s it had increased to three times this level.

The **life expectancy** of those in the highest class increased by two years between 1970 and 2000, compared to an increase of 1.4 years in the lowest class.

Professional workers are much less likely than unskilled workers to suffer from a **limited long-standing illness**, and the inequality in this regard has been increasing.

Evidence shows substantial variations in **mental health**, with 24% of women in social classes IV & V suffering from mental illness but only 15% of those in classes I & II.

Shaw *et al* (1999) found that there were considerable **geographical differences** in mortality even when gender and class factors had been taken into account.

Explanations for health inequality

Artefact explanation

The **artefact explanation** suggests that the apparent rise in health inequality is misleading. **Illsley** (1986, 1987) argues that the emphasis on the relative decline in the health of the lowest socioeconomic class (class V) is misleading, because this class is small and shrinking in size. However, the **Acheson Report** (1998) showed that health inequality was growing even when the top two classes (I and II) were compared with the bottom two classes (IV and V).

Other researchers have questioned whether the **Registrar General's Scale**, the class scheme on which these statistics are based, is a valid and reliable way of recording social class.

Saunders (1993) argues that **consumption groups** have more influence on health inequality than class, with those who own cars and homes enjoying better health than those who do not.

Some sociologists have questioned the direction of the relationship between poor health and social class. **Illsley** (1987) argues that those with poor health are more likely to be in lower social classes because they are less able to obtain and retain higher-class jobs than others as a result of their health problems.

Shaw et al (1999) suggest that the social and economic problems faced by lower classes create the health problems, rather than the other way round.

Cultural explanations

Some sociologists put forward cultural explanations for health inequality, suggesting that the lifestyle of lower social classes is more unhealthy than that of higher classes. Unhealthy **cultural practices** which are more common in the working class include:

- higher rates of smoking;
- greater consumption of fatty foods;
- lower consumption of fruit and vegetables.

All these differences can lead to higher rates of cancer and heart disease.

Cultural explanations tend to blame lower social classes for choosing an unhealthy lifestyle and suggest that improved education will solve the problems.

Critics of cultural explanations argue that risky behaviours cannot be seen as foolish lifestyle choices but are rational responses to class situation. **Graham** (1993) and **Graham & Blackburn** (1998) see smoking as a way in which working-class mothers try to cope with very stressful lives.

Paterson (1981) argues that cultural explanations ignore the underlying structure of society. For example, poverty makes it difficult for lower social classes to afford healthy foods, and capitalists promote unhealthy food through advertising in order to boost their profits.

Materialist explanations

Some sociologists offer materialist explanations, which explain health inequality in terms of the structure of society. Cultural differences, which may be linked to poor health, are shaped by inequalities in society. A range of arguments and studies support this approach:

- Manual workers suffer more accidents at work than non-manual workers.
- **Martin et al** (1987) show a link between poor housing and respiratory disease.
- **Lobstein** (1995) found that healthy diets tend to be expensive and healthy food is more expensive in poor areas than in affluent areas.
- The American **Multiple Risk Factor Intervention Trial** (1996) showed that death rates were considerably higher for lower social classes even when factors such as smoking, blood pressure and cholesterol levels were taken into account.
- **Doyal & Pennell** (1979) claim that the capitalist desire for profits explains health inequalities, as it creates risks for workers and advertises and sells unhealthy products to consumers.
- **Clapp et al** (2005) suggest that 12% of deaths from cancer are workplace-related.

- **Meldrumm** (2005) found 15-20% of lung cancer deaths are caused by working conditions.

Shaw et al (1999) explain health inequality in terms of the accumulation of disadvantages at crucial points in the **life course**, such as poor nutrition in childhood and job loss in adulthood.

Putnam (1995) argues that **social capital**, particularly networks of contacts, are important in understanding life chances.

Using the concept of **social context**, **Joshi et al** (2000) argues that the relationship of the individual with their physical environment and with people around them must also be considered.

Pevalin & Rose (2004) found that **social capital** had less impact on health than social deprivation.

Wilkinson (1996) found that the health of a population improves once a certain level of Gross Domestic Product (GDP) is reached (around $5,000 per head). At this level, an **epidemiological transition** improves mortality and morbidity rates. However, beyond this level, income inequality is far more important, with better health in countries with less income inequality. This is because countries with high levels of income inequality have greater social divisions and a **culture of inequality** in which there is less trust and sense of community and people develop less social capital.

Scambler (2002) criticizes Wilkinson for failing to spell out how a lack of social trust leads to ill health.

Gender inequalities and health

Evidence from **self-report studies** suggests that women have higher rates of illness and restricted activity than men and suffer more depression. However, they tend to live longer than men. These patterns have been explained in a number of ways.

The **artefact explanation** suggests that women do not really suffer more ill health, but are just more likely than men to perceive themselves as being ill. However, **MacIntyre** (1993) found that men are more likely than women to exaggerate their symptoms.

Genetic explanations may account for part of the difference in health between men and women. For example, **Waldron** (1983) suggests women have more resistance to heart disease.

Many sociologists point to social factors to explain gender inequalities. Social factors include the following:

- **Risk** – a higher death rate amongst 17-24 year-old males than amongst females of the same age may be due to the greater willingness of males to engage in risky behaviour. **Lyng** (1990) suggests that male roles in society encourage them to engage in more **edgework** (risky behaviour).
- **Social deprivation – Millar & Glendinning** (1989) argue that lower wages and higher rates of poverty explain why women suffer more ill health.
- **Female roles – Graham** (1984) argues that women spend less money on themselves than other family members when allocating family budgets, because of their caring role in society.
- **Popay & Bartley** (1989) argue that domestic labour can adversely affect women's health due to long hours and poor conditions.

RACE AND HEALTH

AQA, OCR, WJEC   Textbook pp. 305-306

Pearson (1991) argues that there are inconsistencies in the way ethnic groups are defined, so data is unreliable. However there is clear evidence of some differences – for example, ethnic minorities of Asian origin have high rates of heart disease and those of Caribbean origin have high rates of stroke.

Nettleton (1995) suggests that **genetic factors** play a part.

Cultural factors have also been suggested – for example, lack of vitamin D causing rickets amongst Asian ethnic minorities. However, **Ahmad** (1993) suggests that cultural explanations tend to ignore positive aspects of culture, such as low rates of smoking and alcohol consumption amongst British Asians.

Material factors – for example: poorer housing, employment in hazardous occupations, higher rates of unemployment and lower wages – may account for some ethnic minority health disadvantages. In a study of Asian women in northern England, **Nettleton** (1995) found that the women felt their health was affected by isolation, the fear of racist attack and poor housing.

THE BODY

AQA, OCR, WJEC   Textbook pp. 307-311

The body and high modernity

Anthony Giddens (1991) argues that in high modernity (see p. 139) the body is a crucial source of identity:

- People express themselves by altering their bodies – for example: tattoos, piercings or cosmetic surgery.
- People have a sense of being able to see their bodies from the outside, known as **reflective mobilization.**
- An increased sense of choice creates uncertainty over how people want their bodies to be: the 'manufactured uncertainty of everyday life'.
- Media images of 'perfect' bodies lead people to use drugs or diets which might affect health.
- There is also increased choice in sexuality.

According to **Featherstone** (1991), the body has become the focal point of a new emphasis on consumption and what **Turner** refers to as the **play ethic**, which has largely replaced the **work ethic**.

The body as a project

Shilling (2003) believes that the individuals see their body as a project to be worked at and accomplished. People feel able to exert control over their bodies and technology allows people to shape their bodies in line with lifestyle choices.

Foucault – The birth of the clinic

For **Foucault** (1971), people's beliefs about social reality are created by their actions and the way they talk about particular issues. He refers to this sense of reality as **discourse**. He describes discourses concerning health and illness as the **clinical gaze** (le regard).

According to Foucault, in the late eighteenth century new types of clinic in France introduced a new approach to medicine involving clinical observation and physical examination, particularly using the stethoscope.

New classification systems for diseases developed that saw patients in terms of their bodies rather than as whole people. These developments were part of wider social and political changes in which there was increased **surveillance** of people's activities to establish greater state control over mass populations.

Classifications in medicine helped to establish the distinction between the normal and the **deviant/pathological**. These distinctions were **internalized** by the population who learned to control their own behaviour.

In contemporary society this is reflected in people's willingness to monitor their own health.

Armstrong (1983) argues that in the twentieth century the **clinical gaze** was extended, with dispensaries and the development of social science techniques to map the incidence of disease, and the development of new specialisms such as geriatrics and pediatrics.

Turner (1992) argues that medicine has replaced the law and religion as the key institution controlling the body. He sees control in society as closely linked with control of the individual body.

DISABILITY

AQA, OCR, WJEC   Textbook pp. 311-312

Finkelstein (1980) sees disability as a product of capitalist society. Before industrial capitalism the disabled were simply part of the destitute population. However, this group was not needed for machine-based factory work and they became an isolated group segregated in **institutions**.

In the twentieth century there was a shift away from a view of disability as an **abnormality** to one of **sickness** – a condition which can be partially cured, so that the disabled person can enter or return to the labour market.

Oliver (1990) argues that the **personal tragedy ideology** underpins the way disability is regarded.

Disability is seen as a personal tragedy that ruins people's lives, rather than as a social problem. The alternative **social model of disability** sees the problems of the disabled as resulting from the failure of society to accommodate the needs of disabled people, rather than from the inherent problems caused by the disability.

From this viewpoint, people with impairments are disabled by the prejudice of society.

Bourdieu (1984) argues that the disabled have lower levels of **symbolic** and **physical capital**, which creates a notion of inferiority and dependence.

Charmaz (1983) studied self-image in people who had become disabled through accident or chronic illness. She suggested a range of possible responses, from seeing disability as **normality interrupted** to immersion in a **disabled identity**.

Illness, blame and stigma

Some sociologists stress that illness is often seen as a moral issue rather than as a purely physical one.

Helman (1986) notes how patients often see 'colds' and 'chills' as the fault of their own carelessness whereas 'fever' and 'flu' are not seen as their own fault.

Within a **narrative of risk** people may be blamed for lung cancer because it is associated with smoking, or AIDS because it is associated with sexual activity which may seen as irresponsible or immoral.

Goffman (1968) showed how people with physical deformities suffered stigma. **Discrediting stigma** are clearly visible; **discreditable stigma** are not as visible and people may try to hide them with **impression management**.

Scambler & Hopkins (1986) studied epileptics and how they tried to deal with their illness. They noted two distinctive kinds of stigma:

- **enacted stigma** – in which people suffered discrimination;
- **felt stigma** – in which people feared discrimination or had feelings of shame.

People found ways of dealing with felt stigma such as **selective concealment** of their condition, covering up their condition completely, medicalizing their behaviour or condemning the condemners by challenging the attitudes of others through political movements.

Hall *et al* (1993) studied the stigma of mental illness and found that significant minorities of the population wanted to avoid contact with the mentally ill.

Philo *et al* (1996) found that 66% of all images of the mentally ill in the Scottish media were negative.

Charlton (1998) argues that the reality for disabled people across the world is poverty and exclusion. Emphasis on stigma diverts attention from this.

MENTAL ILLNESS

AQA, OCR, WJEB   **Textbook pp. 314-317**

Labelling theory

Scheff (1966) argues that there is no such thing as mental illness; it is simply a label applied to **deviant behaviour** which other people cannot understand. People are **socialized** into stereotypical views of mental illness which are reinforced by the media.

Goffman (1968) argues that the label of mental illness is used when it is in the interests of the powerful to use it. Once somebody is labelled as mentally ill they are treated differently, reinforcing their behaviour. In *Asylums* (1968) Goffman found that people were often admitted to mental hospitals as involuntary patients when there was little evidence that they were suffering significant problems.

Rosenhan (1973) conducted research in which several researchers were admitted to mental hospitals when they asked for voluntary admission as schizophrenics, even though they had no symptoms of schizophrenia. Their subsequent behaviour was often interpreted as evidence of schizophrenia and the staff paid little attention to what the patients said.

Criticisms

Gove (1982) criticizes labelling theories of mental illness for dismissing real and serious mental problems as simply labels, and for ignoring the fact that most medical staff are supportive and sympathetic.

Miles (1981) argues that the label of mental illness tends only to be used as a last resort.

Foucault

Foucault (1971) argues that the concept of madness derives from an eighteenth-century emphasis on rational and disciplined action.

The emphasis on rationality led to undisciplined, irrational behaviour being defined as madness within the **dominant discourse** of medicine. Mad people were seen as a threat to the **new rationality** and were kept separate from the rest of society in institutions , just as lepers had previously been isolated from mainstream society.

Structural theories

Structural explanations of mental illness accept that mental illness exists but see it as resulting from structural factors such as inequality.

Brown & Harris (1978, 1989) found that depression amongst London women was caused by stressful life events and vulnerability factors (such as the lack of strong social networks). Working-class women were much more likely to suffer stressful life events than middle-class women because they had fewer material resources.

Gomm (1996) finds that poorer people suffer more mental illness than people who are better off.

Gender and mental illness

Women are more likely than men to be diagnosed with mental illness, and six times more likely to be diagnosed with depression.

Such figures may reflect women's greater likelihood of seeking medical help. However, Brown (1995) found that feelings of entrapment and humiliation are linked to depression, and these are linked to the roles of women, especially working-class women, in contemporary societies.

Williams & Watson (1996) adopt a feminist perspective, blaming many of women's psychological problems on physical or sexual abuse by men.

Ethnicity and mental illness

In survey research, Nazroo (1997) found that British African Caribbeans are more likely to receive treatment for depression than other ethnic groups, and that people of South Asian origin have low rates of treatment for depression.

Fernando (2002) believes that such figures result from **cultural bias** in psychiatry, which stems from a lack of understanding of cultural differences between ethnic groups.

Many argue that high rates of deprivation and the experience of racism explain higher rates of mental illness in some ethnic groups.

However, Pilgrim & Rogers (1999) suggest that deprivation and discrimination cannot explain the much higher rates of diagnosed mental illness amongst African Caribbeans than amongst South Asians in Britain, as both groups suffer these problems.

DEVELOP YOUR ANALYTICAL AND EVALUATION SKILLS

Essay plans

For each of the following questions write your own essay plan before comparing it with the suggestions given here. For the final question you can write a full answer and compare it with the provided model answer.

Illness can be defined as a malfunctioning of the body. Discuss.

Background

Sociologists of health and illness would strongly disagree with this statement. It describes the biomedical model, which tries to use an objective and scientific approach based around the ideas of mind-body dualism, specific aetiology and the mechanical metaphor. It can be contrasted with broader definitions, such as that of the World Health Organization, and attacked using evidence of the relative nature of illness. Parsons's idea of the sick role, the political economy perspective, interactionism and feminist approaches all suggest that the definition of illness is influenced by society.

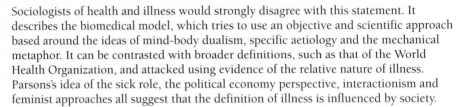

For	Against
• Biomedical model (p. 152)	• Evidence of relative definitions (p. 151)
	• Parsons (p. 151)
	• Political economy perspective (p. 151)
	• Interactionism (p. 151)
	• Feminism (p. 152)

Top Tip

Foucault's work on discourse (p. 156) is also useful for suggesting how social influences shape the definition of illness.

Assess the view that patriarchal capitalism causes ill health.

Background

This view is strongly opposed to biomedical views of health and illness, and combines the views of feminists and the political economy approach to health and illness. Writers from the political economy perspective agree that capitalism is a major cause of ill health, while feminists agree that patriarchy is a major factor. However, only socialist feminists would agree entirely with the view in the question. The biomedical model does not see social factors as important, and the social constructionist approach of interactionists sees illness more in terms of definitions produced during interaction. McKeown is best known for criticising the biomedical model, but his work also suggests the way that improvements within capitalism have reduced illness.

For	Against
• Socialist feminism (p. 152)	• Biomedical model (p. 152)
• Political economy approach (p. 151)	• Interactionism (p. 151)
	• McKeown (p. 152)

For and Against
• Radical feminism (p. 152)
• Liberal feminism (p. 152)

Top Tip

The question might suggest that there are class inequalities in health caused by capitalism (p. 151) and gender inequalities in health caused by patriarchy (p. 152), but it ignores ethnic inequalities, which may be caused by racism (p. 156).

Discuss the view that the main function of medicine is social control.

Background

This view is supported by a range of radical writers who see medicine as part of an oppressive, capitalist system, a prop to patriarchy, and as doing more harm than good. Both Foucault and Illich, in different ways, see medicine as involved in social control. On the other hand, functionalist approaches see medicine and the professions as serving the interests of society, and Weberians tend to see medical practitioners as simply serving their own interests.

For	Against
● Political economy approach (p. 151)	● Parsons (p. 151)
● Feminist approaches (p. 152)	● Millerson (p. 153)
● Illich (p. 153)	● Weberian approaches (p. 153)
● Foucault (p. 156)	● Doctors losing power (p. 153)
	● Biomedical model (p. 152)

Top Tip

Labelling theories of mental illness (p. 157) are worth discussing as another possible example of medicine being used to control the population.

Assess the view that disability is a social rather than a medical problem.

Background

Before the nineteenth century the disabled were part of the destitute population. In the Victorian age, they became seen as not able to do factory work and were isolated in institutions. The idea that disability is a social problem is more recent. It describes the disabled as excluded from society by prejudice and lack of provision for their needs.

For	Against
● Social model (p. 156)	● Finkelstein (p. 156)
● Prejudice of society (p. 156)	● Oliver (p. 156)
	● Bourdieu (p. 156)
	● Charmaz (p. 156)

Top Tip

Even the name disability implies a lack of something important – the ability to lead a normal life. Why might society be keen for the disabled to work?

Assess the reasons for the resurgence of complementary therapies.

Background

Postmodernists see the rise of complementary medicine as part of plurality and choice. Another reason may be the failure of conventional medicine to treat chronic diseases. It is also possible that the market strategy of protectionism by doctors is breaking down.

For	Against
● Sharma (p. 154)	● Dominance of the biomedical model (p. 152)
● Bakx (p. 154)	● Arguments that doctors are losing power (p. 153)

For and Against
● Eisenberg (p. 154)

Top Tip

Using complementary medicine is a personal choice. If patients had total confidence in it would they seek medical help from a doctor? Why don't they tell their doctor about the other therapies they use?

Assess the reasons for the resurgence of complementary therapies.

Bakx identifies three types of medicine – popular medicine, folk medicine and biomedicine. Popular medicine is the informal caring done by women in the home. Biomedicine is based on the theories of science and is dominant in Britain and the United States. Folk medicine is a term for a wide range of therapies, also known as alternative or complementary medicine. Complementary therapies continue to be used in the treatment of populations in all societies.

Complementary therapies are not accepted as part of the biomedical model of health care. However, their use is increasing in modern Britain. Ernst found 20% of the population using complementary therapies at a total cost of £1.6 billion, whilst Eisenberg found 80% of Americans believe in using complementary medicine in conjunction with biomedicine.

Postmodernists explain the resurgence of complementary medicine as a reflection of the move to a postmodern society where there is no longer a belief in science. The biomedical model is deeply rooted in modernism, a period when other therapies were dismissed as purely superstitious. In the postmodern world patients become consumers selecting their treatment from the variety of treatments available, and they may use complementary therapies in conjunction with biomedical ones.

Bakx links the decline in biomedicine and the resurgence of complementary medicine to the failure of biomedicine to treat chronic illnesses. As the population ages, increasing numbers of people are affected by degenerative illnesses that have no biomedical cure, and they use complementary medicine to treat their symptoms. Sharma supports this view and argues that people believe that complementary therapies have fewer side effects than conventional medicine.

Arguing from a Weberian perspective, Friedson attributes the dominance of biomedicine to a successful market strategy by doctors. These professionals have succeeded in ensuring that only scientifically based treatments can be regarded as medicine; all other therapies are marginalized. Saks calls this 'interest-based politics': doctors are ensuring their high social position and high remuneration by using their monopoly over treating the sick. The state and the insurance companies act to protect doctor's monopoly powers by funding biomedicine and not funding alternative therapies.

However, as Saks points out, doctors do not have total power. When doubt emerged about the safety of the MMR inoculation doctors were unable to reassure parents in sufficient numbers and the rate of inoculations fell. Physiotherapy was once regarded as a complementary therapy but is now accepted as part of biomedicine. Also, some NHS hospitals have recently opened homeopathic clinics. All of this may demonstrate that the power of the BMA to protect doctors' monopoly on treating the sick is diminishing.

Bakx argues that there is a decline in the uncritical acceptance of the power of professionals in all spheres, including medicine. The resulting decline in the power of doctors has led to the resurgence of a plurality of alternative therapies. People now feel empowered to take their own decisions about their health and healing. In the postmodern world people expect to be actively involved in choosing solutions to their problems, whilst doctors still expect patients to passively accept their advice. Sharma found people felt they were treated better by complementary therapists than by their doctors. Bakx believes that in the future biomedicine will be one option amongst many.

The evidence suggests that there are a number of reasons for the resurgence of complementary therapies. The increasing questioning of biomedicine, particularly in the treatment of chronic illness, the decreasing power of the BMA to maintain doctors' monopoly over treatment, and people's desire for choice in their treatment are all factors.

RESOURCES

Health, medicine and the body

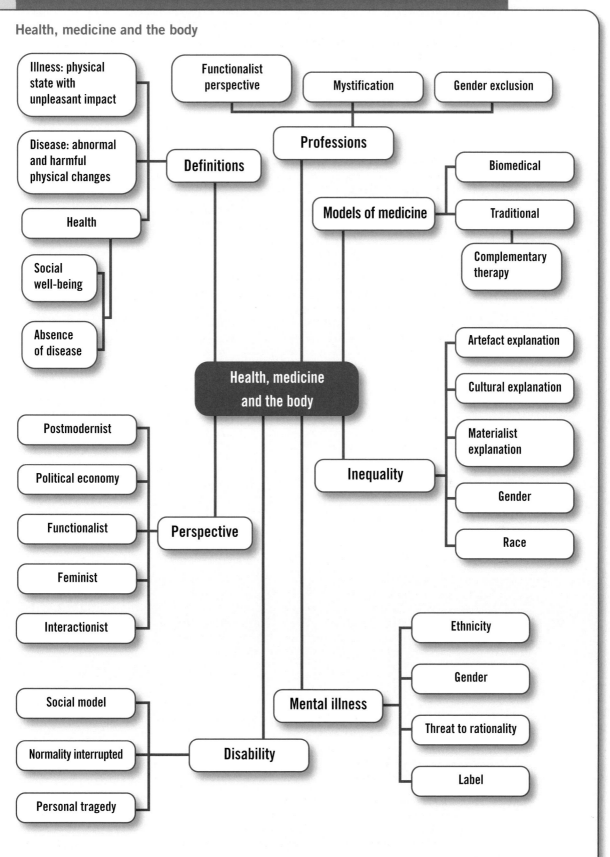

Perspectives on illness and medicine

Perspective	Doctors	Health Inequalities	Mental Illness
Functionalist	Have specialized knowledge. Serve society	May be based on consumption patterns rather than social class	Temporary state; the patient has the obligation to try to get well
Marxist	Serve the needs of capitalism by treating the individual	Capitalists make profits out of medical services and drugs. Inequalities are ignored	Stems from experience of deprivation. Ruling-class ideology ensures negative images in media
Feminist	Disempower women by defining childbirth as a medical process	Women face multiple disadvantages which impact on their health	Result of physical and mental abuse by men
Interactionist	Social factors are as important as medical ones in patients visiting their doctor	Criticized by Day & Day for ignoring health inequalities	No such thing. Label applied to deviant behaviour
Postmodernist	Biomedicine is only one option. Use of complementary therapies rising	The greater people's economic resources the easier it is for them to maintain their self-image during illness	Mad people seen as threat to new rationality and isolated from society

Writers and their work

Writer	Perspective	Concept	Study
Parsons	Functionalist	Obligations and rights of the sick role	Study showing how society controls deviance through the sick role
Navarro	Marxist	Ideological function of sickness	Study showing how medicine benefits capitalism
Doyal	Marxist	Capitalist patriarchy	Study showing how women's health is defined by capitalism
Bury	Postmodernist	Biographical disruption	Study showing how illness affects people's self-image
Williams	Postmodernist	Narrative reconstruction	Study showing how people make sense of their illness
Tesh	Interactionist	Social definitions of illness	Study of Repetitive Strain Injury
Scambler	Interactionist	'Illness iceberg'	Study showing most people with symptoms don't seek medical advice
Becker	Interactionist	Health belief	Study showing the social processes involved in decisions to visit the doctor
Graham & Oakley	Feminist	Medicalization	Study of the medicalization of childbirth
Illich	Marxist	Iatrogenisis	Study of the harm done by the medical profession
Millerson	Functionalist	Professional traits	Study justifying high rewards for doctors
Jamous & Peloille	Weberian	Indeterminacy/ technicality ratio	Study showing how professions maintain social distance from their clients
Witz	Feminist	Gendered exclusionary strategy	Study showing how women are subordinated in health care
Bakx	Postmodernist	Folk medicine	Study showing that most health care happens through folk and popular medicine
Saunders	New Right	Consumption groups	Study showing the influence of car ownership and home ownership on health
Giddens	Late modernist	Reflective mobilization	Study showing the body as a crucial source of identity
Foucault	Postmodernist	Clinical gaze	Study showing how the growth of the clinic led to greater surveillance and control of the masses
Goffman	Interactionist	Discrediting stigma	Study showing how people with physical deformities suffer stigma
Bourdieu	Marxist	Habitus	Study showing how medicine influenced social views on disability
Brown & Harris	Feminist	Stressful life events	Study showing vulnerability of working-class women to stress

Chapter 9

COMMUNICATION & THE MEDIA

SPECIFICATION COVERAGE

Specification	Details
AQA A2 Unit SCLY3: Mass Media	All sections are relevant to AQA
OCR A2 Unit G673: Power and Control	All sections are relevant to OCR except *Disability* and *Sexuality*
WJEC AS Unit SY2: Understanding Culture	All sections are relevant to WJEC except *Age*, *Disability* and *Sexuality*

THE MEDIA

AQA, OCR, WJEC   Textbook pp. 711-712

The media can be usefully distinguished into four structural types:

1 **mass media** – where a message is conveyed from one point to a large number of other points;

2 **interactive media** – where some limited communications back from the points receiving the messages is possible;

3 **interpersonal media** – where messages are conveyed between single points (for example, text messaging between individuals);

4 **network media** – where messages can be conveyed in any direction.

New media refers to media utilizing ICT (information and communications technology) such as the internet and digital multi-channel TV. New media are spreading rapidly: for example, in 2006 57% of people in the UK had internet access and 65% had digital television, increasing from 19% in 1996.

Use of the internet is becoming more dynamic with an upsurge in activities such as blogging and social networking. In 2007 the major social networking sites, such as *Facebook*, reached around a third of the UK online population.

Although the **mass media** communicate the same message to large numbers of people it should not be assumed that the message is always interpreted in the same way by all those receiving it. The audience, in other words, should not necessarily be seen as one 'mass'. Audiences vary – for example, according to class, gender, ethnicity and region.

Postmodernists emphasize that media messages are **polysemic** – they can be interpreted in very different ways by different individuals.

MEDIA STRUCTURE AND CONTENT

AQA, OCR, WJEC   Textbook pp. 713-721

Pluralist theories

Pluralists are sympathetic to the media and see them as acting in a responsible way and reflecting the wishes and interests of their audiences.

For pluralists, society consists of many different groups with diverse interests. Each group has roughly equal **access to power**. The mass media reflect this diversity in what they cover.

The media operate in the **public interest**. They follow **public opinion** rather than shaping it.

Katz & Lazarsfeld (1955) studied the media's influence on political opinion in the USA in the 1940s. They found that:

- people had different amounts of exposure to the media.
- different media had different degrees of influence (television could be more powerful than newspapers when using images).
- the content of the messages determined whether they had much effect.
- people tended to accept messages that supported existing prejudices and reject those that contradicted them.
- messages were mediated by the personal influence of **opinion leaders** and did not directly influence people's attitudes or how they voted.

Many national and international institutions support the idea of media pluralism. The European Broadcasting Union, for example, argues that citizens must have access to a range of diverse opinion, and this should be supported by regulatory authorities and legislation.

Criticisms

Philo (1986) argues that pluralism may be an **ideological justification** for the media, put forward by those who work in the media industry.

Blumler & Gurevitch (1995) argue that journalists and politicians have a shared culture. Under the **lobby system**, journalists rely on politicians for information and will tend to present the politicians' view of the world.

The **pluralist model** assumes that the content of the media is diverse, rather than providing evidence that it is.

The 2003 attack on Iraq shows that diverse viewpoints are not always available. Around 500 journalists were embedded with coalition troops making it difficult to report impartially.

Marxist theories

Marxist theories sharply contradict pluralism.

Marxists see the ownership or control of the media by a capitalist **ruling class** as the key to understanding the mass media.

The media transmit the ideas of the ruling class. The ruling class use the media to promote their **products**, to make a **profit** and to persuade people to accept the **capitalist system**.

The ruling class largely own the **means of production** (TV stations, newspapers, publishers etc.), and huge corporations dominate the media. There is evidence of increased monopolization, as a few big companies such as News Corporation gain domination of the media market. This can be achieved through:

- high levels of **expenditure** – only the biggest corporations can produce blockbuster films, for example; economies of scale mean that vast amounts of merchandise can be produced at low cost.
- **synergy** – a single product such as a film can be used as the basis for other media products (for example, computer games and film soundtracks).
- **branding** – financial muscle is used to market branded products to make them appeal to consumers.

- **globalization** – this involves selling products worldwide; for example, Rupert Murdoch claims his News Corporation satellite and TV channels reach three quarters of the world's population.

The global campaign built around the 2007 film *Transformers: The Movie* offers a good example of these processes. The film was produced by DreamWorks in partnership with Paramount and Hasbro. *Transformers* began as a Japanese toy line which Hasbro began marketing in the USA in the 1980s. Transformers storylines were developed by Marvel comics and in cartoon series. The toy line has been re-launched several times and has featured in video games based on the 2007 film. The film also has tie-ins with businesses whose products feature within it, such as General Motors. The film, the toys and other spin-off products achieve saturation coverage globally and mutually reinforce each other in terms of publicity.

Media ownership

There are four major trends in media ownership in recent decades:

1 **Concentration of ownership** – according to **Bagdikian** (2004), the US media were controlled by 50 corporations in the 1980s, but just five in 2003. These five control the vast majority of the 178,000 media outlets in the USA.

2 **Growth** – the new media company Google offers an example of growth through **acquisition** and **diversification**. Google started out in 1996 as a search engine set up by two students. In 2004 its market valuation was over $23 billion. In 2006 Google acquired the social networking site *YouTube*. Its activities now include email, instant messaging, sale of advertising and reference materials such as mapping.

3 **Integration** – different parts of the media have become united in single companies. For example, Viacom is involved in television, publishing, video and the internet.

4 **Globalization** – Viacom, for example, owns many local companies such as MTV India, MTV Southeast Asia and MTV Nordic to distribute its products throughout the world.

For most Marxists, the **logic of capitalism** dictates the content and effects of the mass media.

The poor and powerless have little money to spend buying media products so their interests are largely ignored – poor consumers bring in little advertising revenue.

Bagdikian (2004) argues that news that is of interest to capitalists (for example, stock market news) gets plenty of coverage. Negative news about capitalism (for example, the living standards of the poor) gets little coverage.

Another strand of Marxism emphasizes **direct interference** in the content of the media by owners. For example, editors of newspapers owned by Rupert Murdoch have told stories of him ringing up to direct the content of the front page.

Criticisms

Marxists may underestimate the importance of **state regulation** – for example, of the BBC.

Not all commentators agree that concentration is occurring rapidly. **Compaine** (2004) states that concentration is only increasing by a small amount.

For **pluralists**, the media must respond to **audience preferences** if they are to survive. Capitalists need to serve audiences to make a profit.

Anti-establishment programmes do get made – for example, *The Simpsons* with its critical portrayal of traditional values.

Postmodernists deny that power is concentrated in the hands of the rich. The public can use the media to oppose the policies of giant corporations – for example, a *Facebook* campaign prevented HSBC imposing overdraft fees for new graduates.

Neo-Marxist theories

Neo-Marxist approaches put less emphasis than Marxism on direct control by capitalists, or the way in which the logic of capitalist competition shapes the media.

They argue that it is the dominance of ruling-class culture (**cultural hegemony**) that shapes the media. Whilst there are competing views within the media, **ruling-class ideology** is the main influence on media content, and on how people understand and make sense of the social world.

Hall – cultural hegemony

Stuart Hall (1995) argues that the way in which the media classify the world assumes a basic **consensus** about how the world works, and this dominant view is taken for granted (for example, the media assume that wage demands cause inflation – rather than, say, profiteering by companies).

There is no conspiracy to manipulate the meanings of the media, simply a widespread acceptance of certain ways of seeing the world.

Discourse analysis

Discourse analysis examines the connections between power and how certain ways of thinking about certain types of event come to be accepted.

For example, **Fairclough** (1995) argues that the television programme *Crimewatch* operates to **legitimate** the role of the police and to encourage the public to believe that they can work with the police in combating crime. It contradicts images of the police as corrupt, inept etc.

Discourse analysis has been criticized for representing only one person's reading: the analyst's. Other viewers might of *Crimewatch* might 'read' the message of the programme differently.

The Glasgow Media Group

The Glasgow Media Group (GMG) has done a variety of research supporting the **cultural hegemony** model. During the 1970s and 1980s their focus was on content analysis of television news. They concluded that:

- the language and visuals of broadcast news favour the viewpoint of powerful groups. For example, in industrial disputes, negative words (such as 'threat' and 'demand') are used to describe strikers, while more positive words (such as 'offer') are used to describe management. Certain visual angles (for example, filming from behind police lines in picket-line clashes) encourage **identification** with the police viewpoint.

- media professionals set the **agenda** about the important issues of the day. For example, the effects of strikes are more likely to be reported than the causes.

- coverage of party politics is sympathetic towards the political **centre ground**.

However, sometimes journalists can escape the pressures on them and present a critical point of view.

In the 1990s and 2000s the GMG focused on **audience studies** using group discussions and activities. Their recent work looks at how audiences 'read' media messages in a variety of ways according to their cultural background.

The GMG identified what they call a **circuit of communication** – a process in which the production, content and reception of media messages are constantly affecting each other. **Philo & Miller** (2005) (see Textbook p. 720) define the four key elements of this circuit:

1 **Social and political institutions** such as businesses and governments, who influence the supply of information to the media.

2 **The media and their content** – within news broadcasting official sources are given more weight and commercial considerations increasingly drive media content.

3 **The public**, who make up the audience for media output; they consist of different social, professional and political groups, with varying levels of prior knowledge and different cultural values.

4 **Decision makers** in government and other social and political institutions.

An example of GMG's approach is their research into audience understandings of the Israeli/Palestinian conflict. They found that most people had little knowledge of the background to the conflict because news broadcasts focus on dramatic images of current events. They also argue that broadcasters avoid challenging the pro-Israeli position of the US establishment.

Criticisms of cultural hegemony theory

Not all journalists share a **dominant ideology**.

There is no **unified culture** among media professionals.

Sections of the establishment are very critical of media reporting, seeing it as promoting a **liberal consensus**.

Organizational factors

Media professions and organizations may have a direct effect on media content.

Galtung & Ruge (1965) identify criteria that journalists are taught to value in stories. These are:

- **frequency** – short-lived events are preferred.
- **threshold** – more intense events are preferred.
- **unambiguity** – especially, events that fit into an established story type.
- **meaningfulness** – relevance to the audience.
- **unexpectedness** – unexpected events are preferred to expected ones.

Other criteria also affect the news agenda:

- **Elite nations** in the story are preferred.
- **Elite individuals** in the story are preferred.
- Reference to **individuals** makes a story more newsworthy.
- **Bad news** is more newsworthy than **good news**.

Boyd-Barrett (1995) criticizes Galtung & Ruge, pointing out that they fail to explain where journalistic values come from, and they ignore **structural factors** and **cultural hegemony** (see above).

MEDIA AND AUDIENCES

AQA, OCR, WJEC   **Textbook pp. 722-728**

The hypodermic model

The **hypodermic model** assumes that media messages are directly injected into audiences as if by a syringe. The media can act like a drug or narcotic, directly changing behaviour.

This process was demonstrated by **Bandura** *et al* (1963), who conducted psychological experiments which showed that boys would imitate aggression in films they had watched (**social learning theory**).

The hypodermic model has been criticized because:

- audiences are very diverse and react in different ways.
- long-term effects may differ from short-term ones.
- it ignores the different uses audiences make of the media – for example, TV programmes may be used only as background noise.
- it ignores other media effects – for example, watching violent films may act as an outlet for aggression rather than a cause of it.

Nevertheless, many politicians and other commentators are still influenced by the hypodermic model.

The two-step flow model

Merton (1946) and **Katz & Lazarsfeld** (1955) argued that media effects may not be direct, but that messages are interpreted by key individuals who then influence others:

- Step 1 – the media message reaches the audience.
- Step 2 – the message is interpreted by the audience and it influences them.

Social interaction is an important element of step 2. **Opinion leaders** interpret messages for others and shape what influence the messages might have.

Advertising campaigns often exploit this two-step flow. **Vernette** (2004) shows how the women's fashion industry uses opinion leaders:

1 Opinion leaders are identified (female employees or students aged 15-35).

2 Magazines that appeal to these opinion leaders are identified.

3 Advertisements are placed in these magazines.

The **multi-step flow model** refines the two-step flow model by recognizing that there may be several stages in the interpretation of media messages. For example, **Hobson** (1990) shows how discussions about soap operas at work may change people's interpretation of them.

Criticisms

There may be no dominant opinion leaders or consensus about the meaning of media messages.

The two-step flow model ignores the possibility that the meaning of media messages might be imposed by the powerful.

The uses and gratifications model

This model is based on the idea that people use the media in a variety of ways. **McQuail** (1972) suggests four possible uses:

- **diversion** or escape;
- **personal relationships** – for example, feeling part of a soap opera community;
- **personal identity** – confirming or weakening the sense of who we are by using certain media messages;
- **surveillance** – finding out what is going on.

The uses made of the media may vary according to age, gender etc.

Criticisms

The model fails to explain why people use the media in different ways.

It ignores the possibility that the media can create people's needs.

It focuses on individuals rather than social, cultural and structural factors.

The interpretative model

In the interpretative model, the audience filters messages, ignoring, rejecting, accepting or reinterpreting them.

Fiske (1988) uses the idea of **intertexuality** – relating different texts/contexts to one another (for example, relating soap operas to your own life or relating interviews with actors to their performance in a film).

Audience members can move between different levels of involvement in watching TV: engagement, detachment and reference (relating events to one's own experiences).

Buckingham (1993) explores how individuals' **media literacy** (their degree of knowledge, and understanding of the media) affects how they interpret media output. More sophisticated viewers can understand the codes, or rhetoric, of TV language and the meanings that can be inferred from the way programmes are produced.

Criticisms

The interpretative model may underestimate the power of media messages and how strongly they can be reinforced.

It is an individualistic approach, which neglects the role of **subcultures** in shaping interpretations.

The structured interpretation model

This model argues that audiences do interpret the meaning of the media, but there is a **preferred reading**, influenced by the way in which the message is encoded. However, researchers need to be aware that different subcultures (class, gender, ethnicity, age, religion etc.) will tend to interpret the messages in different ways.

For example, a young Muslim audience may react differently to footage of the war in Iraq compared with a young non-Muslim audience. However, those Muslims may also respond as British citizens and as young people. Their reactions may also link to their gender and education.

Morley's influential research (1980) showed how the audience of the BBC TV news magazine *Nationwide* interpreted a story differently:

- Trade unionists saw it as biased towards management.
- Managers accepted the news coverage as unbiased.
- Middle-class students saw the programme as superficial.
- Black, mainly working-class students saw it as boring.

Thus the media can be read/interpreted in many different ways – they are **polysemic**. Different groups bring different languages, concepts and assumptions to interpreting messages.

Criticisms

This approach can be seen as presenting an **over-determined** view, as it sees the audience as being controlled by the social groups to which they belong.

Postmodernists stress that the same programme can be interpreted differently by the same audience member in different **contexts**.

Audience reception and postmodernity

Postmodernists adopt views that question the idea of 'the audience' as conceived in other approaches.

Baudrillard (1988) argues that media-saturated societies have produced **hyperreality**, in which objectivity breaks down and images can be interpreted in many ways, even by the same people at different times.

Turkle (1996) sees TV as part of the postmodern culture of **simulation** – we identify more with the fictional life of TV than we do with real life. According to Turkle:

- we treat media messages as if they were real – for example, real *Cheers* bars have opened.
- the distinction between image and reality has broken down. People no longer search for the real meaning of media messages but use media images in the playful creation of different identities.
- the media have become part of lifestyle rather than conveyors of information.

Criticisms

Webster (1999) argues that:

- the social context still influences the way in which the mass media are used and interpreted.
- the question of who creates media information and for what purposes is still important (as Marxists, for example, would argue).

Lerner (1994) argues that postmodernism obscures inequality and prevents attempts to improve the world.

The media and violence

There is concern that the portrayal of violence in media such as TV and video games can breed aggression in viewers. School violence, such as the Columbine High School shootings in 1999 where two male students killed 13 people, has come to symbolize these fears.

There is very little empirical evidence, however, to support the idea of '**copycat**' violence.

Doyle (2006) identifies the following problems in using empirical evidence to establish the impact of the media on levels of violence:

- The effects of the media cannot be inferred just by analysing the content of media texts.
- The media are very diverse – there is no single representation of violence.
- Audiences are not homogeneous – they differ in many respects.
- Defining and measuring influence creates serious problems for researchers.
- Working out a **causal relationship** is very difficult – for example, there is a link between fear of crime and viewing crime programmes but it is difficult to establish which causes which.
- Much research has taken place in **artificial conditions**, so it is difficult to generalize to real-life situations.

MEDIA AND SOCIAL GROUPS

AQA, OCR, WJEC　　　　　Textbook pp. 728-741

Media messages can be seen as passing through four phases:

1. Formulation of the message
2. Message content – the 'text'
3. Audience reception
4. Effects of message

The sections below discuss these four phases in relation to different social groups.

Gender and media representation

Formulation

Most media workers are women, but **Croteau & Hoynes** (2001) found that in the USA in the mid-1990s women made up only 6% of top newspaper managers and wrote 20% of TV news reports.

This '**glass ceiling**' in the media means that issues of particular concern to women are frequently ignored or trivialized.

Message content

Males outnumber females in all TV programme types – for example, there is a ratio of seven males to three females in some soaps, there are few women in cartoons and there are three all-male TV ads for every one all-female ad.

The portrayal of women is changing – for example, the role of *Buffy the Vampire Slayer* is quite different to roles in earlier decades, and in Bond films women have become increasingly strong and resourceful. However, stereotypical gender roles are reinforced in a number of ways:

- Old films and TV programmes with stereotypical female and male roles are recycled on cable and satellite.
- **Ivory** (2006) argues that female characters in video games are under-represented and often portrayed in a heavily sexualized way.

- News presenters are more likely to be female than in the past, but they are generally young and attractive. **Ross** (2002) argues that they are used to make news more 'human' and watchable. 'Fanciable' news readers are used as sex objects despite the seriousness of the news.

- Advertising often portrays women in domestic roles. **Scharrer et al** (2006) found that men were usually portrayed as amusingly incompetent in a domestic role.

Gauntlett (2002) found that women's magazines still emphasize personal beauty and sex, while men's lifestyle magazines such as *FHM* and *Maxim* reassert traditional masculine values.

New media, such as the internet, offer a vast range of representations of men and women, but women tend to be portrayed as sex objects in the widely available pornography.

Audience reception

Radical feminists argue, in recent studies, that women are active interpreters of messages and may reject stereotypical and **patriarchal** messages.

Ang (1985) argues that women may get pleasure from soap operas, such as the 1980s hit series *Dallas*, and are not just the passive victims of stereotyping.

Skirrow (1986) uses the concept of **gender valence** – the relationship between gender identities and technology. Women reject video games because they are part of a technology associated with male power.

Turkle (1988) argues that women reject computers because they do not want a close relationship with a machine. **Livingstone & Bovill** (2001) found girls are more likely to read books than boys, who are more likely to have computers in their bedrooms. Games consoles are very important in boys' culture although there is evidence that differences between the sexes are decreasing.

Gray (1987) argues that telephones are a more female technology because they allow human contact.

Lewis (1990) argues that music videos have a **male gender valence** because they are based on male adolescence – rebelliousness, sexual promiscuity and female conquest. However, girl bands, which encourage female friendship and solidarity, may be changing this.

The postmodernist **Hermes** (1995) argues that some women find women's magazines educative and relaxing. She stresses that the way in which these magazines are used by women can change.

The picture of **gendered technology** may be changing. In 2006 **Ofcom** reported that young girls were more likely than boys to use the internet and also spent more on mobile phone use.

(See also the discussion of class and audience reception, below.)

Media effects

To those using the **hypodermic model**, the media socialize women to be dependent and men to be dominant.

Frueh & McGhee (in **Tuchman**, 1978) claimed that heavy TV viewing amongst US children correlated with traditional **sex-role stereotyping**.

Beuf (1974) argues that children model themselves on TV **role models**, and this leads many girls to abandon their ambitions before they reach the age of 6. The media also make females concerned about their **body image** and the need to get and keep a man.

For socialist feminists, such as **Kath Davies** (1987), the media encourage women to accept **patriarchal capitalism**.

McRobbie (1991) uses a **cultural hegemony** approach, suggesting that an interest in make-up and appearance is taken for granted in girls' magazines.

Liberal feminists find evidence of sex-role stereotyping in the media and argue that it influences behaviour. **Tuchman** (1978) argues that TV advertisements **symbolically annihilate** women through ignoring them or through negative stereotyping. She accepts that representations may change with time; however, media images tend to lag behind changes in society.

Ethnicity and media representation

Formulation

Although there are many black and Asian television presenters in the UK, there are few people from ethnic minorities in senior management positions. In the US the media are more open to minorities but inequalities remain.

Message content

Representations of ethnicity are varied. Some are very sympathetic to ethnic minority worldviews (for example, Asian TV programmes and films), and some 'white establishment' programmes are quite sympathetic.

However, there is also evidence of stereotyping:

- Tabloid newspapers tend to portray ethnic minorities as a threat.

- TV tends to portray ethnic minorities in a restricted range of roles. The **Broadcasting Standards Commission** (1999) found that black people tend to be portrayed in arts, media, entertainment, health and caring, sports and police roles, and Asians in arts, media, entertainment, health and caring and student roles. There are few portrayals of minorities in roles such as that of the legal professional.

- **Malik** (2002) believes there is a **racialized regime** of representation within which black people are portrayed as having different experiences from other groups. 'Whiteness' is portrayed as the norm.

- Newer studies emphasize the beliefs to which media messages appeal, rather than relying simply on content analysis. **Cottle** (2000) suggests that coverage of ethnic minorities that emphasizes multiculturalism reinforces stereotypes of ethnic minorities as the 'other'.

Audience reception

Research suggests that the interpretation of representations of ethnicity can be quite varied. The Broadcasting Standards Commission (**Fletcher**, 2003) found that some saw representation of ethnic minorities as stereotypical or **tokenistic** while others saw it as positive.

Ross (2000) used focus groups of people from different ethnic minority groups. She found that they believed that the media portrayed individual ethnic groups in a rather stereotypical way. Each group was portrayed as homogeneous. For example, 'blackness' was emphasized more than differences between individual black people.

Gillespie (1995) studied 14-18 year-old Punjabis in Southall, London. They used the media to define their own ethnicity, comparing themselves to characters in Indian 'soaps' such as *The Mahabharata* and non-Asian soaps such as *Neighbours*.

Gillespie describes how the young people reflect on cultural differences between themselves and others, and dream of aspects of American culture, but recognize that their culture is different. They develop a **hybrid** national and cultural identity, combining elements of **Islam** and **Westernization**. This leads to some critical evaluation of their parents' culture.

Media effects

Van Dijk (1991) argues that newspapers have a major impact in developing a perception of immigration as a problem. He uses a **hypodermic model**, arguing that this perception may lead to racist attacks etc.

Hartmann & Husband (1974) studied the impact of media messages in different areas. In areas with a large Asian population (for example, the West Midlands) race relations were seen as less of a threat than in areas with few Asians (for example, Glasgow).

Factors such as class and gender also influence the degree to which media reporting of ethnicity affect the audience.

Class and media representation

Formulation

Most people in senior positions in the media are of middle-class origin.

Message content

Glennon & Butsch (1982) studied class lifestyles in family contexts on US TV and found that:

- working-class families are under-represented.
- two thirds of programmes had managers or proprietors as heads of household.
- only 4% had blue-collar heads of household.
- middle-class parents are usually portrayed as good at dealing with problems.
- working-class fathers are often portrayed as figures of fun.

The **GMG** (see above, p. 166) have found that the working class are often associated with 'trouble'.

Audience reception

Gray (1992) conducted a study of women from different classes and their use of TV and video. She concluded the following:

- Lower social classes both used and accepted TV and video more than higher classes.
- Higher classes were more anxious about children using TV.
- Context (i.e. who you watched TV with) was important to viewing.

- Men enjoyed current affairs, documentaries and sport more than women.
- Men tended to control viewing more than women.
- In the highest classes, both men and women valued 'quality' and 'classics' and disliked 'popular' and 'trash' genres.
- In lower classes, women liked 'soppy', 'fantasy' and 'soft' genres; men preferred 'hard', 'tough' and 'factual' genres.
- In all classes, men preferred 'heroic', 'public', 'societal' and 'physical' programmes; women preferred 'romantic', 'domestic', 'familial' and 'emotional' programmes.

Age and media representation

Formulation

Media workers in senior positions tend to be older than those in junior ones.

Message content

According to **Pearson** (1983), adolescents have long been portrayed as a problem by the media. There has been a long-standing myth of a **golden age** when youth was less troublesome (usually twenty years previously), but there have always been problem groups of youths (Victorian hooligans, Teds in the 1950s, 'hoodies' today).

Estrada (2001) examined responses to youth violence in Sweden. In the early 1980s the young offender was represented as a 'problem child with a difficult family background'. By the mid 1980s the representation had changed to a cold ruthless thrill-seeker. Estrada identifies aspects of a **deviancy amplification spiral** in relation to youth crime (see p. 194).

Amongst older age groups, **Sontag** (1978) finds a double standard: women have to match up to a youthful ideal, men do not.

Signorelli (1989) analysed 14,000 US TV characters and found that the very young and the very old were under-represented. Older characters were less likely to be represented as 'good' but also less likely to be involved in violence.

There is some favourable treatment of older people. **Dail** (1988) claims that they often have a positive image in soap operas; **Featherstone & Hepworth** (1995) show how, in a growing market, magazines like *Retirement Choice* generally present more positive images.

Audience reception

Gunter & McAleer (1997) found that the young (aged 4-24) watch less TV (2.8 hours per day) than older people.

Those with access to more media watched less TV, and TV did not seem to displace other activities.

For older viewers, TV was a comfort and company; and for those who did not get out much it offered 'virtual mobility'.

Although older people are now using the internet in greater numbers only 1 in 6 internet users are 65 or over. However, this group do spend more time per month online than any other.

Buckingham (1993) has examined whether children are less **media-literate** and more 'taken in' by media messages than adults.

He found that most children were aware of the purpose of advertising. They were sometimes critical of the quality of what was being sold and cynical about 'free' gifts.

Some were 'wise consumers', trying out advertised toys before purchase. Less of a **hypodermic** effect and more of a **uses and gratifications** effect was found – for example, they used adverts to generate lists of requests for Christmas presents, but were realistic about what parents could afford.

Buckingham found children to be active interpreters but he also notes that:

- they were enthusiastic about watching adverts.
- they did not always view adverts critically.
- the interviews may not have revealed the extent to which children accepted adverts.

Media effects

Hebdige (1988) argues that the media structure the way in which the young perceive society. Youth subcultures are based partly on these perceptions but also on the reality of situations. Hebdige, as a **neo-Marxist**, sees the media as absorbing and neutralizing rebellious **youth subcultures** – for example, by marketing aspects of youth culture as mass-market products.

Gillespie (see above, p. 170), in her research on young Punjabi Londoners, sees youth as more empowered.

The media can promote a **culture of consumerism** to children. **Wall** (2007) shows how the Webkinz range of soft toys uses the internet to keep children spending money.

Disability and media representation

Formulation

Few senior people in the media are disabled.

Message content

The **Broadcasting Standards Commission** (1999) found that:

- disabled people appeared in 7% of TV programmes but only accounted for 0.7% of all those who spoke.
- there were three disabled males to every one disabled female.
- only one in ten were both ethnic minority members and disabled.

Longmore (1987) found that disabled people and disability were commonly portrayed in the following ways:

- disability as an emblem of evil;
- the disabled as monsters;
- disability as representing the loss of one's humanity;
- the disabled as recipients of substitute gifts (for example, the blind having special powers) in compensation;
- disability as leading to courage or achievement against the odds;
- disability as a form of deviancy and sexual menace.

Cumberbatch & Negrine (1992) suggest that the disabled are often seen as the objects of pity or charity, but rarely as a normal part of life. Disability is normally portrayed as their key characteristic.

Harnett (2000) examines images of disability in popular television. He highlights the stereotypes of the 'evil avenger' – associated with malice and wrongdoing – and the 'supercrip' – overcoming disability in a spectacular way.

Representations are less stereotyped when disabled people are involved in creating representations. **Thoreau** (2006) analyzed *Ouch*, a BBC web magazine produced mainly by people with disabilities. Disability was discussed with humour and irony, though even this magazine did not convey a fully comprehensive or diverse representation of people with disabilities.

Audience reception

Cumberbatch & Negrine (1992) found that people with disabilities, or those in close contact with disabled people, were less likely to accept media portrayal of disability.

Media effects

Cumberbatch & Negrine found that for those without close contact with disabled people, disability is seen as a problem. This may make it difficult for disabled people to be integrated into everyday life. However, they conclude that more than changes in media coverage are needed to improve the lot of the disabled.

Sexuality and media representation

Message content

Some writers have found aspects of media representation of sex and sexuality as resembling a **moral panic**.

For example, **Critcher** (2003) argues that sections of the press depicted HIV/Aids as a 'gay plague', blaming a 'deviant minority' for the problem. He notes, however, that other representations were more positive: gay and medical groups were able to use a range of media to argue for a more balanced view.

The moral panic about '**stranger danger**' has constructed a figure of fear and hate under the term '**paedophile**'.

McRobbie & Thornton (1995) point out that early versions of the moral panic model saw society as one unified entity whilst more recent understandings, influenced by postmodernism, would take a more differentiated approach.

Audience reception

Younger viewers are more susceptible to depictions of sex and sexuality as they have less real-world experience. **Gunter & McAleer** (1997) argue that this can lead to unrealistic expectations.

Gender is another variable. Men and women can both be aroused by representations of consenting sex but women react much more negatively to scenes of sexual violence.

DEVELOP YOUR ANALYTICAL AND EVALUATION SKILLS

Essay plans

For each of the following questions write your own essay plan before comparing it with the suggestions given here. For the final question you can write a full answer and compare it with the provided model answer.

The mass media are dominated by capitalist interests. Discuss.

Background

This statement reflects Marxist views on the media. Some versions of Marxism see direct interference by media moguls as crucial, whilst others put more stress on the logic of capitalism, but both would agree with this statement. Neo-Marxist theorists of cultural hegemony largely agree, but would qualify the statement, arguing that capitalist domination is not complete. Pluralists disagree with the statement, arguing that the media reflect the interests and wishes of audiences rather than those of capitalists, Some sociologists believe that organizational factors influence the media more than capitalism.

For	Against
● Marxism (p. 165)	● Pluralism (p. 164)
● Logic of capitalism (p. 165)	● Organizational factors (p. 166)
● Neo-Marxism (p. 166)	

Top Tip

Postmodernists (p. 168) also strongly disagree with this statement, arguing that the media are an integral part of society, allowing people to create lifestyles and identities. They deny that Marxism can explain the role or content of the media.

Discuss the view that the portrayal of disadvantaged groups in the media is no longer stereotypical.

Background

You can discuss groups such as women, ethnic minorities, the young, the old, the disabled and the working class. Much of the evidence does suggest that there has been a change in media portrayal away from crude stereotypes, but if you look carefully some stereotyping is still present. Some of the findings are contradictory and it may be difficult to reach a single conclusion about all groups in every part of the media. The following are some examples of studies supporting the different viewpoints.

For	Against
● Non-stereotypical roles (p. 170)	● Gender: Gauntlett (p. 169), Ivory (p. 168), Scharrer (p. 169)
● Age: Dail (p. 170); Featherstone & Hepworth (p. 170)	● Ethnicity: Broadcasting Standards Commission (p. 169), Malik (p. 169)
● Disability: Thoreau (p. 171)	● Class: Glennon & Butsch (p. 170)
	● Youth: Pearson (p. 170)
	● Disability: Longmore (p. 171), Cumberbatch & Negrine (p. 171)

Top Tip

Gillespie's study (p. 170) suggests that there are now quite diverse portrayals of ethnic minorities which are interpreted in a variety of ways.

Discuss the view that the mass media have little effect on society because the audience interprets the messages in very different ways.

Background

This statement supports the view that interpretations of the media are polysemic. It is certainly supported by postmodernists and to a certain extent by the interpretative, structured interpretation, uses and gratifications, and two-step flow approaches. All of these believe that any effects of the media are indirect and mediated by individual and social interpretations of messages. The hypodermic model gives little credit to the possibility of different interpretations. This model is largely discredited; however, the hegemonic model suggests that certain types of message are so dominant in the media that such viewpoints come to dominate others.

For	Against
• Two-step flow model (p. 167)	• Hypodermic model (p. 167)
• Postmodernism (p. 168)	• Neo-Marxism and cultural hegemony (p. 166)
• Interpretative model (p. 167)	
• Structured interpretation approach (p. 167)	
• Uses and gratifications approach (p. 167)	

Top Tip

The sections on audience reception for different minority groups are useful for discussing this issue.

Both the selection and presentation of news is ideologically controlled. To what extent do sociological arguments and evidence support this view?

Background

An introduction needs to explain what the statement in the question actually means: that the news reflects the interests of powerful groups. Then Marxist and neo-Marxist positions that take this position can be explained. The traditional Marxist argument has two key strands: that the logic of capitalism dictates that the media will inevitably take the side of the powerful; that ruling-class owners of the media may directly intervene in the news process. The answer can then move on to look at neo-Marxist positions that stress the role of cultural hegemony rather than direct control. These positions will then need to be evaluated before the alternative view is presented: that the news is not ideologically controlled. The pluralist view is the key one here, but it would also be helpful to stress the practical and organizational pressures on the news media.

For	Against
• Marxist theories (p. 165)	• Pluralist theories (p. 164)
• Neo-Marxism: cultural hegemony (p. 166)	• The importance of organizational factors (p. 166)
• The Glasgow Media Group (p. 166)	

Top Tip

One conclusion could be to stress the diversity of news outlets associated with digital TV and the fact that TV news has been attacked as biased by both left- and right-wing commentators. The idea of a circuit of communication could be mentioned, as it helps understand the process of news production and reception as a whole.

Model answer

Both the selection and presentation of news is ideologically controlled. To what extent do sociological arguments and evidence support this view?

Many of the public believe that news – particularly TV news – is a 'window on the world', an accurate and objective picture of events. The statement in the question suggests that both the items chosen to be news and the way they are put across – the language and visuals used – are controlled to put across a particular view of the world, a view that reflect the interests and concerns of the powerful.

This view is associated with Marxist and neo-Marxist perspectives. Marxists see ownership of the media by a capitalist ruling class as the key to understanding the mass media. For example, Bagdikian points out that the US media were controlled by just five corporations in 2003. A main ideological function of the media is to transmit the ideas of the ruling class and to persuade people that these ideas are 'normal'. Marxists have different views about how this process occurs. For some it is simply the logic of capitalism that dictates the content of the mass media such as news and current affairs broadcasts. Bagdikian argues that news that is of interest to capitalists, such as the stock market, gets plenty of coverage, whilst negative news about capitalism, such as rising poverty figures, is often ignored. Another strand of Marxism emphasizes the direct influence of wealthy owners such as Rupert Murdoch on the content of the news.

Neo-Marxists place less emphasis on the direct influence of capitalists on news and current affairs broadcasting. Instead they point out the ways in which ruling-class ideology becomes seen as 'common sense' – they refer to this process as cultural hegemony. Hall argues that the media assume a basic consensus about the way the world works and that this dominant view is taken for granted by most people. For example, the media assume that the cause of inflation is wage demands rather than the profiteering of big companies. Another example is provided by Fairclough, who uses discourse analysis – the detailed examination of words and images – to argue that the TV programme Crimewatch legitimates the role of the police and contradicts images of the police as corrupt and incompetent.

The Glasgow Media Group (GMG) have undertaken a variety of research supporting the cultural hegemony model. They have used content analysis to analyse news broadcasts and found that the language of news broadcast favours the views of powerful groups. For example, in industrial disputes negative words such as 'threat' and 'demand' are used to describe strikers while more positive words (such as 'offer') are used to describe management. Also, angles of filming from behind police lines encourage identification with the police. Recent work by the GMG shows how the public has little knowledge of the Israeli/Palestinian conflict because news broadcasters focus on dramatic images rather than the background to the conflict. Broadcasters also avoid challenging the pro-Israeli position of the American government.

Marxist and neo-Marxist positions have been criticized. For pluralists, the media must respond to audience preferences if they are to survive, so the news will reflect public opinion. Society is made up of a range of different groups and media content will reflect this diversity. Other critics of Marxist positions point out that not all journalists share a unified culture which reflects dominant ideology. Anti-establishment programmes such as Unreported World do get made. Postmodernists point out the ways the public can use the media to oppose the policies of giant corporations – for example, the Facebook campaign that prevented HSBC imposing overdraft fees for new graduates.

Another way of looking at the issue is to focus on the organizational and bureaucratic routines that influence journalists' work. From this point of view the news is influenced more by practical pressures than ideology. Galtung & Ruge identify a number of features that journalists are taught to value in news stories. These include preferences for short-lived, intense and unexpected events that fit into established story types; if these events feature elite nations and individuals and are 'bad' rather than 'good' news then all the better. However, Boyd-Barrett criticizes this emphasis on practical factors. He points out that Galtung & Ruge fail to consider the cultural hegemony which is the source of these news values.

In the digital age, where there are multiple news outlets, it seems strange to argue that there is an ideological bias in news programmes — surely, the sheer number of newspapers and news channels means that a variety of viewpoints and voices will be heard? But in fact the selection and presentation of news is very similar in most of these. They all rely on official and other powerful sources of information and work with a broadly shared consensual understanding of the world. Nevertheless the news, especially on the supposedly impartial BBC, has been criticised by both right- and left-wing commentators in recent years.

In the end it is difficult to judge the significance of any ideological bias in the news without understanding all elements of the production and reception of news — what Philo & Miller refer to as the 'circuit of communication'. These elements include the organizations that supply information to the media, the content of the media, the prior understandings of the public and the role of decision-makers in key institutions.

RESOURCES

The mass media

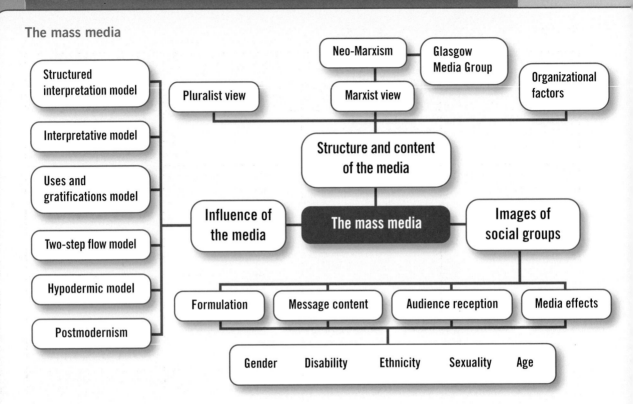

Writers and their work

Writer	Perspective or approach	Concept(s)	Study
Katz & Lazarsfeld	Pluralism	Opinion leaders	Media influence on political opinion in the USA in the 1940s
Hall	Neo-Marxism	Cultural hegemony	Study of ideology
Fairclough	Discourse analysis	Discourse	Study of *Crimewatch*
Glasgow Media Group	Neo-Marxism	Circuit of communication	Content analysis of TV news and audience studies
Galtung & Ruge	Emphasis on organizational factors	News values	Analysis of journalists' practices
Bandura *et al*	Hypodermic model	Social learning theory	Psychological experiments
Vernette	Two-step flow model	Opinion leaders	Study of advertising in women's fashion industry
Morley	Structured interpretation model	Polysemic messages	How audience respond to TV news show *Nationwide*
Skirrow	Feminism	Gender valence	Video games
McRobbie	Neo-Marxist/cultural hegemony model	Inner logic (of magazines)	Study of women's magazines
Tuchman	Liberal feminist	Symbolic annihilation	Study of portrayal of women in advertising
Hebdidge	Neo-Marxism	Neutralizing subcultures	Study of youth subcultures

Sociological perspectives on media effects

	What effect does the mass media have on its audiences?	Writers	Criticisms
Hypodermic model	Media messages are directly injected into audiences	Bandura *et al*	Audiences are diverse and react in different ways
Two-step flow model	Media messages are interpreted by opinion leaders who then influence others	Vernette	Meaning of media messages may be imposed by the powerful; there may be no consensus about the meaning of media messages
Uses and gratifications model	The media audience is active and people use the media in different ways	McQuail	Fails to explain why people use the media in different ways; the media may create needs; ignores wider structural factors
Interpretative model	The audience filters messages, ignoring some and reinterpreting others	Buckingham	Underestimates the power of media messages; ignores role of social groups in shaping interpretations
Structured interpretation mod	Audiences do interpret media messages in different ways but there is a dominant preferred reading	Morley	Social groups may not have such a strong influence on interpretations
Postmodernism	Societies saturated with media images, so much so that it is difficult to distinguish fact from fiction	Baudrillard, Turkle	Still need to look at who creates media content and why; postmodernism obscures issues of inequality

Chapter 10 | CRIME AND DEVIANCE

SPECIFICATION COVERAGE

Specification	Details
AQA A2 Unit SCLY 4: Crime and Deviance; Stratification and Differentiation, Theory and Methods: Crime and Deviance option	All sections are relevant. Other aspects of this unit are covered in the *Sociological Theory* and *Methodology* chapters
OCR A2 Unit G673: Power and Control – Sociology of Crime and Deviance	All sections are relevant
WJEC A2 Unit SY3: Understanding Power and Control – Option 1, Understanding Crime	

INTRODUCTION

AQA, OCR, WJEC   Textbook pp. 321-322

Crime consists of activities that break the law and are potentially subject to official punishment. However, not all criminals are caught and not all laws are strictly enforced. There is often room for interpretation about whether a law has been broken or not.

At its simplest, **deviance** is behaviour that does not follow the norms and expectations of a particular social group.

Deviance can sometimes be seen in a positive light (for example, an unusually dedicated worker could be seen as deviant) but in practice most deviance is seen negatively. The sociology of deviance concentrates on deviance that is viewed negatively.

All societies attempt to prevent and reduce **criminal**, and undesirable **deviant** behaviour. The ways in which this is done is through mechanisms of **social control**.

Mechanisms of social control

Mechanisms can be **formal** or **informal**:

- **Formal mechanisms** include the criminal justice system, involving the police, courts and prisons.
- **Informal mechanisms** consist of mechanisms which are not based upon formal rules but are carried out by members of society in everyday life.

The use of **negative** or **positive sanctions** (punishments or rewards) are crucial in maintaining social control.

Deviance is often **negatively sanctioned** (punished). For example, murderers deviate from the value society places on human life. Their behaviour generally results in widespread disapproval and punishment through formal mechanisms if they are caught.

More minor acts of deviance, for example rudeness, may be subject to **informal negative sanctions** such as criticism or exclusion from a social group.

Positive sanctions are used to encourage behaviour which is deemed desirable. For example, hard work can rewarded with bonuses, praise, promotion or other positive sanctions which raise individual status.

Social control is also achieved through the **socialization** process, whereby members of society learn the behaviour that is deemed desirable in their culture.

Delinquency consists of antisocial or criminal acts committed by young people.

Sociologists who study crime are often referred to as **criminologists**.

FUNCTIONALIST PERSPECTIVE

AQA, OCR, WJEC   Textbook pp. 322-325

The functions of deviance

A **functionalist** analysis of deviance looks for the source of deviance in the nature of society rather than in the biological or psychological nature of the individual. Although functionalists agree that social control mechanisms such as the police and the courts are necessary to keep deviance in check, many argue that a certain amount of deviance can contribute to the well-being of society.

Durkheim – functional crime

Durkheim (1895) believed that crime is an 'integral part of all healthy societies'. This is because individuals are exposed to different influences and will not all be committed to the shared values and beliefs of society. Even in a 'society of saints' where everybody tries to obey the norms, complete conformity will be impossible – even the most minor, perhaps unintentional act of rudeness will be seen as serious deviance.

Crime can also be **functional**. All societies need to progress and all social change begins with some form of deviance. In order for change to occur, yesterday's deviance must become tomorrow's normality. (For example, Nelson Mandela, once imprisoned as a 'terrorist', eventually became president of South Africa.)

Durkheim believed, however, that very high rates of crime or deviance indicated that something had gone wrong with society (see Durkheim's views on **egoistic** and **anomic suicide**, p. 196).

Societies need both crime and punishment. These help to highlight society's norms and define **moral boundaries**. Without punishment the crime rate would reach a point where it became **dysfunctional**.

Durkheim's views have been developed by **Cohen** (1966) who discussed two possible functions of deviance:

- Deviance can be a 'safety valve', providing a relatively harmless expression of discontent. For example, prostitution enables men to escape from family life without undermining family stability.

- Deviant acts can warn society that an aspect is not working properly – for example, widespread truanting from school.

Merton – social structure and anomie

Merton (1968) explains how deviance can result from the **culture** and **structure** of society.

He begins from the functionalist position of **value consensus** – that is, all members of society share the same values. In the USA, members of society strive for the goal of success, largely measured in terms of wealth and material possessions. The accepted, legitimate means of reaching this goal are through talent, ambition and effort. Great emphasis is put upon achieving success goals, but less on using legitimate means to achieve success.

The idea of the 'American dream' (that anybody can go from the most humble background to the top of society – 'log cabin to White House') is widely accepted. However, in reality the path to the top is often blocked for those from poorer backgrounds: there is **inequality of opportunity**.

The result is an unbalanced society where winning is all and the 'rules' are not very important. This situation where there is too much emphasis on the **cultural goals** and not enough on the **institutional means** is known as **anomie**. Individuals may respond to this in different ways:

- **Conformity** – the most common response. Conformists strive for success through the accepted channels.

- **Innovation** – people from lower classes may have few qualifications and turn to crime to achieve material success. Anomie can also affect a smaller number of people from the middle class because there is **no upper limit** on success.

- **Ritualism** – some people, particularly from the lower middle classes, may abandon the ultimate goal of wealth but continue to conform to the standards of middle-class respectability.

- **Retreatism** – retreatists are 'drop-outs' who have rejected both the shared value of success and the means provided to achieve it.

- **Rebellion** – rebels reject both goals and means but replace them with different ones. They wish to create an entirely new kind of society.

The solution to these problems is to place more emphasis on **institutional means** (the law and the values and norms of society) and to produce **equality of opportunity**.

Evaluation

Taylor (1971) criticizes Merton for failing to consider wider power relations in society – that is, who actually makes the laws and who benefits from them.

Merton assumes that there is a **value consensus** in American society and that people only deviate because of **structural strain** in society; in reality groups have different values.

Merton's theory exaggerates working-class crime and underestimates **white-collar crime**.

Taylor et al (1973) argue that the theory cannot account for politically motivated crime, where people break the law because of commitment to a cause.

Merton has been defended by **Reiner** (1994), who believes that Merton's theory can be adapted to take most of these criticisms into account.

Merton's theory can be applied to some contemporary trends in crime. For example, **Savelsberg** (1995) argues that Merton's strain theory can help to explain the rapid rises in the crime rate in many **post-Communist** countries, which have experienced anomie with the introduction of capitalism. In Poland, for example, between 1989 and 1990 the official crime rate increased by 69%.

STRUCTURAL AND SUBCULTURAL THEORIES

AQA, OCR, WJEC   Textbook pp. 325-327

Structural theories of **deviance** explain the origins of deviance in terms of the position of the individual in society. **Subcultural** theories of deviance explain it in terms of the subculture of a particular social group. Certain groups develop **norms** and **values** which are different from those held by other members of society.

Cohen – delinquent subculture

Albert Cohen's work (1955) modified Merton's position and combined both **structural** and **subcultural** theories of deviance. Cohen criticizes two aspects of **Merton**'s theory of working-class deviance. According to Cohen:

● deviance is a **collective** rather than an **individual** response.

● Merton ignores **non-utilitarian** crimes. These are crimes that have no financial reward, such as vandalism and joyriding.

Lower working-class boys want success but cannot achieve their goals because **cultural deprivation** leads to educational failure and dead-end jobs. They suffer from **status frustration** and turn to delinquency to gain status within their peer group. An alternative set of norms and values is adopted – a **delinquent subculture** – which reverses mainstream culture by valuing activities such as stealing, vandalism and truancy. This solves the problem of status frustration, as they gain high status from other members of the subculture for their delinquent behaviour.

Evaluation

Box (1981) argues that Cohen's theory only applies to a minority of delinquents; most delinquents never accepted mainstream success goals in the first place.

Matza (1964) conducted research which suggested that most delinquents are not committed to a delinquent subculture, nor are they totally opposed to society's values. Rather they drift in and out of delinquency, so the idea of highly integrated and distinctive subcultures is a myth.

Cloward & Ohlin – delinquency and opportunity

Cloward & Ohlin (1961) accept **Merton**'s explanation of deviance in terms of the legitimate opportunity structure, but they argue that he failed to consider the **illegitimate opportunity structure**. Just as the opportunity to succeed by legitimate means varies, so does the opportunity to succeed by illegitimate means. For example, in one area there may be a thriving **criminal subculture**, while in another area this subculture may not exist. Thus, in the first area, the adolescent has more opportunity to become a successful criminal.

Like Merton, Cloward & Ohlin believe that there is greater pressure on the working classes to deviate because they have less opportunity to succeed by legitimate means. They identified three possible responses to this situation:

● Criminal subcultures emerge in areas of established **organized crime** where young people are exposed to **deviant values** and **role models**. In this situation

young people have the opportunity to rise within the established criminal hierarchy.

● **Conflict subcultures** develop in areas where there is little access to either legitimate or illegitimate opportunity structures. The response to this situation is often **gang violence**, which serves as a release from anger and frustration and as a means of achieving **prestige** in terms of the values of the subculture.

● **Retreatist** subcultures are organized mainly around illegal drug use and occur because members are 'double failures', who have failed to succeed in both legitimate and illegitimate opportunity structures.

Evaluation

Taylor *et al* (1973) criticize Merton, Cohen, and Cloward & Ohlin for assuming that everybody is committed to the **success goal** of achieving wealth. They point out that there are other possible goals and that some groups, such as 'hippies', make a conscious choice to reject conventional goals.

The **marketization** of capitalist societies has made these theories increasingly relevant. **South** (1997) believes that the British drug trade is largely based around '**disorganized**' crime, which can be compared to Cloward & Ohlin's conflict subcultures, although some of it is based around professional criminal organizations and more closely resembles a criminal subculture. Many of the drug users themselves are part of a **retreatist** subculture.

THE UNDERCLASS AND CRIME

AQA, OCR, WJEC   Textbook p. 327

Murray – welfare, culture and criminality

Some sociologists have suggested that an **underclass** now exists which does not share the same values as other members of society. **Charles Murray** (1989) believes that the underclass is responsible for a large proportion of crime, and he blames welfare benefits which have made it possible for young women to become single parents and for young men to reject the idea that it is important to hold down a job.

Inequality, the underclass and crime

Other sociologists reject Murray's **New Right** views but still believe that an underclass exists. **Taylor** (1997) argues that young, unskilled working-class males have been affected by increasing inequality and declining job prospects. Underclass criminal activity is the result of **material deprivation** rather than an unacceptable culture.

Evaluation of underclass theories

Many sociologists have questioned the idea that there is a distinctive underclass culture. Most criticisms refer to the views of Charles Murray.

Tham (1998) compared **welfare policies** and crime rates in Britain and Sweden. During the 1980s and 1990s he found that crime increased more rapidly in Britain than in Sweden, which had a more generous welfare state. He claims that crime rates are closely linked to levels of inequality.

Mooney (1998) argues that there is no link between single parenthood and criminality. Her research indicates that single parents are more likely to become the victims of crime than to become criminals themselves.

CRIME AND OFFICIAL STATISTICS

AQA, OCR, WJEC   **Textbook pp. 328-334**

Many theories of crime are based on the official statistics provided by government organizations such as the police and the courts. This information is often taken as an accurate measure of the total amount of crime. The data allows comparisons to be made between crimes, and with previous years. These statistics tend to show two main trends:

- Some social groups appear to be more involved in crime than others.
- **Crime rates** in Britain increased from the 1950s to the 1990s.

Social groups more involved in crime are:

- the working class;
- the young;
- males;
- some ethnic minorities for some crimes.

These groups appear to be more likely to commit crimes than comparable groups: the middle class, the elderly; females; whites (for some crimes). Sociologists such as **Merton** and **Murray** have taken these statistics at face value and gone on to explain why these groups appear to commit a disproportionate amount of crime.

Crime rates

Crime rates in Britain remained low until the 1950s but then increased rapidly until the mid-1990s. There was then a period when the crime rate fell, although with the start of the recession in 2008 there was some evidence of rates starting to rise again. In recent years the vast majority of offences have been **property offences**. Often the release of crime figures receives widespread publicity and leads to concern that the country is experiencing a '**crime wave**'.

Maguire (2002) points out that the official crime figures do not include all crimes. Many crimes are dealt with by other agencies such as the British Transport Police. Tax evasion and benefits fraud, for example, are not included in official crime figures.

Statistics are also affected by changes in **recording policies** – for example, after 1997 offences of criminal damage involving property worth less than £20 were included for the first time. In 1997 and 2002 changes in recording practices led to an increase in crimes recorded by the police.

Unrecorded crime

Not all the crimes that take place are recorded by the police. For a crime to be recorded at least three things must happen:

- Somebody must be **aware** that a crime has taken place.
- The crime must be **reported**.
- The police or other agency must accept that a law has been broken and decide to **record** it.

Some crimes, such as tax evasion, do not have an obvious victim, and it is these that are least likely to be reported. However, attempts have been made to estimate the amount of crime which victims are aware of but which is not reported to the police or not recorded as a crime.

Victimization studies

In 1983 the Home Office published the first **British Crime Survey**. Since 2000 this survey has taken place annually and represents an attempt to overcome the limitations of police crime statistics. Instead of relying on police records, it uses **victimization studies**. These involve asking individuals if they have been the victim of crime in the previous year, whether they reported the crimes, and whether the police recorded them. These surveys reveal that the police crime statistics are highly unreliable.

Some of the key findings of the 2006/7 British Crime Survey are as follows:

- Less than half of all crimes (41%) were reported to the police. Reporting varied enormously according to the crime – 93% of vehicle thefts were reported, compared to just 36% of assaults without injury and 32% of vandalism.
- Most crimes are not reported because they are thought to be too trivial or it is felt that the police cannot do anything about them. For many violent offences people felt the offence was a private matter or said they would deal with it themselves.
- Up to 40% of all incidents reported to the police were not recorded as crimes. This was because the police judged the incident as too trivial, did not believe that it had taken place, felt that there was insufficient evidence to proceed, or the victim did not want them to pursue the matter.

In terms of trends in the overall crime rate, figures from the British Crime Surveys are broadly in line with the official police figures, with the overall crime rate beginning to fall in the mid-1990s.

Crime Survey and police statistics are now published together by the government and are used together to give an overall picture of crime trends.

Data from the British Crime Surveys are still not entirely reliable. **Croall** (1998) identifies four main problems:

- Crimes can only be reported if victims are aware of them.
- The results are limited by respondents' memory and their definition of events.
- The survey is restricted to households so does not cover crimes committed against businesses or organizations.
- The sample does not include people under 16.

So the findings of the British Crime Survey should be treated with caution. However, they are probably more reliable than the official statistics because they include so many crimes that are not reported.

Self-report studies

Only a small proportion of offenders are convicted of crimes. In 2006/7 only 26% of crimes known to the police were cleared up (**Nicholas** *et al*, 2007).

Self-report studies attempt to discover the **characteristics** of criminals. They use questionnaires or interviews and ask individuals to admit to the number and types of crime they have committed. The data can then be compared with official conviction rates to discover which types of offender are most likely to be convicted.

Using data from 40 self-report studies from different countries, **Box** (1981) rejected the impression created by official statistics that working-class youths are more likely to engage in delinquency than middle-class youths.

A more recent study by **Graham & Bowling** (1995) found that social class had no influence on whether young British males and females would admit to having committed offences, although lower social classes were more likely to admit to more serious offences.

Evaluation

Individuals may wish to conceal their criminal acts. However, it is estimated (using lie detector tests) that around 80% of those who reply do tell the truth.

It is likely that self-report studies identify many more offenders than the official statistics.

Victims of crime

Statistics on crime from the police and victim studies indicate that the chances of being a victim are not equally distributed:

- The most likely victims of **violent crime** are young males who live in poorer areas and go out three or more times a week drinking.

- Victims of violence are most likely to be attacked by somebody they know, and in the case of women especially by partners or ex-partners.

- 79% of **rapes** are committed by men known to the female victim and over half of rapes are repeat rapes by the same offender.

- People from **minority ethnic groups** are most at risk from personal crimes such as street robbery, partly because they are more likely to live in inner-city areas, be poor and be single parents.

The British Crime Survey of 2006/7 found that 32% of victims of vandalism were victims more than once, as were 28% of victims of violence. Some people are particularly prone to **multiple victimization**.

White-collar crime and corporate crime

Many criminologists suspect that middle-class offenders are less likely than working-class offenders to be convicted of offences they commit, but due to lack of **self-report studies** with adults it is not possible to compare the results with official statistics. However, there is evidence that offences committed by individuals of **high social status** do not often appear in the official statistics.

Edwin Sutherland (1960) was the first sociologist to study '**white-collar crime**'. He defines it as 'crimes committed by persons of high social status and respectability in the course of their occupations'.

Nelken (2002) questions Sutherland's definition. White-collar crimes may be committed outside the course of occupations and some crime may be the responsibility of organizations or corporations (often called corporate crime) rather than individuals.

There are various types of white-collar crime:

- Commercial corruption and fraud – one common type of fraud is insider dealing, in which shares in a company are bought by individuals who know that, for example, the company is about to be the subject of a takeover bid. In 2008 a massive alleged fraud involving $50 billion came to light. Bernard Madoff, the manager of a US hedge fund, admitted a pyramid scheme in which he used new investment to pay interest to old investors, leaving the fund unable to return the original investments.

- Crimes that cause personal harm – according to **Streeter** (1997), in the late 1990s the effects of asbestos were killing 3,500 people per year. The actions which resulted in these deaths may not have been illegal but their consequences in terms of loss of life were extremely serious.

- Political and organizational corruption – the MP Jonathan Aitken, a member of the last Conservative government, was found to have accepted hospitality at the Paris Ritz from Mohammed Al Fayed in return for asking questions in Parliament. He was later imprisoned for trying to cover this up.

Corporate crimes are committed by businesses or corporations usually to increase the profits of the corporation rather than benefit individuals. Such offences could involve massive losses of money. For example, false accounting by the US company Enron led to its bankruptcy in 2001 leaving debts of some $50 billion.

Corporate **negligence** can lead to massive physical harm. Inadequate safety at a factory in Bhopal India in 1984 led to an escape of poisonous gas which left more than 3,000 people dead and more than 20,000 permanently injured.

A number of factors combine to reduce the apparent extent and seriousness of white-collar and corporate crime:

- White-collar crimes are difficult to detect as many do not have obvious victims.

- In cases of bribery and corruption all those involved can sometimes benefit, so nobody is likely to report the offence.

- In cases where the victim is the public at large (such as tax fraud) individual members of the public have no knowledge of the offence or the expertise to realize that they are being misled. Government agencies lack the resources to follow up more than a few cases.

Even if they are detected, few white-collar crimes lead to prosecutions. The power and influence of many of those involved mean that a 'blind eye' is often turned or only an official warning given. Cases of professional misconduct are usually dealt with by the relevant professional association, which may simply hand out a reprimand.

Official statistics probably significantly underestimate the extent of white-collar and corporate crime. As a result, crime is viewed as predominantly working-class behaviour.

In the case of corporate crime it can be difficult to attribute blame to particular individuals so in many cases prosecutions never take place.

State crime

Textbook pp. 390-393

Cohen (2001) argues that the scope of criminology should be expanded to include crimes committed by the state, and **human rights abuses**. States, and their agents, may commit crimes and illegal human rights abuses which contravene the laws of their own countries or binding international agreements.

The 'War on Terror' has highlighted crimes committed by terrorists who are sometimes state-sponsored, but also by national governments themselves. The USA has been accused of human rights abuses including **torture**, and other such abuses have recently been reported in many countries including China, Chechnya (in Russia), Iran, Syria and Burma.

State crimes are often covered up and rarely result in prosecutions because the state has the power to decide what offences are prosecuted. One shocking example of a state crime which did come to light was carried out by the French government, when its secret service blew up a Greenpeace ship, the Rainbow Warrior, in 1985, murdering one of the crew.

Some criminologists go further and have introduced the idea of **trangressive criminology** – which believes that criminologists should study actions which do harm to others, whether or not they are conventionally regarded as crimes.

Chambliss (1989) studied the crimes of the state from a **Marxist** perspective, and found the US state was involved in money-laundering, arms smuggling and state-sponsored assassinations.

McLaughlin (2001) studied state crime from a **Weberian** perspective, arguing that because the state claims a monopoly of the **legitimate use of force**, it can claim the right to use force whenever it is seen as in the **public interest**. However, there is often no agreement about what constitutes the public interest. For example, the actions by the British and US governments in Iraq and Afghanistan are regarded as illegal by some people while the US and UK governments see them as legitimate.

'Green crime'

Green criminology follows studies of state crime in extending the definition of what is seen as criminal beyond conventional law-breaking.

It sees actions which harm animal and plant species and the environment as a form of criminal activity whether or not they are illegal.

Lynch & Stretsky (2003) believe green criminology should study 'individuals or entities who/which, kill, injure and assault other life forms (human, animal, plant) by poisoning the earth'.

There are three approaches to green criminology:

- **Situ & Emmons** (2000) study offences which damage the environment and break national or international laws.
- **Braithwaite & Drahos** (2000) extend green criminology to include legal actions which damage the environment. For example, **Halsey & White** (1998) believe that the World Bank, the global capitalist system and capitalist countries all put economic development before environmental well-being. For example, the US company Union Carbide was allowed to locate a dangerous chemical plant in a residential area in Bhopal, India (see above, p. 182).
- **Beck** (1992) puts green criminology in the context of major changes in society. He argues that we have entered a **risk society**. Technological developments have reduced the scarcity of goods leading to a decline in class conflict but this has resulted in massive damage to the environment, increasing the risks of man-made disasters (such as nuclear accidents, and the effects of air pollution on health and the earth's climate).

South (1998) gives examples of what he calls **primary crimes** – crimes which directly harm the environment even thought they are currently legal. These include:

- air pollution caused by governments, big business and consumers;
- deforestation, which destroyed about 20% of the world's tropical rainforests between 1960 and 1990;
- species extinction, which he predicts will lead to the loss of 10 million species by 2020;
- water pollution, which kills 25 million people each year.

South also gives examples of **secondary crimes** which result from the flouting of environmental laws. An example is pollution in the Bay of Naples caused by the illegal dumping of toxic waste by the Camorra crime organization.

Evaluation

A problem with wider definitions of 'green crime' is that there may be no agreement on what constitutes harm to the environment.

INTERACTIONIST THEORIES

AQA, OCR, WJEC Textbook pp. 334-339

Most of the theories considered up to this point have looked at the factors that supposedly direct the behaviour of deviants. This emphasis on the idea that deviants simply react to external forces is similar to a **positivist** position.

Interactionists take a different approach. They examine:

- how and why particular individuals and groups are defined as deviant.
- the effects of such a definition on their future actions.

Becker – labelling theory

Becker (1963) suggests that there is really no such thing as an inherently deviant act. An act only becomes deviant when others perceive it as such. He writes: 'Social groups create deviance by making the rules whose infraction constitutes deviance and by applying those rules to particular people.'

He gives the example of a brawl involving young people. In a low-income neighbourhood this may be defined by the police as **delinquency**; in a wealthy neighbourhood it may be defined as youthful high spirits. The acts are the same but the meaning given to them is different. If youngsters are defined as delinquent and convicted, then they have become deviant. In other words, they have been labelled as deviants.

Possible effects of labelling

Once an individual or group is labelled as criminal, mentally ill or homosexual, others see them only in terms of that label. It becomes what Becker calls a **master status**. Labelling also causes the labelled group or individual to see themselves in terms of the label. This may produce a **self-fulfilling prophecy** in which the label actually makes itself come true.

Becker identifies a number of stages in this process:

1   The individual is labelled as deviant and may be rejected from many social groups.

2   This may encourage further deviance. A drug addict may turn to crime because employers refuse to give him/her a job. Ex-convicts find it difficult to get jobs and may be forced to return to crime.

3   The **deviant career** is completed when individuals join an organized deviant group, thus confirming and accepting their deviant identity.

4   Now a **deviant subculture** may develop which includes norms and values which support their deviant behaviour.

Young – labelling and marijuana users

Becker's approach is used by **Jock Young** (1971) in his study of 'hippie' marijuana users in Notting Hill London:

1   The police see hippies as dirty, lazy drug addicts.

2   Police action against marijuana users unites them and makes them feel different.

3   As a result they retreat into small **subcultures**.

4   **Deviant norms** and **values** develop in these closed groups. Hair is grown longer, clothes become more unconventional and drug use becomes a central activity.

Thus a self-fulfilling prophecy is created.

Lemert – primary and secondary deviance

Lemert (1972) distinguishes between 'primary' and 'secondary' deviance.

Primary deviance consists of deviant acts before they are publicly labelled. Trying to find the causes of primary deviance is not very helpful because:

●   samples of deviants are inevitably based only on those who have been labelled, and they are therefore unrepresentative.

●   most deviant acts are so common that they are, in statistical terms, normal.

Most males may at some time, for example: commit a homosexual act; engage in delinquency.

Primary deviance therefore has little effect on the person's **self-concept** and behaviour. The important factor in creating deviance is the **reaction of society** – the public identification of the deviant. **Secondary deviance** is the response of the individual to that societal reaction.

Labelling theory and social policy

Jones (2001) identifies two main policy implications of labelling theory:

●   As many types of behaviour as possible should be **decriminalized**. For example, in some countries (such as the Netherlands) cannabis has been effectively legalized.

●   When the law has to intervene, it should avoid giving people a self-concept in which they view themselves as criminals. For example, warnings and cautions could be used to deal with delinquents rather than placing them in institutions.

These policies became less popular during the 1990s. Recently the emphasis has been on the 'naming and shaming' of offenders such as paedophiles and kerb crawlers.

Evaluation of interactionist theories

Labelling theory enjoyed great popularity in the 1960s and it has influenced subsequent theories. However, it has also been strongly criticized. The key criticisms are as follows:

●   **Taylor et al** (1973) argue that labelling theory is wrong in suggesting that deviance is created by the social groups who define acts as deviant. Some acts – such as premeditated killing for personal gain – will always be regarded as deviant in our society.

●   Many sociologists claim that the interactionist approach fails to explain why individuals commit deviant acts in the first place (**primary deviance**).

●   It is claimed that labelling theory is too **deterministic**. It assumes that once a person has been labelled their deviance will automatically increase. **Ackers** (1975) suggests that individuals might simply choose to be deviant, regardless of whether they have been labelled.

●   The interactionist approach fails to explain why some people are labelled rather than others and why some activities are against the law and others are not. It ignores the wider issue of the distribution of power in society.

Interactionists such as **Plummer** (1979) have strongly defended labelling theory against these criticisms. He argues that it is a very useful perspective if you distinguish between **societal deviance** (the types of behaviour society disapproves of) and **situational deviance** (what is defined as deviant in a particular situation).

It is certainly true that the interactionist approach has had a significant influence on the sociology of deviance, particularly more recent approaches such as **new left realism** (see p. 186).

PHENOMENOLOGICAL PERSPECTIVE

AQA, OCR, WJEC   Textbook pp. 339-340

The phenomenological approach is similar to labelling theory as it concentrates on the process of labelling in enforcing the law. However, phenomenology focuses purely on the way in which some individuals and groups come to be labelled as deviant.

Cicourel (1976) applies a phenomenological approach to understanding the treatment of delinquency in two Californian cities.

Cicourel observed how the police used **stereotypes** of the 'typical delinquent' when selecting who to stop and question. They were more likely to stop juveniles in 'bad', low-income areas of town with high crime rates.

Once arrested, the juvenile was more likely to be charged if they fitted the picture of the 'typical delinquent': broken home, 'bad' attitude to authority, low-income background, ethnic minority etc.

Middle-class juveniles were less likely to be charged with an offence. They were seen as 'ill' or temporarily straying from the correct path with a real chance of reform. Their parents were better able to present them as respectable and reasonable and **negotiate justice** on their behalf.

Cicourel concludes that delinquents are produced by the agencies of social control.

Criticisms

Cicourel has been criticized by **Taylor** *et al* (1973) for failing to explain where stereotypes of the typical criminal come from in the first place – i.e. he has no **theory of power**.

MARXIST PERPECTIVE

AQA, OCR, WJEC   Textbook pp. 340-343

Who makes the law? Who benefits?

From a Marxist perspective, laws are made by the state, which represents the interests of the **ruling class**.

Snider (1993) notes that the capitalist state is often reluctant to pass laws that threaten the **profitability** of large businesses. Often the state has worked hard to attract large corporations and does not want to risk alienating them.

Pearce (1976) argues that many laws which appear to benefit only the working class, in reality benefit the ruling class as well. Factory legislation protecting the health and safety of workers benefits capitalists by keeping workers fit for work and loyal to their employers.

Chambliss (1976) suggests that much of what takes place in the creation of rules is '**non-decision-making**'. Many issues – such as the way wealth is distributed – never reach the point of decision.

Who breaks the law? Who gets caught?

Marxists argue that crime is widespread in all parts of society. There are many examples of illegal behaviour by **white-collar** criminals and **corporations** (see p. 182).

Snider (1993) argues that many of the most serious deviant acts in modern societies are **corporate crimes**. She claims that corporate crime costs more in terms of loss of money and life than crimes such as burglary and robbery. She estimates street crime costs $4 billion per year in the USA but losses from corporate crime are more than twenty times greater,

Why break the law? Why enforce the law?

Many Marxists see crime as a natural 'outgrowth' of capitalist society.

Chambliss (1976) argues that the greed, self-interest and hostility generated by capitalist society motivate

crimes at all levels within society. Members of all classes use whatever opportunities they have to commit crime.

Given the nature of capitalist societies, crime is rational. **Gordon** (1976) argues that in a society where competition is the order of the day, individuals must fend for themselves in order to survive.

Gordon goes on to suggest that law enforcement in the USA supports the capitalist system in three main ways:

- Individuals who commit crimes are defined as '**social failures**' and seen as responsible for their actions. In this way blame and condemnation are directed at the individual rather than the capitalist system.
- The imprisonment of selected members of the working class neutralizes opposition to the system. For example, American blacks are heavily over-represented amongst those arrested for street crimes such as robbery and aggravated assault.
- Defining criminals as 'animals and misfits' provides a justification for their imprisonment. This keeps them hidden from public view and so the embarrassing extremes produced by the capitalist system are swept under the carpet.

Evaluation

Conventional Marxist theories have come in for some heavy criticism.

Feminists have argued that Marxist theories ignore the importance of **patriarchy** in influencing the criminal justice system. Marxists have also been accused of neglecting the importance of **racism** in the enforcement of the law.

Crime was not been eradicated in **Communist societies** based on Marxist principles.

Jones (2001) points out that capitalism does not always produce high crime rates. For example, in Switzerland the crime rate is very low.

Perhaps the distribution of power is not as simple as some Marxists suggest. Jones gives the example of insider trading (taking advantage of 'insider' knowledge to make huge profits on the stock exchange). This is illegal, which suggests that capitalists do not always get the laws they want.

Left realists (see p. 186) believe that Marxists put too much emphasis on corporate crime. **Street crimes**, such as burglary, cause greater harm than Marxists imply. Their victims are usually working-class and the consequences can be devastating for them.

Postmodern criminology rejects Marxist criminology as being neither believable nor defensible (see p. 196).

Despite these criticisms, Marxism has had an influence on a number of critical perspectives on deviance. Some have drawn their inspiration from Marxism and can be referred to as **neo-Marxist** approaches. Others owe less to Marxism and are better defined as **radical** approaches.

NEO-MARXIST AND RADICAL PERSPECTIVES

AQA, OCR, WJEC   Textbook pp. 343-344

Neo-Marxist approaches to deviance are strongly influenced by Marxism but do not accept that there is a straightforward link between the structure of capitalist society and deviance.

Taylor *et al* – The New Criminology

In 1973, **Taylor**, **Walton** & **Young** published *The New Criminology*. This influential book criticizes many existing theories of crime. The authors accept some key assumptions of Marxism but adopt a more liberal and tolerant view, influenced by labelling theory.

They outline what they call a 'fully social theory of deviance'. They believe that some criminals act like Robin Hood – stealing from the rich to give to the poor – and believe some offences should be **decriminalized**. Others are political crimes where a person chooses to support a just cause.

The criminologist must consider the following aspects of deviance:

- the way in which **wealth and power** are distributed.
- the **circumstances** surrounding the decision of an individual to commit an act of deviance.
- the **meaning** of the deviant act for the person involved. Was the individual 'kicking back' at society through an act of vandalism, for example?
- the ways in which other members of society, such as the police, **respond** to the deviant act.
- the meaning of this response in terms of the way in which society is organized. Who has the **power** to make rules and decide how deviant acts should be dealt with?
- the impact of the **deviant label**. This may have a variety of effects – the deviant may accept the label as justified, or they may ignore the label, or it may lead to greater deviance.

Finally, criminologists need to look at the relationship between all these different aspects so that they can be fused into one complete theory of deviance.

Evaluation

The New Criminology has been criticized in a number of ways.

Feminists have criticized its concentration on male crimes.

Some **new left realist** criminologists have accused it of neglecting the impact of crime on victims and romanticizing working-class criminals (see below).

In 1998, **Paul Walton** and **Jock Young** re-evaluated their earlier work. They accept some of the criticisms but argue that recent approaches such as 'realist criminology, feminist criminology and postmodern criminology are all committed to creating a more equitable and just society'. In this respect they are each continuing in the tradition of *The New Criminology*.

LEFT REALIST PERSPECTIVE

AQA, OCR, WJEC Textbook pp. 345-343

Left realists see their position as close to the British **Labour Party**. Most left realists describe themselves as socialists and argue for reform of society rather than revolution. Left realism has developed since the 1980s and is particularly associated with **Jock Young**.

The problem of crime

Left realists take the view that crime is a real problem which must be taken seriously, and they present a number of criticisms of previous criminology:

- Some sociologists have tried to explain the huge rise in **street crime** since the Second World War by pointing to the unreliable nature of criminal statistics. **Young** (1993) argues that the rises have been so great that they cannot simply be explained by changes in reporting and recording.

- Some sociologists have advanced the view that the chances of being a victim of street crime are minimal. However, **Lea & Young** (1984) point out that, while this is true, particular groups face high risks. These groups are the poor and deprived, ethnic minorities and inner-city residents. Those with low incomes also suffer more if they are robbed or burgled.

Left realists have carried out a number of **victimization studies** and found widespread **fear of crime**. Many people, particularly women, alter their behaviour to avoid becoming victims of crime.

Lea & Young attack the idea that offenders can sometimes be seen as promoting justice. They attack the image of the criminal presented in parts of *The New Criminology* as a type of modern-day 'Robin Hood'.

While accepting that **white-collar** and **corporate crime** are commonplace and serious, left realists argue that recent criminology has concentrated too much on such crimes.

Left realists have acknowledged the importance of under-reported and under-recorded crimes such as sexual assaults and harassment, racially motivated attacks and domestic violence. They claim to take all crimes equally seriously.

The explanation of crime

Lea & Young (1984) base their attempt to explain crime around three key concepts: relative deprivation, subculture and marginalization.

Relative deprivation

Deprivation will only lead to crime where it is experienced as **relative deprivation**. A group experiences relative deprivation when it feels deprived relative to similar groups or when its expectations are not met. In modern societies advertisers stress the importance of economic success and promote middle-class lifestyles and patterns of consumption. Rather like **Merton** (see p. 193), Lea & Young argue that rising crime is partly the result of rising expectations of high standards of living, combined with restricted opportunities to achieve this.

Subculture

Groups develop lifestyles to cope with the problem of relative deprivation, and subcultures can form as a result. However, these vary. Second-generation West Indian immigrants' **subcultural solutions** include the Rastafarian and Pentecostal religions as well as 'hustling' for money and street crime.

Marginalization

Marginal groups are those that lack organizations to represent their interests in political life. These groups tend to use violence and rioting as forms of political action. The key to avoiding marginality is employment, as workers have clearly defined objectives, such as higher wages. Young, unemployed West Indians do not have clearly defined aims or pressure groups to represent them. They feel a general sense of resentment which can lead to them taking to the streets and rioting.

Dealing with crime

Policing problems

Kinsey et al (1984) argue that there are a number of flaws in policing:

- The clear-up rate is very low so the police are unable to deter criminals.
- The police spend little time actually investigating crime.
- The police rely on a flow of information from the public, but public confidence in the police is declining, particularly in inner-city areas and among members of ethnic minorities.

Without the support of the public, the police have to resort to what the authors call **military policing** – stopping and searching large numbers of people or using surveillance technology. As a result, those who are not directly involved with the police come to see them as an alien force intent on criminalizing local residents – a process known as the '**mobilization of bystanders**'.

Improving policing

Kinsey et al argue that the key to police success lies in improving relationships with the community. To achieve this they recommend that:

- the public should have much more say in shaping police policy.
- the police should spend as much time as possible actually investigating crime.

Young (1992) believes that certain crimes are **over-policed** and others **under-policed**. In the former category are minor drug offences and under-age drinking. In the latter are racially motivated attacks, corporate crime, pollution and domestic abuse.

Social causes of crime

Young (1992, 1997) does not believe that crime can be dealt with simply by improving the efficiency of the police. Left realists see the problem of crime as rooted in **social inequalities**. Young suggests that policies should aim to:

- improve leisure facilities for the young;
- reduce income inequalities;
- raise the living standards of poorer families;
- reduce unemployment and create jobs with prospects;
- provide community facilities which enhance a sense of belonging.

The square of crime

Left realists believe that crime can only be understood in terms of the relationship between the four elements in the 'square of crime', as shown in the diagram below (see Textbook p. 348).

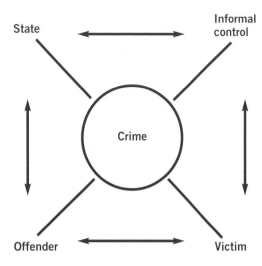

It is important to understand:

- why people offend.
- what makes the victims vulnerable and whether they choose to define incidents as criminal and report them.
- the factors that affect public attitudes and responses to crime.
- the social forces that influence the police and the rest of the criminal justice system.

Evaluation of left realism

Hughes (1991) argues that it fails to explain the causes of street crime. Left realists have not gathered empirical data about offenders' motives.

Hughes also attacks left realism for its reliance on **subcultural theory** which has been heavily criticized (see p. 180).

Jones (1998) argues that left realism fails to explain why some people who experience relative deprivation turn to crime while others do not.

Jones also identifies flaws in the emphasis on victims. Left realists take victims' accounts of fear of crime at face value and never ask victims for their views about the causes of crime. They also only take into account the views of victims in urban areas where crime rates are high, thus giving a misleading impression of how harmful crime is.

Ruggiero (1992) argues that left realists have neglected corporate and organized crime and that this type of crime cannot really be understood within the framework of their theory.

Hughes points out, however, some strengths of left realism:

- It has revived useful concepts such as **relative deprivation**.
- It has promoted debate and theoretical development within sociology.
- It has highlighted the problem posed by street crime for weaker members of society.
- It has explored the position of victims much more than previous theories.
- It avoids the worst excesses of both right- and left-wing approaches by neither glorifying nor attacking the police.

Left realism and social policy

Left realism has had more influence on crime policies than other theories. The police in Britain now employ civilians to do routine tasks, thus freeing police officers to investigate crime. The police are also beginning to take crimes such as **domestic violence** more seriously.

Labour's slogan 'Tough on crime, tough on the causes of crime' echoes the ideas of left realists. However, the reduction of inequality – a key factor underlying crime rates for left realists – has not been addressed as much as they would have liked.

Young – The Exclusive Society

Recently **Young** (1999) has argued that we are entering a period of **late modernity** which is making the problem of crime worse in a number of ways.

Late modernity is characterized by great uncertainty and instability in areas such as family life and work, which make people feel less secure and stable.

There is less consensus about moral values. Instead an increasing variety of subcultures claim that their values are legitimate.

In the world of **leisure** there is an emphasis on immediacy and personal pleasure. People expect to be able to buy the consumer goods of their choice and to have lots of fun. At the same time there are fewer secure jobs and there is rising inequality. In these circumstances increasing numbers of people are likely to experience **marginalization** and relative deprivation.

Informal social controls are becoming less effective as families and communities disintegrate.

Relative deprivation

A major reason for rising crime rates is the problem of relative deprivation (see p. 186). There are a number of reasons why this is significant:

- **Inequality** has increased in recent years.
- **Marketization** places great emphasis on individual material success.
- High levels of **cultural inclusion** (such as access to glamorous TV shows and advertising of designer brands) are combined with social and economic **exclusion**.
- Many people feel they are not properly rewarded for their efforts at work.
- The middle classes feel discontented because of their long working hours and they sense that other groups are now becoming part of the mainstream without necessarily making the sacrifices they have.
- Everybody's feelings of relative deprivation are made worse because of the **proximity** of different social groups. For example, the excluded carry out much routine work for the middle classes such as working in shops and restaurants.

Crime in the exclusive society

Crime becomes more widespread – it is no longer confined to a **deviant minority**.

Crime becomes nastier – there is an increase in hate crime such as racially motivated attacks.

The consensus of what constitutes crime breaks down – for example, the boundaries of acceptable violence are disputed (as in the debate about the smacking of children).

Crime and social policy

Young believes that the Labour government's attempts to reduce crime by forcing truants to go to school and unemployed youth to work, and clamping down on **antisocial behaviour**, (for example through **ASBOs**) will not be a success because these policies are trying to recreate a 'golden age' of community (with stable families and close communities) that does not exist anymore. Young believes that a sense of relative deprivation will only be reduced if rewards in society are seen to be distributed more fairly. This would mean dealing with inherited wealth, discrimination on the grounds of race, sex and so on.

RIGHT REALIST PERSPECTIVE

AQA, OCR, WJEC   Textbook pp. 353-355

Wilson – Thinking About Crime

James Q Wilson (1975) denies that trying to get rid of poverty will lead to reductions in crime. This policy failed in the USA in the 1960s, and many poor people (for example, those who are elderly or sick) do not commit crimes.

Wilson concentrates on **street crime**, which he believes the general public are most concerned about.

He sees crime as the result of **rational calculation**. People will commit crime if the likely benefits exceed the likely costs. In reality the chances of getting caught for a particular crime are quite small. If offenders do not believe they are going to get caught, or if punishments take place long after offences, then even severe punishments will not deter people.

Strong **communities** are an effective way of dealing with crime. People who are disgraced by their involvement in crime will lose their standing in the community. The problem is that crime itself undermines communities.

Wilson & Kelling (1982) believe that it is crucial to try to maintain the character of neighbourhoods and prevent them from deteriorating. The role of the police is to clamp down on the first signs of undesirable behaviour. They should try to keep drunks, prostitutes, drug addicts and vandals off the street so that law-abiding citizens feel safe.

If a single broken window is left unrepaired the area will start to deteriorate, law-abiding citizens will feel safe on the streets and **informal social control** will break down.

The answer is to concentrate on areas that are starting to deteriorate before they get too bad. Some areas are too far gone to save.

Wilson & Herstein – Crime and Human Nature

Wilson & Herstein (1985) argue that some people are born with a **predisposition** towards crime. Their potential for crime is likely to be realized if they are not properly **socialized**. Where close-knit **nuclear families** are absent, effective socialization is unlikely. (This links to **Murray**'s views of the **underclass** and **single parents**, see p. 180.)

Wilson & Herstein still believe that people have free will. Ultimately, they choose whether to commit crime by weighing up the costs and benefits. Unfortunately, it is too easy to live off welfare benefits, and the potential gains from crime are increasing as society becomes more affluent.

For many people the benefits of crime come to outweigh the costs, and the crime rate increases.

Evaluation of right realism

Some aspects of right-realist thinking have been influential. 'Zero tolerance' policing is based on the idea that it is effective to clamp down at the first sign that an area is deteriorating, as is the use of ASBOs. Generally both Labour and Conservative governments in Britain have been keen to increase the number of police, have stricter sentences and build more prisons in order to catch and punish severely more criminals.

The views of Wilson and others have come under serious attack. Matthews (1992) finds little evidence that tolerating broken windows and minor incidents has led to an increase in crime.

Jones (1998) argues that:

- factors such as lack of investment are far more important in determining whether a neighbourhood declines.
- concentrating attention on minor offenders means that more serious offenders are more likely to get away with their crimes.
- if some neighbourhoods are made more orderly then the disorderly and criminals will simply move their activities.
- the biological approach ignores the role of inequality and unemployment in causing crime and neglects white-collar and corporate crimes.
- despite the influence of right realist policies, the crime rate in the USA continued to rise.

MARKET FORCES AND CRIME

AQA, OCR, WJEC   Textbook pp. 355-359

Some sociologists are particularly critical of the increasing importance of market forces in Western capitalist societies and have analysed the impact this has had on crime.

Taylor – The Political Economy of Crime

Taylor (1997) is interested in how changes in the global economy and the ways in which some politicians have responded to these changes have affected crime. He argues that:

- the deregulation of financial markets has provided increased opportunities for crimes such as insider trading, where financiers use privileged knowledge to make illegal profits.
- marketization has increased opportunities for crimes such as insurance fraud and false claims for subsidies from the European Commission.
- unemployment has become a more or less permanent feature of some areas – lack of opportunity and hope leads some to turn to crime.
- Changing patterns of work have created more opportunities and incentives for criminal activity.

Ruggiero *et al* (1998) believe that subcontracting encourages the employment of people who are working illegally, or in conditions and wage levels that fail to conform to national laws.

- success is increasingly associated with expensive consumer goods. At the same time, inequalities have increased rapidly. Taylor sees crimes such as car theft as related to these changes.
- there are few opportunities for young working-class men in cities which are suffering from deindustrialization (such as Los Angeles). At the same time, the culture of entrepreneurship encourages many young blacks, who confront the additional problem of racism, to pursue illegitimate opportunities in the drugs business.
- for less successful, Third World countries, producing the crops from which drugs are derived requires little technology or investment and offers high profits.

Hobbs & Dunningham – 'glocal' crime

Hobbs & Dunningham (1998) studied organized crime in Britain and found that crime had global links.

However, many criminals operated mainly in a local context and they found no evidence of integrated criminal organizations or close-knit subcultures or gangs. Instead they found networks of criminals who worked with each other from time to time. Crime was organized on the basis of a 'glocal' system: there were some global connections but most networks were largely locally based.

For example, criminals mainly involved in locally based crimes (such as robbery, disposing of stolen goods or fixing greyhound races) might also get involved with global criminal activities such as drug smuggling or importing cut-price alcohol from abroad (for example, one criminal described in the study had moved to the Costa del Sol but still kept business and criminal contacts in Britain).

Hobbs & Dunningham's study suggests that the global aspects can be exaggerated, though they are of growing importance, and it also suggests that networks might be more important than subcultures. (See also the discussion of state crime, p. 183, and 'green crime', p. 183, which can have a global dimension).

CULTURAL CRIMINOLOGY

AQA, OCR, WJEC   Textbook pp. 376-380

Most of the theories of crime and deviance discussed above claim or imply that crime is committed for material gain, or because people rationally calculate they will gain from crime in some way. Right realism particularly emphasizes rationality (see above, p. 188) as does administrative criminology (see p. 196).

However, some criminologists argue that most theories of crime neglect the importance of the emotional and irrational aspects of crime and the importance of self-image for explaining crime. Jeff Ferrell (2004) calls these alternative approaches cultural criminology.

Cultural criminology generally rejects positivist research methods, arguing that an understanding of offenders' emotional states is crucial to understanding crime.

Studies in cultural criminology

Matza (1964) is opposed to **deterministic** theories which suggest that some delinquents are trapped by circumstances into offending. His research used **unstructured interviews** with young males. He argues that it is always a choice to offend. He does not believe (as subculture theories claim) that delinquents are committed to the values of a delinquent subculture. Instead he argues that they use **techniques of neutralization** to temporarily suspend their belief in mainstream values and make it possible for them to offend. Nor are delinquent subcultures well structured and integrated; instead, people drift into and out of delinquency. The final decision to commit crimes only happens when delinquents feel pushed around and unable to shape their lives – the '**mood of fatalism**' – and decide to take action to restore the '**mood of humanism**' – a sense that they can shape events around them.

In *Seductions of Crime* **Katz** (1988) argues that emotions of humiliation and rage play an important part in causing crime. Crime is used to resolve an intolerable situation – for example, many murderers kill their victim because they have humiliated them and killing them is the only way to overcome shame. Minor crimes such as shoplifting are often carried out for 'sneaky thrills' rather than for material gain.

Lyng (1990) argues that offenders in general, and young males in particular, put themselves in risky circumstances because they enjoy being on the edge of danger and using their skill to avoid coming to harm. Lyng uses the term '**edgework**' to describe this and uses the theory to explain offences such as joyriding.

Presdee (2004) studied **arson** by asking sixth-formers to write about the meaning of fire for them. Based on accounts of school-leavers 'burning their blazers' he argues that arson can be seen to **symbolically destroy** the power of adults or to mark a **rite of passage** from one status to another. He also observed young people on bonfire night engaging in risky behaviour with fireworks and bonfires. He argues that in highly regulated, rational **late modern** societies people need to transgress established rules to find space away from such an organized society.

Cultural criminology tends not to be based upon systematic evidence, and it tends to explore marginal issues; however, it does show that the emotional aspects of crime are ignored by other approaches.

RACE, ETHNICITY AND CRIME

AQA, OCR, WJEC   **Textbook pp. 359-367**

Croall (1998) argues that the association of criminality with different racial groups dates back to the nineteenth century when the Irish were portrayed as part of the 'dangerous classes'.

Phillips & Bowling (2002) argue that in more recent years the issue returned to public attention because of the question of whether the over-representation of **African Caribbean** people in prison was the result of their being more criminal than other groups or because of **discriminatory** treatment by the criminal justice system.

Phillips & Bowling point out that **British Asians** were usually seen as well regulated because of close-knit communities and families. But by the 1990s they too were beginning to be seen as a problem. In 2001 riots involving Asians in Oldham, Burnley and Bradford led parts of the media began to develop an image of the 'Asian gang'.

In the 1990s the **Macpherson Inquiry** into the racially motivated murder of the African Caribbean teenager Stephen Lawrence, and the failure of the police to bring his killers to justice, raised the issue of **institutional racism** (a failure of the institution to treat minority ethnic groups as well as other groups) within the Metropolitan Police.

The 'myth of black criminality'

Paul Gilroy (1983) argued that black criminality was a myth. British Asians and African Caribbeans originate from former colonies of Britain. Their struggle against British **imperialism** allowed these groups to learn how to resist exploitation. Demonstrations and riots represented resistance to a society that treated them unjustly.

Gilroy claims that a myth of black criminality has been created as a result of the police's **negative stereotypes**. High levels of crime among ethnic minority groups are the result of police prejudice.

Lea & Young – ethnic minority criminality

Lea & Young (1984) attack Gilroy for suggesting that the disproportionate number of black males convicted of crimes is the result of police racism. They argue that:

- most crimes are reported by the public, not uncovered by the police.
- the crime rates for whites are slightly lower than that for Asians. If Gilroy is right, then the police can only be prejudiced against African Caribbeans.
- statistics suggest that **first-generation immigrants** were highly law-abiding. It is hard to see how they could have passed down the tradition of 'anti-colonial struggle' to their children. What is more, many of the victims of the crimes committed by African Caribbeans are from the same ethnic group.

Lea & Young accept that police racism may exaggerate the ethnic minority crime rate, but believe there has been a real increase in the number of crimes committed by ethnic minorities. They believe that this is largely the result of **relative deprivation**, **marginalization** and the formation of **subcultures** (see p. 180).

The debate about the real incidence of crime among ethnic minority groups was based on limited evidence. It was only in 2000, in response to the **Macpherson Inquiry** (1999), that the government first started publishing detailed statistics on ethnicity and crime.

Hall *et al* – Policing the Crisis

The views of **Gilroy** are supported to some extent by **Hall** *et al* (1979) in their explanation of the crime of **mugging** in Britain in the 1970s.

The authors argue that there was a **moral panic** (an exaggerated outburst of public concern over the morality and behaviour of a group in society) about crime, and about mugging in particular – a crime associated with black youth. Hall *et al* found no evidence to indicate that the crime of mugging was new or increasing.

The moral panic over mugging could only be explained in the context of the problems facing capitalism at the start of the 1970s. Economic problems and industrial and social unrest meant that the **hegemony** (ideological domination) of the ruling class was under threat and it had to turn to force to control the crisis. Mugging was presented as a key element in the breakdown of law and order.

The moral panic over mugging helped capitalism in two ways:

- The public was persuaded that society's problems were caused by 'immigrants' rather than the faults of the capitalist system.
- The government was able to justify the use of force to suppress the groups that were challenging them.

The **societal reaction** to the threat of violence led to the **labelling** of large numbers of young blacks as deviants. Labelling helped to produce the figures that appeared to show rising levels of black crime, which in turn justified stronger police measures.

Evaluation

Downes & Rock (1988) identify two weaknesses:

- The study was contradictory, claiming both that black street crime was not rising while at the same time arguing that it was bound to rise as a result of unemployment.
- The study fails to show how moral panic over mugging was caused by a crisis of British capitalism.

Young (1993) argues that the study provides no evidence that the public was panicking about mugging, nor does it show that the public identified the crime with blacks. However, he adds that it would have been quite rational if the public had been concerned about street crime.

Studies of British Asian crime

Bowling & Phillips (2002) review a number of ethnographic studies of crime among British Asians.

Early studies linked a low crime rate among Asians with strong families and communities. For example, **Mawby & Batta** (1980) found that most Asians in Bradford are relatively poor and living in inner city areas. However, the study found they committed few crimes because of the emphasis on family honour, or *izzat*, which encouraged conformism. They were afraid of dishonouring the family name.

More recent research by **Desai** (1999) found that young Asian men were taking a more aggressive stance in combating racist attacks. Some **Bangladeshi** boys were making a self-conscious attempt to counteract the image of themselves as weak and passive.

Alexander (2000) argues that the media image of a growing problem of **Asian gangs** is something of a myth. Although there was some violence in the area of south London covered by her study, it was greatly exaggerated by the media.

Patterns of criminality

Black ethnic groups are **over-represented** in criminal statistics. For example, in 2004-5 they made up only 2.8% of the population but 13.5% of the prison population.

Over the same period **Asian** ethnic groups were slightly over-represented in terms of the prison population (5.4% of those in prison as opposed to 4.7% of the population); 7.4% of those appearing in Crown Court were of Asian ethnic origin. **White** ethnic groups were under-represented, in terms of population ratio, amongst those who were cautioned, arrested or imprisoned.

Racism and the criminal justice system

Stops and searches

In 2004-5 official figures show that black ethnic groups were five times more likely to be stopped and searched than the average for the population as a whole. Asian ethnic groups also had an above average chance of being stopped and searched. However, this may be partly because there are simply more members of ethnic minority groups in the urban areas where most stops are likely to take place.

The **Macpherson Inquiry** (1999) into the Stephen Lawrence case examined a range of evidence and concluded that there was **institutional racism** in the police, which was reflected in statistics such as those on stop and search.

Arrests

Bowling & Phillips (2002) note that in 1999-2000 about four times as many African Caribbean people were arrested as would be expected in terms of their proportion in the general population.

The difference was even greater in terms of imprisonment, with African Caribbeans having an imprisonment rate that is much higher than that of whites (see above).

Prosecuting and sentencing

Hood (1992) found that, when other factors were taken into account, black men were 5% more likely than white men to be given a **custodial sentence**. They were also given sentences which were on average three months longer than those of whites who had committed equivalent offences. The discrepancy was even greater among Asian men.

A **Home Office** study of 16 police areas (2006) found that black offenders were more likely than other offenders to be given a custodial sentence for drugs offences but were less likely than whites to be found guilty of offences in Crown Courts. However, this study did not take any account of the seriousness of offences.

Self-reported crime

Self-report studies have been used to try to discover whether the rate of offending among ethnic minority groups really is higher than among whites. Despite the methodological problems associated with this approach (see p. 213), according to **Phillips & Bowling** (2002) the surveys have produced similar results: that official crime statistics exaggerate the extent of offending among ethnic minority communities.

Race and victimization

There is clear evidence that most ethnic minorities are more likely to be victims of most crimes than whites are.

Clancy et al (2001) argue that much of the difference in **victimization** can be explained in terms of social factors such as higher rates of unemployment among ethnic minorities and the younger **age structure** of those groups.

Data from the **British Crime Survey** indicates that there is increased fear of crime among ethnic minorities. This is compounded by their lack of faith in the ability of the criminal justice system to deal with racially motivated crimes.

Race, ethnicity and crime – conclusion

Bowling & Phillips (2002) argue that black people are more likely to be criminalized. This in turn leads to greater **social exclusion** and therefore to a greater chance of criminalization – a vicious circle.

WOMEN AND CRIME

AQA, OCR, WJEC   Textbook pp. 367-374

In 1976 **Carol Smart** put forward the following reasons to explain the neglect of women in criminology:

- Women tend to commit fewer crimes than men.
- Most crimes committed by women tend to be of a comparatively trivial nature.
- Sociology and criminology tend to be dominated by men.
- Traditional criminology is motivated by a desire to control **problem behaviour**. As women's behaviour is less of a problem than men's it has received less attention.

Official statistics indicate that women in all age groups appear to commit far less crime than men. This pattern has raised three main questions:

1   Do women really commit fewer crimes than men, or are the figures misleading?

2   Is the proportion of crimes that are committed by women increasing, and is this linked to 'women's liberation'?

3   Why do some women break the law?

Statistics on criminality and gender

According to official statistics, in 2005 79% of known offenders were male and 21% female.

Just over half of offences committed by women were thefts but thefts accounted for only a third of men's offences.

Statistics from other countries and from Britain in the past show that women are generally convicted of far fewer crimes than men.

Pollak – the 'masked' female offender

Otto Pollak (1950) argued that official statistics on gender and crime seriously underestimated female criminality. He argued that many crimes predominantly committed by females went unreported and unrecorded. Examples included **shoplifting** and **prostitution**.

He also gives reasons why there should be an under-recording of female crime:

- The criminal justice system tends to be made up of men. Brought up to be chivalrous, they are usually lenient with female offenders.
- More importantly, women are very good at hiding their crimes because they are used to deceiving men in matters such as revealing pain and faking orgasm.

Heidensohn (1985) regards Pollak's work as based on an inaccurate stereotypical image of women. His work has little credibility today.

Leniency towards women – the 'chivalry' thesis

Graham & Bowling (1995) conducted a self-report study of 14-25 year-olds and found that 55% of males but 35% of females admitted an offence in the last twelve months. This suggests that males do commit more offences than men but the difference is not as great as that in official statistics.

The **Youth Lifestyles Survey** (2000) found that, excluding drug offences, 11% of females and 26% of males had committed a fairly serious offence in the last 12 months. One in 11 **self-reported offences** by women had resulted in a caution or prosecution compared to about one in 7 of the offences admitted by males.

Allen (1987) found women were less likely than men to be given custodial sentences for indictable motoring offences.

Evidence against the 'chivalry' thesis

Box (1981) reviewed the data from self-report studies in Britain and the USA and concluded that the official statistics on gender and crime were fairly accurate.

The studies discussed above by Graham & Bowling and the Youth Lifestyle Study both found that males tended to be involved in more serious offences which could explain the higher proportions of men among the convicted and cautioned. Furthermore, it is possible that males are more likely than females to admit offences in self-report studies.

A direct observational study of shoplifting by **Buckle & Farrington** (1984) found that men were twice as likely as women to shoplift even though official figures suggest almost as many women as men are shoplifters.

Double standards in criminal justice

Heidensohn (1985) argues that the justice system is influenced by attitudes to gender in society as a whole. Women are treated more harshly when they deviate from norms of **female sexuality**. Sexually promiscuous girls are more likely to be taken into care than similar boys. On the other hand, courts may be reluctant to imprison mothers with young children.

Carlen (1997) found in a study of Scottish courts that women are more likely to be sentenced according to the court's assessment of them as wives, mothers and daughters rather than the seriousness of their crimes.

Heidensohn and **Carlen** therefore believe that the criminal justice system is **gendered** – it treats men and women differently

The causes of female crime

Physiological causes

Some of the earliest attempts to explain female criminality were based on **biological theories**.

Lombroso (1895) compared the anatomical features of female criminals and non-criminals. He believed that male criminals could be identified by physical abnormalities such as having an extra toe or nipple. Few women had these features; therefore they were not 'born criminals'.

Lombroso's work has long been discredited. However, biological theories have recently reappeared. **Moir & Jessel** (1997) explain some violent crime as being linked to Prementstrual Syndrome (PMS).

Most sociologists, however, focus on **social causes** of female crime.

Women's liberation

Adler (1975) claimed that **women's liberation** had led to a new type of female criminal and an increase in women's contribution to crime. Women were taking on male social roles in both legitimate and illegitimate areas of activity. Instead of confining themselves to 'feminine' crimes such as shoplifting, women were getting involved in robbing banks, mugging and even murder.

Heidensohn (2002) accepts that the proportion of crimes committed by women in Britain has increased from about one seventh of recorded crime in the 1950s to about one sixth in 1999. However, Heidensohn argues that the women who do commit crime are generally poor and are amongst those who have been little affected by women's liberation.

Carlen – women, crime and poverty

Carlen (1988) conducted **unstructured interviews** with 39 convicted female offenders. She argues that working-class women have been controlled through the promise of rewards stemming from the workplace (**the class deal**) and family (**the gender deal**). When these rewards are not seen as worth the sacrifice, then criminality becomes a possibility.

Female conformity

Heidensohn (1985) attempts to explain why women commit fewer crimes than men. She argues that **patriarchal** societies control women more effectively than men, making it more difficult for them to break the law. Control is exerted at home, in public and at work:

- The time that women spend on housework and in caring for children means that they have little time for crime. Daughters are given less freedom than sons to come and go as they please.
- Women often choose not to go out in public places because of fear of becoming a victim of crime or harassment. They also limit their behaviour in public for fear of being labelled a 'slag, slut or bitch'.
- Women are usually controlled by male superiors at work and may be intimidated by various forms of harassment.

MASCULINITIES AND CRIME

AQA, OCR, WJEC   Textbook pp. 380-386

Messerschmidt's masculinities

James W Messerschmidt (1993) analyses why different groups of males turn to different types of crime in their attempts to be masculine.

In order to achieve success white middle-class boys have to be subservient to schoolteachers. Outside the school they try to demonstrate some of the characteristics they repress within school. This may involve pranks, vandalism, minor thefts and excessive drinking. Such young men adopt an **accommodating masculinity**.

White working-class boys have less chance of academic success and tend to construct masculinity around the importance of physical aggression. They try to be tough and oppose the authority of teachers. Theirs is an **oppositional masculinity**.

Lower working-class ethnic minority boys do not expect to be able to hold down a steady job and support a family. They may use violence to express their masculinity, or they may become involved in more serious property crime than white working-class youths. This offers them some prospect of material success.

Evaluation

Jefferson (1997) acknowledges the importance of Messerschmidt's work but points out that he fails to explain why particular individuals commit crimes when others don't. He tends to assume that all men in the same circumstances will be socialized to express their masculinity in the same ways.

Messerschmidt has also been accused of putting forward views that are rather stereotypical and negative towards men.

Simon Winlow – Badfellas

Winlow (2001) conducted an ethnographic study using **participant observation** and **unstructured interviews** of changing masculinities amongst bouncers in Sunderland.

The area had experienced rapid **deindustrialization**, a decline in manual work for men and a growth of the night-time economy and the service sector. It had also been influenced by **globalized culture** (for example, gangster films and hip hop).

With few opportunities in traditional manual work for unskilled men, being a 'hard man' by working as a bouncer was a way for some men to convert **bodily capital** into a source of status and income. Door work spilled over into other criminal activities such as protection rackets and the sale of drugs.

CRIME AND SOCIAL CLASS

AQA, OCR, WJEC

The distribution of crime by social class is covered in sections throughout this chapter.

The work of **Merton** (1968, first published 1938), and **subcultural theories** (p. 180), are largely based upon the idea that crime is a predominantly working-class activity. However, Merton does recognize there is some middle-class crime – as there is 'no upper limit on success'.

Murray (1989) (p. 180) believes crime is particularly common in an underclass made up of **benefit claimants** and the children of **unmarried mothers**.

Official statistics generally support the view that crime is concentrated in the working class.

However, many sociologists believe that criminal statistics are a social construction and do not give a reliable and valid picture. Convicted criminals may be unrepresentative of all criminals.

Studies of white-collar crime, corporate crime, state crime and environmental crime suggests crime is common in all social strata.

Although **labelling theory** (p. 183) does not address class issues directly, **Becker** (1963) does suggest that those from lower income backgrounds may be more likely to be labelled than those from higher income backgrounds. This is supported by the study of the treatment of juvenile offending conducted by **Cicourel** (p. 184).

Marxists (p. 185) emphasize the importance of the crimes committed by the ruling class and argue that there is class bias in the law and in the administration of justice. They acknowledge that crime is present in all classes because of the effects of capitalism which encourages greed, though the crimes of higher classes do most harm.

Left realists (p. 186) accept all classes commit crime but emphasize that street crime should not be ignored. They argue that relative deprivation, marginalization and subcultures might cause high levels of street crime in lower social classes. They also emphasize that the working class are more likely to be the victims of crime.

Although crime is found in all social classes, the type of crime committed tends to vary by social class. Studies by **Hobbs & Dunningham** (1998) (p. 189) and **Winlow** (2001) (p. 193) show how typical working-class crimes are very different to upper- and middle-class crimes.

The sections on *Women and Crime* (p. 192) and *Race, Ethnicity and Crime* (p. 190) show how class interacts with other social divisions such as gender, ethnicity and age to shape the amount and type of offending and the **social distribution** of victims.

AGE AND CRIME

AQA, OCR, WJEC

According to **Newburn** (2007), more than 20% of offenders cautioned or convicted of offences in England and Wales are aged 10-17 and over one third are aged under 21. Amongst middle-aged and older people offending rates decline.

Research by **Graham & Bowling** (1995) for the Home Office found the highest offending rates for property crime (excluding fraud) for males was 14, for violent crime it was 16 and for serious offences it was 17. However, once fraud and forgery were included the peak offending rate for property crime was 22-25. Amongst females the peak offending ages were a little lower, at 15 for serious and property offences and 16 for violent offences.

Studies of youth offending

Cohen (1955) (Textbook pp. 325-326) sees youth crime as the result of the formation of subcultures reflecting **status frustration** amongst working-class boys who do poorly at school (see p. 180).

Matza (1964) (Textbook pp. 377-378) denies there are cohesive subcultures, arguing that young people drift in and out of delinquency but may get involved to restore the **mood of humanism** (see p. 190).

Lyng (1990) (Textbook pp. 378-379) believes youth offending is the result of testing boundaries, or **edgework** (see p. 190).

Presdee (2004) (Textbook p. 379) believes that young people use fire generally, and arson in particular, as a way of symbolically destroying the power of adults and marking **rites of passage** (for example, destroying uniforms when finishing school – see p. 190).

The Birmingham Centre for Contemporary cultural Studies (**CCCS**) (1976) (Textbook pp. 771-782) relates crime and deviance to the existence of youth cultures such as punks, teddy boys, and skinheads. This **neo-Marxist** approach sees youth culture as a creative response to changes in the class structure. For example, **Jefferson** (1976) believed teddy boys were part of a white working-class attempt to recreate **class loyalty** where they felt it was threatened by ethnic minorities, urban redevelopment and growing affluence.

Critics have argued that the CCCS exaggerate the degree to which youth culture was oppositional to society and neglect female participation in subculture – for example, **Reddington** (2003) points out that many punks were female.

Hodkinson (2004) (Textbook pp. 780-782) studied goths, finding that though they are deviant in some ways (such as dress) this youth culture is not **oppositional** to society, but is more concerned with dressing up, socializing with friends and having fun.

Whatever the differences in the explanations of youth crime and deviance, they all tend to assume that the official statistics or self-report studies are correct to see young people as heavily involved in crime and deviance.

Questioning 'youth crime'

There are many problems with accepting police statistics (see p. 181).

Self-report studies may not be valid (see p. 213) and in any case most of the offending that young people admit to is relatively trivial.

Both police statistics and self report studies fail to reveal the extent or the importance of white collar, corporate, environmental and state crimes (Textbook pp. 331-334 and 390-393) which are almost entirely committed by adults.

Pearson (1983) believes there have always been **moral panics** about certain types of crime, and youth crime in particular, which exaggerates the fears. **Cohen** (2002, first published 1972) (Textbook pp. 730-731) showed how an exaggerated moral panic about violence between mods and rockers in the 1960s amplified what deviance there was amongst these youth groups. This suggested that youth deviance could, in part, be a media creation.

Despite the above problem nearly all the available data does suggest that there is more petty crime amongst younger people than older people.

Control theory

Control theory or **social bond theory** offers arguably the best explanation for the apparent decline in offending as people age.

Developed by **Travis Hirschi** (1969), control theory argues that all individuals are likely to commit criminal and deviant acts unless they have a reason not to. What prevents some people from becoming criminals or deviants is the existence of **social bonds**. When bonds to society are weak or broken then crime takes place. In some ways this is similar to **Durkheim**'s (p. 179) idea that **egoism** or **anomie** were responsible for crime.

Hirschi identified four aspects of social bonds:

- **Attachment** – this involves socialization resulting in the development of a conscience which prevents us doing harm to others.
- **Commitment** – is the time and energy we put into certain activities which gives us a stake in society and something to lose if we are found to be criminal.
- **Involvement** – concerns spending time on socially conforming activities which gives us little time to be deviant.
- **Belief** – involves commitment to **cultural goals**.

Generally, these types of bond develop as we get older. For example, getting a job, getting married, having children, buying a house and getting a mortgage are associated with greater attachment, commitment and involvement than we have as children or adolescents. This means that as we age we are less likely to be criminal or deviant. It can also lead to a change in our beliefs, which also increases the likelihood of conforming.

The theory explains both low offending rates among older people and higher rates of crime and deviance among the young.

Criticisms

Control theory can't explain why people engage in particular types of deviant behaviour.

Writers such as **Matza** (1969) deny that delinquents have weak bonds to society.

It cannot explain white-collar and corporate crimes which are committed by people who, by Hirschi's criteria, have strong social bonds.

Nevertheless, it may go some way to explaining why in nearly all societies crime rates are highest in younger age groups.

CRIME AND LOCALITY

AQA, OCR, WJEC   **Textbook pp. 374-376**

Socio-spatial criminology examines where offenders live and where crimes are committed, and sees neighbourhood (**spatial characteristics**) as a factor in crime rates.

Shaw & McKay – urban delinquency

Shaw & MacKay (1942) of Chicago University (often called the **Chicago School**) used a system devised by **EW Burgess** in which the city was seen as divided into five concentric circles radiating from the centre.

The central business district was found in the centre of cities with the next circle consisting of the **zone of transition**. The zone of transition had the highest offending rate.

Shaw & McKay explained this offending as the result of a high rate of population turnover, poverty and poor housing, which combined to create **social disorganization** – a situation where there was no strongly established community and therefore no shared values which could prevent offending.

Shaw & McKay later amended the meaning of social disorganization to mean a distinct set of **non-conformist values** which encouraged offending.

These were passed on from generation through socialization or **cultural transmission**.

Criticisms

Bottoms (2007) argues that Shaw & McKay confused where people lived with where they committed offences – people from outside the zone of transition could have committed the offences there.

Bottoms also points out that the concentric circles model does not fit the town planning and social housing model of most European cities.

Later studies have looked more at where offences take place than where offenders live. **Wilkstrom** (1991) found the highest offending rates near the centre of Stockholm, in poorer areas, and in rich areas adjacent to poor areas.

Opportunity theory

Felson (2002) argues that crime rates are related to opportunity. This depends upon:

- **target attractiveness** – for example, thieves prefer portable and valuable items above large lower value items;
- **accessibility** – how easy the object is to steal and escape without being witnessed.

Routine activity theory

Felson (2002) also develops **routine activity theory**, which argues that more crime takes place where suitable targets and likely offenders are in close proximity – offenders are most likely to commit offences in areas in which they spend time or are close to where they live.

Cohen & Felson (1979) argue that burglaries tend to take place where there is no **capable guardian** (for example, police or neighbours) to see and report an offence. They also argue that the time of day could be important – for example, town centres see more crime at night than during the day because more people are out drinking. Together these factors influence where and when offences take place.

People's routine activities also influence the risk of being victims – for example, those who go out drinking in city centres several times a week have a high risk of being victims of violent crime.

Brantingham & Brantingham – cognitive maps

Brantingham & Brantingham (1991) argue that people have different perceptions of areas of towns and cities depending on where they live, where they work, where they go for leisure, and their routes between these different areas. The map a person carries in their mind of an area is called a **cognitive map**. Offences are most likely to take place when the opportunity arises in an area with which a potential offender is cognitively familiar. A study of Sheffield by **Wiles & Costello** (2000) found that burglars travelled on average only two miles to commit an offence.

Evaluation – administrative criminology

Opportunity theory, routine activity theory and cognitive map theory are together known as **administrative criminology**. These approaches have been used to try to reduce burglary through measures such as better lighting, blocking access to the backs of houses, marking objects with indelible ink etc. Administrative criminology also encouraged flexible licensing laws to reduce violence when pubs or clubs closed at the same time.

These approaches do not explain why people commit offences, merely the circumstances in which they commit them. Furthermore, they assume all offenders are rational – a view challenged by **cultural criminology** (see p. 189).

POSTMODERNISM AND CRIMINOLOGY

AQA, OCR, WJEC   Textbook pp. 386–390

Smart – unique criminality

Smart (1995) argues that traditional approaches to crime all adopt a version of **positivism**:

- They try to find the causes of criminality.
- They try to find ways of eradicating crime.
- They assume that scientific methods are the best way of discovering the truth about crime.
- They believe that it is possible to find an overall theory to explain crime.

Postmodernists reject these traditional approaches to crime. They do not believe that crimes can be linked together and that common factors which cause them can be identified. They regard each criminal act as unique. They do not believe that it is possible to engineer reforms to improve society. Effective ways of dealing with crime must be local and individual.

Collier – masculinities

Collier (1998) (Textbook pp. 382–383) believes that there are stereotypes of masculine behaviour which affect people's understanding of masculinity, but that these are misleading.

In the **postmodern** era masculinity is **multi-faceted** and the individual's identity is also multi-faceted. There is increasing uncertainty about what it means to be a man – for example, homosexual masculinity is increasingly as accepted as heterosexual masculinity.

Therefore, you cannot generalize about how masculinity relates to crime, but need to examine individual cases.

Collier uses the example of Thomas Hamilton, who shot dead fifteen primary school children and their teacher in Dunblane, Scotland, in 1996. Collier explains his behaviour as an attack upon the feminized world of the primary school by a man whose sense of masculinity came from a desire to control boys.

Criticisms

Collier can be criticized for sometimes making generalizations about masculinity despite arguing that such generalizations should not be made.

Evaluation of postmodern approaches

Lea (1998) believes that postmodernism has made a useful contribution to the study of the control of crime. In the postmodern world **informal control mechanisms** can come to dominate at the expense of the state. Private security firms watch over shopping malls, and closed-circuit TV (CCTV) follows our movements around town and city centres. Security firms prevent 'undesirables' from entering some estates. People are treated differently in different areas and seen increasingly as customers and consumers.

However, Lea also believes that postmodernism is **regressive** since it denies the possibility of being able to do anything to change unequal and unjust societies.

THE SOCIOLOGY OF SUICIDE

AQA

Suicide is no longer a criminal act in Britain, but it is still widely regarded as deviant since it contravenes norms relating to the sanctity of human life.

This topic provides a good illustration of different research strategies.

Durkheim – four types of suicide

Durkheim (1970, first published 1897) tried to show that suicide was not just a product of individual psychology and that **positivist** methods could be used to study and explain acts of suicide and suicide rates.

He showed that suicide rates varied fairly consistently. High suicide rates were correlated with:

- Protestants rather than Catholics or Jews.
- married people rather than single people.
- parents rather than the childless.
- political stability and peace rather than political upheaval and war.
- economic booms and slumps.

From the statistical patterns, Durkheim claimed to have identified four types of suicide:

- **Egoistic suicide** was caused by insufficient integration into social groups (for example, Protestants had less connection to their church than Catholics).
- **Anomic suicide** resulted from too little regulation in industrial societies at times when rapid social change disrupted traditional norms (for example, both economic booms and depression led to a rise in suicide rates).
- **Altruistic suicide** resulted from too much integration in non-industrial societies (for example, the practice of **suttee** – Hindu widows throwing themselves on their husbands' funeral pyres).
- **Fatalistic suicide** resulted from too much regulation in non-industrial societies (for example, the suicide of slaves).

Despite his association with positivism, Durkheim used elements of a **realist** approach in looking for **unobservable structures** underlying suicide rates.

Responses to Durkheim

Positivists have generally supported the principles on which his work was based but have modified details.

Halbwachs (1930) argued that Durkheim overestimated the importance of religion. He also found that living in urban areas was an important factor correlated with high suicide rates.

Gibbs & Martin (1964) tried to define integration in a more precise way than Durkheim, by using the concept of **status integration**.

Interpretive theories of suicide

Douglas (1967) points out that suicide statistics are based on coroners' interpretations and negotiations between the parties involved. The relatives/friends of an individual might persuade the coroner not to record a death as suicide.

Douglas believes that there are different types of suicide, based on their **social meanings**. There are different meanings in different societies – for example, in Innuit society elderly Eskimos were expected to kill themselves in times of food shortage.

Baechler (1979) develops Douglas's approach, defining suicides in terms of the types of solution they offer to different types of situation:

- **Escapist** suicides involve fleeing from an intolerable situation.
- **Aggressive** suicides are used to harm others.
- **Oblative** suicides are used to obtain something that is desired (for example, saving another or getting to heaven).
- **Ludic** suicides involve taking risks for excitement or as an ordeal.

Dorais (2004) has used an **interpretative** approach to understanding high rates of suicide amongst young men. He conducted **in-depth interviews** with 32 Canadian men who had attempted suicide.

He found that many of the men had attempted suicide because they were, or were perceived by others to be, gay or bisexual in a society which was still **homophobic**.

As a result many of the men felt isolated from social groups; gay men who did not consider suicide tended to be better integrated into social groups.

Dorais concludes that although **interpretative** methods are needed to understand suicide, his research still finds evidence to support aspects of **Durkheim**'s theory.

Criticisms of interpretive theories

A problem with interpretive theories is that the categories used to classify suicides are simply a matter of the researcher's judgement.

Atkinson – phenomenonology of suicide

Atkinson (1978) develops a **phenomenological** view. He believes that it is impossible for coroners or researchers to objectively classify suicides. The 'facts' are simply a **social construction**.

From studies of coroners' courts he finds that four factors shape the common-sense theories of coroners:

- The presence of a suicide note is taken to indicate suicidal intent.
- Some types of death (for example, hanging) are seen as more likely to be suicide.
- Location and circumstances are important.
- Evidence of depression or particular difficulties tends to encourage suicide verdicts.

In Atkinson's view, when positivists study suicide statistics, all they uncover are the common-sense theories of coroners – for example, a tendency to record the deaths of depressed or lonely people as suicides.

Criticisms

Critics of phenomenology, such as **Hindess** (1973), point out that the logic of this view can be turned against phenomenologists' own theories of how deaths are categorized as suicides – i.e. they are no more than their own interpretations and cannot be supported by objective data.

Taylor – Underground suicides

Taylor (1982, 1989, 1990) tries to move beyond **positivism** and **phenomenology**, using a **realist** approach.

He agrees with phenomenologists that certain factors influence coroners. From a study of deaths on the London Underground he found that evidence of **social failure** or **social disgrace** tended to lead to suicide verdicts.

However, Taylor claimed that evidence from **case studies** revealed underlying patterns of suicide. Suicides could be seen as one of four types, based on a person's certainty or uncertainty about themselves or others:

- **Submissive** suicide involves certainty that your life is over – for example, in response to terminal illness.
- **Thanatation** involves uncertainty about yourself and whether you should live – for example, playing Russian roulette.
- **Sacrifice** involves certainty that others have made your life unbearable – for example, rejection by a lover.
- **Appeal** suicide involves uncertainty about others – for example, suicidal behaviour which may win back a lover if they save you from death.

Evaluation

Taylor explains some variations in suicide – for example, why some suicide attempts are more serious than others – but his theory is hard to test and relies upon the interpretation of sometimes limited secondary data.

DEVELOP YOUR ANALYTICAL AND EVALUATION SKILLS

Essay plans

For each of the following questions write your own essay plan before comparing it with the suggestions given here. For the final question you can write a full answer and compare it with the provided model answer.

Official criminal statistics cannot be trusted. Discuss.

Background

Many early theories of crime were based on the assumption that official criminal statistics were an accurate reflection of the crime rate. However, the reliability of these figures has been questioned as many crimes go unreported and unrecorded. Alternative methods such as victimization and self-report studies have now been developed to reveal more of the 'dark figure' of crime.

Statistics cannot be trusted	Statistics give a good indication of patterns of crime
• Crime and official statistics (p. 181) • Labelling theory (p. 183)	• Left realism: the problem of crime (p. 186) • Merton and subculture theory (p. 179)

Top Tip

The sections on *Race, ethnicity and crime* and *Women and crime* include debates about the accuracy of official crime figures. Although it is right to question the reliability of official figures, perhaps they should not be dismissed altogether. There are some crimes – for example murder, burglary and car theft – where they are likely to be quite accurate.

Is the criminal justice system more lenient towards women than men?

Background

Official statistics reveal that the crime rates of women are far lower than those of men. Some sociologists believe that one reason for this difference is the 'chivalry' factor. This means that agents of social control (usually men) treat women more leniently than men.

For	Against
• Pollak (p. 192) • Allen (p. 192)	• Box (p. 192) • Farrington (p. 192) • Carlen (p. 192) • Heidensohn (p. 192)

For and against
• Graham & Bowling (p. 192)   • Youth Lifestyles Survey (p. 192)

Top Tip

It is necessary to distinguish between different parts of the criminal justice process in dealing with this issue, such as police arrest rates and court sentencing. It is not possible to identify clearly one of these two positions as representing a feminist view, as feminist writers take a range of positions in this debate.

Durkheim showed that suicide can be explained using positivist methodology. Discuss.

  Background

This topic links to methodology because Durkheim used suicide as an example to illustrate the usefulness of positivism. Durkheim, however, only tried to explain suicide rates rather than the causes of individual suicides. Interpretative approaches (for example: Baechler, Dorais and Douglas) believe you cannot do this without looking at the meanings of suicide, whereas positivists don't believe it is scientific to study unobservable meanings. Atkinson, using a phenomenological approach, questions the idea that there is any validity in suicide statistics as coroners' verdicts are simply opinions. However, Taylor suggests that qualitative data can be used to produce case studies which allow a scientific understanding of suicide.

For	Against
• Durkheim (p. 196)	• Douglas (p. 197)
• Gibbs & Martin (p. 197)	• Dorais (p. 197)
• Halbwachs (p. 197)	• Baechler (p. 197)
	• Atkinson (p. 197)
	• Taylor (p. 197)

 Top Tip

You can discuss whether Atkinson is right to regard suicide statistics as completely invalid. In some cases there is very strong evidence that a person intended to kill themselves; and statistics in one country might give a reasonable indication of trends over time. Furthermore, some qualitative studies have supported some of Durkheim's views – for example, that lack of integration into society can be a cause of suicide.

Crime is a growing problem in modern Britain. Discuss.

This is a widely held view in the media and is supported by some theories. Both left realism and right realism (though right realism is concerned with America) see crime as a growing problem since both believe that there has been real increase in street crime. They give different reasons for this, with left realists blaming it on growing inequality leading to marginalization and relative deprivation, and right realists blaming over-generous welfare and inadequate policing and punishment. Ian Taylor sees globalization, marketization and inequality as a cause of rising crime. Similarly, Marxists see corporate, state and white-collar crime as growing problems. However, all the critics believe that official figures cannot be trusted. The study of mugging by Hall *et al* demonstrates that media-led moral panics can exaggerate crime. Labelling theory implies there may just be more labelling of acts as criminal rather than a real increase.

For	Against
• Left realism (p. 186)	• Criticisms of statistics (p. 181)
• Right realism (p. 188)	• Hall *et al* (p. 190)
• Taylor (p. 186)	• Labelling theory (p. 183)
• Official statistics (p. 181)	
• Marxism (state, white-collar and corporate crime) (p. 185)	

Top Tip

Both official statistics and the British Crime Survey suggest that crime has been falling since the late 1990s.

Conflict theories provide the best explanations of crime and deviance. Discuss.

Background

Conflict theories consist of all theories which believe that society is divided into different groups that have different interests. These include Marxist and other socialist-influenced theories that emphasize class divisions, feminist theories that emphasize gender divisions, and theories which stress the existence of ethnic divisions and racism. On the other hand, functionalists believe there is a consensus in society, and sociologists such as Merton and Cohen agree there is a basic consensus (although it does come under strain at times). Cultural criminology provides an alternative perspective of crime, focusing on the emotional and irrational aspects of criminal behaviour.

For	Against
● Marxism (p. 185)	● Durkheim (p. 179)
● Neo-Marxist and radical perspectives (p. 185)	● Merton (p. 179)
● Left-realism (p. 186)	● Cohen (p. 180)
● Taylor (p. 186)	● Right realism (p. 188)
● Paul Gilroy (p. 190)	
● Hall *et al* (p. 190)	

Top Tip

Many conflict theories assume there is one dominant type of conflict, but it can be argued that class gender and ethnicity (as well as perhaps age and sexuality) are all important social divisions which can be linked to crime in society.

Some theories explain crime and deviance in terms of the background of offenders while others concentrate on the societal reaction to crime and deviance. Explain and evaluate these two approaches.

Background

Define some basic terms first and explain the question. Theories which emphasize the background of the offender examine the causes of criminal behaviour and tend to assume that offenders are a relatively small and distinct minority. On the other hand, labelling theory argues that most people are offenders, but only a few are labelled as deviants or criminals. Therefore, they believe societal reaction is more important than actual offending. Some recent perspectives (such as left realism) combine the two approaches.

For	Against
● Merton (p. 179)	● Evidence from self-report studies (p. 181)
● Subculture theories (p. 180)	● Labelling theory (p. 183)
● Shaw & McKay (p. 195)	
● Charles Murray (p. 180)	
● Desai (p. 191)	

Top Tip

Theories which look both at the background of the offender and the societal reaction to crime and deviance include Taylor, Walton & Young (p. 186) and left realism (p. 186).

Some theories explain crime and deviance in terms of the background of offenders while others concentrate on the societal reaction to crime and deviance. Explain and evaluate these two approaches.

Crime is behaviour which contravenes the formal, written laws of a society. Most early theories of crime adopted an essentially positivist approach to explaining these types of behaviour. They assumed that criminals and deviants were a relatively small minority of the population who were different to the conforming majority. The key to understanding crime was to identify how deviants/criminals were different and explain why that difference caused their behaviour. For example, many early theories of crime (such as Robert Merton's) assumed that crime was predominantly a male and working-class activity, and then proceeded to explain why these groups were more involved in criminality.

This approach, which concentrated on the background of offenders, was challenged in the 1960s by criminologists who began to question the reliability and validity of criminal statistics, and by labelling theory. When the first victim studies and self-report studies were carried out, it became apparent that there were many more offenders and offences than were recorded in official statistics. This led to the development of new approaches, such as labelling theory, which saw crime and deviance as a social construction rather than as a social fact. More recently, approaches such as left realism have examined both the background of offenders and the societal reaction to crime.

An example of the first approach is Robert Merton's influential functionalist theory. This argued that crime and deviance were caused by a structural imbalance in society, with too much emphasis on the cultural goals and not enough emphasis on the institutional means – a situation he called anomie. As a result, the working class – whose opportunities were blocked, preventing them from achieving the 'American dream' and with it the goals of money and power – were likely to innovate and try to achieve these goals through crime for material gain.

The subculture theory of Albert Cohen developed Merton's theory. This argued that Merton ignored the collective nature of some criminality and the existence of non-utilitarian crime such as vandalism and joyriding. Cohen attributed delinquent behaviour to status frustration amongst boys who failed to achieve success and status in the education system; this frustration was resolved through the creation of a deviant subculture in which the values of society were reversed.

A more recent approach which concentrates on the background of the offender is Charles Murray's theory; this attributes offending to the generosity of welfare payments which have created an underclass of unmarried mothers, their children and the long-term unemployed.

A major problem with all the above approaches is that they concentrate almost entirely on male, working-class crime, paying little or no attention to other social factors correlated with crime, such as ethnicity and age. Other sociological theories of crime and deviance have looked at factors other than class (for example, Desai looked at the incidence of crime amongst Bangladeshis). A further problem with the theories discussed above is that, with the exception of Merton, they show little awareness of the existence of white-collar, corporate, state and 'green crimes', which research suggests are widespread, but are unlikely to be committed by working-class men.

The issue of crimes committed by middle- and higher-class individuals highlights the problem with taking statistics on the social distribution of criminality and the background of offenders at face value. Research by Graham & Bowling found little difference in the class background of those who admitted offences; self-report studies have shown that the majority of the population sometimes break the law. Furthermore, there are unlikely to be many people who never commit a deviant act.

In the 1960s a theoretical approach developed which took account of the research revealing that crime and deviance were widespread in all social groups. The labelling theorist Becker argued that deviance was not a quality of the act committed, but a quality given to an act by a social audience. Deviance was socially constructed and deviants only appeared to come from a similar background to one another because they fitted stereotypes of deviants held by police and others in the criminal justice system.

A major problem with labelling theory is that it generally does not explain why some individuals are more likely to commit serious deviant acts (such as murder) than others. Although most people commit some offences and are sometimes deviant, very few commit the most serious offences. It seems unlikely, therefore, that it is possible to fully understand crime and deviance simply by examining the social reaction to crime or deviance: there must also be some consideration of the offender and his or her background.

Recent theories of crime and deviance have acknowledged that both the background of the offender and the social reaction are important. For example, the left realist approach of Lea & Young developed the 'square of crime', which looks at informal and formal social control (the social reaction to crime and deviance) as well as at the offender. To left realists, offending is constituted through the interaction between these elements; the perspective of victims must also be part of the equation. Left realists see relative deprivation, marginalization and the formation of subcultures as important in explaining offending; but they also see interaction between offenders, victims and the police, and informal social control, as crucial to understanding the societal reaction which determines how an act is dealt with and what its consequences are. For example, domestic violence has increasingly been seen as criminal and victims or neighbours have been more willing to report the offence and the police more willing to take reports seriously.

Labelling theory contributed a great deal to the development of theories of crime but did tend to neglect the offender with its their emphasis on societal reaction. It can be concluded that a complete theory of crime and deviance can only be developed by looking both at the background of the offender and the societal reaction, not forgetting the victim and the social structure of the society in which crime and deviance occur.

RESOURCES

Research methods in the study of crime and deviance

Author: Matza (1964) **Research:** Victim survey of unreported crime and other issues in England and Wales (Textbook pp. 377-378)
Research methods: Unstructured interviews with delinquents
Strengths: Able to get subjective views of delinquents. Could ask about motivation and get in-depth qualitative data
Weaknesses/problems: Possibility of lying. Interviewees may have changed their interpretation of their own behaviour over time (interviewed after conviction). Lack of reliability

Author: British Crime Survey (annual) **Research:** Delinquency and the lack of subcultures (Textbook pp. 329-30)
Research methods: Social survey using interviewers with a sample of 47,000, questionnaire interviews with one adult in each household
Strengths: Large sample. High reliability. Replicated annually to show trends. Uncovers unreported crime and can be used with police statistics to give a more accurate picture of overall crime
Weaknesses/problems: Doesn't cover crimes without obvious victims, crimes against under-16s, or crimes against those without private addresses. Non-response (usually around 25%) may make generalizations dangerous. People may lie, forget offences or not remember if offence was in last 12 months. Interpretation needed to decide if some events were crimes

Author: Graham & Bowling (1995) **Research:** Study of youth offending (Textbook p. 366)
Research methods: Self-reported crime questionnaire administered to around 2,500 people in England and Wales aged 14-25
Strengths: Useful for estimating offending rates in different social groups and evaluating whether the criminal justice system treats groups equally. Large sample, quantitative methods, possible to generalize and replicate
Weaknesses/problems: Respondents may lie; problem of non-response. Box estimates about 20% lie in self-report studies. Males may exaggerate compared to girls. Individual has to interpret whether an incidence was an offence. Questionnaire can't include every possible offence and is therefore selective

Author: Home Office Police Crime Statistics (annual) **Research:** Government data on extent of offending (Textbook pp. 228-234)
Research methods: Compiled from reports by police stations
Strengths: Comprehensive coverage of crimes recorded by police. Reliable data on what has been recorded, no sampling involved. Based upon official judgements about whether incidents are offences
Weaknesses/problems: Major problem of the 'dark figure' of unreported and unrecorded crime. Police have considerable discretion. May be class, gender or ethnic bias in administration of justice. Some types of offence dealt with by other agencies (e.g. tax fraud) who may be less likely to record offences. Marxists see statistics as ideologically biased

Author: Jock Young (1971) **Research:** Amplification of deviance amongst hippies in Notting Hill (Textbook pp. 335-336)
Research methods: Participant observation
Strengths: In-depth picture of a community and the subjective meanings they attached to drug use. High in validity. Real behaviour observed not reported behaviour (as in questionnaires and interviews)
Weaknesses/problems: Relied on observer's interpretations. Can't be replicated so lack of reliability. Problem of researcher 'going native'. Small sample, can't be generalized. Ethical problems of studying illegal behaviour and maintaining confidentiality

Author: Becker (1963) **Research:** Study of becoming a marijuana smoker (Textbook p. 336)
Research methods: In-depth interviews with 50 users of the drug
Strengths: Interviews allow study of past behaviour and meanings and motives attached to it. In-depth qualitative data, high in validity
Weaknesses/problems: Interviewees might lie, or reinterpret past events. Relatively small sample. Data requires subjective interpretation. Ethical problem of confidentiality

Research methods in the study of crime and deviance, (*continued*)

Author: Winlow (2001) **Research:** Bouncers in Sunderland (Textbook pp. 283-286)
Research methods: Participant observation and interviewing plus secondary sources
Strengths: High in validity. Ease of access because of familiarity with area. Extra reliability from triangulation. Secondary sources allow discussion of social changes. Actual behaviour observed for ecological validity
Weaknesses/problems: Possibility of Hawthorne effect (the experiment itself affecting the results) and/or going native. Ethical issues of witnessing illegal behaviour and difficulty of getting informed consent. Personal danger to researcher from violence. Practical issues of recording data and gaining acceptance. Time consuming. Small sample so generalization not possible

Author: Presdee (2004) **Research:** Study of feelings about fire and arson (Textbook p. 379)
Research methods: Observation of bonfire night; sixth-formers asked to write about attitudes to fire
Strengths: Allows exploration of subjective states. Some cross-checking of findings from triangulation
Weaknesses/problems: Small sample. Writing may not have been truthful. Had to interpret scenes witnessed on bonfire night with little check on the validity of the interpretations

Author: Steve Taylor (1982) **Research:** Realist study of suicide (Textbook p. 802)
Research methods: Use of qualitative secondary sources such as biographies, autobiographies and suicide notes and statement of people who had attempted suicide
Strengths: Allows interpretation of the meanings behind suicide which statistics alone (as used by Durkheim) do not
Weaknesses/problems: Problems of the authenticity, representativeness, meaning and credibility of sources. Relied heavily on Taylor's own interpretation

Writers and their work

Writer	Perspective or approach	Concepts	Study
Durkheim	Functionalism/ positivism	Anomie/egoism/ fatalism/altruism	Suicide
Merton	Functionalism	Anomie	Crime rates in USA
Cohen	Subculture theory	Status frustration	Delinquent boys
Cloward & Ohlin	Subculture theory	Illegitimate opportunity structures	Crime in USA
Becker	Labelling theory	Deviant career	Marijuana smoking
Cicourel	Phenomenology	Stereotypes	Juvenile justice in California
Snider	Marxism	Corporate crime	Crime of companies
Lea & Young	Left realism	Square of Crime	Victim studies
Charles Murray	Right realism	Underclass	Study of unemployed and unmarried mothers
Ian Taylor	Radical/socialist criminology	Globalization, marketization	Study of crime and contemporary capitalism
Matza	Cultural criminology	Techniques of neutralization	Subcultures of delinquency
Lyng	Cultural criminology	Edgework	Study of youth crime
Shaw & McKay	Socio-spatial criminology	Zone of transition	Crime in Chicago
Heidensohn	Feminism/control theory	Patriarchy	Gender and crime
Hall *et al*	Neo-Marxism	Moral panic	Mugging and race
Collier	Postmodernism	Multi-faceted masculinity	Study of Thomas Hamilton
Brantingham & Brantingham	Administrative criminology	Cognitive maps	Study of the location of criminality

Chapter 11 | METHODOLOGY

SPECIFICATION COVERAGE

Specification	Details
AQA AS Unit 2 SCLY2: Education, Health and Sociological Methods A2 Unit 4 SCYL4: Crime and Deviance, Stratification and Differentiation, Theory and Methods	The chapter covers the specifications for AS and A2 level. A2 Methodology starts with the section on *Critical Social Science* (p. 215)
OCR AS Unit G671: Exploring Socialisation, Culture and Identity; A2 Unit G674: Exploring Social Inequality and Difference	Note that the following topics do not need to be studied until A2 for OCR: sampling techniques, longitudinal studies, case studies, pilot studies. Otherwise the content is the same as AQA
WJEC AS Unit SY2: Understanding Culture; A2 SY4: Understanding Social Divisions	The split between AS and A2 is similar to AQA (A2 starts with the section on *Critical Social Science*, p. 215); theoretical issues underlying methods (particularly positivism and interpretivism) do not need to be studied until A2

INTRODUCTION

AQA, OCR, WJEC   Textbook pp. 787-788

Methodology is concerned both with research methods and with the philosophies underlying them. It tries to establish accepted ways of getting the best possible data about the social world. Broadly, some sociologists support using **scientific methods** and **quantitative data** (numerical, statistical data), while others see such methods as inappropriate in the study of human society and prefer **qualitative data** (non-numerical data – words, for example).

QUANTITATIVE METHODOLOGY

AQA, OCR, WJEC   Textbook pp. 788-793

Positivism

Positivism is an early influential approach, advocated by **Auguste Comte** (1986, first published 1840s) and **Emile Durkheim** (1938), which suggests that sociology can be **scientific**.

Positivism argues the following:

- There are **objective social facts** about the social world. These facts can be expressed in **statistics**.

- These facts are not influenced by the researcher's personal opinion (their **subjective viewpoint**) or their beliefs about right and wrong (**values**) and are therefore **value-free**.

- Researchers can look for **correlations** (patterns in which two or more things tend to occur together).

- Correlations may represent **causal relationships** (one thing causing another).

- **Multivariate analysis** (analysing the importance of many different possible causes) can help researchers find what the true causes of things are.

- It is possible to discover **laws of human behaviour** – causes of behaviour which are true for all humans everywhere and throughout history.

- Human behaviour is shaped by **external stimuli** (things that happen to us) rather than **internal stimuli** (what goes on in the human mind).

- To be scientific one should only study what one can **observe**. It is **unscientific** to study people's emotions, meanings or motives, which are internal to the **unobservable mind**.

Experiments

Many sciences make use of **experiments.** In experiments, theories can be tested in precise conditions (often in a **laboratory**) controlled by the researcher. The researcher develops a **hypothesis** – a prediction of what will be found – which is then tested.

Experiments involve trying to **isolate** the effects of **independent variables** (possible causes) on a **dependent variable** (the thing to be explained). A **control** (in which everything is held constant) and an experiment (in which one independent variable is changed) are compared, allowing scientists to find precise causes. Experiments can be **replicated** (reproduced exactly) to test the reliability of findings.

Sociologists rarely use **laboratory experiments** because:

- laboratories are **unnatural settings** and people may not behave normally.

- it is impractical to conduct laboratory experiments on large numbers of people or over long periods.

Field experiments

Field experiments take place outside the laboratory in 'natural' settings.

Examples of field experiments include: **Rosenthal & Jacobson** (1968) on labelling in education (p. 54); **Brown & Gay** (1985) on racial discrimination by employers (p. 17).

Field experiments avoid unnatural laboratory situations, but it is difficult to **control variables**, and if those being studied are aware of the experiment, this may alter their behaviour (the '**Hawthorne effect**'). If subjects are unaware that they are being studied, this raises **ethical issues** (see p. 208).

The comparative method

This involves using the same logic as the experiment, but using events that have already taken place rather than creating artificial situations. Social groups, times or places are **systematically** compared to try to **isolate variables**. When it is impractical or unethical to use experiments, the comparative method is used instead.

The comparative method has been very widely used. Examples include **Durkheim** on suicide (see p. 196), **Weber** on the Protestant ethic (p. 71) and **Marx** on social change (p. 5).

It is more difficult to isolate variables than in controlled experiments, but the comparative method is based upon real social events and is the only systematic way to study long-term or wide-scale social change. It is central to sociology.

QUALITATIVE METHODOLOGY

AQA, OCR WJEC   Textbook pp. 793-795

Qualitative data usually takes the form of words. Compared to statistics, qualitative data tends to be richer and to have more depth.

The interpretive approach

Interpretivists usually advocate the use of qualitative data to interpret **social action**, with an emphasis on the **meanings** and **motives** of actors.

Interpretivists often see sociology as different from the natural sciences in that it requires the understanding of **meaningful behaviour** by humans.

This often requires imagining the situation from another person's viewpoint, which involves the development of **empathy**.

According to interpretivists, people do not simply react to external stimuli but interpret the **meaning of stimuli** before reacting. An understanding is therefore required of people's **unobservable subjective states**, which cannot be reduced to statistical data.

Weber – social action

Max Weber (1948) sees sociology as the study of **social action** (or meaningful behaviour).

This requires *verstehen* (understanding), to explain why people behave in particular ways. For example, in *The Protestant Ethic and the Spirit of Capitalism* (1958) Weber tries to understand why Calvinists reinvested their money and became early capitalists (see p. 71).

Symbolic interactionism

Symbolic interactionists see individuals as possessing a **self-concept**, or image of themselves. This is largely shaped through other people's **reactions** to them.

Herbert Blumer (1962) argues that sociologists need to understand the viewpoint of the people whose behaviour they are trying to understand. They cannot do this simply by using statistical data.

Interactionists prefer methods such as **in-depth interviews** and **participant observation**.

Labelling theory is the best-known version of interactionism (see p. 183).

Phenomenology

Phenomenologists go further than other interpretivist approaches, rejecting the idea that causal explanations are possible.

To them the social world has to be **classified** before it can be measured. Classifications (for example, whether an act is suicide, or whether somebody is a criminal) depend upon the judgements of individuals. These judgements reflect the common sense and stereotypes of individuals rather than some objective system.

Since there is no way of choosing between classification systems, no hard facts can be produced, so causal explanations are not possible.

Phenomenologists try to understand the classifications people use to give order and meaning to the social world. See, for example, **Cicourel's** (1976) study of juvenile justice (p. 184).

(For a useful example of how the above approaches can be applied, see section on the sociology of suicide, p. 196.)

Feminism

Most feminists support interpretivists methods (see Textbook pp. 808-809). They tend to reject 'masculine' scientific approaches which lack **empathy** for those being studied.

For example, **Ann Oakley** (1981) supports **feminist interviewing**, in which the researcher gets to know the respondent and collaborates with them rather than just exploiting them for information. This often involves the development of **rapport** – a relationship in which the researcher and interviewee can understand and relate to one another. This may increase the **validity** of the findings, although **positivists** believe it can prevent the researcher being **objective**.

THE RESEARCH PROCESS

AQA, OCR, WJEC   Textbook pp. 814-815

To begin research, sociologists have to select an area to study. This is influenced by multiple factors, including:

- the **values** and **beliefs** of the researcher (**Paul Heelas**, for example, sees the New Age as a significant phenomenon, see p. 75);
- developments in the **subject** – issues such as globalization, and theories such as postmodernism have been in fashion in recent times while other issues such as class inequality and theories such as Marxism and feminism have rather fallen out of fashion; researchers may tend to favour subjects which offer career advantages.
- developments in the **social world** (for example, the emergence of fundamentalist religion).
- **government policies** – researchers tend to investigate the effects of new initiatives (for example, research into marketization in education or changes in the NHS).
- **research funding** – funding organizations act as gatekeepers deciding which research is worth funding and which is not (see below).
- **practicalities** such as time, money and access.

Funding

Much research funding in sociology comes from the **ESRC** (Economic and Social Research Council), which derives its funds from government.

It tends to favour research which is relevant to government policies or concerned with social problems which are government priorities. **Tim May** (2001) argues that government is hostile to research which is critical of its policies.

Business funding tends to favour research which can increase the profitability of business.

Some independent or charitable sources of funds (for example, the Joseph Rowntree Foundation) may fund research which is more critical of the government.

Ethical issues

Israel & Hay (2006) describe ethical behaviour as behaviour which 'helps protect individuals, communities and environments, and offers the potential to increase the sum of good in the world'. Israel & Hay identify the following ethical principles which should influence the choice of methods:

- **Informed consent** – the aims and methods of the study are explained to participants, who then agree to take part. This avoids deceit, but poses problems for experiments which use covert methods – for example, **covert participant observation**. Many codes require **parental consent** for research involving children. Without informed consent there is a danger that research can be an invasion of privacy – prying into areas of people's lives which they prefer to keep private.

- **Confidentiality** – this can pose a problem in some studies: for example, if authorities demand information from researchers or if it is difficult to disguise the identity of respondents. Confidentiality can be particularly important when dealing with sensitive issues such as sexuality or health.

- **Avoiding doing harm and doing good** – this is the ultimate aim of ethical codes. It can involve minimizing risks of harm to participants (**non-maleficence**) or actively promoting their well-being (**beneficence**). For example, studies of domestic violence might consider how they can minimize psychological trauma or help victims escape from violence.

The above ethical principles can be contested – for example, some researchers justify covert research in some circumstances, such as in investigating wrongdoing.

PRIMARY SOURCES

AQA, OCR, WJEC   Textbook pp. 815-838

Primary sources are data collected by sociologists themselves. **Secondary sources** are pre-existing sources of data.

Choosing a primary research method

Like choosing a topic, the choice of method may be influenced by factors such as funding (it is usually easier to get funding for quantitative studies).

The nature of the topic may make particular methods more appropriate, and the approach of the researcher (for example, **positivist** or **interpretivist**) will influence the choice. Also important are questions of:

- **reliability** – whether another researcher using the same procedure would obtain the same results. Quantitative methods are sometimes seen as more reliable.
- **validity** – whether the data produce a true reflection of social reality. Some see **qualitative data** as offering a more valid picture of social reality.

According to **Bryman** (2001), there are four types of validity:

1 **Measurement validity** (or **construct validity**) concerns whether something really measures what it claims (for example, whether IQ tests measure intelligence).

2 **Internal validity** concerns whether a causal relationship is real or not.

3 **External validity** concerns whether results can be generalized.

4 **Ecological validity** concerns whether social science theories hold true in everyday settings.

Research methods are also determined by practical considerations – particularly issues of time, money, sample size and access.

Sampling

A **sample** is a part of a larger **population**, often chosen as a **cross-section** of the larger group – so that the sample is **representative**.

Sampling is used in order to **generalize** about the larger population (to make statements about a group bigger than the one actually studied).

The **population** is the total group the researcher is interested in.

The **sampling unit** is the individual thing or person in that population.

The **sampling frame** is a list of all those in the population (for example, the electoral register is a sampling frame of those eligible to vote). There is no comprehensive sampling frame of everyone in Britain, but the **Postcode Address File** is often used (by the British Crime Survey, for example).

There are a variety of ways of producing a sample.

Random sampling

In this approach every sampling unit has an equal chance of being chosen. It relies upon **statistical probability** to ensure a representative sample, so a large sample is needed to give a high chance of representativeness.

Stratified random sampling

To ensure representativeness, the population is divided into groups according to important **variables** such as class, gender and ethnicity, and the sample is then chosen in the same proportions as their preponderance in the population. This method ensures a good cross-section and requires a smaller sample than random sampling, but it is only possible with a **sampling frame**

containing all the relevant information about members of the **population**.

Quota sampling

In this method **quotas** are established which determine how many people with particular characteristics are studied. Once a quota is filled no more people in that category are studied. It is useful if the proportions of different types of people in a population are known and if there is no suitable sampling frame. It is often used in **opinion polls** and is generally quicker and cheaper than random sampling.

However, the results may be distorted if, for example, the researcher questions people in one particular place at a particular time, since the sample will not then be representative. Also, people may be unwilling to reveal personal details that would allow them to be placed into a quota category, and there may be practical difficulties in finding members of particular quota groups.

Multi-stage sampling

This involves getting a sample of a sample – for example, a sample of voters in a sample of constituencies. It can save time and money but it makes a sample less genuinely representative.

Snowballing

In snowballing, a member of a sample puts the researcher in touch with other potential members of the sample. It is useful for studying groups who cannot be easily located, but the networks connecting them make it less than representative.

Non-representative sampling

This occurs when members of a sample are picked because or despite them being untypical, or to study specific characteristics. It is used:

- to **falsify** a general theory by looking for exceptions to a rule (see, for example, Oakley on gender roles, p. 33).
- to find the **key informants** who can provide most information about an area of social life.
- in a **convenience sample** (where you use the easiest people to contact) to save time and money.

Case studies

Case studies involve the study of a single example of something. They can be used:

- to develop a comprehensive understanding of something by studying it in depth (for example, Willis's study of a group of 'lads', p. 48).
- to develop a general theoretical approach by **falsifying** a theory (for example, **Gough**'s study of the Nayar, falsifying **Murdoch**'s theory that the family is universal, p. 26).
- to develop a **typology** (for example, **Douglas**'s typology of the social meanings of suicide, see p. 197).
- to generate **hypotheses**.

A problem with case studies is that you cannot generalize from them. **Bryman** (1988) suggests that this can be overcome through **multiple case studies** – for example, **Edwards & Scullion** (1982) compared industrial relations in several British factories. However, it can be difficult to compare the findings of case studies carried out by different researchers.

Life histories

A life history is a case study of one person's life. An example is **Thomas & Znaniecki's** (1919) study of Jenny, an ageing woman.

Plummer (1982) suggests that they are useful for helping to understand the world from an individual's point of view. They provide rich detail and can help to generate **hypotheses**.

Some **feminists**, such as **Mies** (1993), think that life histories can be used to help women understand their own situation and perhaps change their lives – for example, life histories discussing domestic violence may help a woman decide to leave a violent partner.

Postmodernists sometimes use case studies to explore the increased **fluidity** and **variation** in peoples' experiences – for example, **Stacey's** (1996) study of family life, see p. 29.

Pilot studies

Pilot studies are small-scale preliminary studies carried out before a bigger study to improve, help to design, or test the feasibility of proposed research.

They can be used:

- to test how useful and unambiguous interview questions are (for example, **Young & Willmott**, p. 27).
- to develop ways to gain the cooperation of respondents.
- to develop research skills.
- to decide whether or not to proceed with research.

Social surveys

Social surveys are **large-scale** studies which collect **standardized data** about large groups, often using questionnaires. There are three main types:

- **Factual surveys** collect descriptive information – for example, **Gordon** *et al* (2000) on poverty.
- **Attitude surveys** examine subjective opinions – for example, opinion polls.
- **Explanatory surveys** test theories or produce hypotheses – for example, the study of class by **Marshall** *et al* (1988).

Questionnaires

Questionnaires consist of written questions.

When administered by an interviewer, a questionnaire becomes a **structured interview**. This allows clarification of questions but introduces the possibility of **interviewer bias**.

Postal questionnaires avoid interviewer bias but have low response rates.

Telephone questionnaires tend to result in unrepresentative samples.

Questionnaires involve **operationalizing concepts**, turning concepts – such as educational achievement, religiosity and intelligence – into questions.

A problem with **operationalization** is that the researcher imposes their own meaning on a concept – they choose what questions to ask – and this may not correspond with the respondents' meaning. For example, they might see intelligence as something different to the qualities measured in intelligence tests.

Questions may be **open-ended** or **fixed-choice**:

- **Open-ended** questions may give more valid data, as respondents can say what is important to them and express it in their own words. However, the data is difficult to **quantify**, and **interpretation** is required when using the data. **Coding** of the answers (putting them into categories) distorts the actual replies given by respondents by linking responses that are not identical.
- **Fixed-choice** questions are easy to classify and quantify, but respondents are limited to using the concepts and categories predetermined by researchers. The answers may be **reliable** but lack some **validity**.

Questionnaire data is often analysed using **multivariate analysis** and **statistical techniques**.

Advantages of questionnaires:

- Large amounts of data can be collected quickly.
- There is little personal involvement by researchers.
- Access to subjects is easy.
- It is easy to **quantify** the results, find **correlations** and use **multivariate analysis** to look for causes.
- **Positivists** see differences in answers as reflecting real differences since everyone responds to the same **stimuli**.
- **Comparative analysis** and **replication** (repeating the questionnaire) are easy, making the results reliable.
- A large, geographically dispersed sample can be used, increasing the **representativeness** of the data and the ability to **generalize**.
- For **positivists**, the **statistical patterns** revealed can be used to develop new theories; and questionnaires can be devised to test existing theories.
- Non-positivists see questionnaires as useful for collecting straightforward **descriptive data**.

Disadvantages of questionnaires:

- Different answers may not reflect real differences between respondents since they may interpret questions differently.
- In designing questionnaires, researchers assume they know what is important, and therefore it is difficult to develop **novel hypotheses**.
- The **operationalization of concepts** distorts the social world by shaping concepts in line with researchers' rather than respondents' meanings.
- The **validity** of the data may be undermined by deliberate lying, faulty memories or respondents not fully understanding their own motivations. People may not act in line with questionnaire answers. For example, **La Pierre** (1934) found that US hoteliers were racist when replying to questionnaires but not when faced with real situations.

- Researchers are distant from their subjects, making it difficult to understand the social world from their viewpoint (*verstehen*) or develop **rapport**. **Interaction** cannot be understood through questionnaires. For **feminist** researchers, questionnaires preclude the possibility of subjects evaluating the research.

- The **coding** of open-ended data distorts the distinct answers given by individuals.

Most sociologists accept that surveys are useful for collecting factual or descriptive data, but there is more controversy over their use in explanatory studies.

Interpretive sociologists question the use of questionnaires, while **phenomenologists** reject them altogether.

Interviews

Structured interviews are questionnaires administered by a researcher.

Unstructured interviews do not have preset questions and are more like a conversation.

Many interviews are **partly structured**, with some preset questions, or the researcher has a list of topics to cover. Some interviews allow prompts where interviewers can clarify questions or stimulate responses.

Most interviews are **non-directive** – they try to avoid influencing the interviewee, in order to increase the objectivity of the research. **Becker** (1970) suggests, however, that more **aggressive** interviewing is useful for some topics – for example, hidden racist feelings may be revealed through confrontation.

Some **feminists** believe that interviewees should be **collaborators** in the research.

Group interviews are sometimes used to put respondents at ease or to make respondents more reflective and more likely to open up as a result of interaction between interviewees.

Focus groups are a type of group interview often used by political parties. According to **Bryman** (2001), they emphasize the 'joint construction of meaning'. Focus groups can lead to greater probing of why people do things and they allow the researcher to observe how people construct meaning in groups. They are therefore favoured by **interactionists**. They are sometimes regarded as more **naturalistic** (closer to the real social world) than one-to-one interviews. However, the answers given may be influenced by the most prominent members of the group and they are not effective for collecting **systematic data**.

Advantages of interviews:

- **Quantitative researchers** prefer interviews to **participant observation** because: larger **samples** can be used; **statistical data** can be produced with the **coding** of questions; the research can be **replicated** to increase **reliability**.

- **Qualitative researchers** prefer interviews to questionnaires because: **concepts** can be clarified; there is more opportunity for respondents to express ideas in their own way, say what is important to them and explore issues in depth.

- Interviewing is a practical and flexible method of research. Interviews can examine past, present or future behaviour, subjective states, opinions, attitudes or simple factual information. They can be as in-depth or as superficial as the researcher wants.

- Interviews are useful for studying groups who might not return questionnaires or consent to participant observation – for example, **Laurie Taylor**'s (1984) study of professional criminals.

- For **feminists**, interviews have theoretical advantages since they provide space for **critical reflection** and **interaction** between interviewer and interviewee.

A variety of sociologists use interviews. They may not be ideal for **positivists** or **interpretivists**, but are useful to both.

Disadvantages of interviews:

- As with questionnaires, the **validity** of interview data may be affected by respondents being untruthful, having faulty memories or not fully understanding their own behaviour. People may have **reinterpreted** past events in the light of later experience – for example, **Matza**'s (1964) delinquents disapproved of delinquent behaviour.

- The presence of the researcher may influence answers (**interviewer bias**). **Labov** (1973) found that the race of the interviewer affected young black children in speech tests. Interviewers might consciously or unconsciously lead respondents towards preferred answers.

- **Social factors** such as ethnicity may influence the sort of answers members of different social groups are willing to give.

Evaluation

Despite their imperfections, the practicality and flexibility of interviews make them attractive to researchers using different theoretical perspectives, and they are widely used. **Hammersley & Gomm** (2004) believe that interview data should be handled carefully but that interviewing remains useful when combined with other methods.

Observation

Observation is used by a variety of sociologists. **Positivists** see observation as essential. **Interpretive** sociologists tend to particularly support **participant observation**, in which the researcher becomes part of the social life being studied.

Ethnography is the study of a way of life and often uses participant observation.

Participant observation

Overt participant observers are open about doing research. This method is adopted because:

- it is regarded as **unethical** to mislead subjects.

- it allows the observer to ask questions.

- the observer can retain some **detachment**.

However, the observer may influence the subjects' behaviour if they know they are being observed.

In **covert participant observation**, the researcher does not reveal that they are doing research. This method is adopted because:

- respondents may act more **naturally**.
- some groups would not allow an overt observer, thus it allows **access**.
- the observer becomes fully engaged with the group and can develop an **insider's perspective**.

However:

- some regard it as **unethical** to lie.
- it may be difficult to opt out of illegal/immoral activities.
- the observer may 'go native' and lose objectivity.

Recording data from participant observation can be a problem, as the use of cameras/tape recorders may not be possible. Researchers usually write up **field notes** when they can, but they may forget things or be highly selective about what they do record.

Advantages of participant observation:

- Researchers are less likely than in other methods to impose their own **concepts**, **structures** and **preconceptions** on the data.
- They may gain answers to questions which they hadn't anticipated – see, for example, **Whyte** (1955).
- It is difficult for respondents to lie or mislead.
- For these reasons many see participant observation as having a high degree of **validity**.
- **Symbolic interactionists** support participant observation because it allows an understanding of the subjective viewpoints of individuals and the processes of **interaction** in which people's meanings, motives and **self-concepts** constantly change. It therefore avoids a static picture of social life.
- The researcher understands subjects better because they experience some of the same things.
- It provides in-depth studies which can be useful both for developing new theories and for falsifying existing ones.

Limitations and disadvantages of participant observation:

- It can be time-consuming and expensive for the researcher.
- The researcher is limited to studying a small number of people in a single place.
- It will be impossible to join some groups to carry out observation.
- Researchers' lives may be disrupted; they may need to do illegal/immoral/unethical things or they may face dangers.
- **Samples** may be too small for generalizations.
- Studies cannot be **replicated**, so the results may be unreliable, and comparisons difficult.
- The **interpretations** are rather **subjective** as the researcher has to be very selective about what is reported.

- The presence of the researcher will change group behaviour and affect the **validity** of the data.
- The researcher may become too involved with the group ('go native') and therefore lose their objectivity.

For **positivists**, participant observation is an unsystematic, subjective and unscientific method.

Evaluation

Participant observation is the only research method that gets very close to real social life, but it is rather subjective. It is strong on **validity** but weak on **reliability**.

Longitudinal research

Longitudinal research (**panel** studies) follows a group of people over an extended period, using periodic data collection.

Examples include **JWB Douglas**'s (1964) study of home life and education; the *Child Health and Education Survey* and the *British Household Panel Survey* used by **Berthoud & Gershunny** (2000) in their study of family life.

Longitudinal studies are usually large-scale quantitative studies, but participant observation can also be longitudinal.

Advantages of longitudinal research:

- People don't have to report on events retrospectively so problems of faulty memory or reinterpretation of events are reduced.
- It can be used to examine a large number of variables.

Disadvantages of longitudinal research:

- The size of the participating sample may drop over time, affecting the reliability of findings.
- Whatever method is used (for example, questionnaires or structured interviews) will have its own specific limitations.
- Taking part in the study might affect subjects' behaviour.

SECONDARY SOURCES

AQA, OCR, WJEC   Textbook pp. 838-845

Secondary sources are data that have already been produced – by, for example, the government, companies, or individuals (personal documents).

Existing sociological studies become secondary sources when used by other sociologists.

Secondary sources can be quantitative (for example, government statistics) or qualitative (for example, letters and diaries). They can be **historical** or **contemporary**.

Secondary sources are used for practical reasons. They save time and money and may include data that is beyond the scope of sociologists to collect (for example, census data). There are fewer problems of **access** than with primary data. Secondary data that is already public generally does not have **ethical problems**. Secondary sources allow the study of past societies, for which it is impossible to produce primary sources.

Official statistics

Government statistics cover a wide range of topics including **demography** (census statistics); crime; employment and unemployment; industrial relations; educational achievement; family life (for example, divorce statistics); household composition data and so on. The government conducts **statistical surveys** such as the *General Household Survey* and the *British Crime Survey*, and since 1801 has carried out a **census** every decade.

Such sources are invaluable because they are easily accessible and much more thorough than any data sociologists could produce. The census is the only survey that tries to include the whole of the population, and participation is legally **compulsory**.

Some **positivists**, such as **Durkheim** (1970), have seen official statistics as both **valid** and **reliable** (see Durkheim's study of suicide, p. 196). However, many official statistics are highly unreliable – for example, many crimes are not reported, or not recorded by the police (see p. 181).

Some sociologists believe that it is possible to produce valid and reliable statistics by doing research. For example, they believe that reliable crime statistics can be produced using surveys. Survey methods include:

- **self-report studies** – questionnaires asking people if they have committed crimes; for example, **West & Farrington**'s (1973) study of delinquency.

- **victim studies** – asking people if they have been the victims of crime; for example, the government's *British Crime Survey*.

However, such studies may not be entirely reliable, due to factors such as **non-response** and the limitations of sampling.

Some argue that the results are invalid. **Box** (1981) argues that in self-report studies people may lie, hide or exaggerate crimes or simply forget them. The total number of crimes recorded in studies depends on the willingness and ability of respondents to be honest, and the interpretation of the researcher as to whether a crime has taken place. The researcher also chooses what offences to include.

Phenomenological view of statistics

Phenomenologists regard all crime statistics as invalid. They are simply the product of the **categorization** procedures used to produce them. For example, **Atkinson** (1978) sees suicide statistics as the product of coroners' assumptions about the sort of people who commit suicide. For **Cicourel** (1976), all statistics are based on subjective classifications.

Conflict theorists' views

Conflict theorists see statistics as the product of **inequalities in power**. For **Miles & Irvine** (1979), government statistics are not lies, but collection procedures and definitions are manipulated by governments. Examples include frequent redefinitions of unemployment which reduce official unemployment figures, and the manipulation of data on NHS hospital waiting lists by removing people who have missed appointments for an operation. Poverty statistics rely on government definitions.

Some conflict theorists question the categories used in statistics. For example, the Marxist **Theo Nichols** (1996) argues that official definitions of social class ignore the existence of wealth inequalities. From this point of view, statistics reflect ideological frameworks which in turn reflect power inequalities rather than individuals' assumptions.

Historical sources

These are vital for studying long-term social changes.

Laslett (1972, 1977) used parish records and **Anderson** (1971) used census data to show that industrialization led to an increase in extended family households in Britain (see p. 27).

Parliamentary investigations, diaries, letters, autobiographies, speeches and mass media reports are all useful sources.

Statistical sources suffer, however, from the same possible problems of reliability and validity as contemporary statistics. Qualitative sources reflect the subjective views of those who produced them. Sometimes this is nevertheless useful – for example, when studying the effects of religious beliefs on the development of capitalism.

Life documents

These are documents created by individuals which record subjective states. They include diaries, letters, photos, biographies, memoirs, suicide notes, films, pictures etc.

Thomas & Znaniecki (1919) used letters and statements to study Polish peasants who emigrated to the USA.

Plummer (1982) argues that personal documents are rarely used by contemporary sociologists because:

- surviving documents may not be representative.

- they are open to differing interpretations.

- they are highly subjective – the same events discussed in a document such as a diary might be described very differently by someone else involved.

- the content may be influenced by the identity of the person or the intended readers of the document.

Plummer believes, however, that life documents are still very useful because they allow insights into people's subjective states.

Symbolic interactionists see them as revealing the personal meanings and self-concepts which they see as shaping behaviour.

The mass media and content analysis

The mass media may be unreliable for providing factual information, but may themselves be the objects of study. Some researchers see such studies as useful for revealing the **ideological frameworks** of those who produce the mass media. This is important because of the influence of the media.

Pawson (1995) describes different ways of analysing the content of the mass media:

- **Formal content analysis** involves classifying and counting content. For example, **Lobban** (1974) and later **Best** (1993) counted the appearances of girls and boys in different gender roles in children's books. This technique is reliable but it involves inferring the meaning of words within a text from numbers alone.

- **Thematic analysis** examines a topic and looks for the messages that lie behind the coverage. For example, **Soothill & Walby** (1991) found that newspaper coverage of rape emphasized the pathological nature of individual rapists and largely ignored rapes by partners and friends. Studies using thematic analysis rarely use representative samples and don't examine the impact of the messages on the audience.

- **Textual analysis** involves the detailed analysis of small pieces of text. For example, the **Glasgow Media Group** (p. 166) looked at the words used to describe managers and strikers. Textual analysis relies heavily on the researcher's interpretation and may therefore be unreliable.

- **Audience analysis** examines how the audience interprets the messages of the media – for example, **Morley's** (1980) study of responses to *Nationwide* (p. 168). The honesty and openness of respondents may be questionable, and studies cannot reveal long-term effects of media messages.

Assessing secondary sources

John Scott (1990a, 1990b) argues that the following criteria can be used to assess secondary source material:

- **Authenticity** – determined by its **soundness** (whether the document is complete and reliable) and its **authorship** (whether it was written by the claimed author).

- **Credibility** – determined by its **sincerity** (whether the author intended to provide a true account or was trying to mislead the reader) and its **accuracy** (whether the author is able to be truthful – for example, whether faulty memory might affect accuracy).

- **Representativeness** – whether the material is typical or representative of what is being studied. **Survival**, or lack of it, may mean that representative documents do not exist; **availability**, or lack of it, may mean that researchers cannot gain access to representative samples even where they have survived.

- **Meaning – literal understanding** involves being able to read, decipher or translate the content; **interpretative understanding** involves interpreting what the document signifies – there may be very different possible interpretations.

Stein (2002) identifies particular problems in using the internet as a secondary source. Unlike published sources there are no editorial or review processes, which are designed to ensure the reliability and validity of the data. Consequently, data needs to be used with caution, particularly in relation to the identity, credibility and authority of the author(s).

TRIANGULATION

AQA, OCR, WJEC   Textbook pp. 845-847

Bryman (1988) argues that most sociologists use a mixture of quantitative and qualitative sources. Sociologists as far back as Weber have combined methods.

Examples include:

- **Eileen Barker's** (1984) study of the Unification Church (the 'Moonies') which used observation, questionnaires and interviews;

- the use of statistical (quantitative) computer programmes to analyse data from ethnography (based on qualitative research);

- **Winlow's** (2001) study of bouncers in Sunderland which used participant observation, interviews and secondary sources.

Hammersley (1996, in **Bryman**, 2001) distinguishes three ways of combining methods:

- **triangulation** – in which findings are cross-checked using a variety of methods;

- **facilitation** – in which one method is used to assist or develop the use of another method;

- **complementarity** – in which different methods are combined to dovetail different aspects of an investigation.

Bryman (2001) describes how **multi-strategy** research is used in different ways and for different purposes:

- **triangulation** to check the reliability of data produced using different methods;

- **qualitative** research facilitating **quantitative** research – for example, by designing questionnaire questions;

- **quantitative** research facilitating **qualitative** research – for example, by helping to identify people for a sample.

Multi-strategy research:

- fills in the gaps where the main research method cannot produce all the necessary data.

- uses some methods to study **static** features of social life and others to study **processual** features – i.e. changes.

- uses different methods to obtain different perspectives from research subjects.

- uses different methods to help to generalize.

- uses qualitative research to understand the relationship between variables revealed in the quantitative research.

- studies different aspects of a phenomenon.

- solves a puzzle by using a different method to that initially used.

Bryman sees multi-strategy research as very useful in that the limitations and disadvantages of each individual research method can be partially overcome.

CRITICAL SOCIAL SCIENCE

AQA, OCR, WJEC   Textbook pp. 804-808

The following sections cover the requirements for A2 Methodology for AQA, OCR and WJEC. See Specification Coverage at the beginning of the chapter for more details.

Critical social science develops methods of study which are critical of society and have the aim of improving it. They therefore reject the view that sociology can be value-free and should not be used to try to change the social world.

Harvey (1990) sees a crucial aspect of critical social science as **deconstruction** – taking apart an aspect of the social world to understand how it really works.

This is followed by **reconceptualization** so that the social world can be thought of in a different way.

This in turn leads on to **praxis** – practical activity designed to improve the social world.

Critical social science methods involve **reflexivity**: the researcher reflects upon the social world and tries to understand it. These reflections then create changes in the social world they are observing. For example, studies of domestic violence identified it as a form of male oppression; this led, in turn, to domestic violence being taken more seriously as a crime. Reflexivity means that methods reflect back on the social world and may change it.

FEMINIST METHODOLOGY

AQA, OCR, WJEC   Textbook pp. 808-811

Feminist methodology is one form of critical social science.

Feminists such as **Abbott & Wallace** (1997) criticize 'malestream research' (male-dominated mainstream research) for:

- researching only men and using male-only samples.
- ignoring women's issues, such as housework.
- neglecting sex and gender as variables.

However, there is increasing attention to women and gender in sociology, and research is becoming less dominated by the 'malestream'.

Feminist research methods

Oakley (1981) argues that in a **masculine** approach to interviewing:

- there is an emphasis on objectivity and detachment.
- interviewees are manipulated as sources of data and have an entirely **passive** role.
- the emphasis is on **reliability**.

Oakley believes that in a **feminist** approach to interviewing:

- the interviewer should be willing to answer questions and provide helpful information to respondents.
- the research should be **collaborative** – researchers should always gain consent and even help out those being interviewed.

- interviewees can help improve the validity of the results by becoming increasingly reflective about their own lives and by checking on whether the findings reflect their own experiences.

Oakley (1981) uses this approach in her study of childbirth.

Evaluation of Oakley

Pawson (1992) criticizes Oakley for simply adopting the techniques of unstructured interviewing. However, Oakley's approach has novel features, such as advising and helping the interviewees (which other theorists see as unduly influencing those being studied).

Feminist standpoint epistemology

Feminist standpoint epistemology argues that women have a unique insight into the social world by virtue of being an oppressed group.

Some **standpoint feminists**, such as **Stanley & Wise** (1990), believe that researchers should examine a plurality of women's viewpoints (for example, women of different ethnic groups).

Critics such as **Pawson** (1992) suggest that:

- some feminist researchers will not accept the viewpoints of women they disagree with (such as those who don't think they are oppressed).
- standpoint epistemology neglects the **oppressors** (usually men) and therefore makes it difficult to understand how oppression comes about.
- it can be **relativistic** – i.e. accepting a variety of women's viewpoints as valid without any way of distinguishing between more and less useful ones.

POSTMODERN METHODOLOGY

AQA, OCR, WJEC   Textbook pp. 811-815

Epistemological postmodernists reject the idea that any research procedure can produce a single 'true' description of the world.

Lyotard (1984) sees all knowledge as **story-telling**, with no way of distinguishing between true and untrue stories.

Postmodern **ethnography** involves the collection of different people's stories. **Tyler** (1986) sees postmodern ethnography as designed to stimulate the **imagination**, like a work of literature. He believes that ethnography should simply be used to record the viewpoints of the many different groups in society. The researcher has no special ability to interpret the accounts of subjects.

Some postmodernists are simply concerned to reveal the **contradictions** in other sociological theories, using the technique of **deconstruction**.

Evaluation

Many critics regard postmodernism as too **relativistic** (knowledge simply depends on your point of view). They point out that postmodern 'stories' about the social world cannot be shown to be better than any other stories. Ethnography becomes similar to fiction, with no special claim to describe a real world.

Alvesson (2002) believes that postmodern methodology can be used to refine traditional methodology rather than to reject it altogether. For example, he believes that you cannot take data from interviews at face value and as the 'truth'. People's stated beliefs can be challenged to see if they really hold them. This can form the basis of **reflexive pragmatism** – the researcher produces the best data they can without seeing it as absolutely true.

SOCIOLOGY AND SCIENCE

AQA, OCR, WJEC   **Textbook pages 847-851**

Positivism

Positivists see sociology as a science based on the use of objective observation, statistics, a search for correlations, causal relationships and laws. They use an **inductive** approach in which the researcher starts with evidence and induces theories from the evidence.

Popper – falsification and deduction

Popper (1959) argues that you cannot ever be sure that you have found the truth. What is considered true today may be disproved tomorrow.

A scientific theory is one that can be tested. From the theory one can deduce **hypotheses** and make precise **predictions** (a **deductive** approach). If repeatedly tested and found to be correct, a theory may be provisionally accepted, but there is always the possibility that it will be proved wrong (**falsified**) in the future.

Scientific theories are ones that make **precise predictions**. Popper regards some sociology (such as Marxism) as unscientific because the predictions are not precise enough.

Popper uses a deductive approach: this means deducing hypotheses from a theory then checking that they are correct. (This is unlike **positivism**, which is **inductive** – it induces theories from the data collected).

Both Popper and positivists see a scientific methodology as desirable. Positivists see science as producing objective truth, while Popper sees science as getting as close as possible to the truth, since it is always possible that a theory will be falsified in the future.

Phenomenology

Phenomenologists reject the idea of a scientific sociology because:

- the social world cannot be objectively classified and measured; classification reflects the subjective categories and interpretations of individuals.

- sociologists can only study the way classifications are made; they cannot discover some underlying objective truth.

Social context of science

Some sociologists argue that science does not follow any single methodology. It takes place in a **context** and often does not involve an objective search for truth.

Kaplan (1964) distinguishes:

- **reconstructed logics** – the methods scientists claim to use;

- **logics in use** – the actual methods they use.

Lynch (1983) illustrates this by showing how scientists studying rats' brains ignored slides that contradicted their theories, dismissing them as **artefacts** (mistakes produced during the laboratory procedures). Scientists look for evidence to confirm theories, ignoring evidence that might falsify them.

Gomm (1982) argues that Darwin's theory of evolution was accepted because the social context of Victorian Britain, with its laissez-faire capitalism, welcomed the ideas of natural selection and survival of the fittest. Opposition to revolution encouraged acceptance of evolutionary theory, and evolutionary thinking allowed Victorian Britons to see themselves as superior to the people in conquered colonies. Lack of fossil evidence of evolution was ignored because of the social context.

Kuhn – scientific paradigms

Kuhn (1962) argues that **scientific communities** develop a commitment to a particular **paradigm**, a set of shared beliefs about some aspect of the physical world: how it works, how to study it and how to interpret evidence. A paradigm provides the complete framework within which scientists operate. Ideas from outside the paradigm are normally dismissed.

During a **scientific revolution**, however, **anomalies** which the paradigm cannot explain come to the fore. One paradigm is rejected and replaced by another, and science returns to its normal state, in which the paradigm is not open to question. An example is the move from Newtonian to Einsteinian physics.

From this point of view, sociology can be seen as **pre-scientific** because there are a variety of paradigms (or perspectives), such as feminism, Marxism, postmodernism etc.

It may not be desirable for sociology to become scientific, in Kuhn's sense, because the conflict between perspectives is a critical element of sociology.

Anderson et al (1986) criticize Kuhn for underestimating the extent of disagreement between scientists, and question whether his approach has much relevance to sociology.

Realist view of science

Realists such as **Bhaskar** (1979) and **Sayer** (1984) believe that it is both possible and desirable for sociology to be scientific. They see physical and social sciences as similar.

Sayer argues that some sciences have **closed systems** in which all variables can be measured. However, many sciences are open, in that all variables cannot be measured nor precise predictions made (for example, seismology and meteorology). Sayer therefore rejects Popper's view that a scientific theory must make precise predictions.

Sayer believes that sociology is scientific but societies are **complex open systems**, making it impossible to make precise predictions.

Keat & Urry (1982) argue that some sciences deal with things that cannot be directly observed – for example, subatomic particles, continental drift and magnetic fields. They therefore reject the positivist view that science confines itself to studying the observable. They argue that sociology can still be seen as scientific even if it studies **unobservable meanings** and motives.

Realists believe that scientists try to discover the underlying structures and processes that cause observable events (for example, evolution). Sociologists try to do exactly the same, looking for social structures (for example, in Marxism: the economic base, superstructure and social classes) and **processes** (for example, capital accumulation). Realists therefore argue that much sociology is scientific.

METHODOLOGY AND VALUES

AQA, OCR, WJEC   Textbook pp. 851-853

There are different views on whether sociology is, or can be, objective or value-free:

- **Bierstedt** (1963) defines objectivity in terms of investigators not being influenced by their own beliefs.
- **Comte, Durkheim** and **Marx** all thought they were objective and scientific.
- **Weber** argued that the selection of a topic for research was bound to be influenced by values, but that the research itself could be value-free.

However, many sociologists who considered their work value-free have been accused of being value-laden:

- **Functionalists** have been seen as having a conservative bias in stressing the usefulness of institutions.
- **Durkheim**'s values are revealed in his opposition to inherited wealth.
- **Marx** was committed to revolutionary politics.
- **Weber**'s values influenced his view that bureaucracy could stifle human freedom.

Can values be eradicated from sociology?

As Weber suggested, values are bound to influence what topics sociologists think are important enough to study.

Sociologists' values may also influence which aspects of a topic they study. **Gouldner** (1971) argues that all sociologists make **domain assumptions** – for example, about whether humans are rational or irrational, whether society is essentially stable or unstable, etc.

All research is selective – for example, what questions are included in a questionnaire or what aspects of a social setting an observer takes note of – and values may influence the selection process.

All research involves some degree of interpretation which may be influenced by values. For example,

interpretive sociologists see questionnaires as distorting the real nature of the social world in line with the researcher's assumptions and values. **Positivists** see **participant observation** research as based on the subjective and value-laden perceptions of interpretive researchers.

Phillips (1973) concludes that values influence the choice of topic and the methods and sources of data used in research.

Gouldner (1975) argues that **fact** and **value** cannot be separated in sociology, just as the bull and human in a mythological minotaur cannot be separated. He argues that sociologists should bring their values into the open so that others are aware of any possible bias.

For many **postmodernists**, knowledge is simply the reflection of the values of the social groups that create the knowledge.

Other sociologists, however, argue that sociology is not simply an expression of people's values. **Carspecken** (1996) argues that there is a real, objective social world, and this makes it possible to reject some claims about the truth which do not fit reality. Thus, while values will always influence sociology, research can show that some theories are more supported by evidence than others.

This view is also supported by the **realist theory of science**.

DEVELOP YOUR ANALYTICAL AND EVALUATION SKILLS

Essay plans

For each of the following questions write your own essay plan before comparing it with the suggestions given here. For the final question you can write a full answer and compare it with the provided model answer.

Secondary sources tend to be unreliable and invalid and are therefore of little use to sociologists. Discuss.

Background

Reliability and validity need to be defined to answer this question, and what is meant by secondary sources also needs to be explained. Different sociologists tend to see different types of secondary data as reliable and valid. For example, positivists tend to favour official statistics, though Marxists and interpretivists see them as invalid. Interpretivists see life documents as largely valid but positivists do not. All secondary sources have problems attached to them and there might be particular biases built in, but the same is true of primary sources. Secondary sources are the only option for historical sociology and when sociologists can't afford to collect their own data, so they are certainly of some use to sociologists.

For	Against
• Positivist perspectives (p. 216)	• Positivist views on statistics (p. 213)
• Interpretivist, phenomenological and conflict views on statistics (p. 213)	• Interpretivist views on life documents (p. 213)

Top Tip

John Scott's work (p. 214) is useful for showing the caution needed with the use of secondary sources, but also for suggesting that they can be very useful when used with care.

Experimental methods are of little use to sociologists. Discuss.

Background

You will need to explain what experimental methods are, using terms such as dependent and independent variables, control groups, replication and hypotheses. Remember to distinguish between laboratory and field experiments. Include some examples of each.

For	Against
• Sociologists rarely use experiments (p. 207)	• Positivism (p. 216)
• Interpretivist objections to scientific sociology (p. 207)	• Examples of field experiments (p. 207)

Top Tip

You can explain how the comparative method acts as an alternative to experiment for many sociologists (p. 207).

The advantages of participant observation outweigh the disadvantages. Discuss.

Background

In answering this you need to consider the practical, ethical and theoretical advantages and disadvantages of the method. Theoretical issues are the most complex and it is essential to discuss reliability and validity. Participant observation is usually seen as very unreliable because it relies so heavily on the interpretations of the individual researcher, and studies are impossible to replicate. On the other hand, its supporters see it as highly valid as being close to real social life. Critics question the validity though, pointing to the possibility of influencing the group or 'going native'.

For	Against
● Practical advantages (p. 211)	● Practical problems (p. 212)
● Closeness to real social life (p. 211)	● Ethical issues (p. 212)
● Interpretivists, interactionists (p. 212)	● Theoretical issues (p. 212)
	● Positivists (p. 212)

 Top Tip

Be sure to mention different types of participant observation (e.g. covert and overt) and to illustrate your answer with examples.

All research methods have their uses, especially when combined together. Discuss.

 Background

This is a view originally put forward by Weber, but which rather fell out of favour when positivists, phenomenologists, and interpretivists argued either for quantitative or qualitative methods. The advocates of both quantitative and qualitative approaches exaggerated their case, and in practice most sociologists do use a full range of methods. All research methods have particular advantages (as well as disadvantages), and sociologists such as Bryman believe that triangulation and other forms of methodological pluralism are the way forward.

For	Against
● Triangulation (p. 214)	● Positivism (p. 216)
● Weber (p. 207)	● Phenomenology (p. 208)
	● Interpretivist sociology (p. 207)

 Top Tip

Bryman believes that most sociologists use a mixture of methods (p. 209).

Essay plans for A2 questions

Sociology is a scientific subject. Discuss.

 Background

Positivists support this view, at least when sociology uses statistical data and quantitative methods. However, interpretivists and phenomenologists do not think the subject matter of sociology can be studied using a scientific approach because humans are unpredictable and act on unobservable meanings and motives. From Thomas Kuhn's viewpoint, sociology is not scientific because a single paradigm is not accepted by all. Popper thinks much sociology is not objective and scientific, although it is possible for it to become so if it sticks to precise predictions. Critical realists would agree with the essay title because they do not believe that precise prediction is necessary to be scientific.

For	Against
● Positivism (p. 216)	● Phenomenology (p. 208)
● Realism (p. 216)	● Kuhn (p. 216)

For and against
● Popper (p. 216)

 Top Tip

The answer to this question hinges on how you define a scientific subject. Kaplan and Lynch (p. 216) show that the theory of science may be different to the reality.

It is both desirable and possible for sociology to be objective. Discuss.

Background

This view was originally supported by positivists, but was attacked by phenomenologists and interpretivists. Most of the classical sociologists (e.g. Marx, Durkheim, Comte) thought that their approaches to sociology were objective. Popper thinks much sociology could be objective and scientific – if it sticks to precise predictions. However, many sociologists who believe that sociology can be value-free have been attacked for putting forward value-laden theories. Gouldner, and many others, do not believe sociology can be value-free. Critical realists do not believe it is desirable to be value-free, although they do believe systematic and scientific knowledge can be produced by sociology.

For	Against
• Positivism (p. 216)	• Phenomenology (p. 208)
• Marx (p. 217)	• Interpretivist sociology (p. 207)
• Popper (p. 216)	• Popper (p. 216)
• Durkheim, Comte (p. 217)	• Gouldner (p. 217)
• Postmodernism (p. 215)	

For and against

• Critical realists (p. 216)

Top Tip

Weber (p. 207) is useful for arguing you cannot be value-free in selecting topics for research, but that value-freedom is possible and desirable in the research itself. Carspecken (p. 217) is useful for a conclusion.

Model answer

It is both desirable and possible for sociology to be objective. Discuss.

Robert Bierstedt sees objective, or value-free, sociology as sociology where, 'the conclusions arrived at ... are independent of the race, colour, creed, occupation, nationality, religion, moral preference, and political predisposition of the investigator'. From this point of view, value-free research is based entirely on the data found during investigation and is not affected by what the researcher wanted to discover or expected to find, or their existing ethical or theoretical assumptions. This viewpoint suggests that sociology can be scientific if the researcher puts their own views to one side, uses scientific – or at least systematic – methods, and is open to results which might contradict what they expected or wanted to find.

Both Comte and Durkheim believed that sociology could be and should be value-free. Value-freedom could be achieved by using positivist methods in which only observable social facts were studied. The researcher could look for correlations and causal relations, and even discover laws of human behaviour, by using statistical methods. Karl Marx also believed that his approach was scientific and value-free, although many sociologists believe it was very strongly influenced by his communist political ideology.

The idea that sociology can be and should be value-free is supported by the philosopher Karl Popper. However, Popper denied that Marxism was either scientific or objective. He believed that a truly scientific subject uses a deductive approach, making precise predictions on the basis of theories. Popper believed that Marx's predictions were too imprecise to qualify as scientific. For example, Marx predicted a proletarian revolution but failed to say when it would happen. Without a timescale specified, Marx could never be proved wrong, his theory could never be falsified and the theory was not therefore scientific.

In Popper's philosophy a theory might be value-laden, but theories which are not objective will soon be falsified; only theories which have stood the tests of time and investigation will continue to be accepted. However, many sociologists believe it is impossible to keep values out of sociology and believe the whole process of research is bound to be influenced by a sociologist's values — however objective they try to be.

Weber thought that most aspects of research could be value-free, but even he accepted that the initial choice of research topic would inevitably reflect the issues that the researcher thought were important according to their values. The values of sociologists are evident in their choice of topic, whether it is Marx studying class inequality, functionalists studying how society is integrated, feminists looking for oppression in relationships between husbands and wives, or Weber examining the problems created by rational bureaucratic organizations.

The theoretical approach and research methods chosen also reflect the researcher's values. Gouldner argues that all research is based upon 'domain assumptions' about the nature of society which reflect their values. Furthermore, all research is selective, and the sort of data collected is likely to reflect the researcher's assumptions and values. In questionnaire research and interviews questions have to be chosen, and in participant observation only some of what happens can be recorded by the researcher. Values will influence what is seen as being important enough to generate data. Interpretive sociologists emphasize that all research involves a process of interpretation where the researcher will be influenced by their own experience and understanding of the social world. Phenomenologists go further, and see all knowledge as a product of categorization procedures, so that it can never be objective and value-free. For example, Maxwell Atkinson believes suicide statistics are a product of the assumptions of coroners, and Cicourel believes that crime statistics reflect the assumptions of officials in the criminal justice system. From this point of view, it is impossible to keep values out of research. Postmodernists such as Lyotard agree that knowledge is relative and there is no way of distinguishing fact and opinion.

Alvin Gouldner, supports these types of argument in his 1975 essay 'Anti-Minotaur', arguing that it is as impossible to separate fact and value in sociology as it is to separate the bull and the man in the mythological minotaur. Gouldner and critical social scientists (including many Marxists and feminists) believe that sociology should be concerned with values since they see the whole point of social science as being to improve the social world.

Despite their commitment to the importance of values, critical social scientists such as Phil Carspecken believe that sociology is more than just personal, value-laden opinion. Following the realist theory of science, they believe that it is possible to test theories against the evidence to discover the underlying structures and processes shaping the social world. Researchers are bound to be influenced by their values, and without values about how the social world should be improved their work has little value. However, they should also be open to rational argument and should not let their values distort their interpretation of data to the extent that it prevents them from accepting when their theories are wrong.

RESOURCES

Quantitative and qualitative studies

	Quantitative studies	Qualitative studies
Theoretical approach favoured	Positivist	Interpretivist
Primary methods favoured	Questionnaire/social surveys	Unstructured interview/ participant observation
Secondary sources favoured	Official statistics	Personal documents
Ease of replication	Easy to replicate	Difficult to replicate
Scientific/non-scientific	Scientific	Non-scientific
Statistical or non-statistical	Statistical data	Non-statistical
Validity versus reliability	More reliable?	More valid?
Size of sample	Large sample	Small sample
Emphasis on internal or external stimuli	Internal stimuli	External stimuli
Closeness to real social world	Distant from real social world	Close to real social world
Better for discovering new theories of testing existing ones?	Better for testing existing theories	Better for discovering new theories
Better for which kind of data?	Better for simple factual data	Better for more in-depth data
Does researcher assume or discover what is important?	Researcher assumes they know what is important, e.g. by choosing questionnaire questions	Researcher discovers what is important during research
How easy to generalize from findings	Relatively easy to generalize	Relatively difficult to generalize
How time-consuming per person studied	Relatively quick	Time-consuming
Main practical problem in obtaining data from primary research	Problem of non-response	Problem of access

A2 Sociology and science

	Positivism	Popper	Phenomenology	Kuhn	Realists
Theorists	Durkheim, Comte	Karl Popper	Atkinson Cicourel	Thomas Kuhn	Bhaskar Sayer Keat & Urry
Is it possible for sociology to be scientific?	Yes	Yes	No	Yes	Yes
Is it desirable for sociology to be scientific?	Yes	Yes	No	Possibly not – would limit perspectives and critical debate	Yes
How is science defined?	Inductive – based on using objective, statistical data to look for correlations, causal relationships	Precise predictions are derived from theories; research attempts to falsify them	Science socially constructed; influenced by factors other than search for objective truth	Science follows generally accepted paradigm until a paradigm change takes place	Science uses observable data to uncover the unobservable structures and processes
How far does science produce true knowledge?	Science is seen as objective and able to reveal universal laws	Science never final because theories can be falsified in future, but it can rule out theories that are false	Science is a social construction with no greater claim to truth than any other sort of knowledge	Science is what a particular paradigm deems to be true; after scientific revolutions what is considered true changes	Science reveals underlying structures and processes, but cannot make precise predictions in open systems
How much sociology is scientific now?	Most quantitative sociology	Only a small amount of sociology which makes precise predictions. Marxism is not scientific	No sociology can be truly scientific because human behaviour is meaningful and unpredictable; meanings and motives cannot be observed	No single paradigm so sociology is pre-paradigmatic and therefore pre-scientific	Structural sociology, e.g. Marxism, is considered scientific

Chapter 12 | SOCIOLOGICAL THEORY

SPECIFICATION COVERAGE

Specification	Details
AQA A2 Unit 4, SCLY4: Crime and Deviance; Stratification and Differentiation; Theory and Methods	This chapter covers the Theory component of the AQA specification. Note that a basic introduction to theories is provided in chapter 1.
OCR, WJEC	There is no specific unit covering theory in the OCR and WJEC specifications, but a knowledge of theory is embedded in all units.

INTRODUCTION

AQA   Textbook pp. 855-856

Structural versus social action theories

There are two main types of sociological theory:

- **Structural** or **macro** perspectives examine the way in which society as a whole fits together. Examples include **Marxism** and **functionalism**. They tend to see human activity as a product of **social structure**.

- **Social action, interpretive** or **micro** perspectives examine smaller groups of people in society and are concerned with the **subjective states** of individuals. They tend to see society as a product of human activity. Examples include **symbolic interactionism** and **Weber**'s theory of **social action**.

Many theories do not fit neatly into one category or the other; there are variations within perspectives and some perspectives and individual studies combine elements of both approaches. For example, **Weber** used both structural and social action perspectives in his general approach, and **postmodernism** cannot be clearly categorized in terms of these concepts.

FUNCTIONALISM

AQA   Textbook pp. 856-863

Functionalism views society as a **system** with interconnected parts.

Early functionalists used a biological analogy, comparing parts of society to parts of the human body (for example, the government was compared to the brain). In terms of this analogy, both humans and societies have certain basic needs (or **functional prerequisites**) that must be met if they are to survive.

Social institutions exist to meet these basic needs (for example, families provide socialization, which helps meet a basic need for a common culture).

Institutions are studied by identifying the ways in which they contribute to meeting needs. The function of an institution is seen in terms of its contribution to the survival of the whole – i.e. society.

Some functionalists accept that there may be aspects of society which are **dysfunctional** – which prevent it from operating smoothly – but they generally pay little attention to them.

Functionalism has been accused of having a conservative ideology. It tends to support preservation of the status quo, since anything that persists in society is seen as serving a useful function.

Emile Durkheim

Durkheim believed that people were constrained by **social facts**: ways of acting, thinking and feeling in a society. Shared **moral codes** shaped individual consciousnesses.

Social facts were caused by other social facts – for example, Durkheim found that religion had an influence on suicide rates (see p. 196). Social facts could also, however, be explained in terms of the functions they performed for society. Parts of society would only persist if they served useful functions.

Societies needed a **collective conscience**, or shared morality, in order to function successfully.

Modern industrial societies could be disrupted by the existence of **anomie** (normlessness) and **egoism** – where individuals are not integrated into social groups. Both anomie and egoism stemmed from a complex division of labour. People did specialist jobs, and this weakened solidarity in society.

Talcott Parsons

Parsons believed that all societies needed a value consensus based upon shared goals. Societies developed rules based upon this value consensus and norms about how people should behave, which fitted in with these overall goals.

When individuals are socialized to accept the values, goals and norms, and where this works smoothly, social equilibrium is achieved.

Parsons saw society as a system with four basic needs, or functional prerequisites:

1 **Adaptation** – the need for an economic system to ensure the survival of members of society.

2 **Goal attainment** – the need to set goals, a function primarily carried out by the government.

3 **Integration** – the need to control conflict, a function carried out by the legal system.

4 **Pattern maintenance** – the maintenance of values, achieved largely through education, religion and family life.

Parsons saw change in terms of a shift in values from pattern **variables A** to pattern **variables B**. Under *variables A*, status was based on **ascription**, and people were treated as specific individuals. Under *variables B* – the dominant pattern in modern societies – status is based upon achievement, and individuals are judged according to impartial **universalistic standards** (for example, exam systems).

Social change also involves the development of specialist institutions, such as those of the welfare state – a process called **structural differentiation**.

Robert Merton

Merton was a functionalist, but he accepted that societies did not always work smoothly. He argued that parts of society could be dysfunctional and might prevent society from running smoothly. For example, Merton thought crime and deviance could result from anomie – a situation where people put too much emphasis on goals and not enough on using legitimate means (see p. 179).

Evaluation of functionalism

Functionalism has been accused of being **teleological** – that is, it confuses cause and effect. In other words, the functions of an institution are the effects it has rather than the reasons why it exists.

Functionalism assumes, without putting forward evidence, that a value consensus exists, and it ignores conflict and diversity in society (for example, **class conflict** as discussed by Marxists and **gender conflict** as discussed by feminists).

Functionalism is too **deterministic**. It sees human behaviour as shaped by the needs of the social system, and makes no allowance for the fact that individuals have choices about how they behave.

Gouldner (1975) argues that functionalism ignores the extent to which people are **coerced** in society to do things they do not wish to do.

Lockwood (1970) argues that functionalism ignores **conflicts of interest** between groups, which tend to destabilize social systems.

Turner & Maryanski (1979) argue that functionalism remains useful for understanding social structures and how they influence behaviour, although it does have many flaws.

CONFLICT PERSPECTIVES

AQA   Textbook pp. 866-867

Conflict perspectives take many forms – for example, Marxism, feminism, anti-racism – but all agree that there are different groups in society with conflicting interests.

MARXISM

AQA   Textbook pp. 867-872

Karl Marx saw history in terms of conflict between social classes.

Marxism is based upon a philosophy of **dialectical materialism**, the idea that history proceeds through the clash of material forces, particularly classes.

Marx saw human society as having a **material base**, based on work and the production of goods.

In the earliest stages of history, under **primitive communism**, there was no economic surplus and no private wealth, so classes did not exist.

As some individuals began to accumulate wealth (for example, herds of animals), and passed it down to their children, classes emerged.

Power tended to be monopolized by a ruling-class minority (those who owned the **means of production**) who dominated a subject-class majority. This caused tension and provided the potential for conflict.

The ruling class used their control over institutions such as organized religion to justify, or **legitimate**, their position and persuade the subject class that they were not being exploited.

Humans became increasingly **alienated** from their true selves and their true interests. Religion was a form of alienation, since people created in their minds a non-existent alien being which then controlled their behaviour.

In capitalist societies, where people worked for wages, and companies made profits (**surplus value**), workers were alienated from their work. They were alienated because they worked for other people, lacked control over their work and did not own the products they produced.

An end to alienation and exploitation could only be achieved in a **communist society**, in which there was no private property. Instead there would be communal ownership of the means of production. There would be no classes and therefore no exploitation. Instead of working for others to make a profit, people would work for the good of the society as a whole.

In Marxist theory, all societies apart from communist ones have two main classes: the owners of the means of production (the ruling class) and the non-owners of the means of production (the subject class). The means of production are those things that are necessary to produce other things, such as land, capital, raw materials, machinery and labour power.

In capitalist societies, the ruling class, or **bourgeoisie**, own capital (money used to finance production), while the subject class, or **proletariat**, own only labour power which they have to sell to the bourgeoisie.

The bourgeoisie use the **superstructure** – the non-economic parts of society such as education, religion and the state – to stabilize society. They encourage the development of **false class consciousness** whereby people see society as fair and just.

Eventually, Marx predicted, the proletariat (or working class) would become aware that they were being exploited, and they would develop class consciousness (an awareness of their true class interests).

The proletariat would be increasingly exploited, and suffer from crises in the capitalist system. They would become aware of increasing inequality between themselves and the bourgeoisie.

They would organize themselves into trade unions, political parties and revolutionary movements, overthrow capitalism and establish a communist society.

Criticisms

Critics have argued that as capitalism has developed, class consciousness has reduced rather than increased.

The Communist societies established in the twentieth century did not end inequality and exploitation, and they tended to be unpopular and to restrict individual liberty. By the early 1990s most Communist regimes had collapsed.

Marxism seems to exaggerate the importance of economic factors, ignoring the influence of ideas and culture.

Marxism has been accused of **economic determinism** – seeing individuals' behaviour as determined by the economic system and neglecting the extent to which individuals have free choice.

Marxism emphasizes class differences and pays too little attention to gender, ethnicity, sexuality, age, lifestyle etc.

Defenders of Marxism argue that it is not truly an economically deterministic theory. Marx emphasized that individuals and groups had to make their own history, but that the economic structure determined the context in which that process took place.

Neo-Marxism

Neo-Marxists are strongly influenced by Marx but reject one or more aspects of his work.

Antonio Gramsci (1971) (see p. 136) suggested that ownership of the means of production was not enough to guarantee control for the ruling class. It needed to make alliances with other classes and make some real concessions in order to attain **hegemony** (political domination).

Gramsci saw aspects of the superstructure as having some independence from the ruling class.

Neo-Marxists tend to place more emphasis on cultural and ideological factors than Marx did, and focus less exclusively on economic factors.

CONFLICT THEORY

AQA   Textbook pp. 866-874

Conflict theories emphasize the importance of conflict between different groups in society.

Weber (see p. 6) is seen as the pioneer of conflict theory. He argued that other groupings in society may be in conflict as well as status groups (groups with different amounts of prestige).

Conflict may take place between occupational groupings, men and women, ethnic or religious groups, different age groups, heterosexuals and homosexuals, the disabled and able-bodied, and so on.

Criticisms

A problem with conflict theory is that so many groups can be seen as being in conflict that it is difficult to get a clear picture of how society works.

Postmodernists argue that social divisions and conflicts are no longer of great significance.

FEMINISM

AQA   Textbook pp. 91-92

Feminism is a type of conflict theory which sees a conflict of interest between males and females as the most important type of conflict in society.

Feminists believe that most or all existing and historical societies are **patriarchal** (male-dominated).

Feminist theories try to explain inequalities and differences between men and women, and suggest what should be done about them.

Many feminists believe that much mainstream sociology (which they call '**malestream**' sociology) has a masculine bias. **Abbott *et al*** (2005) identify the following ways in which sociology has been seen as 'malestream':

- More research has been conducted about men than women, and it has been generalized to people in general even when all-male samples have been used.

- Issues of particular concern to women have been neglected.

- Women are often presented in sexist ways.

- Gender is often just added on to existing variables and is not seen as having the central importance feminists believe it should have.

However, Abbott *et al* believe that considerable progress has been made in countering 'malestream' sociology.

Although feminists broadly agree that society is patriarchal and 'malestream', and that sociology needs to change, there are a number of distinctive feminist perspectives.

Radical feminism

Textbook p. 101

Radical feminists believe that women are exploited by, and subservient to, men. Society is patriarchal, or male-dominated. Men are the **ruling class** and women the **subject class**.

Radical feminists explain the inequality in various ways, some seeing biology as the cause, others seeing culture or male violence as more important.

Female supremacists see women as superior to men, while female separatists believe that women should stay completely independent of men.

Origins of gender inequality

Radical feminists explain the origin of gender inequality in a variety of ways (see Textbook pp. 104-6 and 109-110).

Firestone (1972) argues that the sexual class system is the most fundamental form of stratification. The **biological family** results from women being burdened by pregnancy, childbirth, breastfeeding and menstruation. They become dependent on men and **power psychology** develops, which maintains female oppression.

Critics point out that in some societies women seem less disadvantaged by biology than in others.

Ortner (1974) sees female oppression as cultural. Because women give birth they are defined as closer to nature than men, who are seen as more cultural. Culture is seen as superior to nature.

Millett (1970) believes that several factors are important in maintaining female oppression:

- Biology plays some part, through superior male strength and the use of violence (though this is now more psychological than real).
- Ideological factors and socialization are important, as are sociological factors, such as the woman's role as mother in family life.
- Women have a **caste-like status** which means that even higher-class women are subordinate to men.
- Educational and economic inequalities hold women back.
- Myth and religion are used to justify male dominance.
- Psychology causes women to **interiorize** patriarchal ideology.
- Rape, sexual violence and the use of force underpin male power.

Critics such as **Rowbotham** (1982) question the usefulness of a vague term like patriarchy. Rowbotham also denies that all men exploit all women.

Marxist and socialist feminism

Textbook pp. 101-111

Marxist and socialist feminists see the capitalist system as the main source of women's oppression. They stress the importance of the exploitation of women as paid and unpaid workers.

Some would like to see a communist society established.

Origins of gender inequality

Marxist and socialist feminists have put forward a number of explanations of how the oppression of women started:

- **Engels** argued that gender inequality had a **materialist** base. The **monogamous family** only developed once herding of animals replaced hunting and gathering. Men used monogamous marriage to control women's sexuality so that they could identify their own biological children and pass down their herds of cattle to them. Engels's theory is, however, not based on sound empirical evidence.
- **Coontz & Henderson** also provide a materialist explanation. They argue that men became dominant due to the practice of **patrilocality**, whereby a wife went to live with her husband's family. This tended to mean that men gained control of women's labour and the wealth they produced.

Marxist and socialist feminists have also explained how gender inequality is maintained:

- **Engels** argued that men retained power because of access to work, particularly well-paid work, and he expected inequalities to reduce once women gained greater access to well-paid employment.
- Marxist feminists such as **Benston** (1972) argue that women are used as a **reserve army of labour**, benefiting capitalism by keeping wages low. They are a relatively docile, easily exploited workforce.
- **Hartmann** (1981) argues that capitalism might create low-paid jobs and a reserve army of labour, but this does not explain why women occupy these positions. She argues that **patriarchy** provides the key. Men maintain their control over women by exploiting their labour and denying them access to jobs that pay a living wage, so that they stay dependent on their husbands.

Liberal feminism

This perspective is associated with campaigners for equal rights, who want reforms to improve women's position, rather than revolution (see Textbook pp. 102-103, 132-135).

They often attribute inequality to sexism, discrimination, and sex-role stereotyping, and socialization.

Liberal feminists accept, much more than other feminists, that women have made considerable progress in gaining rights and improving their position in society. However, they still believe there is some way to go before equality is achieved.

Walter (1998) believes there is still much that feminists need to change. She believes that continuing problems of inequality affect all women. Women still tend to suffer from problems such as low pay, lack of childcare, the dual burden of paid employment and domestic labour, poverty, and domestic and sexual violence.

Whelehan (2000) believes that some of the gains of feminism are being lost. She argues that:

- there is evidence of **retrosexism** in the laddish culture of much of the popular media.
- the idea of the **singleton** – the ageing 'ladette' getting too old to have children – plays upon women's fears of being without a man.
- popular culture creates the myth of liberation for women through 'girl power', while disguising the continuing existence of oppression and discrimination.

Black feminism

Black feminists (see Textbook pp. 103-104) believe that racial/ethnic differences between women have been neglected by white feminists, and they stress the particularly deprived position of black women.

Brewer (1993) argues that class, race and gender combine to create multiple sources of deprivation for black women.

Postmodern feminism

Postmodern feminism (see Textbook pp. 115-119) generally rejects the idea that all women share the same interests and that their position can be explained in terms of a single theory. It emphasizes differences between groups of women – for example between lesbian and heterosexual women, women from different classes and ethnic groups, and women of different ages. Postmodern feminism celebrates these differences.

Postmodern feminists:

- reject the idea of progress, seeing it as a product of **male rationality**, and the idea of a single path to female liberation.
- argue that women's position can be improved by **deconstructing** (taking apart and criticizing) masculine language and thinking. **Cixous** (1993) describes language as **phallocentric** – male-dominated and reflecting a male view of the world.
- attack the male way of thinking of women as the 'other' (as different from and inferior to men). By allowing the voices of different women to be heard, the idea of women as an inferior 'other' can be broken down.

Criticisms

Walby (1992) criticizes postmodern feminism for losing sight of the importance of inequality and the degree to which the experience of oppression and inequality gives women shared interests. Walby accepts that there are differences between groups of women, but many still suffer from the effects of **patriarchy** – particularly older women, poorly qualified young women and single parents. Most elite positions continue to held by men.

Postmodern feminists tend to neglect important areas such as male use of violence to maintain power and gender inequalities at work.

Evaluation of feminism

Feminism has made a substantial contribution to sociology and understanding society. Feminism has:

- highlighted the problems of '**malestream**' sociology.
- introduced new topics which were previously neglected – for example, housework and childbirth.
- ensured that we know almost as much about women in society as about men.
- highlighted and contributed to reducing the oppression of women, faced by domestic violence, sexual discrimination and sexist socialization.
- helped to increase opportunities for women and raised consciousness of gender inequality.

Criticisms of feminism

Postfeminists such as **Brooks** (1997) (Textbook p. 132) believe that most feminists fail to acknowledge the progress made by women.

Marxists criticize feminists for neglecting class inequality.

Postmodernists believe that gender identities are no longer fixed, inflexible and oppressive.

Pollert (1996) (Textbook pp. 114-115) attacks the use of the term 'patriarchy', the key concept for feminists. The idea of patriarchy, Pollert says, involves a circular argument – it is used both as a description and as an explanation of inequality between the sexes. Pollert argues that capitalism is a system with an internal dynamic, but that patriarchy is not. She prefers empirical studies of how class, gender and ethnicity relate to one another, rather than abstract theorizing about the relationship between these different sources of inequality.

SOCIAL ACTION PERSPECTIVES

AQA   Textbook p. 874

Some **social action** and **interpretive** perspectives deny the existence of a clear social structure that tends to direct individual behaviour. Others accept the existence of a structure but see it as shaped by individuals.

Max Weber

Weber combined a consideration of **social structure** (classes, status groups and bureaucracies) with a consideration of **social action**.

He described sociology as the study of social action – which he defined as any intentional, meaningful behaviour which takes account of the existence of other people.

Explaining social action requires *Verstehen*, or understanding. One needs to understand what actions mean to people – for example, it is possible to understand that a woodcutter with a piece of wood and an axe is chopping wood. But one also needs to understand the **motive** behind an action.

An example is Weber's study of the Protestant ethic (see p. 71), in which he discusses the meaning of

Protestantism to some of its followers and the **motives** they have for working hard to reinvest money.

Weber accepts the existence of institutions such as bureaucracies, but he sees them as consisting of individuals carrying out social actions. Bureaucracies:

- are organizations with sets of rules and **hierarchical relationships** (for example, the civil service or large corporations).
- are composed of individuals pursuing **rational social action** – social action intended to achieve particular goals, such as increasing the profits of a company.

Weber saw the modern world as increasingly governed by rational social action (the process of rationalization). **Premodern** societies were regulated more by traditional social action – people behaved in certain ways because their ancestors had behaved in those ways.

In modern societies, governed by rational social action, there was far more scope for innovation, but to some extent bureaucracies with strict rules stifled individual creativity.

Weber was neither a **materialist** (like Marx) who believed that material forces shaped history, nor an **idealist** who believed that ideas shaped history. Instead, Weber believed that both materialism and idealism played a part in explaining human history. For example, the development of capitalism required both the right material conditions and the religious ideas of Protestantism.

Criticisms

Weber has been criticized by **Lee & Newby** (1983) as a **methodological individualist** – somebody who reduces everything to the actions of individuals and ignores how social structure shapes society.

To the extent that Weber does deal with social structure, what he says seems to contradict some of his ideas on the importance of individual social action.

Postmodernists deny that the contemporary social world is increasingly characterized by rationalization.

However, **Ritzer** (1996) supports Weber's view that capitalist societies drive towards bureaucratic organization and rationalization in the pursuit of profit. He sees the fast-food giant McDonald's as representing a contemporary and extreme form of **bureaucratization** which he calls 'McDonaldization'. McDonald's is based on rational principles such as:

- **efficiency** – the 'optimum method in getting from one point to another', achieved using the principles of the conveyor belt to feed people as rapidly as possible;
- **calculability** – the precise measurement of all products;
- **predictability** – achieved by standardizing the physical environment and operating methods in all branches;
- **control** – providing precise directions to workers and monitoring them, and controlling customers through the use of drive-thrus and security guards.

Ritzer believes these principles have spread to many areas of social life.

SYMBOLIC INTERACTIONISM

AQA   Textbook p. 881-884

George Herbert Mead

Mead (1934) is usually seen as the founder of **symbolic interactionism**.

Human behaviour is social because people interact in terms of symbols. Symbols (for example, words or flags) stand for other objects and imply certain behaviour – for example, the symbol 'chair' implies an object that you can sit on.

Humans do not have instincts, and thus they need symbols in order to survive and interact. For example, they need symbols for different plants which indicate whether they are edible or poisonous. Meanings and symbols are largely shared by members of society.

In order to understand the behaviour of others, it is necessary to take the **role of the other** – to imagine that one is that person in order to try to understand the reasons for their behaviour.

Individuals have a **self**: an image of what sort of person they are. This largely reflects how other people react to them. By taking the role of the other (imagining how others see us) we build up a **self-concept**. For example, we come to see ourselves as brave or cowardly, hard or soft.

Society has a culture and a **plurality of social roles** – for example, the roles of husband and wife. These roles imply certain behaviours, but the roles are flexible and can change. For example, there is considerable leeway in how people carry out different family roles.

Herbert Blumer

Other interactionists, such as **Blumer** (1962), have developed Mead's approach. Blumer emphasizes that people do not react automatically to external stimuli but interpret their meaning before reacting (for example, interpreting the meaning of a red light before deciding how to react to it).

Meanings develop during interaction and are not fixed.

Rules and structures restrict social action and shape the interpretation of meaning to some extent, but they are never absolutely rigid and fixed.

Evaluation of symbolic interactionism

Interactionists fail to explain where the norms which partly shape behaviour come from.

They may underestimate the degree to which human behaviour is constrained.

They neglect the role of structural factors – such as the unequal distribution of power and the existence of inequality – in shaping human societies.

PHENOMENOLOGY

Phenomenology is a European philosophy. Like other social action approaches it is concerned with subjective meanings, but unlike them it denies that one can produce causal explanations of human behaviour.

According to its founder, **Edmund Husserl** (1931), individuals organize chaotic sensory experience into **phenomena**.

Phenomena are things which are held to have characteristics in common – for example, the category 'dog' includes a range of animals with particular characteristics.

The emphasis is on the **subjective** nature of the categorization. Although a real world exists, how it is categorized is a matter of human choice rather than an objective process.

The purpose of phenomenology is to understand the **essence of phenomena**: the essential characteristics which lead to something being placed in a particular category.

An example of phenomenology is **Atkinson's** (1978) work on suicide, which looks at why certain events are categorized as suicides, rather than looking at the causes of suicide (see p. 197).

UNITING SOCIOLOGICAL APPROACHES

AQA   **Textbook pp. 887-890**

As discussed at the beginning of this chapter, there are two main approaches in sociology: **structural** approaches (which emphasize how social structures shape social action) and **social action** approaches (which emphasize how social groups produce society through their actions).

Sociologists have increasingly tried to combine these two approaches.

In *The Sociological Imagination*, **Mills** (1959) suggested that one needed to understand how the larger historical scene affected individuals.

Giddens – theory of structuration

Anthony Giddens (1979) advocates **structuration** theory. He sees structure and action as two sides of the same coin: structures make social action possible, but social actions create the structures. Giddens calls this the **duality of structure**.

This duality can be illustrated by considering **language**. Grammar is the structure of language, but individuals create the structure by talking and writing in ways that follow grammatical rules. If people start to use language in a different way, then grammatical rules will change. However, people can only use language and understand each other because there is some grammatical structure.

In the same way, **societal structures** and institutions are reproduced through people's actions, but if their actions change the structures and institutions change.

Critics of Giddens, such as **Archer** (1982), argue that he puts too much emphasis on people's ability to change society by acting differently, and he underestimates the constraints under which people operate.

MODERNITY AND POSTMODERNITY

AQA   **Textbook pp. 890-894**

It is possible to distinguish two types of theoretical approach within sociology:

- **Modern theories** – such as those of **Durkheim**, **Marx** and **Weber** – argue that the objective truth about society can be discovered.

- **Postmodernism**, on the other hand, argues against the idea of objective truth.

Some sociologists distinguish different eras in human development and argue that there has been a move from **modernity** to **postmodernity**, although others dispute this.

Modernity

Many sociologists have distinguished between **premodern** and **modern** societies. The change is often associated with industrialization.

Marx, Weber, Durkheim and most classical sociologists see the development of modernity as progress.

The **Enlightenment** (an eighteenth-century intellectual movement) is often seen as the starting point of modernity. The Enlightenment rejected the idea that thinking should be limited by religious beliefs and tradition and argued that humans could work out the best way to organize societies for themselves.

Weber, in particular, saw the change to modernity in terms of the triumph of **scientific rationality** over superstition, tradition and religious faith.

Postmodernism

Postmodern theorists reject the idea that human society can be perfected through rational thought; they reject the idea that grand theories can discover the truth.

Postmodernism first developed in architecture. It rejected modern concrete, steel and glass tower blocks, which some modern architects saw as the solution to the problem of accommodating people.

Postmodern architecture uses a greater variety of styles and uses the architecture of earlier eras rather than just using modern materials and designs.

There are two particularly influential postmodern theorists: **Lyotard** and **Baudrillard**.

Lyotard – postmodernism and knowledge

Jean-François Lyotard (1984) is a French social theorist. He argues that the move to postmodern culture started in the 1950s.

The transition to postmodern culture involves changes in **language games**. Preindustrial societies had a language game based on **narrative**. Narrators of stories have **legitimacy** because of who they are (for example, their position within a tribe).

With the Enlightenment, **denotative** language games became dominant. In these, statements are judged in terms of abstract standards of proof, deriving from science.

Science itself is based upon **metanarratives** – big stories which give meaning to other narratives. Scientific metanarratives include the idea of progress through science and the possibility of conquering nature. Such metanarratives influenced events such as the French Revolution and helped to make Marxism popular in the twentieth century.

Postmodernism leads to 'incredulity towards metanarratives'. The metanarratives of the twentieth century failed to solve the world's problems and in fact made things worse. For example, Marxism led to tyranny in the communist USSR. People no longer believe in a simple recipe for progress.

In postmodernism, denotative language games are replaced by **technical** language games. These are not judged by standards of truth, but by standards of usefulness.

Postmodern society is based upon producing saleable, useful knowledge rather than searching for eternal truths. It is more **diverse**, **pluralistic** and **tolerant** than modern societies in which doctrinaire metanarratives dominated.

Criticisms

Critics argue that Lyotard's theory is itself a sweeping metanarrative about the development of society.

Lyotard advances little evidence to support his theory.

The Marxist critic **Terry Eagleton** sees Lyotard's theory as justification for uncontrolled capitalism which puts profit before human well-being.

Baudrillard – simulations

Like Lyotard, **Baudrillard** (1983) sees society as moving through several stages. He argues that Marxists are wrong to see contemporary society as based on the production of material goods. The economy is increasingly based on the production and sale of **signs and images** – for example, the image of pop stars is what sells rather than the content of their records.

Signs have developed through four stages:

1 Signs are a reflection of a basic reality.

2 Signs become a distortion of reality.

3 Signs disguise the absence of reality (for example, images of a non-existent God).

4 Signs bear no relation to any reality – signs become **simulacra**.

Examples of simulacra are:

- Disneyland, which reproduces imaginary worlds such as 'Future World'.

- The mummy of Rameses II, which was transformed by attempts to preserve it.

- Los Angeles, which Baudrillard sees as an 'immense script ... a perpetual motion picture'.

Baudrillard believes that politics has imploded into a meaningless exchange of signs in which politicians have no real power. People become trapped in a situation where image and reality cannot be separated, particularly through watching TV.

Criticisms

Baudrillard's arguments are highly abstract and not based on systematic research.

Harvey (1990) suggests that the decisions made by politicians make a real difference to people's lives.

Baudrillard makes absurd statements, such as claiming that the first Gulf War was simply a series of images on TV screens.

Postmodernism and contemporary society

Postmodernism is seen as having a number of consequences for contemporary society.

According to **Pakulski & Waters** 1996 (Textbook pp. 84-86), class differences largely disappear and image becomes much more important in determining **status**.

Other sources of identity such as age, gender and ethnicity become less significant as people can choose what identity to adopt. For example **Featherstone & Hepworth** (1991) (Textbook pp. 754-756) believe **deconstruction of the life-course** has taken place – people no longer have to 'act their age' but can act however they like.

Crook et al (1992) (Textbook pp. 682-684) believe that postmodern culture is characterized by people being able to choose their own lifestyle options. The consumption of goods – for example, through shopping – becomes more important than the production of goods through work.

Strinati (1995) (Textbook pp. 684-686) describes postmodernism as typified by:

- the triumph of style over substance (for example, the popularity of films which look good but have little plot);

- the breakdown of the distinction between low and high culture (for example, the high status given to pop art);

- confusions over time and space (for example, films which jump backwards and forwards in time).

Postmodernist feminists such as **Cixous** (1981) (Textbook pp. 117-118) believe that the use of **language** has much more influence on society than inequality between social groups.

Philo & Miller – critique of postmodernism

Philo & Miller (2001) make a number of criticisms of postmodernism:

- It encourages **political apathy**, as it denies the existence of an objective reality that social scientists can analyse.

- The emphasis on language detracts attention from real social problems.

- Postmodernism fails to challenge distorted or misleading images of reality presented by the media – for example, about the Israeli-Palestinian conflict.

- Postmodernism ignores the growing inequalities of wealth and income, the growing power of corporations and the increasing influence of market forces on social life.

Philo & Miller believe that the growth of consumerism and the fragmentation of styles does not represent the development of a new type of society.

MODERNITY AND MODERN THEORY

AQA   Textbook pp. 895-899

Numerous sociologists reject postmodern theories and argue that societies can be understood, explained and improved.

Anthony Giddens

Giddens believes that societies have entered an era of **high modernity**. Despite important changes, such as **globalization**, key features of modern societies remain.

In particular, societies are still based upon the modern characteristic of **reflexivity** – this involves people reflecting upon the world and thinking about acting differently in the future to improve things.

People increasingly reflect upon all aspects of their lives and consider changing them. This makes contemporary culture increasingly unsettled and changeable. This is not, however, a feature of postmodernity but an extension and development of a key feature of modernity.

SOCIOLOGY AND SOCIAL POLICY

AQA

Sociology and social policy can have a number of relationships.

Some sociologists believe that sociology should be **value-free**, and should be concerned only with trying to describe and understand the social world (Textbook pp. 850-853).

Others believe that the whole point of sociology is to try to make a difference and improve the world. For example **Gouldner** (1975), feminists (Textbook pp. 100-121), and **critical social scientists** (Textbook pp. 804-808) all believe that sociology should try to influence social policy.

What influence sociology does have on social policy is open to question. There are a number of possible relationships between the two:

- Sociology may be influenced by social policy.
- Sociology may directly influence social policy.
- Policy-makers might use sociology selectively to justify policies.

The influence of social policy on sociology

There are many examples of how sociology research has been influenced by social policies followed by governments. For example:

- The introduction of choice and **quasi-markets** into education stimulated much research into its effects on education (Textbook pp.634-635).
- Changes in the welfare state have been researched (Textbook pp. 259-276).
- Researchers have studied the impact of social policies on the family (Textbook pp. 508-512).

To some extent, social policies may even have helped to introduce new theories into sociology. For example, following the **New Right** policies of Conservative governments after 1979, New Right perspectives on welfare developed in sociology (for example, **Marsland**, 1996) (Textbook pp. 238-239) and **Bartholomew** (2006) (Textbook pp. 269-272).

Sociology's influence on social policy

Sociology has affected social policy in a number of areas:

- The **social democratic** perspective on education encouraged the introduction of comprehensive schools by Labour governments in the 1960s and 1970s (Textbook pp. 612-613).

- **Feminist** campaigns have led to changes in education to prevent bias against girls (Textbook pp. 642-647) and have led to offences such as domestic violence being taken more seriously by the police (Textbook p. 370).
- The development of the concept of **relative poverty** by **Peter Townsend** (1979) (Textbook pp. 217-219) led to anti-poverty programmes by Labour governments of the 1960s and 1970s and by New Labour.
- The **right realist** perspective on crime of **James Q Wilson** (1975) has led to some new policies, such as the introduction of ASBOs aimed at preventing areas from deteriorating due to antisocial behaviour (Textbook pp. 354-355).
- **Anthony Giddens** was one of Prime Minister Tony Blair's main advisers following New Labour's victory in 1997. Giddens helped devise the political philosophy of the 'Third Way' combining elements of traditional left- and right-wing policies (Textbook pp. 273-275). This influenced the idea of **active welfare** and the whole direction of social policy for recent Labour governments.

The selective use of sociology

Many sociologists do not believe that the government simply consults sociology, accepts the findings of the most rigorous research and then uses it to devise the best possible social policies. There are many other influences on social policy and, in general, governments are only likely to take note of research which supports their existing policies, fits with their ideological position and is likely to win votes.

Crouch (2005) (Textbook pp. 595-596), for example, believes that **New Labour** used the idea of the Third Way to justify a shift in ideology in the Labour Party towards much greater acceptance of free markets. According to Crouch, this change in policy direction was influenced more by capitalists than by sociologists.

Right realist views on crime and deviance (Textbook pp. 353-355) may have influenced governments more than **left realist views** (Textbook pp. 345-350) because politicians believed that 'hard' policies on crime were more likely to win votes.

Conclusion

Sociology is unlikely to have a direct influence on social policy where sociologists are strongly opposed to the policies supported by a particular government, and more likely to be adopted by policy-makers where sociological research fits the existing policies or can be used to justify the policies of policy-makers.

To some extent governments influence sociological research anyway by deciding on priorities for research funding (Textbook p. 814).

The influence of sociology varies depending on the government in power. **New Right**-influenced **Conservative** governments between 1979 and 1997 were generally hostile to sociologists, apart from a handful of right-wing sociologists who supported their views. **New Labour** governments since 1997 have taken sociology more seriously and sociology has had some influence on the shape of policies in areas such as criminal justice, welfare, education and health.

DEVELOP YOUR ANALYSIS AND EVALUATION SKILLS

Essay plans

For each of the following questions write your own essay plan before comparing it with the suggestions given here. For the final question you can write a full answer and compare it with the provided model answer.

Structural perspectives are superior to interpretative perspectives. Discuss.

Background

Structural perspectives include Marxism and functionalism and perhaps some versions of feminism (particularly Marxist feminism and approaches which see patriarchy as a structure). They see society as having a structure which shapes action. Interpretative perspectives include interactionism and phenomenology; postmodernism is also critical of structural approaches. Although both structural and interpretative approaches have their advocates, it can be argued that they look at different aspects of society and are stronger when combined than when used in isolation.

For	Against
● Marxism (p. 225)	● Symbolic interactionism (p. 229)
● Functionalism (p. 224)	● Phenomenology (p. 229)
● Marxist/functionalist feminism (p. 227)	● Most types of postmodernism (p. 230)
● Other feminists (Walby, p. 228)	

Top Tip

Giddens (p. 232) and Weber (p. 228) both advocate combining structural and interpretative approaches; many types of neo-Marxism combine elements of both as well (p. 226).

We now live in postmodern societies. Discuss.

Background

You will need to discuss the differences between modern and postmodern societies (see p. 230) and between postmodernity and postmodernism. Marxism and functionalism provide arguments against this statement, while Weber saw societies as becoming modern with greater bureaucratization and rationalization. This could be illustrated with Ritzer's work (p. 229). Postmodernists such as Baudrillard and Lyotard would clearly agree with this statement, but remember there are criticisms of their views. You could look at the arguments on both sides in some of the other chapters on issues such as popular culture (p. 93), religion (chapter 4), and race/ethnicity and nationality (p. 101).

For	Against
● Baudrillard (p. 231)	● Marxism (p. 225)
● Lyotard (p. 230)	● Functionalism (p. 224)
● Postmodern feminism (p. 228)	● Weber (p. 228)

Top Tip

Giddens (p. 232) is useful for accepting some aspects of postmodernism but arguing for the idea of high modernity, which does not see societies as having moved fully into postmodernity yet.

Marxists place too much emphasis on classes and material factors. Discuss.

Background

It is worth looking at the materialist basis of Marxism in some detail in discussing this statement, with a discussion of issues such as dialectical materialism, and alienation (p. 225). Some neo-Marxists (such as Gramsci, p. 136) would agree with this view up to a point, but remember there are many interpretations of Marx and not all see him as an economic determinist. You can contrast materialism with idealism – a useful way of illustrating this is Weber's Protestant ethic theory (see p. 71). Weber certainly thought Marx was too much of a materialist and most postmodernists and symbolic interactionists would also be critical of materialism.

For	Against
● Weber (p. 71) ● Symbolic interactionism (p. 229) ● Postmodernism (p. 230) ● Some neo-Marxists (p. 226) ● Feminists, other than Marxist/socialist feminists (p. 227)	● Marx (p. 225) ● Marxist/socialist feminists (p. 227)

 Top Tip

Chapter 1 has an analysis of whether class is still an important social division. Although not Marxists as such, Philo & Miller (p. 231) hold that class inequality is still a key feature of society.

Can inequality between men and women be explained by the concept of patriarchy?

 Background

You need to define patriarchy before answering this question. It can be defined simply as male domination in society; note, however, that it is a rather imprecise term and may be used in different ways by different feminists. Give an indication of the views of different types of feminists (radical, Marxist, socialist, liberal, black and postmodern). Most tend to approve of the use of the term patriarchy but postmodern feminists see it as too sweeping. Pollert is useful for criticizing the concept of patriarchy (p. 228).

For	Against
● Radical feminists (p. 227) ● Walby (p. 228)	● Pollert (p. 228) ● Postmodern feminists (p. 228)

For and Against
● Marxist and socialist feminists (p. 227) ● Black feminists (p. 228)

 Top Tip

Think about whether the idea of patriarchy is more a description than an explanation of inequality.

Functionalism is of little use for understanding contemporary society. Discuss.

 Background

Functionalism now looks a rather dated perspective and it has been heavily criticized. There are few, if any, sociologists who would call themselves functionalists today, but some functionalists, particularly Durkheim, still have an influence on sociology. His ideas have strongly influenced the study of suicide and his ideas about the problems of modern societies (anomie and egoism) are regarded as important by some sociologists. Merton's ideas on anomie and crime and deviance are also influential (see p. 225).

For	**Against**
● Marxism and neo-Marxism (p. 225)	● Durkheim (p. 225)
● Feminism (p. 226)	● Parsons (p. 225)
● Interpretivist perspectives (p. 229)	● Merton (p. 225)
● Postmodernism (p. 230)	

Top Tip

Merton's idea of dysfunction shows that functionalists don't always emphasize the positive.

Conflict theories are the most useful theories for understanding contemporary society. Discuss.

Background

Conflict theory is a term specifically applied to theories which argue that there are many different sources of conflict in society, but other theories which stress one type of conflict (for example, Marxism and feminism) are also types of conflict theory. The main challenges to conflict theory come from functionalism and postmodernism.

For	**Against**
● Conflict theory (p. 226)	● Functionalism (p. 224)
● Marxism (p. 225)	● Postmodernism (p. 230)
● Feminism (p. 226)	
● Weber (p. 226)	

Top Tip

It is useful to talk about concrete examples to evaluate the importance of conflict theory.

Model answer

Conflict theories are the most useful theories for understanding contemporary society. Discuss.

The term 'conflict theory' was developed to describe any theory that believes there are divisions within society between social groups which have different interests. There are many varieties of conflict theory and the theories emphasize different types of conflict and sources of conflict, but they all agree that conflict is a central feature of society. From the viewpoint of conflict theory, society involves a struggle over scarce resources by competing social groups; members of each group share, or believe they share, common interests. Conflict theory has been opposed in the past by functionalism, and more recently by postmodernism, both of which deny there are fundamental differences of interest which lead to conflict in contemporary societies.

One of the earliest conflict theories to develop was Marxism. In this theory, class divisions are the main source of conflict. Marx believed that, until a communist society was established, there was a fundamental division between the owners of the means of production and the non-owners of the means of production. In capitalism, the bourgeoisie who owned capital exploited the wage labour of the proletariat by paying them less than the full value of their work and thereby extracting surplus value or profit. To Marx, this was a form of exploitation, through which wealth and power became concentrated in the hands of the bourgeoisie. They used this power to control the superstructure of society (for example: education, the state and the media) in order to foster false class consciousness and prevent revolution. Eventually, however, class consciousness would develop as a result of growing inequality between rich and poor and crises of capitalism. Marxism has been further developed by a range of neo-Marxists, such as Antonio Gramsci, who move away from the apparent economic determinism of some of Marx's writing, giving more emphasis to culture and stressing that false class consciousness is always partial.

Marxism has been heavily criticized for placing too much emphasis on class differences and underestimating the importance of ideas in history. To some postmodernists, such as Pakulski & Waters, class differences are irrelevant as they have largely disappeared. However, studies of social mobility and of income and wealth inequality show that class inequality has certainly not disappeared and class still has a very strong influence on life chances. Research (for example, by Wilkinson) suggests that even life expectancy is strongly influenced by class.

More convincing criticisms of Marxism have come from other theorists who argue that class is not the only or main cause of conflict. Most prominent of these are feminists. Radical feminists such as Firestone and Millett argue that patriarchy and gender divisions are the fundamental organising principles of society today, rather than capitalism and class divisions. Firestone believes there is a sexual class system that pre-dates and is more important than social class in the Marxist sense. Millett believes that gender inequality is perpetuated by a range of patriarchal structures including the family, religion, ideology, the education system and male violence. Liberal feminists have less extreme views and accept that women have made progress in western societies, but still believe that there is conflict between men and women and that problems still remain. They point to the continuing lower levels of pay for women than men and the lack of women in elite positions in society. Some feminists recognize that gender may not be the only source of division in society. For example, Marxist and socialist feminists see class and gender divisions acting in tandem, while Black feminists insist that racism should also be brought into the equation.

Feminists have been criticized by Anna Pollert for using the concept of patriarchy both to describe and to explain gender inequality. Postfeminism goes further, arguing that older types of feminism are no longer needed because inequalities and conflict between men and women are largely a thing of the past. However, sociologists such as Sylvia Walby have carefully documented continuing inequality. Walby accepts that patriarchy has changed (from private to public forms), but she does not accept that it has disappeared.

The critics of conflict theory examined so far have not convincingly argued that conflict has disappeared, but they have shown that there is more than one source of conflict. Max Weber recognized that conflict could occur between status groups (groups with a particular status in society) as well as between classes which were distinguished by economic inequalities. Status groups include males and females and racial/ethnic groups, but might also include age groups, the disabled and the able-bodied, groups with different sexualities, and so on. From Weber's point of view, there is likely to be some degree of conflict between numerous class and status groups as each tries to increase its share of scarce resources. Weber's theory offers no clear pointers as to which sources of conflict will be most prominent in society, but it does recognize that is not safe to assume that a single source of conflict will be dominant.

Functionalists, such as Parsons, question the whole idea that conflict is an important feature of contemporary societies. For Parsons, countries such as the USA had little conflict because there was a value consensus in which shared beliefs united social groups, thus preventing conflict. Indeed, Parsons believed that without a value consensus society could not function effectively. Parsons accepted that there could be challenges to this consensus, but he thought that equilibrium would soon be restored.

Parson's idea of a value consensus is not hard to challenge. There are numerous differences in values in society — for example between atheists and the religious, religious fundamentalists and others, the political left and the political right, strong environmentalists and those who prioritize economic growth above the environment, and so on. Parsons, therefore, was wrong to claim that the USA and similar countries had a value consensus. Durkheim was nearer the mark arguing that society needed some degree of social solidarity, but he accepted that egoism and anomie might weaken solidarity in modern societies with a complex division of labour.

The most recent challenge to conflict theory has come from postmodernists such as Lyotard, Baudrillard and Crook, Pakulski & Waters. Lyotard argues that the great metanarratives of modernity, for example communism and fascism, are no longer taken seriously, removing ideological sources of conflict. Baudrillard believes that reality has dissolved into simulacra and in a world where reality is so distant from experience there is little basis for conflict. Crook et al believe that old social divisions on which conflict were based have dissolved. People are free in consumer societies to choose their own identities and change them at will. Society is therefore too fluid to create clear divisions between groups which are likely to come into conflict with one another.

Postmodernists are undoubtedly right that important social changes have taken place, consumerism is more important than it was, and social divisions have become somewhat blurred. However, they greatly exaggerate the extent of these changes and ignore a wealth of sociological evidence that class, gender, ethnic and other divisions remain very important. The sources of conflict may have broadened (for example, there is increased conflict now over the environment) but conflict has certainly not disappeared. Conflict theory therefore continues to be crucial for understanding contemporary society. Without understanding struggles over power between different social groups it is impossible to understand and explain most of the social changes taking place in societies today.

RESOURCES

Sociologists, perspectives, concepts and studies

	Functionalism	Marxism	Feminism	Weber	Symbolic interactionism	Postmodernism
Structural or social action theory	Structural	Structural	Varies – Marxist feminism is structural but postmodern feminism is not	Both structural and social action	Social action	Doesn't fit neatly but is not a structural approach
Conflict or consensus theory	Society characterized by consensus	Class conflict theory	Gender conflict theory	Conflict exists between multiple groups	Society is not based on consensus but conflict is viewed in micro terms rather than structural divisions	Closer to consensus perspective as it believes conflict has lost importance
View of stability in society	Society normally stable	Stability can be maintained through false class consciousness but ultimately revolution will occur in capitalist societies	Patriarchy encourages stability but gender conflict can make society unstable	Instability always possible with the diverse interests of particular groups	Stability created through social roles but these are not fixed	Major conflict likely to be avoided in tolerant, pluralistic postmodern societies without metanarratives
View of change in society	Gradual, evolutionary change	Revolutionary changes with development of new modes of production until communism ends history	Varies. Some see patriarchy as in decline (e.g. liberal feminism) but radical feminism sees it as maintaining its power	Society moves towards rational modernity with bureaucracy increasingly dominant	Change tends to come from below and small-scale change happens continuously	Shift from modernity to postmodernity takes place
View of power distribution and sources of power	Power widely distributed	Ruling class monopolize power	Men monopolize power (radical feminists); ruling class men (Marxist feminists); white men (Black feminists)	Higher classes and status groups have more power than others	Some have more power than others but all groups have some power	Power is widely distributed

Sociologists, perspectives, concepts and studies *(continued)*

	Functionalism	Marxism	Feminism	Weber	Symbolic interactionism	Postmodernism
Main method-ologies	Functional analysis or positivism	Analysis of economy and history though some Marxists do qualitative research	Feminist methodology favoured, e.g. collaborative interviewing	Interpretive qualitative methods favoured though quantitative analysis accepted as well	Favours qualitative methods, especially participant observation	Postmodern methods, allowing different people to tell their stories. Relativistic methods
Major criticisms	Ignores conflict and dysfunctional aspects of society	Ignores non-class divisions. Too much emphasis on economics and too little on culture	Patriarchy a vague concept. Ignores other types of social division apart from gender. Underesti-mates progress towards gender equality	Methodological individualism. Postmodernists don't believe rationalization is taking place. Combined social action and structural approach may be contradictory	Doesn't explain where norms come from and neglects constraint and structural factors	Neglects inequality and power differences, and encourages political apathy. Many sociologists believe we still live in modernity

Writers and their work

Sociologist	Perspective	Concept	Application/study
Durkheim	Functionalist	Anomie	Statistical study of suicide
Lyotard	Postmodernist	Incredulity towards metanarratives	Attitudes towards science and political theories
Parsons	Functionalist	Pattern variables	Changing patterns of cultural values
Mead	Symbolic interactionism	The self	Labelling theories of crime and education
Weber	Weberian sociology	*Verstehen*	*The Protestant Ethic and the Spirit of Capitalism*
Firestone	Radical feminism	Sexual class system	Biology and gender inequality
Atkinson	Phenomenology	Categorization of phenomena	Study of coroner's courts
Giddens	Theory of high modernity	Reflexivity	Study of the development of modernity
Robert Merton	Functionalism	Dysfunction	Theory of anomie as a cause of crime
Weber	Weberian sociology	Rational social action	Study of modernity and bureaucracy
Coontz & Henderson	Marxist/socialist feminism	Patrilocality	The origins of gender inequality
Giddens	Structuration theory	The duality of structure	Grammar and speech
Whelehan	Liberal feminism	Retrosexism	Gender and popular culture
Marx	Marxism	Alienation	The experience of work under capitalism/ analysis of religion
Ritzer	Weberian sociology	'McDonaldization'	Study of organizations in modern societies
Benston	Marxist/socialist feminism	The reserve army of labour	Gender inequality in the labour market
Gramsci	Neo-Marxism	Hegemony	Theory of how power is maintained by a dominant group
Cixous	Postmodern feminism	Phallocentric language	Study of gender and language
Baudrillard	Postmodernism	Simulacra	The development of signs
Karl Marx	Marxism	Dialectical materialism	Theory of history

USEFUL WEBSITES

A-level sociology sites

The list below is a selection of the most useful websites aimed at AS/A-level sociology students. Access is free, unless otherwise stated.

Collins Sociology Website

www.collinseducation.com/sociologyweb

The site which accompanies this book, the main textbook on which this book is based (*Sociology Themes and Perspectives, Seventh Edition*), and Collins's other sociology books. It requires a subscription but a free trial is available, and there is also free material including mind maps and multiple choice questions on all the Handbook chapters.

ATSS

www.le.ac.uk/se/centres/ATSS/atss.html

The site of the Association for the Teaching of Social Science; particularly useful for its comprehensive links page.

Sociology Central

www.sociology.org.uk

One of the most comprehensive and useful sites for A-level sociology, providing links, notes on most topics, textbook reviews and much more.

Tamara O'Hara's sociology site

www.quia.com/pages/sociologytamara.html

A lively site containing articles, notes, revision exercises and more. Largely based on AQA but useful for other exam boards as well.

Cool Revision

www.s-cool.co.uk

Very good for revision materials, not just for sociology but most other topics too.

Sociology online

www.sociologyonline.co.uk

This is particularly strong on quizzes and games and is well worth exploring in depth.

David Abbott's Sociology Blog

www.tutor2u.net/blog/index.php/sociology

An interesting blog which has up-to-date commentary on sociology issues in the news. It is very useful for giving your answers a contemporary feel.

Get Revising

http://getrevising.co.uk

Get revising is an innovative revision site covering many A-level subjects but particularly strong on sociology. It allows students to share resources and approach revision in an interactive way.

Sociology Review

www.philipallan.co.uk/sociologyreview/index.htm

There are no resources on this site, but it's where you can order *Sociology Review*, the only magazine specifically aimed at A-level sociology students. You can buy it yourself, or ask your college or school library to order it, as it is one of the most useful resources for A-level sociology students.

Wales Virtual Teacher's Centre

www.ngfl-cymru.org.uk/vtc-home/vtc-aas-home/vtc-as_sociology

Lots of resources for the WJEC specification as well as useful links.

School Sociology

www.barrycomp.com/bhs/index.htm

This site is run by Barry Comprehensive School, originally for the OCR specification but now for WJEC. 'Duffers' guides', revision materials and self-support pages are all included.

Other sociology sites

These sites are not designed specifically for A-level and may therefore include material that is more advanced than you need for most A-level work. However, they can still be very useful for students looking to extend themselves further.

Allyn and Bacon Sociology Links

www.fsu.edu/~crimdo/soclinks/soclinks.html

This is an American site with links arranged by topic area to a wide range of sites of interest to sociologists. One of the most complete listings of useful material.

Intute Sociology

www.intute.ac.uk/socialsciences

Edited by the University of Surrey, with wide-ranging links.

Socioweb

www.socioweb.com

Quite an advanced academic site but with links to a wealth of sociological material.

The British Sociological Association (BSA)

www.britsoc.co.uk

The site of the main UK academic organization for sociologists, it provides an interesting introduction to the subject and is excellent for anybody thinking of studying at undergraduate level: it lists the HE institutions which offer sociology and gives information on their courses.

Exam boards

Every student should familiarize themselves with the site for the exam board whose specification they are following. The specification itself is obviously vital, but even more important for revision purposes are the past papers, mark schemes and examiners' reports, which all help you to know what is expected of you in the exams and increase your chances of getting high grades.

AQA
www.aqa.org.uk/index.php

OCR
www.ocr.org.uk/index.html

WJEC
www.wjec.co.uk

News and media sites

As a sociology student you should, of course, try to keep up with events in the real world, and use them where appropriate in your answers. The BBC and all the serious newspapers are useful, with *The Independent, The Guardian* and *The Observer* offering, arguably, the most articles of sociological interest. It is well worth searching the archives for articles relevant to topics you are studying, such as education, families, crime and deviance, politics.

The Independent
www.independent.co.uk

The Guardian
www.guardian.co.uk

The Observer
http://observer.guardian.co.uk

The BBC
www.bbc.co.uk

The Times/Sunday Times
www.timesonline.co.uk/tol/news

The Telegraph
www.telegraph.co.uk

Statistical and research data

These sites are important for staying up to date on the latest trends which are of interest to sociologists, and they provide information which is more contemporary than in textbooks. Government statistics are relevant to many topics; the Joseph Rowntree Foundation is the leading research body on poverty, welfare and related issues; The Sutton Trust on educational inequality and opportunity. The IFS (Institute for Fiscal Studies) covers economic issues – particularly income and wealth, and the Equality and Human Rights Commission researches issues related to race, gender and disability. Amnesty International, the human rights organisation, raises many issues which sociology students should be interested in, for example concerning state crime and world sociology.

UK National Statistics
www.statistics.gov.uk

Sutton Trust
www.suttontrust.com/index.asp

Joseph Rowntree Foundation
www.jrf.org.uk

Institute for Fiscal Studies
www.ifs.org.uk

Equality and Human Rights Commission
www.equalityhumanrights.com

Amnesty International
www.amnesty.org.uk

INDEX

A

Abbott, P & Wallace, C 36, 215
Abbott, Pamela 16, 226-7
Aboriginal societies 79
Abraham, J 56
absolute poverty 111
academies 51
Acheson Report 38, 154
achieved status 4, 13, 27, 47
achievement *see* education, attainment
Ackernecht, E A 150
Ackers, P 184
Adkins, Lisa 16
Adler, F 193
administrative criminology 189, 196
affluent worker studies 10
African Caribbean communities 16, 76, 77, 100, 157; and crime 190, 191; educational achievement 57-9
age 17-18; and crime 194-5; effect of ageing population on society 38; and identity 102; and media representation 170-71; and religiosity 77; strata 71
ageism 18
Ahmad, W I U 156
Al Qaeda 81
Alcock, P 115, 117, 119, 123
alienation 69-70
Allan, G 36
Allan, G & Crow, G 31, 36
Allen, H 192
Almond, B 36
Almond, B, Appleby, R S and Sivan, E 81
alternative medicine 154
Alvesson, M 215
America *see* United States of America
Amnesty International 34, 134
Anderson, M 27, 213, 216
Ang, I 169
Annandale, Ellen 151

anomie 179, 195, 225
Ansley 28
anti-capitalism 139-40
anti-globalization 139-40
Arber, Sara 18
Archer, L 59
Archer, M S 230
Aries, Phillippe 34
Armstrong, D 156
Armstrong, Karen 70, 81
arranged marriage 32
arrests 191
arson 190
artefact explanation of illness 154, 155
ASBOs (anti-social behaviour orders) 188, 189
ascribed status 4, 13, 27, 47
Asian communities 100, 157, 170; crime 190, 191; educational achievement 57-8; families 32; health issues 156; *see also* Bangladeshis, Indians, Pakistanis, South Asians
asylum seekers 115, 134
Atkinson, J 213, 197, 230
Atlee, Clement 121
attainment *see* education, attainment
audiences, and media 167-8
authority 132, 133

B

baby boomers 38
Back, Les 100
Badawi, L 70
Baechler 197
Bagdikian, B 165
Bakx, K 154
Ball, Stephen J 50, 53; Beachside Comprehensive 54
Ballard, Roger 32
banding of pupils 54
Bandura, A 167
Bangladeshi communities 16, 17, 76-7; and crime 192; educational achievement 57-9;

families 32; *see also* Asian communities, South Asians
Bara, J & Budge, I 141
Barber, Bernard 8
Barker, Eileen 214
Barlow 35
Barrett, M 78
Barron, R D & Norris, G M 16
Barrow, Jocelyn 32
Barry, B 118
Bartholomew, James 123, 232
Bartle, J & Laycock, S 141
Bartlett, W & Le Grand, J 50
Baudrillard, Jean 138, 168, 231
Baumann, Zygmunt 81-2, 101
Beachside Comprehensive (Ball) 54
Beck, Ulrich 14, 57, 183
Beck, Ulrich & Beck-Gernsheim, Elisabeth 30, 35, 37
Becker, M H 152, 183-4, 194, 211
Beckford, James 74, 82, 83
bedroom culture 95
Beechey, Veronica 16
beliefs *see* religion
benefits system *see* welfare benefits
Bennett, A 95
Bennett, A & Kahn-Harris, K 95
Benston, Margaret 28, 84, 227
Benzeval, M 117
Bernades, John 35
Bernard, J 10
Bernstein, Basil 52-3
Berthoud, R & Beishon, S 32
Berthoud, R & Gershuny, R 212
Best, L 214
Beuf, A 169
Beveridge Report 121
Bhaskar, R 216
Bhatti, Ghazala 32
Bhopal, India 182, 183
Bierstedt, Robert 83, 217
Bin Laden, Osama 81

biomedical model of health 85, 151, 152-3, 154
Bird, John 77
Birmingham Centre for Contemporary Cultural Studies (CCCS) 94, 95, 194
birth rates 35, 37
Black African families 32
Black Caribbean families 32
black communities 16, 26; crime 192; underclass 17
black culture 100; educational achievement 57-9; masculinity 58-9; subcultures 94
black feminism 15, 84, 101, 228
Black Muslim sect 74
Black Report 154
black women, and the labour market 16, 17
Blackburn, R M & Mann, M 11
Blackledge, D & Hunt, B 48
Blackman, S 117
Blackstone, T & Mortimore, J 52
Blaikie, Andrew 18, 38
Blair, Tony *see* Labour Government
Blanden, J 13
Blaxter, M 150, 153
Blumer, Herbert 207, 229
Blumler, J & Gurevitch, M 165
body, the 156, 169
Borderless World 137
Bottoms, A 195
Bourdieu, Pierre 12, 53, 98, 156
bourgeoisie 2, 5, 8, 83, 110, 226; embourgeoisement 10; *see also* middle classes
Bowles, S & Gintis, A 47-8, 83
Bowling, B & Phillips, C 191, 192
Box, S 180, 182, 192, 213
Boyd-Barrett, O 167
Bradley, H 14, 101
Braithwaite, J & Drahos, P 183

Branch Davidian sect 72, 74
Brannen, J 30
Brantingham, P J & Brantingham, P L 195-6
Braverman, H 8, 9
Breen, R 13
Brewer, R M 228
Brierley, P 76, 77, 78
British Crime Survey 181-2, 192
British Social Attitudes Survey 35, 36
Britten, N & Heath, A 13
Broadcasting Standards Commission 169, 171
Brooks, A 228
Brown, C & Gay, P 17, 207
Brown, G W & Harris, T O 157
Brown, Gordon *see* Labour Government
Brown, M 31
Brown, P 48, 157
Bruce, S 70, 72, 74, 76, 77, 78, 79, 80, 81, 82, 83
Bryman, A 209-210, 214
Bryson, V 84
Buchanan, J & Tullock, G 49
Buckingham, D 167, 171
Buckle, A & Farrington, D P 192
Budge, I 141
budget standard, and poverty 111-2
Burchardt, T 113, 118
Burgess, E W 195
Burghes, L & Brown, M 31
Bury, M 151
business elite 134-5
Butler, D & Rose, R 140
Butler, D & Stokes, D 140
Byrne, D 113, 118

C

Calhoun, C 29
Callahan, S 27
Callender, C & Jackson, J 54
Callinicos, A 139-40
Campbell, R & Lovenduski, J 141
cannabis use 184
Cant, S & Sharma, U 154
capitalism 1-2, 5, 28, 110, 136, 152; anti-capitalism 139-40; spirit of 71-2; and the welfare state 122

capitalist schooling 47
Carlen, P 192, 193
Carpenter, M 153-4
Carricaburu, D & Pierret, J 151
Carspecken, P 217
Casanova, J 32, 78, 80
case studies (research methodology) 209-10
Cashmore, E E 32
Castles, S & Kosack, G C 17
Catholic Church *see* Roman Catholic Church
causal relationships 207
CCCS (Birmingham Centre for Contemporary Cultural Studies) 94, 95, 194
Chambliss, W J 183, 185
Chandler, J 35
Charlesworth, Simon 12
Charlton, J I 157
Charmaz, K 156
Chester, R 32
child mortality 34, 37
Child Poverty Action Group 113
childhood 34-5
children, oppression of 18
Chinese communities 16, 76
chivalry thesis 192
Chomsky, Noam 136-7
Christianity 78; New Christian Right 70, 86
chronic illness 150, 151
Chryssides, G 77, 79
Chubb, J & Moe, T 49
church attendance 77-8
Church of England 70, 77
Cicourel, A V 184-5, 194, 208, 213
circumcision, female (female genital mutilation) 70
civil partnerships 37
Cixous, H 228, 231
Clancy, A 192
Clapp, R 155
Clark & Goodman 117
Clarke, H 141
class *see* social class
class consciousness 5, 11, 14
class culture 12
class identities 12
classification 208
clinical gaze 156
Cloward, R A & Ohlin, L E 180
club culture 95
Coard, B 58
coercion 132

cognitive maps 195-6
cohabitation 35, 37
Cohen, A K 194
Cohen, Albert 180
Cohen, L E & Felson, M 195
Cohen, R & Rai, S M 139
Cohen, Robin 100
Cohen, S 183
cohort 18
Colley, A 56
Collier, R 196
commodification 97
communication 164-71
communism 2, 6, 69, 110, 135, 226
Compaine, B 166
comparative method 207
compensatory education 53
complementary medicine 154
Comte, Auguste 206, 217
confidentiality in research 208
conflict, and religion 81
conflict perspectives 2, 47-8, 213, 225, 226
conjugal roles 10, 33
Connolly, P 59
Connor, H 57
Conrad, P & Schneider, J 153
consent, informed 208
Conservative Party 140, 141, 142, 232; *see also* John Major, Margaret Thatcher
consumer culture 76, 80, 82, 83, 97, 99, 171
consumerism, and identity 102
content analysis 213-4
Coontz, S & Henderson, P 227
Cooper, D 28
corporate crime 182-3
correlations 207
Cottle, S 169
counterculture 75
counter-school culture 48
Cracknell, D 135
Craik, J 102
credit crunch 109-10
Crewe, I 11, 142
Crewe, I & Thompson, K 141
Criddle, B 135
crime 116, 178-9; and age 194-5; cultural criminology 189-90; ethnicity 190-92; functionalist perspective 179; interactionist theories 183-4; left realist perspective 186-8; and

locality 195-6; Marxist persepective 185; and masculinities 193; neo-Marxist perspective 185-6; official statistics 181-3; phenomenological perspective 184-5; and postmodernism 196; rates 181; right realist perspective 188-9; and social class 193-4; structural theories 180; subcultural theories 180; and the underclass 180-81; and women 192-3; youth offenders 194
Critcher, C 171
critical social science 215, 232
Croall, H 181, 190
Crompton, R 16
Crompton, R & Jones, G 9
Crook, S 97, 139, 231
Croteau, D & Hoynes, W 168
Crouch, C 142, 232
cults 72, 73-4, 79
cultural capital 12, 53, 98
cultural criminology 189-90, 196
cultural deprivation 52, 53
cultural hegemony 166, 169
culture 1, 92-4; consumer 76, 80, 82, 83, 97, 99; global 96; and intelligence 52; mass 95-6
culture of dependency 115, 118, 120, 121, 123
culture of necessity 12
culture of poverty 116
Cumberbatch, G & Negrine, R 171
Cumming, E & Henry, W E 18
Curtice, J & Park, A 141

D

Dahl, R A 133
Dahrendorf, R 11
Dail, P W 170
Darwin, Charles 85, 216
Davie, G 80
Davies, Kath 169
Davis, K & Moore, W E 5, 47, 110
Day, R & Day, J 152
de Beauvoir, Simone 70
dealignment 140-42

Dean, H & Taylor-Gooby, P 12, 116
death rates *see* mortality
deindustrialization 10
delinquency *see* crime
Delphy, C & Leonard, D 28
Democratic Unionist Party, Northern Ireland 79
demography 37-8, 213
Dench, G, Gavron, K & Young, M 32
denominations, religious 72, 74
Denver, D 141
Department for Work and Pensions (DWP) 114
dependency culture 115, 118, 120, 121, 123
deprivation index 112
desacrilization 80
Desai, P 191
deskilling 8, 9
deviance *see* crime
Devine, F 10, 11
difference feminists 2, 29, 33
direct action 134, 139
disability 18, 156-7; and media representation 171; and poverty 115
discourse analysis 84, 166
discrimination *see* racism
disease *see* health
disengagement: of churches 78; of older people from society 18
Disney 82
dissolute living 115
divorce 35, 36
doctors *see* medical profession
domestic violence 188
Dorais, M 197
Douglas, J D 197, 209
Douglas, J W B 52, 212
Downes, D & Rock, P 191
Doyal, L 152
Doyal, L & Pennell, I 151, 155
Doyle, A 168
Drane, J 75
dual labour market 11, 16
Duncombe, J & Marsden, D 33
Dunne, G A 33
Durkheim, Emile 2, 119, 206, 217, 225, 230; and crime 179, 195; and culture 93-4; and education 46-7; and

religion 68-9, 77, 79; on suicide 196-7, 207, 213

E

Eagleton, Terry
economic crises 6, 140
economic growth, and education 49
Edgell, S 33
education 46, 122; ability grouping 54-5; attainment 51-4; compensatory 53; conflict perspectives 47-8; and economic growth 49; the education market 50, 53; functionalist perspectives on 46-7; further education 51; and gender 55-7, 99; hidden curriculum 47-8, 98; higher education 49, 51, 53-4, 117; the interactionist perspective 54-5; Labour policies 49, 50-51, 232; market liberal perspectives 49-50, 51; pupil subcultures 55; social democratic perspectives 48-9, 50-51
Education Action Zones 51, 53, 122
Education Maintenance Allowances 51
Education Reform Act (1998) 49
Edwards, P K & Scullion, H 210
egoism 195, 225
Ehrenreich, B & Ehrenreich, J 8
Ehrenreich, B & English, D 152, 153
Eisenberg, L 150, 154
El Saadawi, N 70
elite theory 7, 134-5
embourgeoisement 10
employment: and class 6-12; and gender 15-16; unemployment 113, 116
Engels, Friedrich 28, 83, 135, 227
environment, and intelligence 51
environmental crime 183
Equal Opportunities Report (2006) 15
Equal Pay Act (1970) 15

equality of opportunity 5, 13, 179; within marriage 33-4
Equality Act (2006) 15
Ernst, E & White, A 154
ESN *see* special schools
ESRC (Economic and Social Research Council) 208
Estrada, E 170
ethics, in research 207, 208
ethnicity: and age 18; and crime 182, 190-92; and educational achievement 57-59; and family diversity 32; and health 156; and identity 100, 101-2; and inequality 14, 16-17; and media representation 169-70; and mental illness 157; and poverty 115; and religion 76-7, 79; and voting patterns 141
ethnography 211, 215
evolution 85, 216
Excellence in Cities programme 51, 53, 117
experiments 207
extended families *see* families

F

Fairclough, N 166
false class consciousness 2, 5, 69, 94, 226
families 26-7, 47; changing functions of 32-3; childhood 34-5; conjugal roles 33-4; demography 37-8; diversity 30-32; diversity and ethnicity 32; feminist perspective on 28-9; functionalist perspective on 27; historical development of 30; Labour policies 37; low income 113; marriage and marital breakdown 35-6; Marxist perspective on 28; and modernity 29-30; postmodern perspective on 29: and social policy 36-7
Featherstone, M 93, 156
Featherstone, M & Hepworth, M 18, 34, 170, 231

Feinstein, L 52
Felson, M 195
female circumcision (female genital mutilation) 70
female underachievement 55-6
feminism 2, 98, 115, 226-8, 232; and age 18; black 15, 84, 101, 228; and the family 33, 37; and health 152; and ideology 84; liberal 15, 227-8; postmodern 228; radical 15, 16, 84, 227; and religion 70-71; research methodology 208, 210, 211, 215; socialist 15, 227; and socialization 98-9; and welfare provision 120, 121, 122, 124: *see also* gender, women.
Fernando, S 157
Ferrell, Jeff 189
Ferri, E & Smith, K 33
fertility rates 35, 37
field experiments 207
Fieldhouse, E & Cutts, D 141
financial elite 134-5
Finkelstein, V 156
Finn, D 50
Firestone, S 15, 227
Fiske, J 167
five-class model 140
Flaherty, J 114, 115
Fletcher, D 169
Fletcher, R 33, 36
focus groups 211
folk culture 92, 97
folk medicine 154
Fordism, post-Fordist theory 16, 118
Foucault, M 96, 156, 157
Fourth Age 18, 38
Fox Harding, L 36
Francis, B 56
Francis, B & Skelton, C 56, 57
Fraser, D 122
Fraser, Nancy 138
Freud, S 99
Freund, P E S & McGuire, M B 152
Friedson, E 151, 153, 154
Fruch & McGhee 169
Fuller, M 54
functionalism 2, 3, 224-5; and age 18; and crime 179; and education 46-7; and families 33, 36; and illness 151; and the professions 7; and religion 68-9, 71;

and social stratification 4-5; and socialization 98; and the state 133
fundamentalism 71, 78, 81, 83
funding of research 208
further education 51

G

Gaine, C & George, R 53
Gallie, D 11
Galtung, J & Ruge, M 166-7
gang culture 59, 180
Gannon, L R 18, 38
Gans, H J 96
Garnett, M 133
Gauntlett, D 169
gay and lesbian households 27, 31
gender: and crime 192-3; and educational achievement 55-7; and employment 15-16; and identity 101, 102; and illness 155; and inequality 14, 15, 227; and media representation 168-9, 171; and mental illness 157; and poverty 115; and religion 70-71, 76; and social class 12, 13-14; and social mobility 13; and socialization 98-9; stereotyping 16, 169; and subcultures 95; and voting patterns 141: see also feminism, women.
generation 17
genes, and intelligence 52
George, V & Wilding, P 121
Gershuny, J 33
Ghail, M Mac an 55, 58
ghetto poor 17
Gibbs, J & Martin, W 197
Gibson, C 36
Giddens, Anthony 1, 3, 9, 11, 17, 18, 29, 35, 82-3, 93, 123-4, 137-8, 139, 156, 230, 232
Giles, C & Johnson, P 117
Giles, C & Webb, S 113
Gillborn, D & Mirza, H S 58
Gillborn, D & Youdell, D 52, 55, 58
Gillespie, M 170, 171
Gilroy, Paul 190
Ginsburg, N 117, 122

Glasgow Media Group (GMG) 166, 170, 214
Glass, D V 13
Glennon, L M & Butsch, R 170
global culture 93, 96
globalization 7, 14, 71, 83, 100, 118, 137-8, 139, 165, 189, 232; anti-globalization 139-40
'glocal' crime 189
Glock, C Y & Stark, R 81
GNVQ (General National Vocational Qualifications) 49, 50
Goffman, E 99, 157
Goldthorpe, J H 9, 10, 11, 13-14
Goldthorpe, J H & Payne, C 13
Gomm, R 85, 157, 216
Google 165
Gordon, D M 185, 185
Gordon, David 112, 210
Gordon, L 48
Gosling 16
Gough, Kathleen 26, 209
Gouldner, A W 217, 225, 232
Gove, W 157
Graham, H 155
Graham, H & Blackburn, C 155
Graham, H & Oakley, A 152
Graham, J & Bowling, B 182, 192, 194
Gramsci, A 28, 83, 98, 136, 226
Grant, W 134
Grant, W & Marsh, D 133
Gray, A 169, 170
Greeley, A 79
green crime 183
Greer, Germaine 28, 84
group interviews 211
Gunter, B & McAleer, J 170, 171

H

habitus 12, 53
Hakim, C 15-16
Halbwachs, M 197
Hall, P 157
Hall, Stuart 99-100, 166, 190-91
Hallsworth, S 138-9
Halsey, A H 48
Halsey, A H & Floud, J 48
Halsey, M & White, R 183
Hamilton, M 68, 69
Hammersley, M 214

Hammersley, M & Gomm, R 211
Handel, G 93, 98
Hardill, I, Green, A & Owen, D W 33
Hargreaves, D H 47, 55
Harnett, A 171
Hart, N 151
Hartmann, H 227
Hartmann, P & Husband, C 170
Harvey, D 231
Harvey, L 215
Haug, M 153
Hawthorne effect 207
health 150-57
health belief model 152
Heath & Evans 141
Heath, A 13, 117, 140
Hebdige, D 94-5, 171
Heelas, P 75, 76, 77, 79, 82, 83, 208
Heelas, P & Seel, B 80
Heidensohn, F 192, 193
Held, D & McGrew, A 138
Helman, C G 157
Herberg, W 80
Hermes, J 169
Hernstein, R & Murray, C A 52
Hewitt, C J 133
hidden curriculum in education 47, 48, 98
high culture 92, 97
higher education 49, 51, 53-4, 117
Hill, Michael 120-21, 123
Hills, J 117, 118
Hills, J & Stewart, K 124
Hindess, B 197
Hinduism 70, 77
Hirschi, Travis 195
Hirst, P & Thompson, G 137
Hispanics 17
historical data sources 213
HIV/Aids 171
Hobbs, D & Dunningham, C 189, 194
Hobson, D 167
Hockey, J & James, A 18, 38
Hodkinson, P 95, 194
Holm, Jean 70-71
Hood, R 191
housing, council 123
Houston, D M & Marks, G 16
Howard, M 112
Howlett, B C 150
Hughes, G 187
human capital theory 15
human rights abuses 183
Hunt, S 18

Huntingdon, S P 81
Husserl, Edmund 229
hypodermic model (of media) 167, 169, 170, 171
hysteria 150

I

iatrogenesis 153
ICT (information and communications technology) 164
identity 1, 93, 99-102
ideology 83; and feminism 84; and Marxism 83; and neo-Marxism 83-4; and postmodernism 84-5; and science 85
illegitimacy 116
Illich, Ivan 8, 153
illness see health
Illsley, R 154, 155
in-depth interviews 207
income 6-7, 108-9; see also wealth
Indian communities 16; families 26; see also Asian communities, South Asians
individualization 14, 30, 35, 37
Industrial Revolution 1
industrial societies 1-2, 30
industrialization 1
inequality 1; and ethnicity 14, 16-17; and gender 14, 15, 227; in health 154-6; in marriage 33; and poverty 111; social 14-15
infant mortality see child mortality
informed consent 208
Institute for Fiscal Studies (IFS) 109
intelligence, and education 51-2
interactionist perspectives 2-3, 101; on age 18; on crime 183-4; on education 54; on illness 151-2
interactive media see media
interest groups 133
interpersonal media see media
interpretative approach (qualitative research) 207
interpretative model (of media) 167

interviews 211
IQ 52, 54, 55
Iran 71
Iraq War 165, 168
Ireson, J 55
Islam 70, 72, 81, 170;
  Islamophobia 84;
  see also Muslims
Israel, M & Hay, I 208
Ivory, J D 168

J

Jackson, C 57
Jackson, S & Scott, S 17
Jamous, H & Peloille, B 153
Jefferson, T 94, 193, 194
Jehovah's Witnesses 73
Jencks, C 92
Jenkins, R 99, 101
Jenks, C 35
Jessop, B 136
Jewson, N 37-8
Johnson, D 36
Johnson, T J 8
Johnstone, R 141
Jones, S 184, 185, 187, 189
Jordan, B 116
Joseph Rowntree Foundation 116
Judaism 70

K

Kaplan, A 216
Katz, E & Lazarsfeld, P 165, 167
Katz, J 102, 190
Kautsky, K 72
Kavanagh, D & Butler, D 141
Keat, R & Urry, J 217
Keddie, N 54
Kellner, P & Wilby, P 13
Kempson, E 116
Kendal Project 79
Kepel, G 77, 80
Kerr, C 10
King, Martin Luther 72
Kinsey, R 187
Klein, Naomi 140
Kuhn, Thomas 85, 216

L

La Pierre, R T 210
labelling theory 183-4,
  194, 207; mental
  illness 157; pupils 54,
  58
Labour Force Survey 16
Labour Government 133,

188, 232; action on
  poverty 117, 119;
  composition of 135;
  education policies
  50-51, 232; family
  policies 37; 'Third
  Way' 123-4; and the
  welfare state 124
labour market: dual 11,
  16; and ethnic
  minorities 17; and
  poverty 117-8
Labour Party 140, 141,
  186
Labov, W 211
laddish behaviour 48, 57,
  98
Lader, D 33
Lansley, Stewart 7, 109
Laslett, P 18, 27, 213
Lauder, H 50
Laurie, H & Gershuny, J 33
Lawler, S 12
Lawrence, Stephen 190,
  191
Lawson, R 113
Lea, J 196
Lea, J & Young, J 186,
  190
Leach, E 30, 36
league tables (schools)
  49, 50
Learning to Labour
  (Willis) 48
Lee, D & Newby, H 1-2,
  229
left realist perspective
  232; on crime 185,
  186-8, 194
leisure 102
Lemert, E M 184
Lerner, A 168
lesbian households 27,
  29, 31, 33
L'Esperance, J 150
Levin, H M & Belfield,
  C R 50
Levitas, R 114-15, 119
Lewis, L 169
Lewis, Oscar 116
liberal democracy 2
liberal feminism 15,
  169, 227-8; and the
  family 28-9; and
  health 152
liberation theology 70,
  72, 76
life chances 4, 6
life course 34
life cycle 34
life documents 213
life expectancy *see*
  mortality
life histories 210
lifestyle choices 14, 35,
  84

Lincoln, S 95
Ling, R 102
linguistics 96
Lister, R 115
Livingstone, S & Bovill, M
  169
Lobban, G 214
lobby system 165
Lobstein, T 155
locality, and crime 195-6
Lockwood, David 9, 10,
  225
Lombroso, C 193
London Underground,
  suicides on 197
lone parenthood *see* single
  parents
longitudinal research 211
Longmore, F 171
Lovering, J 16
low income families 113
lower middle class *see*
  middle class
lower strata 11-12
Lukes, Steven 132, 134
Luton, affluent worker
  studies 10
Lynch, M 216
Lynch, M & Stretsky, P
  183
Lyng, S 190, 194
Lyon, David 82
Lyotard, Jean-Francois 3,
  84, 85, 138, 215, 230-
  31

M

McCuire 72
Macdonald, D 95
Macdonald, K 8
McDonough, F 101
McDowell, L 16
McGlone, F 30
McIntosh, M 31
MacIntyre, S 155
Mack, Joanna & Lansley,
  Stewart 112-3
McKeown, T 38, 152-3
McKinley, J & Arches, J
  153
McKnight, A 51, 117
McLanahan, S & Booth, K
  32
McLaughlin, E 183
Macpherson Inquiry 190,
  191
McQuail, D 167
McRobbie, A 95, 102,
  169
McRobbie, A & Thornton,
  S 171
Maduro, O 70, 76
Maguire, M 181
Major, John 37, 49, 118;
  see also Conservative

Party, Margaret
  Thatcher
male underachievement
  55, 57
'malestream' 2, 215, 226-7,
  228
Malik, S 169
Malinowski, Bronislaw 69
Mann, M 11, 138
marginalization 186-7
marital breakdown 35-6
market forces, and crime
  189
market liberal
  perspectives 49; on
  education 49-50; on
  social stratification 5;
  on welfare 120, 121,
  122-3, 124
marketization 54
marriage 35-6; arranged
  32; conjugal roles 10,
  33-4
Marsh, D 134
Marshall, G 9, 10, 11, 14,
  72, 101, 210
Marshall, G & Swift, A 5
Marsland, David 115-6,
  121, 232
Martin, D 78, 80, 155
Marxism 2, 3, 217, 224,
  225-6, 230; and crime
  185, 194; and culture
  and identity 94; and
  ethnic inequalities 17;
  and the family 28, 37;
  and feminism 227;
  and ideology 83; and
  illness 153; and lower
  middle classes 9; and
  the media 165-6; and
  the middle class 7-8;
  and poverty 118, 119;
  and power 133; and
  religion 69, 71; and
  social stratification
  5-6; and socialization
  98; and the state
  135-6; and the upper
  class 7; and wealth
  109, 110; and welfare
  provision 120, 121,
  122: *see also* neo-
  Marxism
masculinities 196; black
  58-9; and crime 193
mass culture 93, 95-6
mass media *see* media
matrifocal families 26
Matthews, R 189
Matza, D 180, 189, 194,
  195, 211
Mawby, R I & Batta, I D
  191
Mead, George Herbert
  229
Mead, M 99

media 164; audiences 167-8; content analysis 213-4; ownership 165; and social groups 168-71; structure and content 164-7
media literacy 167, 170
medical profession 153-4
medicalization 153
medicine *see* health
Meldrumm, M 155
mental ill health 154, 157
meritocracy 5, 47-8
Merton, Robert 167, 225, 179, 180, 181, 193-4
Messerschmidt, James W 193
metanarratives 29, 82, 84, 97, 138, 230
Methodism 73, 74
methodology 216; critical social science 215; feminist 215; postmodern 215-6; primary sources 208-12; qualitative 206, 207-8, 214; quantitative 206-7, 214; research process 208; secondary sources 212-4; triangulation 214; and values 217
middle classes 1, 7-10, 53; *see also* bourgeoisie
Mies, M 210
migrant workers 17
Miles, A 157
Miles, I & Irvine, J 213
Miliband, R 135
Millar, J & Glendinning, C 155
Miller, A S & Hoffman, J P 76
Millerson, G L 153
Millett, K 84, 227
Mills, C W 230
Mingione, Enzo 118
minimum wage 124
Mirza, H 17, 58, 84
Mitsos, E & Browne, K 56
mixed ability teaching 54
mobility *see* social mobility
modernity 14, 97; and families 29-30; and modern theory 231-2; and postmodernity 230-31
Modood, T 57, 76, 77, 100
Moir, A & Jessel, D 193
money, control over 33
monotheism 70
Mooney, J 181
morbidity 154
Morgan, D H J 27, 28

Morgan, P 35, 37
Morley, D 168, 214
mortality 37-8, 151, 154; of children 34
Moynihan, R & Smith, R 153
mugging 190-91
Muggleton, D 95
multi-stage sampling 209
multiple deprivation 111
Multiple Risk Factor Intervention Trial 155
multivariate analysis 206, 210
Murdoch, Rupert 165
Murdock, George Peter 26, 27
Murray, Charles 11, 17, 31, 36, 115, 116-7, 119, 180, 181, 194
Muslims 77, 78, 101, 141, 168; Black Muslim sect 74; and education 59 *see also* Islam

N

National Child Development Study (NCDS) 13
National Curriculum 48, 49, 56
National Health Service 121, 150-51
National Insurance 121
National Vocational Qualifications (NVQs) 51
nationalism, and identity 100-102
Navarro, V 151, 153
Nazroo, D Y 18, 157
necessity, culture of 12
Neibuhr, H R 73, 75
Nelken, D 182
Nelson, G K 72
neo-Marxism 226; and crime 185-6; and culture 94; and ideology 83-4; and the media 166; and socialization 98; and the state 136 *see also* Marxism
neo-tribes 95
Nettleton, S 156
network media *see* media
New Age movement 75-6, 79-80, 82, 208
New Christian Right 70, 86
New Criminology, The (Taylor et al.) 179, 180, 184, 185, 186

New Deal for Young People 51
New Labour *see* Labour Government
new media 164, 169
new reproductive technologies 27, 31
New Right 115-6, 232; and educational reform 49; perspective on the family 30, 36-7; perspective on social stratification 5; perspective on upper class 7; perspective on welfare provision 120, 121, 122-3; policies on poverty 118
new social movements 138-40
Newburn, T 194
Nicholas, S 181
Nichols, Theo 213
Nicholson, L 29
Nolan, B & Whelan, C T 113
Norman, F 55-6
norms 1
Norris, P 141
Norris, P & Wlezien, C 141
Northern Ireland 72; Democratic Unionist Party 79
nuclear families *see* families

O

Oakley, Ann 18, 33, 99, 208, 215
observation (research method) 211-2
occupational structure, changes in 6-7
official statistics 213; and crime 181-3
Ohmae, K 137
Oliver, M 156
opinion leaders 167
Oppenheim, C 118
opportunity, equality of 5, 13, 179
opportunity theory 195
Orientalism 84
Ortner, S B 227
Oxford Mobility Study 13

P

paedophiles 171
Page, R M 119, 121
Page, Robert 124
Pahl, R 33
Paisley, Ian 79

Pakistani communities 16, 17, 77; educational achievement 57-9; families 32: *see also* Asian communities, South Asians
Pakulski, J & Waters, M 14, 84, 231
paradigms 85, 216
parental choice in education 50, 53
Pareto, V 134
Park, A 30, 31
Parkin, F 13
Parry, N & Parry, J 8
Parsons, T & Bales, R F 1
Parsons, Talcott 2, 4-5, 225; on education 47; on the family 27, 33, 36; on illness 151, 153; on power 133; on religion 69, 71, 78; on socialization 98
participant intervention 207
participant observation 211-2, 217
Paterson, K 155
patriarchy 2, 16, 70, 84, 152, 169, 193226
Pawson, R 214, 215
Payne, G 12
Pearce, F 185
Pearson, G 170, 194
Pearson, M 156
Penn, R 11
personal service workers 6, 9, 15
Pervalin, D J & Rose, D 155
petty bourgeoisie *see* bourgeoisie
phenomenology 3, 208, 213, 216, 229-30; perspective on crime 184-5
Phillips, C & Bowling, B 190, 191-2
Phillips, D L 217
Philo, G 157, 165
Philo, G & Miller, D 85, 166, 231
Piachaud, D 112
Piachaud, D & Sutherland, H 117
Pierson, C 121, 122, 123, 124
Pilcher, J 18, 34
Pilgrim, D & Rogers, A 157
Pilkington, A 17, 100
pilot studies 210
Pitcher 34
Plummer, K 184, 210, 213
pluralism 7; religious 79, 82

pluralist perspectives: on the media 164-5; on the state 133-4
policing 187, 190
political economy perspective on illness 151
political parties 133
politics and power 132-42
Pollak, Otto 192
Pollert, A 228
Poor Law 120-21
Popay, J & Bartley, M 155
Popper, Karl 85, 216
popular culture 93
positive discrimination 53
positivism 3, 85, 196, 206-7, 216
post-Fordism 16, 118
postindustrialism 142
Postman, N 34, 35
postmodernism 2, 3, 97, 210, 224, 230-31; and age 18; and complementary medicine 154; and criminology 185, 196;and the family 29, 33, 37; and feminism 228; and identity 93, 95, 98; and ideology 84-5; and illness 151; and the media 166, 168; and power 138; and religion 80, 81-3; and research methodology 215-6; and science 85
postmodernization 139
poststructuralism 96
Poulantzas, N 122, 135
Pound, P 151
poverty 38, 111-3; conflict theories of 117-8; cultural theories of 115-6; government policies 118-9; social distribution of 114-5; and social exclusion 113-4, 113-4; and the underclass 116-7; welfare state 119-24
Power Inquiry 142
power and politics 132-42
preindustrial societies 1, 30
premodern societies 1
Presdee, M 190, 194
pressure groups 120, 133
primary deviance 184
primary labour market 16
primary schools, racism in 58

primary socialization 1, 27
primary sources 208-12
private sector welfare providers 120
private sphere 138, 139
professions 8, 134, 8, 134
proletarianization thesis 9
proletariat 2, 5, 10, 110, 226
Protestant ethic 71-2, 207, 229
Prout, A 35
public sphere 138
Putnam, R 155

Q

Quakerism 70
qualitative methodology 206, 207-8, 214
quantitative methodology 206-7, 214
questionnaires 210-11
quota sampling 209

R

race see ethnicity
racism 115; and the criminal justice system 191; and education 57-8; and employment 16; institutional 190; in the media 169-70
radical feminism 15, 16, 84, 169, 227; and the family 28; and health 152
Randall, G J 56
random sampling 209
Ranson, S 50
rape 182
Rapoport, Rhona & Rapoport, Robert 31, 32
Reay, D 53, 54
Reddington, H 95, 194
redistribution of income see income redistribution
reflexivity 14, 82-3, 215, 232
refugees 115
Reiner, R 179
relative deprivation 74, 112, 186, 188
relative poverty 111, 232
religion 68, 93; and age 77; and conflict 81; and ethnicity 76-7, 79; and feminism 70-71; functionalist perspectives on 68-9, 71; fundamentalism

and conflict 71, 78, 81, 83; and gender 70-71, 76; Marxist perspectives on 69-70, 71, 76, 77; New Age beliefs 75-6, 82; new religious movements 73-4; participation 76-77, 77-8; and postmodernity 81-2; religious organizations 72-5; and secularization 36, 71, 77-81; and social change 71-2; and social class 76
reproductive technologies, new 27, 31
research ethics 207, 208; funding 208; process 208
reserve army of labour 118, 122, 124, 227
retirement 113
retreatist subculture 179, 180
rewards system 5
Rex, J & Tomlinson, S 17
Reynolds, D 48
Reynolds, T 32
right realist perspective 232: on crime 188-9
risk society 14, 57, 183
Ritzer, G 229
Roberts, K 11, 12
Robertson, R 72
Rojek, C 102
roles 2; role allocation 5, 47
Roman Catholic Church 70, 72, 73, 77
Roof, W C & McKinney, W 80
Rose, D & Marshall, G 14
Rosenhan, D L 157
Rosenthal, R & Jacobson, L 54, 207
Ross, K 169, 170
routine activity theory 195
Rowbotham, S 227
Rowntree, Seebohm 111-2
RSI (Repetitive Strain Injury) 152
Ruggiero, V 187, 189
ruling class 2, 5, 165
Runciman, W G 12
Russell, A 141

S

Saggar, S & Heath, A 141
Said, E W 84
Saks, M 154
sampling 209

sanctions 178-9
Sanders, D 142
Sarlvik, B & Crewe, I 140, 141
Saunders, Peter 5, 7, 154-5
Saussure, F 96
Savage, M 8, 9, 10, 12
Savelsberg, J J 179
Sayer, A 216-7
Scambler, G 151, 152, 155
Scambler, G & Hopkins, A 157
Scharrer, E 169
Scheff, T 157
schizophrenia 157
science and ideology 85; and sociology 216-7
scientific revolutions 85, 216
Scientology 74
Scott, A 14
Scott, John 7, 214
Scraton, S 102
secondary deviance 184
secondary labour market 11, 16, 17
secondary sources 212-4
sects 72, 73-5, 79
secularization 36, 71, 76, 77-81
self-fulfilling prophecy 54, 184
self-report studies 181-2
semiology 94, 96
Sen, A K 151
separation (marital breakdown) 35
service class 9, 13
setting of pupils 50, 54
Seventh Day Adventists 75, 77
Sewell, T 58
Sex Discrimination Act (1975) 15
sex-role stereotyping see gender stereotyping
sexism 18
sexual harassment 16
sexual work 16
sexuality, and media representation 171
Sharma, U 154
Sharpe, Sue 37, 56
Shaw, C R & McKay, H D 195
Shaw, M 154, 155
Sheeran, Y 27
Shilling, C 156
shop-floor culture 48
Shorter, E 34
sick role 151
Sikhs 77
Sinclair, S 114, 119
single parents 31-2, 58-9, 114, 194

single-person households 31, 35
Situ, Y & Emmons, D 183
Skeggs, B 12
Skirrow, G 169
Sklair, Leslie 7, 96, 137
Skocpol, T 136
Sloane, Peter 15
Smart, Carol 192, 196
Smith, T & Noble, M 54
Snider, L 185
snowballing 209
social action theory 3, 224, 228-9, 230
social capital 12
social class 1; contemporary theories about 14-15; and crime 193-4; and educational achievement 51; and gender 12, 15-16; and identity 101; and religion 76; and voting patterns 141
social control 178-9; and religion 69-70
social democrats influence on government policy 122; perspectives on education 48-9, 50-51; perspectives on welfare provision 120, 121, 124
social differentiation 78
social exclusion 111, 112-3, 119
social inequality 4
social learning theory 167
social mobility 4, 10, 13; and gender 13
social model of disability 156
social policy and families 36-7; and left realism 188; and sociology 232
social science, critical 215
social stratification 4, 13-18; and age 17-18; changes in 6-7; functionalist perspective 4-5; market liberal perspective 5; Marxist perspective 5-6; social classes 7-12; Weber's perspective 6
social surveys 210
socialist feminism 15, 152, 227
socialization 1, 27, 47, 93, 98-9
societalization 79

sociological theory 224; conflict perspectives 225-8; conflict theory 226; feminism 226-8; functionalism 224-5; Marxism 225-8; modernity and modern theory 231-2; modernity and postmodernity 230-231; phenomenology 229-230; social action perspectives 228-9; sociology and social policy 232; symbolic interactionism 229
sociology and science 216-7; and social policy 232
Somerville, J 28-9, 32, 36
Sontag, S 170
Soothill, K & Walby, S 214
South Asians 32, 100
South Asians see also Asian communities, Bangladeshis, Indians, Pakistanis
South, N 180, 183
special needs pupils 50
special schools 58
speech patterns 52-3
Spencer, Herbert 115
Spicker, P 112
square of crime 187
Stacey, J 29
Stacey, M 210
Stanko, E A 16
Stanley, L & Wise, S 215
Stanworth, M 14, 56
Stark, W S & Bainbridge, W A 72, 74
state crime 183
state, the 133
state-centred theories of power 136
statistics 206; analysis 210
status 4, 6, 12, 13, 27, 47
Stein, S 214
stereotyping, gender 16, 169
Stewart, A 9
stigma, and disability 156-7
Stoker, G 142
'stop and search' 191
Storey, J 96
Strathdee, R 51
stratification, social see social stratification
stratified diffusion 30
streaming of pupils 50, 54-5
Streeter, M 182
Strinati, D 96, 97-8, 231

structural differentiation 78, 225
structuralism 96, 224, 230; and crime 180; and mental illness 157
structuration 230
structured interpretation model (of media) 167-8
subcultures 1, 4, 48, 55, 72; and crime 180, 186, 187, 193-4; and gender 95; and the media 167-8; youth 94-5, 98, 102, 171
subject class 5
suicide 196-7, 207, 208, 209, 213, 225, 230
Sure Start programme 51, 124
surrogate motherhood 31
surveys, social 210
Sutherland, Edwin 182
Sutton Trust 135
symbolic capital 12
symbolic interactionism 98, 207, 212, 213, 224, 229
symmetrical families 30

taxation 108-9, 117, 124
Taylor, I 179, 180, 184, 185, 186, 189
Taylor, L 179, 211
Taylor, S 197
Teddy boys 94
Tesh, S 152
testing (education) 49-50
Tham, H 180
Thatcher, Margaret 37, 49, 118: see also Conservative Party, John Major
third age 18, 38
Third Way 123-4, 142, 232
Thomas, W I & Znaniecki, F 210, 213
Thorne, B 99
Thornton, S 95
Titmuss, Richard 121-2
Todd, M J & Taylor, G 139
Tomlinson, S 51
Townsend, Peter 112, 118-9, 232
trade unionists, male 16
traditional medicine 152
Transcendental Meditation 74
transnational corporations (TNCs) 137, 140
triangulation 214
Troeltsch, E 73

Trowler, P 51, 55
Tuchman, G 169
tuition fees, higher education 54
Tumin, Melvin 5, 110
Turkle, S 168, 169
Turner, B S 151, 153, 156
Turner, J H & Maryanski, A 225
Tutu, Desmond 72
two-step flow model (of media) 167
Tyler, S A 215

U

underclass 11-12, 31, 36, 113, 115, 116-7; black 17; and crime 180-81, 194
Underground suicides 197
unemployment 113, 116, 189
United States of America: black underclass 17; media ownership 165; New Christian Right 70; secularization 78, 80
universities see higher education
unrecorded crime 181
Unschuld, P 38
upper class 1, 7
upper middle class see middle class
urbanism 2
Urry, J & Wakeford, J 136
USA see United States of America
uses and gratification model (of media) 167, 171

V

validity, of research 209, 210
value consensus 2, 4, 69, 179
values 1
Van Diyk, T 170
Vernette, E 167
victimization studies 181, 186
Vincent, J A 17-18, 38
violence, and the media 168
Voas, D & Crockett, A 77
vocational education 49, 50, 51
Vogler 33
voluntary sector 120
voting behaviour 140-42

W

Waco, Texas 72, 74
Waitzkin, H 151
Walby, S 16, 228
Waldron, I 155
Walker, A 116
Walker, A & Foster, L 18
Walker, R 113
Wall, M 171
Wallis, Roy 73-4, 75
Walter, N 228
Walton, Paul 186
'War on Terror' 137
Warwick, D & Littlejohn, G 11
Washington Consensus 139-40
Watson, H 70
Waugh, D 37
wealth 7, 38, 108, 109-11: *see also* income
Webb 109
Weber, Max 3, 207, 217, 224, 226, 228, 230; on lower middle class 9; on middle class 8, 9; on power 132-3; on the professions 8; on religion 71-2, 74, 77, 80; on social stratification 6, 117; on wealth 109, 110-11
Webster, F 168
Weeks, J, Donovan, C & Heaphey, B 1
welfare benefits 11, 17, 31, 116, 117
welfare state 117, 118-24
Welfare to Work programmes 124
West, D J & Farrington, D P 213
Westergaard, J 14, 118
Westergaard, J & Resler, H 7, 109, 119, 133, 135-6
Whelehan, I 228
white-collar crime 179, 182-3
Whitely, P 141
Whitty, G 53
Whyte, W F 212
Wiles, P & Costello, A 196
Wilkinson, R 38, 155
Wilkstrom, P-O H 195
Williams, G 151
Williams, H 134
Williams, J & Watson, G 157
Williams, Raymond 83, 94
Willis, P 48, 98, 209
Willmott, P 30
Willmott, P & Young, M 33
Wilson, J Q & Herstein, R 188-9
Wilson, J Q & Kelling, G 188
Wilson, James Q 188, 232
Wilson, W J 17, 75, 77, 79
Winlow, Simon 193, 194, 214
Witz, Anne 153
women: black 16, 17; and crime 192-3; and employment 1; and health 155; and poverty 115; and religion 1; religiosity 76; religious oppression 70-71: *see also* feminism, gender
Woods, P 55
Woodward, K 99
Woolf, A 49
working class 1, 10-11, 53
Wright, A 71
Wright, C 58
Wright Mills, C 3, 134
Wyness, M 34
Wynne, Derek 9-10

Y

Yinger, J M 68
Young, Jock 184, 186, 187, 188, 191
Young, M & Willmott, P 27, 30, 210
youth 170; offenders 194; subcultures 94-5, 98, 102, 171; training schemes 49, 50

Z

Zaretsky, Eli 28
zero tolerance 189